# The Enigma of the
# Oceanic Feeling

# The Enigma of the Oceanic Feeling

*Revisioning the Psychoanalytic
Theory of Mysticism*

WILLIAM B. PARSONS

New York    Oxford  •  Oxford University Press    1999

Oxford University Press

Oxford   New York

Athens   Auckland   Bangkok   Bogotá   Buenos Aires   Calcutta
Cape Town   Chennai   Dar es Salaam   Delhi   Florence   Hong Kong   Istanbul
Karachi   Kuala Lumpur   Madrid   Melbourne   Mexico City   Mumbai
Nairobi   Paris   São Paulo   Singapore   Taipei   Tokyo   Toronto   Warsaw

and associated companies in
Berlin   Ibadan

Copyright © 1999 by William B. Parsons

Published by Oxford University Press, Inc
198 Madison Avenue, New York, New York 10016

Oxford is a registered trademark of Oxford University Press

Library of Congress Cataloging-in-Publication Data
Parsons, William Barclay, 1955–
The enigma of the oceanic feeling : revisioning the psychoanalytic
theory of mysticism / William B. Parsons.
p.   cm
Includes bibliographical references and index.
ISBN 0-19-511508-2
1. Psychoanalysis and religion. 2. Freud, Sigmund, 1856–1939.
I. Title
BF175.4.R44P37   1999
291.4'22'019—dc21        97-18199

1 3 5 7 9 8 6 4 2
Printed in the United States of America
on acid-free paper

For

Jean Lily,

Theodora Rose,

Robert Coleman

# *Preface*

In 1904, Freud traveled to the Acropolis. Standing amid the temple ruins, gazing out over the sea, he fulfilled one of his most cherished wishes. His descriptions of that moment, found in his letters and cultural texts dealing with mysticism, are oddly contradictory, emphasizing his utter joy, astonishment, and sense of reality on the one hand and feelings of derealization and depression on the other. These varying descriptions make the Acropolis a fitting symbol for Freud's perplexity and ambivalence when faced with oceanic feelings. Years later he said that for him mysticism was, like music, a closed book. This "landtier" was more comfortable with worldly themes and cultural selfobjects of western religions; his genius was content to play between their manifest and latent meaning. In 1914, when Jung and Adler had defected and the Great War threatened both Europe and Freud's hopes for the dissemination of psychoanalysis, the introspective doctor, in the throes of self-disintegration, traveled again. This time he visited not the Acropolis and its blue sea, but Rome and its statues, there to gain newfound strength meditating on Michelangelo's Moses.

The legacy Freud bequeathed for the religious of his generation consisted in unearthing the depth-psychological issues surrounding figures like Moses and Oedipus. While present cultures may also serve to shape the psychic structure of its inhabitants in ways that emphasize the preponderance of such developmental themes, it is, at least to much of my generation, Freud's forays into the pre-Oedipal and mysticism that are of more relevance. This is not to be read simply or principally as an indication that recent generations are beset by a culture of narcissism. On the contrary, while depth-psychological ideation of various kinds can be found in contemporary as well as historic expressions of mysticism, the more recent interest in, familiarity with, and investigation of altered states has raised another question: the extent to which existing psychoanalytic models account for the deepest levels of mystical subjectivity. It is here where the other protagonist of this study, Romain Rolland, emerges, for it is he and not Freud who speaks to such possibilities.

The resolution of the two men's debate over the nature of mysticism is not yet in sight. I consider it the scholarly version of good fortune to have come across a correspondence which might, if in a small way, contribute to articulating parameters for further discussion of this important topic. Several people have given generously of their time and energy to nourish what value is contained in these pages. To Harvey Aronson, Bertram Cohler, Peter Homans, Bernard McGinn, and the anonymous readers for Oxford University Press, all of whom critiqued the entire manuscript with painstaking attention to detail, I can only offer my heartfelt thanks. This study has further benefited from the careful eyes of Christopher Fitchner, Sam Jaffe, and Robert Kaplan. A special thanks to my colleague at Rice, Gerald McKenny, who has offered not only emendations but wise counsel and emotional support. Dan Bertsche and Jamie Lee were of immense help in correcting my French translations. Certain persons affected this study by drawing me to the topic of mysticism: William Chen, William Johnson, and Julian Miller. I owe an enormous debt to Boris Lietsky, whose mediation and careful tutelage have made this undertaking possible in ways which cannot be articulated.

The following copyright holders are acknowledged with gratitude for allowing me to reprint excerpts of previously published material:

# Contents

# The Enigma of the
# Oceanic Feeling

# Introduction

## Psychoanalysis and Mysticism

In his landmark biography of Freud, Ernest Jones observed that no single topic in the Freudian corpus, excepting that of sexuality, had evoked more interest than that of religion.[1] Although Freud's views on religion are complex, Jones had in mind the definitive and pejorative conception of religion delineated in *The Future of an Illusion*. There Freud, defining religion in terms of "the final form" taken by our present-day "Christian civilization," sought to undermine religious tenets by interpreting them with respect to childhood development and metapsychological concepts like projection, repression, and the unconscious. His trenchant analysis led to a long and fruitful debate among subsequent psychoanalysts, as well as between psychoanalysis and multiple disciplines within religious studies, concerning the nature and function of religion. The history of this ongoing conversation need not be repeated here, as it is substantial and has been well documented.[2] What is noteworthy about this literature, however, is the dearth of any sustained interdisciplinary dialogue with respect to one of its central themes, the origin and development of the relation between psychoanalysis and mysticism.

The emergence of the psychoanalytic theory of mysticism has come to be associated with one specific phenomenon: Freud's interpretation of the famous "oceanic feeling." This curious and neglected chapter in Freud's oeuvre was a consequence of the furor over *The Future of an Illusion*. Shortly after its publication in 1927, Freud sent a copy to an esteemed friend, Romain Rolland, a French writer, mystic, and social critic renowned for his humanitarianism and pleas for tolerance between peoples and nations. In a letter dated December 5, 1927, Rolland responded, praising Freud's "lucid and spirited little book" for exposing an adolescent form of belief that prevailed among the masses. He further expressed concern that Freud had neglected to treat the true source and nature of religious sentiments. Rolland thought true religion arose from the mystical experience of oneness with the world (*la sensation océanique*). Confessing he was "familiar" with this oceanic feeling and emphasizing its presence in mystics of all religious traditions, Rolland extended an invitation to Freud to analyze mysticism. Freud took up Rolland's request in the first chapter of *Civilization and Its Discontents*, interpreting the oceanic feeling as an instance of the primary narcissistic union between mother and infant.

This one chapter has formed the basis for the common understanding of Freud's interpretation of mysticism. However, an examination of the continued correspondence between the two men reveals complexities unaccounted for by the received view. Freud and Rolland engaged in other debates and raised issues that proved to be central to the subsequent historical interaction between psychoanalysis and mysticism. It was, in the final analysis, a thoroughly interesting but largely unfinished conversation.

The precise details and continued ramifications of their unfinished conversation makes up the subject matter of this study. What were the issues discussed and debates engaged in by Freud and Rolland? How did the Freud–Rolland debate affect subsequent developments in the psychoanalytic theory of mysticism? In what ways does its analysis provoke new avenues for rethinking the relation between psychoanalysis and mysticism? During the course of this study I will seek to answer these and other questions by explicating the Freud–Rolland debate, offering a critique of both men's positions and promoting a new constructive agenda for the psychoanalytic theory of mysticism.[3]

## Mysticism: Definitions and Debates

Before proceeding any further, some preliminary agreement must be reached concerning what is to be understood by the term *mysticism*. Applied to the world's religious traditions in an unsophisticated, conversational sense, the meaning of the term seems readily intelligible. For example, an educated layperson might label St. Teresa of Avila, the Zen master Dogen, the Sufi al-Hallaj, or the Hindu sage Sri Aurobindo as "mystics." Again, the Enneads, the Upanishads, or the Zohar might be adduced as classic "mystical texts." So too might Ramakrishna's first vision of Kali, St. Paul's ascent to Paradise, and Buddha's attainment of nirvana under the Bo tree be singled out as examples of "mystical experiences." But what may at times appear to be a straightforward phenomenon exhibiting an unambiguous commonality has become, at least in the hands of scholars, opaque and controversial. Indeed, even a cursory survey of scholarly literature on mysticism reveals a rich diversity of definitional strategies, theoretical agendas, and methodological concerns.[4]

The variety and complexity of extant strategies and agendas gives one pause to consider. Attempting to circumscribe the "field of religion" in his *Varieties of Religious Experience*, William James states that "being as wide as this, it is manifestly impossible that I should pretend to cover it."[5] The same holds true for any attempt to define the field of mysticism. The vastness of current literature on mysticism precludes a simple presentation of and adjudication between opposed views. James sidestepped his difficulty by refusing to formulate an abstract definition of religion's essence and proceeding "to defend it against all comers," choosing instead to promote an admittedly "narrow view" of religion fit for the purposes of his study.[6] Following in the general direction of James, I choose to engage in an "orienting discussion" that draws forth a cluster of meanings which have become associated with the word *mysticism*. Although these meanings responsibly take in current definitional strategies and debates in the field, they are admittedly tailored to the needs of this study. They provide the indispensable background for the analysis undertaken in Part I, which surveys how Freud came to understand and interpret mysticism, as well as the groundwork for the constructive thesis advanced in Part II, which offers suggestions for the reorientation of the psychoanalytic theory of mysticism.

To begin, then, initial access to the field is needed. Scholars agree that at the outset of inquiry, confined to descriptive accounts before the imposition of theory, mystical phenomena admit of a bewildering variety. The ontological commitments, moral implications, and religious practices associated with mystical encounters are diverse. To create order out of textual chaos, many central works on mysticism have created initial access by offering introductions that champion a particular definitional strategy. These strategies are by no means uniform. They can, however, be characterized as falling along the lines of two basic types: the inclusive (or universalistic) and the restrictive (or particularistic).

Inclusive definitions use comprehensive, abstract, generic terms to circumscribe mysticism. This approach highlights one or more characteristics useful in denoting an experience as mystical. Early attempts stressed the concept of union. The comparativist R. C. Zaehner, for example, defined mysticism as an "experienced fact . . . the essence and keynote of which . . . is a unitive experience with someone or something other than oneself."[7] James also noted the centrality of union: "In mystic states we both become one with the Absolute and we become aware of our oneness. This is the everlasting and triumphant mystical tradition, hardly altered by differences of clime or creed."[8] However, he also emphasized other characteristics—transiency, passivity, ineffability, and, most important, a noetic element above and beyond reason ("insight into depths of truth unplumbed by the discursive intellect")—which further served to qualify a state as mystical.[9] R. M. Bucke, D. T. Suzuki, W. T. Stace, and others have added related characteristics (subjective light, moral elevation, sense of immortality, loss of fear, joy and exultation, authoritativeness, an alteration of space and time, etc.), bringing the total to something resembling a laundry list.[10] The use of this strategy continues, as is evinced in the recent attempt by the Carmodys, who define mysticism as "a direct experience of ultimate reality."[11]

Restrictive definitions, on the other hand, abandon the attempt at abstraction and inclusiveness in favor of defining the topic with respect to terms and criteria endemic to a particular religion. Mysticism is viewed as a historical and relational phenomenon that cannot be defined without recourse to a total religious matrix. What constitutes a mystical experience and how it is evaluated shifts from religion to religion. Gershom Scholem advocated the restrictive approach when, in de-emphasizing the centrality of unitive encounters among Jewish mystics, he insisted on attention to context and warned of the tendency of the inclusive approach to become linked with the promotion of a universal mystical religion.[12] Many Christian theologians have followed suit, preferring to designate Christian mysticism through the felt "presence of God" and pointing to the variety of Christian symbols, metaphors, and categories that have been used to express this presence: deification; the birth of the Word in the soul; "intellectual," "imaginative," and "corporeal" visions; rapture; and so on.[13] Scholars of Eastern traditions have advocated the restrictive approach on cross-cultural grounds. Terms of discourse like *mysticism* and *union*, which have their roots in the Greek Mysteries and the Church Fathers, invariably reflect meanings of the Western religious past.[14] As the Buddhist scholar Robert Gimello writes: "there is a modicum of imprecision in the labeling of the most characteristically Buddhist experience and discourse mystical. . . . . it is difficult to apply any of the widely accepted definitions or descriptions of mysticism to Buddhist praxis without the most serious reservations. There seems always to be some crucial element of the definition, some essential part of the description which just does not fit the Buddhist case."[15]

Taken to their extremes, both approaches are problematic. Inclusive definitions can become so generic as to lose referential meaning. The stress on common characteristics can mitigate against the need for context and the articulation of significant differences between mystical traditions. Restrictive approaches, on the other hand, can become so myopic as to ignore the need to provide grounds for comparative discourse. The emphasis on context should not ignore the need for an ongoing conversation that stresses the search for commonality. It is best, then, to utilize both approaches in dialectical interplay. Thus the meaning of mysticism can be continually monitored and qualified, allowing it to accrue specificity and structural constancy through attention to context and comparativist dialogue.

Given the general aim of this orienting discussion, the definitional strategy just suggested is sufficient to provide the functional task of preliminary access to the field. However, it should be further noted that in many extant studies definitional strategies of the purely restrictive or inclusive kind are linked to, even inseparable from, methodological concerns and normative agendas. In this sense definitions are hardly neutral, functioning only to create initial access. Rather, in being linked to theoretical concerns, definitions are prejudicial, predisposing one to think of mysticism in specific ways.[16] It may be that all attempts at definition are prejudicial in some measure. If so, this awareness should similarly be made explicit and monitored. Keeping in mind the importance and ramifications of the prejudicial nature of any definition, it is still possible to make a functional distinction between definitions (in the sense of initial access to the field) and theories (concerning the nature and meaning of mysticism). Turning to the latter, I would like to briefly highlight two major debates that are central to the current literature and this study in particular.

First, the poles of a long debate that has animated the study of mysticism in this century are represented by the perennialists (or "essentialists") and the constructivists (or "contextualists"). Simply put, the perennialist position gravitates toward the view that all mysticism points toward a transcendent unity and common-core. Although it is acknowledged that the descriptions of mystical experiences differ from tradition to tradition, such variety is attributed to a mystic's set of beliefs and concepts coming into play only after the initial, immediate encounter with the divine. Scholars like Rudolf Otto, Huston Smith, Frithjof Schuon, and Robert Forman, utilizing a broad spectrum of textual, cultural, and philosophical arguments of varying degrees of sophistication, have been identified as proponents of this school of thought. The constructivist or contextualist school, which has become increasingly popular in the last two decades, has been identified with scholars like Bruce Garside, Rufus Jones, and Steven Katz. Rejecting the arguments of the perennialists, constructivists hold that mysticism is irreducibly diverse. Adducing a variety of counterarguments, the constructivists think the conclusion that all mysticism points to a transcendent unity is philosophically untenable. Mystical experiences between traditions are bound to be different, mediated as they are by culture, concepts, expectations, and existing structures of the mind. Opposed to the notion of a common-core, theirs is a plea for differences.[17]

A second debate concerns whether one thinks of mysticism as consisting essentially in experiences per se or in terms of a process. The more familiar view is that mysticism consists of an episodic, ecstatic, intuitive encounter with the divine. Such an encounter may be either spontaneous or deliberately sought through meditation, contemplation, drugs, dance, and other mystical practices. Most definitional strategies, whether restrictive or inclusive, assume this understanding of mysticism.

Mysticism as process shifts the emphasis from mystical experience per se to mystical encounters set in the broad context of a life. Without denigrating the importance of singular epiphanies or deep meditative intuitions about the nature of self and reality, the criteria for evaluation and comparison moves from analysis of the characteristics of mystical experiences as such to how such encounters are linked to the cultivation of a specific set of dispositions, capacities, virtues, and states of consciousness. This general point finds specificity in the diverse ways in which mystical authors have subsumed mystical experiences and meditative insights under the broader umbrella of the spiritual "path." For example, a process view of mysticism is implied in St. John and St. Teresa's use of "mansions" and "stages" [purgation, illumination, union], Buddhaghosa's Visuddhimagga, Zen's Ox-herding pictures, Ramana Maharshi's conception of sahaja samādhi and the Sufi notions of "stages" and "stations."[18] Extending the constructivist–perennialist debate to engage the problem of mysticism as process, the question is whether there exists an underlying common-core of development and the problem is how to articulate an interdisciplinary procedure through which the search for such commonality might proceed.

A central concern of this study is to address the historical relationship between psychoanalysis and these debates. To what extent did Freud and Rolland address views of mysticism as experience and process? What position did they take with regard to the various cultural, textual, and philosophical arguments adduced by scholars of their day? What resources within psychoanalysis exist to advance these debates?

## The Oceanic Feeling and Its Historical Matrix

In order to facilitate the examination of these many issues and questions this study is divided into two parts. Part I details the relationship between Freud and Rolland and how each came to understand and interpret mystical phenomena. Although the two men had noticeable differences concerning the meaning and value of mysticism, they were agreed that psychology could illumine its fundamental nature. Historically speaking, their debate over mysticism took place during the earliest period (1880–1930) of the interaction between religion and psychological studies. While Freud, William James, and Carl Jung are the psychologists most readily associated with this period, other contributors made this a truly exciting time, international in scope, for the psychology of religion. More important, several noted scholars of their generation—Delacroix and Maréchal in France, Flournoy and Morel in Switzerland, Bucke in Canada, Hocking and Leuba in the United States—placed the psychological study of mysticism at the forefront of their research.[19]

Historical shifts in the meaning of the term *mysticism* played no small part in facilitating interest in analyzing it from a psychological perspective. As essays on the history of the word tell us, *mysticism* is derived from the Greek verb *muo*, meaning "to close" (as in one's eyes and lips). Initially, the word lacked any reference to a direct encounter with the transcendent. In the Greek Mystery religions, it referred only to the hidden or secret elements of ritualistic activity (*mystikos*). However, picked up and elaborated by Origen, Dionysius, and the early Church Fathers, it came to refer to that knowledge of God accessed through liturgy and scriptural exegesis. As these early Christians would have it, "mystical theology" and "mystical contemplation" were terms receiving definition only with respect to a total religious matrix. In proclaiming that Christian mystical experience was accessed only through the auspices of church and tradition, the Church Fathers ensured that "mysticism" was devoid of the kind of subjective resonance usually associated with psychological introspective probes. As Bouyer puts it: "We finally understand why mysticism was never reduced by the Fathers to the level of a psychological experience, considered merely, or primarily, in its subjectivity. It is always the experience of an invisible objective world: the world whose coming the Scriptures reveal to us in Jesus Christ, the world into which we enter, ontologically, through the liturgy."[20] Surely mystical practices led a Christian practitioner to probe the deeper recesses of the psyche. However, according to the Church Fathers, these probes encountered an objective, ontological ground above and beyond that inner topography mapped later by metapsychology. Moreover, in contrast to modern psychological construals of mysticism in terms of innate potentialities, peak experiences, and self-actualization, these theologians stressed that access to the further reaches of the divine–human encounter were initiated by God and dependent on his grace.

By the time Freud was writing, one finds the term *mysticism* commonly used as a noun, *mystic* as an adjective, and the delineation of the topic in terms of a subjective "experience" divorced from tradition, capable of being understood with respect to psychological views of the psyche.[21] Many early psychologists gave primacy to a view of mysticism as an "experience." Tradition and its accoutrements were viewed as growing out of the more basic experiential matrix, hence secondary phenomena nonessential for access to the divine. Further, mystical modes of knowing were increasingly conceptualized in terms of developmental or innate unconscious (or subconscious) potentialities. These trends were undoubtedly facilitated by the fact that many researchers were privy to spontaneous, unchurched mystical experiences. Rolland, for example, in his letter to Freud of December 5, 1927, characterized mysticism as the basic experiential matrix that gave rise to scripture, dogma, religious institutions, and theologies. The oceanic feeling, states Rolland, is "totally independent of all dogma, all credo, all Church organization. . . . the true subterranean source of religious energy which . . . has been collected, canalized and dried up by the Churches to the extent that one could say that it is inside the Churches" that one finds the least true religious feeling. He then cited his own unchurched mystical experiences and advocated conceptualizing mystical modes of knowing in terms of innate, untapped potentials existing in a religious subconscious.

Many psychologists of this era proceeded along the same lines. James, for example, in his classic *Varieties of Religious Experience*, defined religious experience as "the feelings, acts and experiences of individual men in their solitude, so far as they apprehend themselves to stand in relation to whatever they may consider the divine" and interpreted it with respect to field theory and subconscious functions.[22] Tradition and its accoutrements—"theologies, philosophies, and ecclesiastical organizations" as James put it—were viewed as secondary phenomena derived from the primary experiential matrix.[23] James's mystical experiences were also unchurched, ignited through experimentation with nitrous oxide ("the opposites of the world . . . were melted into a unity") and the majesty of the mountains ("one of the happiest lonesome nights of my existence").[24]

The Canadian psychologist R. M. Bucke, a friend and correspondent of James, was similarly subject to mystical experiences. His experience of an "intellectual illumination," the essential elements of which consisted of an apprehension of how the universe is composed of "a living Presence" whose essence is love, that "all men are immortal" and that "the happiness of each and all of us is in the long run absolutely certain," was spontaneous and unchurched. It became the experiential basis for his famous notion of "cosmic consciousness," a psychological datum capable of being scientifically analyzed and characterized as the root of the mystical element in all religions.[25] Jung, echoing James, defined creeds as "codified and dogmatized forms of original religious experience." Like James and Bucke, he had several visionary experiences, including what today would be termed a near-death experience. These were attributed to the influence of archetypes, as were mystical experiences from all religious traditions.[26] Lesser known interpretations of this time, such as Janet's case history of Madeleine and Flournoy's of Cécile Vé, as well as pivotal debates, notably the Leuba–Maréchal debate over whether Christian mystics, in the deep introspective probes they called "intellectual visions," encountered psychological or transcendent noumenal ground, similarly addressed this new historical approach to the understanding and interpretation of mysticism.[27]

As with these psychologists as a whole, Freud's encounter with the oceanic feeling has had a definitive impact on the interdisciplinary study of mysticism. Recalling our "orienting discussion," one could categorize Freud's interpretation of the oceanic feeling as a legitimate version of the perennialist or "common-core" approach to mysticism. The oceanic feeling, conceived of as a phenomenological account of mystical experience whose essence and keynote consists in the fact of "unity," has become the psychoanalytic contribution to generic terms for "mysticism everywhere." However, contrary to most who favor a common-core approach, psychoanalysts cast doubt on any transcendent source, interpreting metaphysical claims as projections of developmentally specific modes of apprehension. Fluctuations in mystical texts are explained as cultural elaborations of a universal experience: the unity the infant feels with the nurturing breast of the mother. Combined with this reduction of metaphysics to metapsychology, psychoanalysis is perceived as appending a value judgment that brands the mystic as immature, reveling in illusion and socially retrograde. "Mysticism" becomes but one more form of the "common-man's" religion.

The above elements of what I earlier called the "received view" of Freud's understanding and interpretation of mysticism have been recognized by scholarship in the field. Daniel Merkur, for example, in his survey of psychological contributions to the "common-core" hypothesis, observes that "with the rise of psychoanalysis, the orthodox Freudian school of depth psychology, the unitive factor in mystical union was attributed to manifestations of ordinarily unconscious psychical material of a unitive character. . . . Freud interpreted the union as a regression to immediately postnatal experience."[28] R. C. Zaehner, commenting on Freud and his influence on Jung's early views on mysticism, notes the pejorative element in psychoanalytic evaluations of mysticism: "The commonest symbols of mysticism—the sea, the air, trees, water—are nothing more than symbols of the eternal feminine both in mythology and psychology; and the mystical experience, figured in practically all mystical traditions as a drop of water or a river dissolving into the sea, is simply a sign of infantilism in the adult."[29] More important, Freud's analysis of the oceanic feeling has had substantial impact on psychological forays into mystical phenomena. As Ralph Hood notes, it is "this basic position of Freud" that is "at the basis of most contemporary investigators' efforts to link the mystical process of union with human regressive behavior."[30] Unfortunately, the consequences of the received view have been anything but progressive. Those within the mainstream study of mysticism have tended to dismiss psychoanalysis as reductive and lacking in interdisciplinary awareness and engagement. This state of affairs continues to exist, being buttressed by reductive psychoanalytic studies ranging from Franz Alexander's early attempt to classify Buddhism as inducing pathological states to the more recent portrayals of Indian mysticism by J. M. Masson and Narasingha Sil in terms of regression, manic denial, depersonalization, and derealization.[31]

In actuality, the received view and the religious response to it reflect the hegemony of the reductive models promoted by Freud and his legacy, what can be termed the "classic" school of psychoanalysis. Other psychoanalytic studies, utilizing advances in metapsychology and exhibiting interdisciplinary sophistication, can be found. For example, during the 60s and 70s one can point to the emergence of an "adaptive school." Championed by Prince and Savage, Fingarette, Horton, and Fromm and continuing in recent studies by Meissner and Kakar, these studies utilize advances in ego psychology and object-relations theory and emphasize the healing, adaptive dimension of mystical experiences.[32] In the last decade, studies in Hindu and Buddhist spirituality by Engler, Kripal, and others indicate that not only a revival of interest but also the rudiments of a third school, which can be called "transformational," that utilizes yet goes beyond "classic" and "adaptive" approaches is emerging within the psychoanalytic community. Many transformative studies display cross-cultural sensitivity and, in calling upon theorists like Bion and Lacan, display a marked sympathy with the transcendent, religious claims of mystics.[33]

A detailed analysis of the history and development of these disparate, often conflicting, schools of psychoanalytic theorizing about mysticism must await the later chapters of this study. What is of immediate concern is the fact that the historical roots of these schools can be found in the Freud–Rolland correspondence. Unfortunately, the received view, lacking in any contextualization whatsoever, has obscured this fact. Indeed, it has altogether distorted Freud's understanding and interpretation of mysticism and forestalled inquiry into the substantial theoretical issues entertained by the two men. Any attempt at revisioning the psychoanalytic theory of mysticism, then, should start "at the beginning," that is, by a careful examination of the psychoanalytic theory of mysticism as it first evolved out of the Freud–Rolland correspondence.

Part I endeavors to achieve this end by providing a detailed analysis of the two men's conversations over the nature and interpretation of mystical phenomena. Drawing on psychobiographical and sociohistorical studies of Freud's life and thought, Chapter 1 begins to provide a corrective to the received view by describing the complex relationship between Freud and Rolland, carefully highlighting the themes that form the background for understanding their debate on mysticism. Chapter 2 takes the analysis further by correlating these themes with a detailed exegesis of *Civilization and Its Discontents*. Of particular concern will be to document how Freud, in response to several letters from Rolland, offered two models for the interpretation of two different mystical phenomena, neither of which corresponds to that found in the received view. Chapter 3 turns to Rolland, showing the relevance of his analysis of mysticism and comparative pursuits for his debate with Freud. Finally, Chapter 4 catalogs the vicissitudes of the later stages of their debate as seen in various letters and texts, notably Freud's analysis of his own "mystical" experience as contained in his essay "A Disturbance of Memory on the Acropolis."

## The Psychology–Comparativist Dialogue

Part I can be read as an entity unto itself. It is historical and exegetical in character and is meant to contribute to studies in the first period of the psychology and religion movement. At the same time, by revealing what the two men thought and wrote about mysticism, it demonstrates the fragmentary yet suggestive quality of much of their debate. Perhaps because of age (Freud was ill and over seventy, Rolland over sixty when the debate began), geographical and cultural distance (they met only once, in 1924, with a mutual friend, Stefan Zweig, acting as a translator), political turmoil (between the two World Wars), and a mutual respect which inhibited the full articulation of their very real differences, the two men rarely followed up in detail the substantial issues provoked by their correspondence. Often frustrating, this can be taken as an opportunity, for the unresolved elements of the Freud–Rolland debate offer avenues to address anew the role psychoanalysis can play in the interdisciplinary study of mysticism. In this sense Part I lays the indispensable groundwork for the constructive project to be undertaken in Part II.

Part II takes it cue from recent developments in the field of religion and psychological studies. In the most familiar sense, the latter  designation refers to all psychological theorists and models complicit in the attempt to uncover the origins and meaning of religious ideation and practice—thus the classic term "the psychology of religion," which came into use at the turn of the century to denote a discernible subset within the field of psychology. Most studies of this initial, formative period (1880–1930) of religion and psychological studies locate its development as issuing from a few generations of scholars in the United States, notably William James, G. Stanley Hall, James Leuba, Edwin Starbuck, and James Pratt; European researchers like Joseph Maréchal, Henri Delacroix, Pierre Janet, Theodore Flournoy, Wilhelm Wundt; and, of course, Freud and Jung. Prayer, conversion, revivalism, religious leadership, and mysticism: these were primary topics of interest.[34] Since that time, a diverse body of theorists ranging from Erik Erikson, Heinz Kohut, Ken Wilber, and Bernard Spilka to Brant Wenegrat, Arthur Deikman, Antoine Vergote, and Jacques Lacan have developed and given credence to the use of a wide variety of theoretical models (e.g., ego psychology, object relations theory, humanistic, existential, transpersonal, empirical, experimental, post-structural, sociobiological, and neurological approaches) for analyzing religon.[35]

Psychological analyses of religion have given rise to a long history of responses that have emerged from a variety of institutional settings: multiple departments within the university, the clinic, the church, and the seminary. I also use the term "religion and psychological studies," then, to refer to other, more integrative and dialogical enterprises. For example, one could point to the growing trend to include psychology as part of an inclusive social scientific approach to religion—one that reaches to the shores of political and economic theory while integrating disciplinary partners like sociology and anthropology in explaining religious phenomena. I would include in this category what Peter Homans calls the psychology *and* religion approach, which integrates depth-psychology and social theory in an effort to explain the historical relationship between religion and psychological modes of introspection and theorizing.[36] Such analyses have observed a cultural effect of psychological theorizing and institutionalization that will be particularly important for his study, namely, how psychology has been used for the purpose of organizing and expressing the existential search for wholeness, numinous experiences, and individuation. A third designation alongside the psychology of and psychology "and" religion, which can be called psychology *as* a religion, can thus be noted. Carried on in the Jungian tradition and in theorists like Robert Assagioli, Abraham Maslow, transpersonal psychologists like Stanislav Grof and Ken Wilber, and in contemporary popular books like M. Scott Peck's *The Road Less Traveled*, we have a tradition of psychological theorizing that seeks to not only interpret religious phenomena but quite intentionally offers itself as a modern, unchurched way to frame one's religiosity.

Other enterprises that are explicitly dialogical can be identified. The most obvious of these is the *psychology-theology dialogue*, which reached its zenith during the second major period of the field of religion and psychological studies (1930–1960). Humanistic and existential psychology became popular, while ego-psychology replaced classic Freudian metapsychology as the preferred psychoanalytic school. In contrast to the initial, formative period of religion and psychological studies, a perusal of the classic works of this second historical period reveals a general dearth of serious interest in mysticism. Rather, the hegemony of a Protestant culture insured the ascendancy of the attempt to deconstruct a heteronomous God, the desire to find a psychological space for ethics, the articulation of psychologically sophisticated forms of religious subjectivity, and the development of pastoral psychology. These themes, found in seminal books such as *Young Man Luther* and *The Courage to Be* and furthered through the efforts of pivotal figures like Paul Tillich, Erik Erikson, Reinhold Niebuhr, Rollo May, Carl Rogers, and Erich Fromm, are still very much extant, impacting the works of typical Protestant scholars like Don Browning and James Fowler.[37]

The last few decades have seen the growth of other dialogues. Certainly the explosion of interest in psychology, religion, and gender studies, evident in theorists like Julia Kristeva, Judith van Herik, and Diane Jonte-Pace, belongs here.[38] However, most important for our purposes is the growing popularity and sophistication of what I call the *psychology-comparativist dialogue*. Like the psychology-theology dialogue, it has precedents in scholars of the recent past like Mircea Eliade and Joseph Campbell and in the works of contemporary scholars like Wendy Doniger, Sudhir Kakar, and Luis Gómez.[39] Like the psychology of religion, one can locate its roots in the figures of the initial, formative period of the field. It is well known that one can find comparative interests in the works of James and Jung. But one can also find such interests in lesser known works of the formative period like the Jesuit psychologist Joseph Maréchal's *Studies in the Psychology of the Mystics*, R. M. Bucke's *Cosmic Consciousness*, and Ferdinand Morel's *Essai sur l'Introversion Mystique*.

The interest of these early psychologists in comparative mysticism was spurred on by that intellectual movement Raymond Schwab has referred to as "the Oriental renaissance." Versluis, Welbon, Fields, Tweed and others have since joined Schwab in cataloging how the Western world, particularly at the turn of the century, came to grips with the dissemination of mystical texts and practices from a variety of Eastern religious traditions.[40] The writings of philosophers and poets from Nietzsche and Schopenhauer to Emerson and Hesse exhibited the enormous impact of this intellectual movement. By 1875, with the publication of Max Müller's *Sacred Books of the East*, the parameters of comparativist studies were set and the scholarly interest in mysticism began to perk. Translations of Eastern scriptures and debates over issues like the Indian influence on Plato and the implications of terms like *nirvana* were the order of the day. As we shall see, Freud's thought did not escape the impact of this Oriental renaissance. As early as 1904 one finds him commenting on the European debates over nirvana and the poetic beauty of the Bhagavad Gita. Rolland as well was taken with the East. In the 1880s he was constructing a notebook on "the Buddha Siddhartha," and by 1914, with the advent of the Great War, he began to actively campaign for dialogue with the religious, intellectual, and social traditions of Asia. It was his research into the Hindu saints Ramakrishna and Vivekananda that spurred on his efforts to enlist Freud in the interpretation of the oceanic feeling. Indeed, as we shall see, the Freud–Rolland debate over the nature and interpretation of the oceanic feeling reveals a crucial but unacknowledged dimension of Freud's psychology of religion: his encounter with and reflection on the doctrines and practices of Hinduism.

The historical-exegetical study of Part I, then, can be further specified as a contribution to the roots of the emerging psychology–comparativist dialogue. This dialogue, as reflected in the Freud–Rolland debate, anticipated various cultural, textual, and philosophical arguments found in contemporary debates over the nature and meaning of mysticism. The constructive project of Part II, based on recent developments in the psychology–comparativist dialogue, critiques both Freud's and Rolland's conclusions, offering suggestions for reorienting the psychoanalytic theory of mysticism. At the heart of this project is the elaboration of the tripartite typology of classic, adaptive, and transformational approaches and the articulation of a new dialogical position that grants legitimacy to mystical modes of knowing. In so doing, this project promotes a bona fide dialogue between psychology, comparativist literature, culture studies, philosophical issues in mystical epistemology, and debates over mysticism as experience and process.

I begin in Chapter 5 by reconstructing the totality of Rolland's mysticism as found in his journals, autobiography, biographies, novels, essays, and correspondence. The text restored, it becomes clear that Freud misunderstood, and thus did not do interpretative justice to, Rolland's mysticism. The problem becomes finding resources within psychoanalysis that can address the lacunae in Freud's analysis. In Chapter 6 I seek to unearth some of those resources. In brief, I suggest paths for revision through a historical overview and critique of three major strands of psychoanalytic theorizing about mysticism (the classic, adaptive, and transformational approaches). I do this by bringing these schools into historical relation with the Freud–Rolland correspondence and with contemporary comparativist and philosophical literature on mysticism.

Having delineated the general direction I think psychoanalysis should traverse in its encounter with the mystics, I turn back in Chapter 7 to the mysticism of Romain Rolland. Here I illustrate how a revised psychoanalytic theory of mysticism can account for the discontinuities in Freud's interpretation. First, drawing on the restored text of Rolland's mysticism, I contextualize it with respect to relevant comparativist categories. Rather than reflecting "mysticism every-where," I conclude that Rolland's mysticism reflects the characteristics of what I dub an "unchurched mysticism," which captures his sociohistorical locale and the generic, unchurched nature of his mystical encounters and attempts to conceptualize it and other forms of mysticism with respect to Western psychological frameworks. I then proceed with a fresh interpretation of Rolland's oceanic feeling. The point is to show how psychoanalytic models, in conjunction with studies in mystical epistemology, culture studies, and the comparativist conclusion that Rolland was an "unchurched mystic" can work together in the hermeneutic enterprise that seeks to come to grips with that deep form of mystical subjectivity Rolland called "the oceanic feeling."

The various types of mysticism lightly glossed in Chapter 6, placed alongside the more extensive analysis of Rolland's mysticism in Chapter 7, buttress the conclusion that any single case history, in and of itself, cannot be the basis for generalizations about all mysticism. The nature of mystical experience and mystical process varies from mystic to mystic. The flexible nature of my constructive proposals promotes the emergence of new issues and debates as other cases are analyzed. In other words, not closure but the promotion of fresh arenas of dialogue as research dictates is the anticipated outcome of the reorientation advocated by this study.

PART I

*The Freud–Rolland Correspondence*

## O N E

# *Across All Boundaries*

## The Atheistic Jew and the Apostle of Love

On February 9, 1923, Freud wrote to Edouard Monod-Hertzen, the son of Gabriel Monod, a friend and teacher of Romain Rolland, to relay to the latter a "word of respect from an unknown admirer."[1] Rolland responded with enthusiasm less than two weeks later, praising Freud's person and work. Thus began a correspondence which lasted until Freud's death in 1939, touching on topics ranging from art, psychoanalysis, and mysticism to politics and the Great War. Interestingly enough, what most have come to associate with the correspondence, the debate over the oceanic feeling, did not occur until the years 1927–1930. Up to that time, the topic remained untouched. After 1930, the two men continued their debate on the nature and interpretation of mysticism, although reference to a variety of other topics can also be found. Given this, and drawing on the complete correspondence as cataloged by Ernst Freud, Colette Cornubert, David Fisher, and Doré and Prévost, I divide the correspondence into three parts, which I term, quite simply, the "early," "middle," and "late" periods.[2] The "early period" of the correspondence, then, stretches from the inception of their relationship in 1923 to the beginning of the debate on mysticism, instigated by Freud's gift to Rolland, a copy of *The Future of an Illusion*, late in 1927. The "middle period" formally begins with Rolland's crucial letter of December 5, 1927, and ends with the publication of Freud's analysis of the "oceanic feeling" in *Civilization and Its Discontents*. The "late period" of the correspondence starts with Rolland's gift to Freud in 1930 of his biographies of Ramakrishna and Vivekananda and ends, for all intents and purposes, with Freud's analysis of his "mystical experience" on the Acropolis in 1936.

The analysis undertaken in this chapter will revolve around four topics that were directly addressed in the letters of the early period: politics, morality, art,

and psychoanalysis. The themes that animate this period are crucial, for they occur throughout the correspondence, revealing the dynamics of the relationship
and offering clues as to the social and developmental echoes that the figure of
Rolland caused to resound in Freud. Although these echoes are multiple, I aim
to highlight only those aspects which will demonstrate beyond doubt that
Freud's interpretation of the oceanic feeling cannot be divorced from the figure
of Rolland and the complex symbolic meaning his friendship had for him.[3] The
themes that are isolated form the indispensable background for the proper exegesis of the middle and late periods of the correspondence to be undertaken in
the chapters to come.

## The Conscience of Europe

If there is one outstanding characteristic throughout the Freud–Rolland correspondence, it is the mutual respect, admiration, and love that bonded the two
men. In Rolland's first letter to Freud on February 22, 1923, he wrote how fascinated he was by Freud's "subliminal visions," calling him the "Christopher
Columbus of a new continent of the spirit."[4] On May 3, 1931, he wrote to tell
Freud of his feeling of moral kinship with him and his identification with
Freud's passion for truth. Then, on February 8, 1936, he penned this testament
to their friendship: "Of all the reasons I have to be grateful to Stefan Zweig, the
least of them is not for having introduced us, for it was from this meeting ten
years ago that our friendship was born. You know what respect I have for the
man I have admired for so long, whose fearless glance is able to penetrate into
the depths of the interior abyss. I am happy and proud to have his friendship." In
return Freud was even more effusive: "That I have been allowed to exchange a
greeting with you will remain a happy memory to the end of my days," he wrote
to Rolland in 1923 and again in 1931: "I may confess to you that I have rarely experienced that mysterious attraction of one human being for another."[5] Generally speaking, Rolland appreciated Freud for his intellect and moral courage
whereas Freud admired Rolland for his artistry, politics, and humanity. However,
particularly with respect to Freud, we can be more precise about why it was that
Rolland elicited idealizations that, given the fact that the two met for all of one
afternoon, seem to go well beyond what one might expect.

Jones intimates that it was the horrors of the Great War and Rolland's visible
presence as mediator and "conscience of Europe" during it that moved Freud to
contact Rolland.[6] We know that Freud's first reaction to the outbreak of hostilities was one of enthusiasm and support for the Central Powers, a rekindling of
the nationalistic and political ardors of his university days, and, beyond that, an
apparent regression to the military preoccupation of his youth.[7] This mood was
short-lived, however, as a host of factors—the sheer brutality of the war, the
moral mendacity of statesmen on both sides, the loss of objectivity in the sciences, concern for his sons, and disruption of the psychoanalytic movement—
quickly led him to become more neutral and pessimistic. By November of 1914
he was thoroughly disillusioned, writing to Lou Andreas-Salomé that mankind

was "organically unfitted" for civilization: "We have to abdicate, and the Great Unknown . . . will sometime repeat such an experiment with another race."[8] This slow process of deidealization led Freud to a familiar turn: the generation of new cultural texts. In a state of mourning, Freud gained insight into his own illusions and those of his fellow men and then offered his psychoanalytic ruminations to culture at large in the hopes that a new, more humane and cohesive social whole could be established.[9]

Especially relevant for our purposes is his short essay entitled "The Disillusionment of the War."[10] After describing his disillusionment and the reasons for it, Freud goes on to elaborate how psychoanalytic instinct theory shed light on the nature of war. Mankind is ill fitted for civilization, thought Freud, because of the large number of cultural "hypocrites"—those who behave ethically due to external constraints, the possibility of rewards, and the fear of punishments— who inhabit it. It is these masses who, under conditions of social breakdown such as war or secularization, will not hesitate to regress and then express the most primitive aggressive, antisocial tendencies. In contrast to these masses, Freud pointed to those truly cultured men, much fewer in number, who showed an ability to internalize external constraints and ennoble their instinctual endowment through education, experience, and renunciation. It was these men who could adapt to the demands of civilization by transforming egoistic into altruistic impulses.

One could surmise that the best of these men would make themselves known when society begins to disintegrate morally and structurally. Alexander Mitscherlich cites Rolland as being one of these few and points to his book *Au-dessus de la Mêlée* ("Above the Battle") as evidence to support his claim.[11] The latter was a direct result of the horrors of the Great War on Rolland's sensitive conscience. Rolland, who up to that time had been known only from his duties as a professor of musicology (at the Sorbonne) and his growing fame as a playwright and novelist, embraced the mantle of social activism, embarking on a series of essays, appeals, letters, and moral diatribes. Sixteen of these were then culled from the various newspapers, journals, and reviews in which he had published and subsumed under a single title.[12] The red thread uniting these articles was the reasoned moral appeal to intellectuals, public officials, and governments to create a higher ground of constructive dialogue through which hostilities could be adjudicated. In his articles Rolland called attention to the loss of ethics and common sense, the lack of balanced judgment, and the preponderance of hypocrisy and savagery among the supposed cultured in both France and Germany. Nationalism and its appeal to the baser elements in men was attacked in all of its subtle forms. Rolland exposed the perversion of ideology—its role in undermining reason and its complicity in fermenting a militaristic nationalism. Valued social institutions such as the church and respected classes of individuals such as scientists, political leaders, writers, and academics were portrayed as actively contributing to blind nationalistic fervor. Rolland appealed for heroic individualism free from mendacious ideology and social conformism, dispassionate and reasoned judgment, humanitarianism, fraternity, compromise, and self-restraint. Although he used idealistic terminology to clothe his appeals, Rolland was well aware of the power of psychological and social forces and the probable futility of his efforts. Nevertheless, he never allowed his realism and pessimism to interfere with a conscience that bid him to hope and act. The result was adulation among many (the "conscience of Europe"), outright condemnation and hostility among some, international fame, and a Nobel Prize.[13]

Certainly Rolland, in his first letter to Freud, personalized his efforts at mediation by expressing his disgust at the war and the "lunacy" of mankind and his deep sympathy for the vanquished: "If it is sad to be, as you are, in a country that has been ravaged by war, it is no less sad, believe me, to be, as I, in a victorious country and to feel disconnected from it: for I have always preferred to be among those who suffer rather than among those who cause suffering . . . each victory ruins the victor, and the wheel of misfortune never ceases to turn." In return Freud acknowledged Rolland's status as a cultural leader by sending him a copy of *Group Psychology and the Analysis of the Ego.* Indeed, to the Swiss analyst Charles Baudouin Freud once stated: "The true destiny of the world rests on perhaps a dozen men: Rolland is one of them."[14] David Werman, following Mitscherlich, points beyond *Above the Battle* to Freud's letter of January 29, 1926, as evidence that Freud considered Rolland to be a truly cultured individual, a "great man": "Unforgettable Man, to have soared to such heights of humanity through so much hardship and suffering! I revered you as an artist and apostle of love for mankind many years before I saw you." Indeed, this is a striking, if not extraordinary, remark by a man not easily given to accolades. As Werman points out, Freud's stress on Rolland's achieving a high ethical ideal (the "heights of humanity") through "hardship and suffering" indicates that Freud thought Rolland possessed an unusual capacity to transform egoistic into altruistic impulses.[15]

Further confirmation of this line of thought can be found in an important yet neglected passage in Freud's essay "Dostoevsky and Parricide." There Freud, recalling his essays on the war, draws a contrast between two types of moral character.[16] In the opening pages Freud isolates four facets of Dostoevsky's personality: the creative artist, the neurotic, the sinner, and the moralist. It is the latter Freud finds as the "weak point" in Dostoevsky. Although aware of the true nature of the deepest wishes of mankind, Dostoevsky was unable to exercise the "essence of morality, renunciation." As a result, his moral standards were not indicative of the transformation of egoistic into altruistic inclinations. Rather, they became the means through which untamed instincts could find an excuse to sin again without remorse. In this Freud was reiterating territory he covered in *The Future of an Illusion.* Near the end of the seventh chapter of that work, Freud had spoken of how "Russian introspectiveness" (referring to Dostoevsky) had reached the conclusion that sin is pleasing to God. Institutional religion had adopted this idea in the hopes that in return for such large concessions to man's instincts a modicum of civilized social behavior could be wrought. Freud used this as one more example of how religion ultimately failed in its task to promote morality and "susceptibility to culture." A system based on external compulsion and reward and punishment could not "educate" the instincts and had created a civilization based on a gigantic hypocrisy. In light of the reality of secularization, what little ability religion had to promote moral behavior would soon vanish in the flames of man's uninhibited egoism. Dostoevsky, insofar as he lacked the psychological capacity to be moral unto himself, landed in a retrograde position similar to that of the "common-man." For both, reconciliation between their instinctual life and social being was effected through submission to the "external compulsion" of the state and state-sponsored religion.

Freud countered to this portrait of Dostoevsky the ideal of a man who possessed a full measure of the "essence of morality" alongside the qualities of creative ability, intelligence, and "love of humanity." Such a man would not subscribe to a narrow nationalism, would see through the mendacity of organized religion, and would utilize his writings in the service of "becoming a teacher and liberator of humanity." This way of life, states Freud, could be termed "apostolic." Freud, I believe, had Rolland in mind. Rolland was educated, tolerant, a man who had achieved a depth of "humanity" through "hardship and suffering" and who saw through and wrote about the machinations of culture and religion. And didn't Freud refer to Rolland as the "artist and apostle of love for mankind"? In this connection it is interesting to note that outside of actual historical figures who were saints, the only other person in the entirety of Freud's written corpus and, as far as I have been able to surmise, his correspondence whom he referred to as an "apostle" was Rolland. Not so coincidentally, Freud began writing his essay on Dostoevsky a few months after he had written his letter for the celebration of Rolland's sixtieth birthday, referred to above, in which he called Rolland an "artist and apostle of love for mankind."[17] Finally, as Fisher has noted, Freud and Rolland had discussed Dostoevsky at their luncheon in Vienna in 1924.[18] In other words, Freud linked Rolland with Dostoevsky and the issue of art and morality. It does seem, then, that for Freud Rolland was the cultured man par excellence.

## This One Hope

If Rolland was an ethical exemplar whose internationalist and pacifistic stands influenced Freud, then no less did he touch Freud on a deeply personal level: through Freud's racial and cultural status as a Jew. This theme is apparent from the very first letter Freud sent to Rolland (March 4, 1923):

Dear Sir,

That I have been allowed to exchange a greeting with you will remain a happy memory to the end of my days. Because for us your name has been associated with the most precious of beautiful illusions, that of love extended to all mankind.

I, of course, belong to a race which in the Middle Ages was held responsible for all epidemics and which today is blamed for the disintegration of the Austrian Empire and the German defeat. Such experiences have a sobering effect and are not conducive to make one believe in illusions. A great part of my life's work (I am ten years older than you) has been spent [trying to] destroy illusions of my own and those of mankind. But if this one hope cannot be at least partly realized, if in the course of evolution we don't learn to divert our instincts from destroying our own kind, if we continue to hate one another for minor differences and kill each other for petty gain, if we go on exploiting the great progress made in the control of natural resources for our mutual destruction, what kind of future lies in store for us? It is surely hard enough to ensure the perpetuation of our species in the conflict between our instinctual nature and the demands made upon us by civilization.

My writings cannot be what yours are: comfort and refreshment for the reader. But if I may believe that they have aroused your interest, I shall permit myself to send you a small book which is sure to be unknown to you: *Group Psychology and the Analysis of the Ego*, published in 1921. Not that I consider this work to be particularly successful, but it shows a way from the analysis of the individual to an understanding of society.

Sincerely yours
Freud

Prominent in this letter is Freud's association of Rolland with the love-command that, as Homans has pointed out, is referred to as "this one hope" and can be characterized in psychoanalytic terms as a "good illusion."[19] Freud allies his own personal ideals and those that guided psychoanalysis with the humanity and love of Rolland. At the same time, Freud reveals how the love-command engaged his status as not only German but Jewish. This association of Rolland with the love-command and anti-Semitism had significant precursors in Freud's political and developmental past—precursors which we need to detail to appreciate the deep symbolic meaning Rolland had for Freud.

We know from Jones's biography and more recent historical and sociological forays, particularly those by Schorske and McGrath, the important role fin-de-siècle Viennese politics played in Freud's life and thought.[20] During Freud's childhood and student years (1860–1880), Vienna's sociopolitical atmosphere was suffused with the tolerant air of political liberalism and its attempt to actualize the enlightenment ideals of equality, freedom, human rights, and a secular, rational order. These ideals were championed and mediated to Freud by his father and developed in his school years through his association with close friends like Heinrich Braun, later a pivotal figure in European politics. Freud's early desire to study law, his membership in the radical student group *Lesverin der Deutschen Studenten Wiens*, and inclination to enter politics are all testaments to these early personal and social influences. Like many non-Orthodox, middle-class Jews, he aspired to assimilation and preached the gospel of democracy and nationalism. However, after 1880 any Viennese Jew would survey the political landscape with alarm. The collapse of political liberalism waned in the face of the rise of the anti-Semitic Christian Socialist Party, a trend which reached its apex when, in 1897, Karl Lueger became mayor of Vienna. Freud felt the effects of this movement in many areas of his life, the most important being the continual frustration of his cherished wish to become a professor at the University of Vienna. Doubting the power of a political solution to social injustice, perceiving Catholic complicity in the rise of Lueger, and convinced of the mendacity of religious injunctions to tolerance like the love-command, Freud turned away from the outer religio-political realm to that of the inner world, there to seek another arena for the transformation of self and society. Indeed, as Klein and Homans have pointed out, for Freud psychoanalysis became a new basis on which to construct a social whole. The "cultural texts" were but an extension of the "psychoanalytic movement" and the clearest expressions of Freud's desire to create a social space through which humanity could find its way to increased tolerance and equality.[21]

This religio-political reality, then, invariably affected the motivation behind and expression of Freud's "cultural works." Indeed, while ignited in some way by his sociopolitical surround, these motivations can be found rooted in Freud's developmental past, particularly those famous complexes that have been termed his "Rome Neurosis" and "Hannibal phantasy."[22] As cataloged in *The Interpretation of Dreams*, Freud had a number of dreams during the 1880s and 1890s that betrayed the impact of religion and politics on his unconscious, none of which were more significant than the "Rome Dreams."[23] These dreams occurred during a period in which Freud developed an irresistible and overwhelming desire to visit Rome, a longing that provoked fear and anxiety and was fulfilled only after a period of successful self-analysis. Although seemingly aware of the full import of the latent thoughts and developmental precursors that instigated the dreams, Freud was willing only to divulge that his analysis unearthed his identification with Hannibal. Like Freud, Hannibal had been "fated not to see Rome" and "symbolized the conflict between the tenacity of Jewry and the organization of the Catholic Church."[24] In addition, Freud related the childhood experience that served to extend the behavioral attitudes associated with his identification with Hannibal to the religio-political sphere. That experience consisted of a story his father had related to him concerning an encounter in his youth with anti-Semitism, in which he had been obliged to react to a verbal taunt in a compliant and passive fashion. The intent of the father was to affirm to his son how political liberalism had changed things for the better. Unfortunately, this moral entirely bypassed the young "Sigismund," who remembered only the "unheroic conduct" of his father. Endeavoring to replace the story with one more befitting his budding sense of masculine narcissism, Freud recalled the scene where Hannibal, promoted by his father, swore an oath to "take vengeance on the Romans." As Schorske comments, Freud's identification with Hannibal's oath was both "pledge and project" and, as project, both "political and filial": "He defined his oedipal stance in such a way as to overcome his father by realizing the liberal creed his father professed but had failed to defend. Freud-Hannibal as 'Semitic general' would avenge his feeble father against Rome, a Rome that symbolized the 'organization of the Catholic Church' and the Habsburg régime that supported it."[25]

McGrath has further argued that the antiauthoritarian stance which animated Freud's Hannibal phantasy found its origin in his relationship with his older nephew John. While enemy and competitor in one sense, John also collaborated with Freud in the exploration of sexuality and the overthrow of paternal authority. He was, then, the developmental model for Freud's efforts to find fellow "coconspirators" like Josef Breuer, Wilhelm Fliess, and Jung to help him overthrow social representatives of paternal authority and their institutions.[26] Zilboorg and Grigg enrich this developmental portrait, focusing on the nurse-maid who lived with Freud's family and took care of him in his infancy.[27] The nursemaid, whom Freud was deeply attached to and regarded as a second mother, was a devoted Catholic and introduced Freud to the area churches and teachings about heaven and damnation. The visits and lessons seemed to have made an impact on the young Sigismund, who came home from church preaching "about how God conducted his affairs."[28] Unfortunately the nursemaid, caught stealing, was abruptly dismissed just before Freud's third birthday. Zilboorg thinks that Freud reacted to the loss of his nursemaid with feelings of disappointment and betrayal, feelings which became, alongside his deep affection for her, associated with Catholic Christianity. Grigg adds that Freud's ambivalence toward Rome, his desire to visit it and subsequent feelings of fear and anxiety, finds its developmental precursor in the Oedipal desire for the "second mother" and the castration fear it evoked. These feelings were then invariably associated with Catholicism, with its maternal themes and teachings of damnation. In other words, if at one point Freud hoped for the success of the agenda of political liberalism and assimilation to the Catholic culture of Vienna, Catholic complicity in the rise of Lueger and anti-Semitism surely awakened the developmental complexes associated with his nursemaid and his father.

To return now to Freud's letter to Rolland of March 4, 1923, there is much to suggest that these developmental precursors and the sociopolitical reality of his time played no small part in determining the depth of his love, admiration, and hopes for Rolland (and, as we shall see in the next chapter, with his analysis of the oceanic feeling in *Civilization and Its Discontents*). For example, Freud's bitter portrayal of his plight as a Jew during the war and of Jews during the Middle Ages, his hope for assimilation and the need for tolerance (this "one hope"), and the association of both with Rolland ("for *us* your name has been associated . . .") suggests that Rolland reminded Freud of the liberal political figures of Vienna's past. Although a renounced Catholic, Rolland espoused the ethical ideals Freud associated with Christianity yet proclaimed a liberal, tolerant political agenda. Indeed, available evidence indicates that Freud was aware that Rolland championed the Jewish cause. For example, in *Above the Battle* one can find not only a general appeal for justice and harmony between all races and nations but appeals for Europe to correct past injustices with regard to the rights of smaller nations and groups of peoples. One part of *Above the Battle* contains Rolland's letter of January 12, 1915, to Frederik Van Eeden, the publisher of the newspaper *De Amsterdammer*, in which Rolland proclaims it a "duty" for those who "feel for the brotherhood of mankind" to stand for the rights of the neglected and powerless, among whom he cites "the Jewish people." Because Freud read *Above the Battle* and was also in contact with Van Eeden, writing him a letter on December 28, 1914, concerning a psychoanalytic interpretation of the Great War, it is even more likely that he would have noticed this particular phrase from Rolland's pen.

We also know that Freud was emotionally caught up in the Dreyfus affair and deeply appreciative of Zola's *J'accuse*. Although he preferred to remain neutral in the affair, a position that he regretted years later, Rolland became convinced of the innocence of Dreyfus as a result of Zola's work. Remaining politically inactive, Rolland nevertheless did write a play, *Les Loups*, which stirred controversy in France and was widely perceived by the anti-Dreyfusards in France and by Jewish acquaintances of Freud's in Vienna, such as Stefan Zweig, as proclaiming the innocence of Dreyfus (although pro-Dreyfusards in France found it all too neutral for their tastes). Although there is no direct evidence that Freud read *Les Loups*, we do know he read Rolland's play *Les Leonides*, which was the epilogue of a cycle of eight plays, of which *Les Loups* was the third. It seems likely, then, that Freud would have known of the much more famous *Les Loups*. One can understand why this cycle of dramas would have appealed to Freud, for they were inspired by the French Revolution and had in common the aim of recreating a passion for its major theme and values: the conflict between the individual and the state and the stress on the enlightenment ideals of reason, justice, liberty, and faith. In addition, Freud may have known that Rolland during this time was married to a Jew who was the daughter of Michel Breal, a prominent French academic and pro-Dreyfusard.[29]

Later, when the threat of Hitler and virulent anti-Semitism was on the rise, the question is no longer in doubt. Since 1926, Rolland had been at the very forefront of the battle against fascism, and his anti-Nazi and anti-racist writings were widely publicized. In 1932 Rolland helped to organize the Amsterdam Congress, convened to warn against the coming of a new World War, imperialism, and fascism. Jones states that Freud signed a petition circulated among members of the medical profession to help publicize the Congress.[30] In 1933, in his *I Will Not Rest*, a kind of sequel to *Above the Battle*, Rolland devoted a chapter to racism and fascism, condemning in particular the "disgusting persecution of Jews in Germany today" and the "stupid and disastrous racism of the Hitlerites."[31] In the same year, in a letter to his Indian friend Kalidas Nag, Rolland said of *Mein Kampf*: "One cannot imagine anything breathing a more deadly hatred and a narrower, more inhuman, more ignorant fanaticism."[32] On the topic of race Rolland had this to say:

> In the disgusting persecution of Jews in Germany today, one does not know whether to condemn more severely the stupidity or the savagery of the rulers. . . . Hitler's fist has smashed the author of *Nathan the Wise*. Hitlerism reveals itself to the eyes of the world as an usurpation of power over the great German people by savage illiterates or spiteful malignant creatures like Goebbels, whose weak and violent brain has been turned by Gobinean's ill-digested paradoxes about the "Inequality of Human Races," and by the fumes of a delirious pride intent on believing in the supremacy of his race. . . . I profess my aversion and disgust for all racism. At the present stage of humanity, it is a stupidity and a crime. Without here discussing the absurd and illusory concept of "race" . . . the whole civilization of today is the product of the efforts and combined achievements of all peoples, of all races which have intermingled with each other. It is insane and absurd to pretend to sort them out. It is so, particularly, as concerns the Jewish race, or to be more ex-

act, the Jewish races. . . . They have become an integral element in the wealth
and intelligence of Europe. . . . Hitlerism, which under the pretext of defending
the nation, is persecuting or expelling the Jewish element, is destroying one of the
material and intellectual sources of wealth in the nation. Germany will for a long
time suffer the consequences of this absolutist error.[33]

Freud was also aware of Rolland's refusal to accept the 1932 Goethe Prize, a
prize Freud dearly coveted and was awarded in 1930. Rolland cited as reasons for
his rejection "the crushing of freedoms, the persecution of parties opposed to the
government, the brutal and infamous proscription of the Jews, all of which rouse
the world's revolt and my own."[34] Freud gives an indication of his awareness of
Rolland's political activity in a letter of January 6, 1936, to Victor Wittowski, who
had asked Freud to write something for Rolland's seventieth birthday but to ex-
clude all reference to politics. Freud vacillated, initially refusing, then comply-
ing by writing the famous "open letter" to Rolland concerning his trip to the
Acropolis. During the course of his vacillation, he complained to Wittowski as
follows: "my ability to produce has dried up. . . . [I]f there is something that
makes this refusal easier for me, it is that 'all reference to politics' has to be excluded. Under this paralyzing restriction—not being able to follow my urge to
praise his (Rolland's) courage of conviction, his love of truth and his tolerance—
I couldn't do anything, even if I were in my prime."[35] Once again the key term is
"tolerance," which signifies Freud's opinion of Rolland vis-à-vis Jews.

In sum, Rolland was a symbol for Freud, a symbol who inspired the as yet un-
extinguished hopes and aspirations of his youth—hopes that converged around
the themes of assimilation, anti-Semitism, tolerance, and social justice. Rolland,
the man who embodied love extended to all men, who envisaged a civilization
where all races and peoples could exist in harmony, was a true and trustworthy
exponent of these ideals. As Freud once wrote to Rolland, reciprocating his advocacy of tolerance: "Across all boundaries and bridges, I would like to press
your hand."[36]

## Rolland and the Brother Band

The above indicates that although religious issues were not directly discussed
during the early period of the Freud–Rolland correspondence, they were everywhere present. Given the religious aura of Rolland's cultural presence, the motivations behind Freud's sending Rolland a copy of *The Future of an Illusion* seem
rather straightforward and understandable. On the other hand, the latter monograph was, especially in its time, a volatile and even offensive work, even among
a few affiliated with psychoanalysis. One thus becomes somewhat curious as to
why Freud thought Rolland might be receptive to the methodological and epistemological perspective it championed. On a more sociological level, other suspicions are raised. We know that the period after the Great War was a tenuous
time for the psychoanalytic movement. Previous defections of Carl Jung and Alfred Adler and the destruction of the social fabric wrought by the war had put

Freud's plans for the international dissemination of psychoanalysis in disarray. In short, Freud was actively looking for new contacts to help his cause. One wonders whether Freud had more complex motives for engaging Rolland on the topic of psychoanalysis and culture. These issues lead us to consider another aspect of "assimilation," that dealing with Freud's child, psychoanalysis, and the role of the "interlocutor" in Freud's life and work.

Freud's efforts to insert psychoanalytic modes of practice and thought into mainstream European culture took forms common to many movements: a reigning charismatic founder; the hierarchical arrangement of a group or committee of like-minded followers; the creation of an ideology (the metapsychology); a standard set of practices (clinical techniques) and training institutions to oversee their proper dissemination; the establishment of conferences and journals; and so forth. In this context, as we pointed out earlier, the so-called cultural texts can be viewed as but one more extension of the "psychoanalytic movement." A sociological reading of *The Future of an Illusion* highlighting the role of the interlocutor, which complements but is almost always overshadowed by the more familiar epistemological reading emphasizing the illusory, wish-fulfilling nature of religious belief, makes this particularly clear.

To elaborate: that Freud was concerned with the social dynamics of religion is clear from the outset of *The Future of an Illusion*. Freud thought that in the past religion had provided an inestimable service to mankind in its ability to ward off anomie and neurosis. However, unlike social theorists such as Durkheim, who saw religion as an "eternal" and basic constituent of society, or even Weber, who, despite his proclamation of disenchantment, held out the possibility of the charismatic rebirth of religion, Freud was utterly convinced of the inevitable decline of religion and the irreversible process of secularization. Science, with its appeal to reason and experience "which in the long run nothing can withstand," meant the collapse of the cultural superego and hence the rise of anomie, outbreak of neurosis, aggression, and social dislocation. Civilization had little to fear from "true believers," that minority protected from the vicissitudes of secularization by deep ties of affection to God. On the other hand, again recalling his essays on the Great War, Freud saw the great majority of men as believers in only a nominal sense, being "hypocrites," lacking in "cultural adaptability" and the power to sublimate. These masses, then, who were not "vehicles" of civilization but potential enemies of it, would, upon learning of the decline of religion, pose a direct threat to civilized behavior. This gave rise to what can be seen as the major sociohistorical problem Freud tried to address in *The Future of an Illusion:* that "either these dangerous masses must be held down . . . or else the relationship between civilization and religion must undergo a fundamental revision."[37]

Freud's solution to the problem, which called for the attempt to maintain cohesion and civilized behavior in society on purely secular and rational grounds, is undoubtedly sociologically as well as psychoanalytically naive. Nevertheless, there was some method in his madness, one that had a peculiarly Weberian flavor to it. Aside from the "true believers" and the great masses, Freud isolated a third group in society that consisted of the cultured elite. This group, whom

Freud saw as the "vehicles" and "brainworkers" of civilization, controlled the relation between religion and society. Being somewhat secularized, they were, despite a willingness to defend religion's cause, open to the force of Freud's argument. It was to this group, then, that Freud addressed *The Future of an Illusion.* His hope consisted of inserting his psychoanalysis into Western culture as part and parcel of the emerging scientific attitude toward reality, hence helping to avoid the kind of social dislocation that could result from the historical transition of mankind from childhood to maturity. It was to this end that Freud employed the rhetorical strategy of creating an interlocutor who embodied the characteristics of the cultured elite and was equally capable of using theological arguments and of being swayed by psychoanalysis.

Rolland possessed attributes which made him attractive to Freud as a possible interlocutor and conduit for the dissemination of psychoanalysis. Rolland was a valued member of the intellectual elite, a gentile connected to the reigning Catholic culture in France, a university professor, a Nobel Prize winner, an internationalist and renowned sociopolitical figure and moral exemplar. In this sense Rolland could only have reminded Freud of the sociological role he had envisioned for Jung.[38] Since the turn of the century, Freud had attempted to universalize psychoanalysis beyond the confines of the particularistic, Jewish "band of brothers" who made up the early Viennese circle of analysts. Jung had served Freud well in this sense simply by his status as a gentile and his roots as a Western European. If Freud was Moses, Jung was Joshua, the heir designate who would take psychoanalysis to the promised land. At times Freud's efforts bordered on the grandiose and humorous—had he not asked Jung in 1907 if Jung had any contact who might be used to get Kaiser Wilhelm interested in psychoanalysis?[39] But now the heir apparent had abdicated. Although Rolland could not be an heir, surely Freud could not but perceive him as helping to fill the void.

The letters of the early period buttress this argument, for they clearly indicate that Rolland gave Freud reason to hope that he was predisposed to psychoanalytic thinking about self and society. Here the close affinity between psychoanalysts and artists makes its presence felt once again. Freud thought religion reified unconscious processes for purposes of social control. However, artists, existing at the margins of culture, had unusual access to the unconscious and a unique ability to represent unconscious processes through myth and symbol. Indeed, Freud had often cited great poets and philosophers like Goethe, Plato, and Schiller as prefiguring key insights of psychoanalytic theory. To his contemporary Arthur Schnitzler, Freud wrote: "Whenever I get deeply absorbed in your beautiful creations I invariably seem to find beneath their poetic surface the very presuppositions, interests and conclusions which I know to be my own."[40] Although Rolland's claim to international fame lay in his role as "conscience of Europe" during the Great War, Freud and much of Europe had already come to know of him through novels like *Jean-Christophe* and plays like *Les Loups.* Freud was enamored of Rolland's literary talent, later "revering" him as an "artist" and citing the moments of "exaltation and pleasure" Rolland's plays and novels had given him. Rolland's writings provided comfort and refreshment for readers by providing a socially acceptable outlet for frustrated and repressed wishes and edified them by representing universal features and conflicts of the human soul in an ego-syntonic manner.[41]

More important, Rolland's works clearly engaged the psychic underground that psychoanalysis had made its home. This theme is apparent from Rolland's first letter to Freud. Citing his approval of Freud's "subliminal visions" and their correspondence to some of his own "intuitions," Rolland went on to draw parallels between the insights of the great philosophers and poets and those of psychoanalysis. Whereas the former had arrived at the truths of the unconscious through chance, Freud was truly the "Christopher Columbus of a new continent of the mind" insofar as he was the "first" to have scientifically charted its deeper terrain and provided a systematic map for the benefit of all.[42] In return, Freud noted Rolland's embodiment of mystical-poetic access to the unconscious in exclaiming, as he had with Arthur Schnitzler, that "it is easier for you than for us to read the human soul!"[43] Further, in a letter to Jean Bloch shortly after his luncheon in Vienna with Freud in 1924, Rolland wrote with pride that Freud had approved "sans reserve" of his novel L' Âme enchantée and that Freud's "scientific experiments" had entirely confirmed his own "experiences."[44]

To Freud's surprise, Rolland also revealed that he had been one of the very first Frenchmen to have read and appreciated Freud's works. In his letter of February 22, 1923, Rolland proudly states that while Freud's name was now well known in France, he had found and read "a few" of Freud's books, most notably The Interpretation of Dreams, twenty years before. Jones refers to Rolland's long-standing interest in psychoanalysis as "remarkable."[45] This becomes understandable when seen in the light of the poor reception psychoanalysis initially received in France. Up until 1926, when the first Psychoanalytic Society was formed in Paris, the French medical establishment all but ignored psychoanalysis. Although it was appreciated by those in literature and philosophy, nothing resembling a movement was formed. The most aggressive group that sought an alliance with psychoanalysis was the surrealists, the members of which did not impress Freud, who called them "cranks."[46] In 1907 Freud remarked to Jung how recalcitrant France was to psychoanalysis, and in 1914 he proclaimed that France was the "least disposed" of all the European countries to acknowledge psychoanalysis.[47] In 1925, Freud, remarking on the birth pangs accompanying the growing psychoanalytic movement in France, observed that "the interest in psychoanalysis began among the men of letters. To understand this, it must be borne in mind that from the time of the writing of The Interpretation of Dreams psychoanalysis ceased to be a purely medical subject."[48] Surely the figure of Rolland lies behind these words. After all, Rolland was French, a man of letters who, unlike the surrealists, was held in great esteem by Freud, who had read Freud's book on dreams somewhere around 1903 or 1904 and had recently informed him of that fact. Surely it was Rolland's interest in psychoanalysis that was a contributing factor in freud's sending him Group Psychology and the Analysis of the Ego and The Future of an Illusion. In 1924, Freud also gave Rolland a copy of Introductory Lectures on Psychoanalysis and, in 1933, a copy of the New Introductory Lectures.[49]

Freud must also have felt that Rolland's sympathy for psychoanalysis extended to a similar assessment of institutional religion. Freud may have noted that in *Above the Battle* Rolland had attacked institutional Christianity and what he thought to be its hypocritical actions during the Great War.[50] He may also have known that, although socialized into Catholicism, Rolland had renounced it as an adolescent, never to return.[51] However, it was Freud's direct exchange with Rolland over *Liluli*, a play clearly displaying the latter's distaste for institutional religion, which undoubtedly made the strongest impact on him. *Liluli* was written by Rolland in 1919 as a result of his disillusionment with the behavior of men and nations during the Great War. Rolland took abstract conceptions and values such as Truth, God, Illusion, and Opinion and embodied them as the principal actors in the play. Several lesser parts symbolized professions and groups of peoples—journalists and diplomats, French and Germans, intellectuals and workers. Generally speaking, the play was an ironic farce, a social satire that sought to portray the gigantic hypocrisy of ideology and its role in subverting reason and fraternity and fermenting hatred and fanaticism. Rolland endeavored to illuminate how ideology was manufactured and controlled by various classes, groups, and institutions of society. Although no social group was spared Rolland's pen, it is of particular interest to us that God, symbolized by the character of Maître-Dieu, was portrayed by Rolland as purely an invention of mankind. In cahoots with the character "Liluli" (Illusion), God was seen as chaining and blindfolding Reason and Truth, under the sway of journalists, diplomats, and intellectuals, promoting killing and hatred, and serving nationalistic interests. When asked by Polichinello, a character symbolizing freedom and laughter, whether he (the Maître-Dieu) was fearful of the wrath of the God in heaven for his actions and deceptions, Maître-Dieu laughs uproariously and says: "the Old Fellow up there, sir  .  .  .  is Me."[52]

The impact of *Liluli* on Freud can be gauged by the following interchange with Rolland. Less than a week after receiving Freud's first letter of March 4, 1923, Rolland sent Freud a copy of *Liluli*. On March 12, 1923, Freud responded: "Thank you very much for the small book. I have of course been long familiar with its terrible beauty. I find the subtle irony of your dedication well deserved since I had completely forgotten Liluli when I wrote the silly passage in question in my letter, and obviously one ought not to do that." Rolland's dedication read: "to Freud the 'Destroyer of Illusions.'"[53] The question is the meaning behind Freud's finding this dedication so ironic. I believe the following is a plausible interpretation. In his letter of March 4th, Freud had emphasized his own disillusionment as a Jew and a German and how it had compelled him to destroy the illusions of man. Freud honored and extolled Rolland's efforts to create unity. Yet he associated Rolland with "beautiful illusions" while adding that Rolland's writings, and here Freud undoubtedly had in mind Rolland's novels, sought less to destroy illusions than to give people consolation and comfort. This was well in keeping with Freud's general views on creative writing of all kinds. However, the very fact that out of all his books Rolland chose to send Freud *Liluli* reveals the general tenor of his reaction to Freud's letter. Responding to the "silly passage" in Freud's letter, Rolland sent him an example of his own work that exposed the beliefs and "illusions" of mankind, their danger, and their mendacity.[54] This was appropriate, for, as we shall fully detail later, Rolland was adamant about the need to expose his own illusions as well as those of others. This kinship was not lost on Freud, who explicitly acknowledged Rolland's love of truth in his works and correspondence. It seems likely, then, that *Liluli*, alongside Rolland's interest in psychoanalysis and stature as a cultural figure, was a contributing factor in moving Freud to think Rolland would be receptive to as volatile and potentially controversial a book as *The Future of an Illusion*. We may add that Freud's perception was essentially correct, for although Rolland did promote a mystical religion, he agreed with Freud's assessment of the "common-man's" religion.

What remained unknown to Freud at this point in time was that Rolland had pursued his interest in psychoanalysis with those closer to home. At the beginning of the Great War, Rolland had retired to Switzerland as part of a voluntary exile. Of course, since 1906, Switzerland, through the figures of Eugen Bleuler, Flournoy, and especially Jung, had become a second home for psychoanalysis— a psychoanalysis which was still in formation and, being geographically farther away from Freud, could tolerate more glaring differences in technique and metapsychology. There Rolland became friends with the Swiss psychoanalyst Charles Baudouin.[55] He also read the psychoanalytic writings of Alphonse Maeder, Ferdinand Morel, Th. Flournoy, and psychologists such as Myers, James, and Starbuck and was at least indirectly familiar with Jung.[56] Disillusioned with the performance of his fellow man and with Christianity during the war and, like Freud, aware of the pitfalls of secularization, Rolland looked for new sources that could help to revitalize what he considered to be the moral and spiritual collapse of Europe. As we shall detail in the chapters to come, Rolland, deeply immersed in the "Oriental renaissance" sweeping Europe in the nineteenth and twentieth centuries, became convinced that the source of wisdom that could revitalize Europe lay Eastward, in the mystic personality and philosophy of India. Rolland then used his knowledge of the various models inherent in the emerging field of the psychology of religion to create interest in the scientific study of mysticism. His letter to Freud of December 5, 1927, far from being a reflex action to *The Future of an Illusion*, was an attempt to enlist Freud in his efforts to create a universal "science–religion," one he thought was the answer to the collapse of the cultural superego. This, of course, put him directly in conflict with Freud, for although both saw the value of science and psychology, for Freud that meant secular psychoanalysis whereas for Rolland it meant a religious psychology that was destined to remind Freud of Jung.[57]

For Rolland, then, Freud was a formidable psychologist, the creator of a science of introspection that could be highly useful in investigating the benefits of the mystical personality. For Freud, Rolland served well as a bridge figure who enabled him to continue to address the implications of a psychoanalytic theory of mysticism and culture. An interlocutor? Surely Rolland was what I call the "silent interlocutor," the man behind Freud's ruminations on religion and mysticism in *Civilization and Its Discontents*.[58] A coconspirator and fellow member of the band of brothers? Certainly Freud had high hopes on this score. It soon became apparent, however, that Rolland, far from being a member of the brother band, had his own agenda. Two men with two very different ideas on the relation of psychology to religion and with varying prescriptions for modern culture — this was the unstated background which lurked behind every corner of their debate on mysticism. It is to the exegesis of that debate we now adjourn.

# The Enigma of the Oceanic Feeling

Freud begins *Civilization and Its Discontents* by referring to a friend of his whom he thought to be a great man, one of the "exceptional few" who eschewed "false standards of measurement" such as wealth and power and knew what was of "true value in life" and whose greatness rested on "attributes and achievements which are completely foreign to the aims and ideals of the multitude." The "friend" was, of course, Romain Rolland.[1] Freud then went on to describe how he had received a letter from Rolland, dated December 5, 1927, in response to *The Future of an Illusion*. Rolland "entirely agreed" with his analysis of the "common-man's" religion but pointed out that Freud neglected to treat the true source of religious sentiments. This, stated Freud, by way of summarizing Rolland's letter,

> consists in a peculiar feeling . . . which he would like to call a sensation of "eternity," a feeling as of something limitless, unbounded—as it were, "oceanic." This feeling . . . is a purely subjective fact, not an article of faith; it brings with it no assurance of personal immortality, but is the source of the religious energy which is seized upon by the various Churches and religious systems, directed by them into particular channels, and doubtless also exhausted by them.[2]

Rolland hoped Freud would subject the oceanic feeling to analysis, and now, almost two years later, Freud took him up on his challenge, an attempt which had a formative impact on the psychoanalytic theory of mysticism. As many would have it, the oceanic feeling is but the psychoanalytic version of the perennialist claim that mysticism is "one and the same everywhere," and the occasional regression to the preverbal, pre-Oedipal "memory" of unity, motivated by the need to withdraw from a harsh and unforgiving reality, is the explanation behind the transient, ineffable experience of oneness with the universe.

It is consistent with psychoanalytic theory to utilize the model Freud developed for the interpretation of transient, mystical feelings of unity.[3] Nevertheless, when Freud's interpretation is contextualized with respect to his correspondence with Rolland, one finds a more complex state of affairs. The first chapter of *Civilization and Its Discontents* was actually constructed around five letters, three from the pen of Rolland.[4] When analyzed with respect to these letters, this chapter reveals that Freud offered two models for the interpretation of two different mystical states, neither of which corresponds to the received view of Freud's take on the oceanic feeling.

## The Oceanic Feeling: Mystical Experience or Mystical State?

We can begin our analysis with Rolland's letter to Freud of December 5, 1927. This crucial document contains the definitive description of the oceanic feeling and expresses the numerous issues that form the unstated background of the chapter as a whole:

Dear and Respected Friend,

I thank you for being so kind as to send me your lucid and spirited little book. With a calm good sense, and in a moderate tone, it pulls off the blindfolding bandage of the eternal adolescents, which we all are, whose amphibian spirit floats between the illusion of yesterday and  . . .  the illusion of tomorrow.

Your analysis of religions is a just one. But I would have liked to see you doing an analysis of *spontaneous religious sentiment* or, more exactly, of religious *feeling*, which is wholly different from *religions* in the strict sense of the word, and much more durable.

What I mean is: totally independent of all dogma, all credo, all Church organization, all Sacred Books, all hope in a personal survival, etc., the simple and direct fact of *the feeling of the 'eternal'* (which can very well not be eternal, but simply without perceptible limits, and like oceanic, as it were).

This sensation, admittedly, is of a subjective character. But as it is common to thousands (millions) of men actually existing, with its thousands (millions) of individual nuances, it is possible to subject it to analysis, with an approximate exactitude.

I think you will classify it also under the *Zwangsneurosen*. But I have often had occasion to observe its rich and beneficent power, be it among the religious souls of the West, Christians or non-Christians, or among those great minds of Asia, who have become familiar to me and some of whom I count as friends. Of these latter, I am going to study, in a future book, two personalities who were almost our contemporaries (the first one belonged to the late nineteenth century, the second died in the early years of the twentieth) and who revealed an aptitude for thought and action which proved strongly regenerating for their country and for the world.

I myself am familiar with this sensation. All through my life, it has never failed me; and I have always found in it a source of vital renewal. In that sense, I can say that I am profoundly 'religious'—without this constant state (like a sheet of water which I feel flushing under the bark) affecting in any way my critical faculties and my freedom to exercise them—even if that goes against the immediacy of the interior experience. In this way, without discomfort or contradiction, I can lead a 'religious' life (in the sense of that prolonged feeling) and a life of critical reason (which is without illusion). . . .

I may add that this 'oceanic' sentiment has nothing to do with my personal yearnings. Personally, I yearn for eternal rest; survival has no attraction for me at all. But the sentiment I experience is imposed on me as a fact. It is a *contact*. And as I have recognized it to be identical (with multiple nuances) in a large number of living souls, it has helped me to understand that that was the true subterranean source of *religious energy* which, subsequently, has been collected, canalized and *dried up by the Churches*, to the extent that one could say that it is inside the Churches (whichever they may be) that true 'religious' sentiment is least available.

What eternal confusion is caused by words, of which the same one here sometimes means: *allegiance* to or *faith* in a dogma, or a word of god (or a tradition); and sometimes: a free *vital upsurge*.

This remarkable letter can be unpacked on several levels. First, it is apparent that Rolland was making both a request and a claim. The claim was that "mysticism," that is to say, the "oceanic feeling," was the true source of religion. To buttress this claim, Rolland drew on his personal experience, his friends and correspondence, and, in donning the hat of comparativist, the scholarly evidence he had amassed for a "future study" of two Asian mystics, a clear reference to his soon-to-be-published biographies of Ramakrishna and Vivekananda. Freud must have been impressed by Rolland's learning, for in a later letter (of July 20, 1929) Freud indicated surprise at how well read Rolland was in the comparative study of mysticism: "I cannot imagine reading all the literature which, according to your letter, you have studied." There was some truth in this, for, as we shall detail in chapter 6, Rolland had indeed studied mysticism and espoused, if in an idiosyncratic way, the kind of perennialism that animated many scholarly studies of his day.

If the claim was that the source of true religion lay in mysticism, then the request was for Freud to subject the oceanic feeling to analysis. This could only have caused consternation in Freud. Rolland agreed that, given the postulation of a personal unconscious, the analysis of the "common-man's" religion was essentially correct. Yet he also posited a "subterranean source," a deeper layer to the unconscious, which was religious in nature and capable of being rendered psychologically meaningful. Thus it is that Rolland was careful to qualify the oceanic feeling with the argument of *The Future of an Illusion* in mind. The oceanic feeling was not opposed to reason nor commensurate with wishful thinking or the desire for immortality. Further, it was dynamic, vitalistic, creative, socially adaptive, and completely independent of the various accoutrements of institutionalized religion. In short, the oceanic feeling was in every significant way of a different order than the religion of the "common-man." "True religion" was beneficial to mankind.

Surely Rolland was signifying his status as a competitor in the arena of cultural analysis. Freud had written *The Future of an Illusion* to create a social space for psychoanalysis, a therapy he once described to the Protestant pastor Oskar Pfister as "a profession of *lay* curers of souls who need not be doctors and should not be priests."[5] *Civilization and Its Discontents* continued this agenda, for Freud meant the term *Unbehagen* in the original German title of the book to refer to the "unease" caused not only by the ineradicable aspects of man's nature (notably the aggressive instinct) but also by the structure of social institutions. Institutionalized religion, being essentially "unpsychological," was just such an example. Rolland, on the other hand, wanted Freud's help to scientifically establish the benefits of mystical introversion, what he would refer to in his biographies of the Hindu saints as a "universal science-religion" and "mystical psychoanalysis." A social agenda promoting a mystical, religious psychology: surely on some level this reminded Freud of Jung.

An additional observation can be made at this time. It is clear that Rolland's letter was as much self-confession ("I myself am familiar with this sensation") as it was scholarly statement. We may, then, ask whether this letter faithfully recounts Rolland's personal mysticism. Might there exist additional sources in his written corpus and correspondence which shed further light on this matter? More important, did Freud have any access to further information about Rolland's personal mysticism? There is no evidence to think Freud based his analysis of the oceanic feeling on anything more than Rolland's letter of December 5. This is an important point, for any additional texts in Rolland's corpus that speak to this issue might change our understanding of the nature of the oceanic feeling, perhaps even providing the basis for a critique of Freud's interpretation. This matter clearly deserves some attention, but in due time. We must first explore how Freud came to understand and interpret mysticism.

Freud seems to have been genuinely mystified by Rolland's description of the oceanic feeling. In his letter to Rolland of July 14, 1929, Freud related how the idea of the oceanic feeling left him "no peace" and, in the text of *Civilization and Its Discontents*, that its analysis, because it was not a feature of his own psychic life, had caused him "no small difficulty." However, like any informed intellectual and university professor, Freud was acquainted with mystical literature if only in a general way. As we shall soon see, he had previously addressed, if briefly and inadequately, the noetic claims of mystical experience in the early 1900s and in works like *The Future of an Illusion*.[6] In other words, there do exist "pre-Rolland" texts in which Freud significantly reflected on the problem of mysticism. Although there is no evidence that Freud had read the seminal psychological work on mysticism of his time, the classic *The Varieties of Religious Experience*, an analysis of Freud's pre-Rolland reflections on mysticism indicate that Freud's understanding of its characteristics was similar to that delineated by James: passivity, transiency, ineffability, and noesis. Why then did Rolland's description of the oceanic feeling cause Freud so much consternation? Precisely because the oceanic feeling did not fit the portrait of the transient mystical "experience" familiar to generations of scholars from James onwards. Although Rolland's reference to the "subterranean source" of the oceanic feeling points to the unconscious, he also refers to the oceanic feeling as a "constant state," a "prolonged feeling" that exists alongside the "critical faculties" without, despite its immediacy and constancy, interfering with their proper function. Freud as well understood it as such, for in his summary of Rolland's letter in *Civilization and Its Discontents* he characterizes the oceanic feeling as consisting "in a peculiar feeling, which he himself is never without." Freud's perplexity is understandable, for the notion of a continuous mystical state would raise eyebrows even among most contemporary psychologists, although not, I hasten to add, among scholars of the comparative study of mysticism, who have long noted examples of such phenomena in mystics like St. Teresa of Avila and Sri Ramana Maharshi.[7]

Freud begins his analysis of the oceanic feeling by admitting that although it was recalcitrant to analysis, a psychoanalytic interpretation was possible if one seized its central "ideational" content: "the indissoluble bond of being one with the external world as a whole." This understanding of the essential characteristic of the oceanic feeling stressed its statelike character over its "subterranean" origin and thus mitigated any attempt to interpret it with respect to the unconscious. Rather, Freud employed another strategy: his theory of pre-Oedipal development. First, Freud reasoned that an infant's sense of itself and the world is considerably more unitary than that of an adult: "An infant at the breast does not as yet distinguish his ego from the external world as the source of the sensations flowing in upon him. He gradually learns to do so, in response to various promptings. . . . [o]riginally the ego includes everything, later it separates off an external world from itself."[8]

Freud then went on to claim that our own adult ego-feeling can be conceived of as a "shrunken residue" of this primary ego-feeling:

> Our present ego-feeling is, therefore, only a shrunken residue of a much more inclusive — indeed, an all-embracing — feeling which corresponded to a more intimate bond between the ego and the world about it. If we may assume that there are many people in whose mental life this primary ego-feeling has persisted to a greater or less degree, it would exist in them side by side with the narrower and more sharply demarcated ego-feeling of maturity, like a kind of counterpart to it. In that case, the ideational contents appropriate to it would be precisely those of limitlessness and of a bond with the universe — the same ideas with which my friend elucidated the 'oceanic feeling.'[9]

The question, given the inevitable effect of the reality principle on self- and other-awareness, now became whether or not an early ego awareness of complete unity could indeed "persist" through the various developmental stages leading up to adult maturity. This engaged the subject of the preservation of psychic contents within the mind. Although he admitted that "the subject has hardly been studied as yet," Freud indicated that the results of psychoanalysis had concluded that "it is rather the rule than the exception for the past to be pre-

served in mental life." If this is the case, then one can assume that in many people this early ego-feeling has indeed persisted alongside the adult ego. Thus
Freud concludes, "we are perfectly willing to acknowledge that the 'oceanic'
feeling exists in many people, and we are inclined to trace it back to an early
phase of ego-feeling."[10] In sum, although granting Rolland's assertion that the
oceanic feeling did in fact exist, Freud contested Rolland's suggestion that it was
an innate, religious feature of the psyche while evading any mention of Jung or
the threat to the psychoanalytic conception of the unconscious by showing how
the same feeling could arise from a purely developmental perspective.

Freud also offered other lines of interpretation in this chapter that more directly addressed the cultural implications of the oceanic feeling, its connection
to institutional religion, and its challenge to the analysis contained in *The Future of an Illusion*. For example, late in the first chapter, after having interpreted
the oceanic feeling as the preservation of primary narcissism, Freud reflects on
its role and function within institutionalized religion. Rolland's advocacy of the
oceanic feeling as the *fons et origo* of religion, interpreted by Freud in terms of
pre-Oedipal development, led him to reconsider which parent played the definitive role in religion. In *The Future of an Illusion* Freud had called attention to
the role of the Mother as the child's first protection against the anxiety and fears
that threatened it from the external world—a role taken over in a more thorough
and effective fashion by the Father.[11] Faced anew with the role of the Mother,
Freud simply reiterated what he had stated three years earlier. The existential
needs of helplessness and anxiety are best assuaged with recourse to the Father.
The oceanic feeling became "connected" with religion "later on," for it recalled
the child's first attempt at disclaiming the dangers arising from the outside world.
The religious "need" it appealed to was the desire for "limitless narcissism," the
memory of the state in which one had felt omnipotent and immortal.[12] Thus although the "oceanic feeling" was not to be regarded as the source of institutional
religion, it was co-opted by the latter to provide easy and childish solutions to
universal existential needs.

In addition to the above reflections on the motivations behind what, for reasons I shall elaborate presently, is best referred to as the "common-man's mysticism," Freud used Rolland's letter of December 5, 1927, to reflect on another pivotal instrument in the psychic inventory of institutionalized Christianity: the
love-command.[13] Freud did not actually embark on his critique of the love-
command until the later chapters of *Civilization and Its Discontents*, in a context seemingly far removed from Rolland's oceanic feeling. Nevertheless, it was
Rolland who led Freud to link the love-command with the oceanic feeling and
inspired him to ruminate further on the connection between the two. In order to
show this, we may first draw attention to two associations, both found in the first
chapter of *Civilization and Its Discontents*, that Freud had to the unitive element of the oceanic feeling. The first association is a text from Christian Die-
trich Grabbe's play *Hannibal*:

> If I have understood my friend rightly, he means the same thing by it as the con-
> solation offered by an original and somewhat eccentric dramatist to his hero who is

facing a self-inflicted death. 'We cannot fall out of this world.' That is to say, it is a feeling of an indissoluble bond, of being one with the external world as a whole.[14]

The quote is taken from the end of the play when Hannibal, faced with certain death at the hands of the Romans, opts for a more noble death, which, religiously conceived, is that of martyrdom. The second association takes the form of an analogy. In attempting to convey a picture of the preservation of psychic contents in the mind, Freud draws an analogy between the development of the mind and the historical development of the Eternal City, Rome. Just as one can see remnants of ancient Rome in the midst of its modern developments, so too is it the case that nothing in the mind, once formed, ever perishes. In this analogy, then, the oceanic feeling corresponds to ancient Rome, the Rome of Jupiter and Minerva.

The two associations seem contradictory. Freud's reference to Grabbe's play can be interpreted as a free association that corresponds to his Hannibal Complex. The reference to ancient Rome, however, reveals a wish far removed from Oedipal hostility. Freud's feelings toward ancient Rome, with all of its maternal connotations, were revealed in a letter to Wilhelm Fliess shortly after his first trip to Rome, a trip made possible by the successful analysis of his "Rome Neurosis." Freud wrote that he was unable to enjoy medieval Rome: "I was disturbed by its meaning, and, being incapable of putting out of my mind my own misery and all the other misery which I know to exist, I found almost intolerable the lie of the salvation of mankind which rears its head so proudly to heaven."[15] In contrast, Freud said that he "contemplated ancient Rome undisturbed (I could have worshipped the humble and mutilated remnant of the Temple of Minerva near the forum of Nerva)."[16] Schorske has pointed out that this Rome was not the Rome of Hannibal, the Rome which engendered Oedipal hostility in Freud. Rather, it was the Rome of the art historian and archeologist Joachim Winckleman, who loved Rome because it was "the mother of European Culture." This was a Rome Freud aspired to assimilate to, the city of culture and love.[17]

These seemingly contradictory associations are reconciled through the figure of Rolland. As we saw earlier, Rolland's exhibition of courage and tolerance rekindled the lost political hopes of Freud's youth. Freud referred to Rolland as the "apostle of love for mankind" and portrayed the "oceanic feeling" in terms of maternity and inclusiveness. There was, so to speak, an aura of ancient Rome surrounding the oceanic feeling. Rolland could be counted on to actualize the kind of tolerance and inclusiveness which formed the essence of the love-command. At the same time, in his letters to Rolland, Freud also recalled the horrors of the Middle Ages and the rampant anti-Semitism associated with Christianity and the love-command. From this perspective, Rolland's postulation of a connection between the oceanic feeling and religion created intellectual excitement and Oedipal hostility in Freud by providing him with new material that spurred analytic reflections on the love-command. This analysis found expression in chapter 4 of *Civilization and Its Discontents*, where Freud puts forward the suggestion that the love-command, "Thou Shalt Love Thy Neighbor as Thyself," finds its origin in "the remote regions where the distinction between the ego and objects or between objects themselves is neglected."[18] In other words, to the same developmental stage which, when preserved alongside the more narrow adult ego, is subjectively apprehended as the oceanic feeling.

One can see how this makes sense, for the love-command simply puts into an ideal and reified form the ethical meaning inherent in an early developmental state in which the self is the other and the other the self. It was precisely the privileging of this primitive state, with all of the psychological complications such primitivity implied, that became the basis for Freud's numerous criticisms of the *Unbehagen* or unease created by the love-command, not the least of which was its complicity in the "narcissism of minor differences" and anti-Semitic behavior—both of which, as we have seen, also found expression in Freud's letter to Rolland of March 4, 1923. It seems, then, that if one casts Freud's understanding of the oceanic feeling in terms of the analytic session with Rolland as analysand and Freud as analyst, the latter was guilty of a kind of countertransference that, while certainly serving to further his social agenda, may well have distorted the true nature and meaning of Rolland's oceanic feeling.[19]

One final set of observations can be made. In comparing Freud's analysis of mysticism in *Civilization and Its Discontents* with his high opinion of Rolland throughout their correspondence, one cannot help but note a certain tension. During the letters of the early period, Freud referred to Rolland as an "apostle of love" who had reached the "heights of humanity" through "hardship and suffering"; in the text of *Civilization and Its Discontents* he called him a man whose "attributes and achievements" distinguished him from the masses. Clearly Rolland was an exceptional man and the interpretative implication was that of existential actualization and ethical nobility. Yet in *Civilization and Its Discontents* Freud seems willing to reduce Rolland's love for humanity to a residue of an early phase of ego-feeling, an interpretation that renders his achievements unexceptional and basically aesthetic, the result of a kind of psychological appendix. Similarly, there exists a psychological chasm between Freud's respect for Rolland's love of truth and courage to voice his opinions and his rendering of the "common-man's mysticism" as defensive and regressive, a retreat from reality. It may be that this is simply an unresolved tension in the text. On the other hand, following along the same kind of distinction implicit in my analysis of the love-command, this tension would disappear if one were to make a distinction between the "common-man's mysticism" and the more psychologically sophisticated mysticism of Romain Rolland. Of course Freud did not make this distinction, at least overtly. However, there is a basis in the text to assume that Freud wished to make a similar distinction in a subtle, covert sense and that he did so to protect the analysis and agenda of *The Future of an Illusion*. For example, in the first paragraph of Chapter 2, Freud adds this postscript to his analysis of the oceanic feeling:

> In my *Future of an Illusion* I was concerned much less with the deepest sources of the religious feeling than with what the common-man understands by his religion—with the system of doctrines and promises which on the one hand explains to him the riddles of the world with enviable completeness, and, on the other, as-

sures him that a careful Providence will watch over his life and will compensate him in a future existence for any frustrations he suffers here. . . . The whole thing is so patently infantile, so foreign to reality, that to anyone with a friendly attitude to humanity it is painful to think that the great majority of mortals will never be able to rise above this view of life. It is still more humiliating to discover how large a number of people living to-day, who cannot but see that this religion is not tenable, nevertheless try to defend it piece by piece in a series of pitiful rearguard actions. One would like to . . . meet these philosophers, who think they can rescue the God of religion by replacing him by an impersonal, shadowy and abstract principle, and to address them with the warning words: 'Thou shalt not take the name of the Lord thy God in vain!' And if some of the great men of the past acted in the same way, no appeal can be made to their example: we know why they were obliged to. Let us return to the common man and to his religion—the only religion which ought to bear that name.

Freud's distinction between the "deepest sources" of religion, the highly abstract and intellectually sophisticated philosopher's religion propagated by the intellectual elite, and what the "common-man" understands by his religion acknowledges his awareness of and entry into the methodological debates that still animate the study of religion. How are we to "define" religion, and what kinds of people and attitudes are to be designated "religious"? Indeed, Freud had thoroughly addressed this very problem in *The Future of an Illusion* and taken to task those "philosophers" who defined religion and religious attitudes in highly abstract and sophisticated terminology.[20] So too can this line of approach be detected in Freud's correspondence with other figures like Carl Jung, Ludwig Binswanger, and the pastor and lay-analyst Oskar Pfister. The latter, for example, had taken a humanistic-philosophical approach to religion by interpreting Jesus as a psychoanalyst and Freud as a true Christian and by writing a theological response to Freud's book entitled *The Illusion of the Future*.[21] Surely Rolland, despite his agreement with Freud's analysis of the "common-man"'s religion, was following in their footsteps in trying to "rescue" religion by attempting to replace the Father-God with a more sophisticated, impersonal, and generic "oceanic" Being. In the above passage Freud rebukes Rolland by casting him in the same mold as Pfister and the philosophers. This fact underscores Rolland's role as the "silent interlocutor" of *Civilization and Its Discontents*. Freud used Rolland's ruminations on religion to defend and further the agenda of *The Future of an Illusion* by analyzing aspects of institutionalized religion, which is to say the "common-man's mysticism" and the love-command, and then offering them to the cultured elite as more examples of *das Unbehagen in der Kultur*. The deeper, more sophisticated views championed by theologians like Soren Kierkegaard or Paul Tillich and mystics like Meister Eckhart simply fell outside of what the "common-man" understood by his religion—"the only religion which ought to bear that name."[22]

Further evidence in the text and correspondence can be adduced to buttress this line of argument. In his letter to Rolland of July 20, 1929, Freud had told Rolland not to expect an "evaluation of the 'oceanic' feeling," for he was "experimenting only with an analytic version of it; I am clearing it out of the way, so to speak." What Freud was clearing out of the way, then, was any challenge to his definition and analysis of religion. So too are there an unusual number of qualifications and disclaimers surrounding Freud's analysis of the oceanic feeling. For example, he begins his analysis by saying "I have nothing to suggest which could have a decisive influence on the solution to this problem" and ends it by saying "Let me admit once more that it is very difficult for me to work with these almost intangible quantities" and "There may be something further behind that [referring to his analysis of religion] but for the present it is wrapped in obscurity." Of course it could well be, as a contrary argument would have it, that the observations adduced here are but illustrations of Freud's clever use of rhetoric and sensitivity to his respect for and relationship with Rolland.[23] Be this as it may, there does exist one more neglected passage in the text that indicates beyond the shadow of a doubt that Freud did indeed think, on some level and with respect to a different, if related, mystical phenomenon, that there was a world of psychological difference between the "common-man's mysticism" and that of Romain Rolland.

## The Goetz Letters: The Problem of Mystical Intuition

The text in question occurs in the last paragraph of the first chapter of *Civilization and Its Discontents*. Here Freud has ended his discussion on the nature of the oceanic feeling and its connection with institutionalized religion and turns to a related phenomenon:

> Another friend of mine, whose insatiable craving for knowledge has led him to make the most unusual experiments and has ended by giving him encyclopaedic knowledge, has assured me that through the practices of Yoga . . . by fixing the attention on bodily functions and by peculiar methods of breathing, one can in fact evoke new sensations and coenaesthesias in oneself, which he regards as regressions to primordial states of mind which have long ago been overlaid. He sees in them a physiological basis, as it were, of much of the wisdom of mysticism. It would not be hard to find connections here with a number of obscure modifications of mental life, such as trances and ecstasies. But I am moved to exclaim in the words of Schiller's diver: 'Let him rejoice who breathes up here in the roseate light!'[24]

One cannot help but note the very real difference between this mystical phenomenon and the oceanic feeling. In describing the latter, Freud had emphasized the enduring feeling of connection with the outside world. The unitive, statelike character of the oceanic feeling demanded recourse to a pre-Oedipal model of development and the theory of the preservation of psychic contents. In the above passage, Freud speaks of mystical practices (Yoga), of ecstasies and trances, and of the regressive descent into "primordial states" for the purpose of achieving a particular kind of wisdom. The description is far more like the transient mystical "experience" elaborated by William James. Freud's reference to "another friend" is also of interest. Who did Freud have in mind and what significance might this friend have for the ascertaining the nature and interpretation of this new mystical phenomenon?

Strong evidence can be amassed to indicate that this "friend" was none other than Rolland. This becomes clear when one takes a closer look at the remaining letters of the middle period. To review, the first letter was Rolland's letter of December 5, 1927. Then over two years later, on July 14, 1929, Freud responded, telling Rolland of a work, *Civilization and Its Discontents*, which lay "still uncompleted" before him. He had written an introduction to the work consisting of an analysis of the "oceanic feeling" and wondered whether Rolland would give him permission to use his personal remark in a public forum. Three days later, Rolland wrote granting his permission and added:

> I should only acknowledge that being at a distance of one year and a half, I no longer remember very exactly the text of my letter. I was then no doubt at the beginning of my long studies on the Hindu mind, which I am going to publish in a few months, in three volumes devoted to 'Mysticism and action in living India.' Since 1927 I have been able to delve deeply into that 'oceanic sentiment,' innumerable examples of which I find not only among hundreds of our contemporary Asians, but also in what I might call the ritualistic and multi-secular physiology which is codified in treatises on *yoga*. . . .
>
> At the end of my work, while reading, for comparison, some of the great mystics of Europe and particularly those of the Alexandrian epoch, those who lived in the West during the 14th century—not to speak of the considerable work of Abbé Brémond on French mysticism during the 16th and 17th centuries—I was surprised to observe, once again, that it is not at all true that the East and the West are two worlds separated from each other, but both are the branches of the same river of thought. And I have recognized in both the same 'river ocean.'

Immediately upon receipt of Rolland's letter, Freud, on July 20th, returned Rolland's letter of December 5, 1927, to him and, while thanking him for his permission to use the letter in *Civilization and Its Discontents*, asked him to review it and make any changes if he so desired. He closed the letter by once again exalting Rolland:

> How remote from me are the worlds in which you move! To me mysticism is just as closed a book as music. I cannot imagine reading all the literature which, according to your letter, you have studied. And yet it is easier for you than for us to read the human soul!

Four days later Rolland returned his letter of December 5, 1927, to Freud and affirmed that it still reflected his views on mysticism. He thought Freud distrusted mysticism out of a respect for upholding the integrity of "critical reason." Citing Heraclitus ("The harmony between the opposing forces is that which is the most beautiful"), he added that he was able to participate in both the "intuitive" and "critical" functions of the mind without conflict.

This exchange of letters demonstrates the affinities which abound between the "another friend" Freud mentions in *Civilization and Its Discontents* and Rolland. Both have wide-ranging interests, a love for the truth, encyclopaedic knowledge, and, most significantly, are interested in Yoga, mystical practices, and the physiological basis of mysticism. Of especial interest is Rolland's distinction between the "critical" and "intuitive" functions of the mind and the correlation of the latter with mysticism. The reference to "intuition," which for Freud always meant insight into the inner world, must have recalled Rolland's stress on the "subterranean source" of mysticism in his letter of December 5, 1927, and solidified the impression that he was speaking about transient experiences as well as continuous mystical states.[25] The portrait Freud paints of this other friend, then, could be a composite of two or more people, of which one was Rolland, or it could be an elaborated version of the information contained in Rolland's letter. In either case, it seems likely that Rolland's letter inspired Freud to append the story about this other friend and his researches into yoga at the end of chapter 1. After all, Freud did say in his letter to Rolland of July 14th that *Civilization and Its Discontents* was as yet unfinished. Further, Rolland's initial response was written a scant three days later. Because the book was not sent to the publishers until November of 1929, Freud had plenty of time to amend the text as he saw fit.[26]

The question now concerns the interpretation of this mystical "experience," the regression into the depths of the psyche. Freud characterizes it simply with words from Schiller's *The Diver*. Commentators who have noted this passage have dismissed it as another example of Freud's rhetorical skill, signifying his aversion to phenomena refractory to psychoanalytic investigation and indicative of his preference for the "light" of rational consciousness.[27] Perhaps it is best to let the matter rest, given what appears to be a dearth of material to investigate. On the other hand, Freud never used a literary reference without some particular intention. Indeed, if one undertakes an analysis of the poem as a whole, something previous commentators have neglected, one finds a curious state of affairs: the condensation of Oedipal with "oceanic" imagery. Briefly summarized, *The Diver* portrays a young man who, on two successive occasions, undertakes the heroic task of grappling with the forces of a feared "whirlpool," portrayed as an "ocean womb" that "boils and hisses . . . a gaping chasm . . . leading down to the depths of hell," in order to retrieve a king's goblet. Motivated by the king's blessing and his crown in return, the page dives into the gloomy depths, miraculously emerging:

> Long life to the King! Let him rejoice
> Who breathe up here in the roseate light!
> For below all is fearful, of moment sad;
> Let not man to tempt the immortals e'er try,
> Let him never desire the things to see
> That with terror and night they veil graciously.

Filled with amazement and curiosity, the king asks the page to return to the "purple depths" to bring word to him of the mystery below. With the promise of the king's daughter's hand in marriage, the idealistic page once again enters the fateful whirlpool, never to return.

This powerful poem can be read as a metaphor for the psychoanalytic task. One "dives" into the "whirlpool" of the unconscious, a whirlpool inhabited by powerful and potentially dangerous powers. Furthermore, the theme of *The Diver* is an Oedipal one: winning the favor of the king and gaining his daughter's hand in marriage, only to eventually displace the king himself. Freud's citation of *The Diver* in the passage in question suggests that, far from retreating from psychic reality, the mystic diver goes where few dare to tread. This suggestion is given further nuance in a famous passage at the end of chapter 7—a chapter which for all intents and purposes signals the end of Freud's argument in *Civilization and Its Discontents*. As a way of summing up how the conflicting aims between civilization and individuals lead to an unbearable sense of guilt, Freud, after quoting a phrase from Goethe's *Wilhelm Meister*, goes on to say:

> And we may well heave a sigh of relief at the thought that it is nevertheless vouch-safed to a few to salvage without effort from the whirlpool of their own feelings the deepest truths, towards which the rest of us have to find our way through torment-ing uncertainty and with restless groping.[28]

The imagery of this passage—garnering the deepest truths from the "whirl-pool" of one's feelings—is reminiscent of *The Diver*. It further seems that Freud intended us to make such a connection, for this is the only place in the entirety of his written corpus that he uses the term "whirlpool" to designate the uncon-scious.[29] The immediate referent is Goethe, who "without effort" (the German is *mühelos*) arrived at the "deepest truths" which the "rest of us" arrive at only through "restless groping." However, Freud's inclusion of "the few" extends the meaning from a single writer to a group, one that Ernst Kris, inspired by this *very* passage, dubbed "intuitive psychologists."[30] The latter was a group of poets and philosophers like Goethe, Schiller, Shakespeare, Nietzsche, Plato, and others whom Freud admired and idealized. These introspective geniuses were a source of creativity for Freud, who referred to them on more than one occasion as his "masters" and "teachers" in their anticipation of psychoanalytic metapsychol-ogy.[31] So too did Freud find a rhetorical use for these figures, often merging his ideas with theirs as a way of reproving society at large for rejecting psychoana-lytic insights, which were, after all, but less disguised, more precise and scientific versions of those that were otherwise universally respected. Freud also accorded some of his contemporaries this honor. As we saw in the last chapter, Arthur Schniztler was an "intuitive psychologist." Rolland belongs in this group as well. Indeed Freud, in his letter of July 20, 1929, refers to Rolland, the poet-mystic, as being able to "read the soul" more easily than "us," that is, psychoanalysts (the German reads: Und dabei konnen Sie doch in der menlichen Seele lesen *müh-eloser* als wir). And didn't Freud, in the opening paragraph of *Civilization and Its Discontents*, refer to Rolland as one of "the few" whose aims and ideals, achieve-ments and abilities separated him from the masses?

The conclusions offered here find support in one of Freud's "pre-Rolland" reflections on mysticism. The document in question, which I dub the "Goetz Letters," concerns the recollections of a relatively obscure Swiss poet, Bruno Goetz, concerning his encounter with Freud during his days as a student at the University of Vienna.[32] His impressions, which were recorded in a series of letters to a friend written immediately after his meetings with Freud during the academic year 1904–1905, contained ". . . verbatim, although in fragmentary form, statements made by Freud." Goetz decided to make his letters public upon prodding by friends, psychoanalysts, and his own desire to correct what he perceived to be a common but jaded view of Freud as biased, reductive, and overly intellectual. "As a man," states Goetz, "Freud had greater breadth, richness, complexity and—I'm glad to say—more inherent contradictions than his teaching."[33]

Goetz's encounter with Freud was occasioned by the onset of acute facial neuralgia that was suspected of being psychological in origin. Although this proved not to be the case, Goetz ended up visiting Freud a number of times, engaging him in conversation on a number of topics. In one such visit, Goetz relayed information about his studies at the University and the enthusiasm that the noted Sanskrit scholar, Leopold von Schroeder, had inspired in him through his lectures on the Bhagavad Gita. At this point Freud "sprang briskly to his feet," began to pace, and responded at length:

> Take care, young man, take care . . . You are quite right to be enthusiastic. For out of the abundance of the heart the mouth speaketh. Your heart will always win the day, but keep that cool head which, fortunately, you still have. Don't be taken off your guard. A clear, sparkling intellect is one of the greatest gifts. The poet of the Bhagavad Gita would be the first to affirm that very thing. Always be on the look-out, always keep your eyes open, always be aware of everything, always be of unswerving courage, but never let yourself be dazzled, never let yourself get tied up in knots. Emotion must not become auto-anaesthesia. Dostoevsky's principle: "Head first, head over heels into the abyss" is all very fine, but the enthusiasm which it has aroused in Europe is based on a sad misunderstanding. The Bhagavad Gita is a great and profound poem with awful depths. "And still it lay beneath me hidden deep in purple darkness there," says Schiller's diver, who never returns from his second brave attempt. If, however, without the aid of a clear intellect you become immersed in the world of the Bhagavad Gita, where nothing seems constant and where everything melts into everything else, then you are suddenly confronted by nothingness. Do you know what it means to be confronted by nothingness? Do you know what that means? And yet this very nothingness is simply a European misconception: The Hindu Nirvana is not nothingness, it is that which transcends all contradictions. It is not, as Europeans commonly take it to be, a sensual enjoyment, but the ultimate in superhuman understanding, an ice-cold, all-comprehending yet scarcely comprehensible insight. Or, if misunderstood, it is madness. What do these European would-be mystics know about the profundity of the East? They rave on, but they know nothing. And then they are surprised when they lose their heads and are not infrequently driven mad by it—literally driven out of their minds. . . . The most sensible thing to do is to keep on asking questions.

At the moment you are interested in the Hindu philosophers. They often went so far as to express their answers in the form of questions. They knew why.[34]

Freud's reference to the European fascination with and interpretation of nirvana ("nothingness"; "sensual enjoyment") indicates the influence of that historical movement Raymond Schwab refers to as the "Oriental renaissance"—particularly its role in fomenting the substantial intellectual debate on the meaning of the term "nirvana."[35] Both Rolland and Jung were deeply interested in the turn to the East in the 1920s and 1930s. According to this document, Freud too was aware of and intellectually stimulated by Eastern texts at the beginning of the century.[36] Of especial interest is how Freud addresses three interrelated aspects of the mystical path: (1) the content of nirvana (the "mystical experience"), (2) the mental and emotional requirements of the seeker, (3) the role of the sage-therapist.

Concerning the first of these, Freud states that Nirvana is not nothingness, annihilation, nilhism [sic] or sensual enjoyment but "that which transcends all contradictions . . . (it is) the ultimate in superhuman understanding, an ice-cold, all-comprehending yet scarcely comprehensible insight." So much, at least, is clear from the text. However, exactly how Freud construed the nature of this insight can be further specified. The realm which transcended all contradictions was, for Freud, not some metaphysical or transcendent reality but, as he indicated as early as 1900 in his *Interpretation of Dreams*, that of the unconscious.[37] This is given further content in the characterization of the "awful depths" of the Bhagavad Gita in poetic terms: ". . . 'and still it lay beneath me hidden deep in purple darkness there' says Schiller's diver, who never returns from his second brave attempt." Once again, then, we find Freud using the same text, Schiller's *The Diver*, to characterize the psychological depths of mystical intuition. However, while the poem has a tragic ending, prefiguring Freud's later, more pessimistic views of interminable analysis, intractable conflict, and guilt, Freud's reference to the "ultimate in superhuman understanding" suggests that the mystic, unlike the page, succeeds in gaining insight into the deepest recesses of his Oedipal distress. Surely Freud's observations in the "Goetz Letters" find their echo in the first and seventh chapters of *Civilization and Its Discontents*.[38]

As important are Freud's observations concerning the mental and emotional requirements needed to ensure a successful outcome to the psychic surgery the mystic undertakes. Given the "awful depths" of the Bhagavad Gita and the possibility of madness, Freud cautions Goetz that the enthusiasm and courage of the mystic diver must be subsumed under the guidance of the intellect. Once again there are literary references—to Matthew 12:34 and Dostoevsky's *The Brothers Karamazov*—which reveal a deeper, richer meaning to Freud's admonitions. The latter is of especial interest given that Freud later wrote a short psychoanalytic study of Dostoevsky that centered around his Oedipal struggles and his creative rendering of them in *The Brothers Karamazov*. The figure of Dimitri, whom Freud calls an "impulsive sensualist" and around whom Dostoevsky clusters the themes of unbridled passion, patricide, and intellectual and moral weakness, is appropriately singled out for attention. Not so coincidentally, it is also

Dimitri who utters "head first, head over heels into the abyss" and who is later brought to trial for the public demonstration of his patricidal urges. Once again, then, we see Freud conceptualizing the mystic path in terms of his budding metapsychology. Dimitri embodies what can happen to those who enter the abyss "head over heels," who are given to what Freud called "acting-out" over remembering and "working-through."

Contrasted to the figure of Dimitri is that of the poet-philosopher of the Bhagavad Gita, who, as a seeker, knows the value of the intellect and, as a therapist, the value of posing answers in the form of questions. Psychoanalytically rendered, Freud intimates that the Indian sages had arrived at the therapeutic wisdom that acknowledges the art of holding the tension between instructive guidance and trust in the patient's ability to bring to conscious awareness the "answers" that lie buried within him in a time-appropriate, ego-syntonic way. Insight, sublimation, and working-through preponderate over acting-out. This rendering of mystical therapy recalls another that Freud was familiar with and compared favorably with his own, namely, the Socratic. Generally speaking, the fundamental tenets which guide the two systems of thought—the end (self-knowledge), the means (asking questions), the assumptions (the answers are within), and the form (dialogue)—are similar.[39] So too did Freud utilize Platonic concepts such as Eros and similes, such as that of the charioteer, to help convey the meaning of his own.[40] Given Freud's classical training and evidence of his awareness of the scholarly debates surrounding the question of the extent of Indian influence on Plato, the "Goetz Letters" suggest that Freud merged the two systems of thought, insofar as they both contained the same germinal element of truth, and then read the more detailed and precise empirical findings of psychoanalysis back into them.

The portrait of a Freud who admires and even idealizes mystics is certainly unorthodox. It raises questions about the authenticity of the "Goetz Letters" and the conclusions offered here as a whole. One assumes that Goetz possessed sufficient integrity not to fabricate his recollections. However, it is certainly possible that, in the interval which lapsed between his meetings with Freud and the subsequent documentation of them, some degree of distortion took place. On the other hand, several observations argue to the contrary. First, there is an almost uncanny correlation between the "Goetz Letters" and the passages cited in *Civilization and Its Discontents*. This fits Freud's style, for a discernible and consistent rhetorical logic governed his use of poetic discourse. Indeed, as we shall explore at length in chapter 4, Freud made other comments to Rolland which unequivocally affirm that he thought mystical practices unearthed psychological insight. For example, in his letter to Rolland in January of 1930 Freud admits that the "intuition" of "your mystics" could be "valuable for an embryology of the soul." Again, in 1933, in his *New Introductory Lectures*, Freud drew a parallel between "mystical practices" and psychoanalysis, emphasizing how both employed a similar line of approach as concerns the investigation of the unconscious and the gaining of insight.

Second, for those wedded to the orthodox view, the interpretation offered here may become more palatable when qualified with respect to the relationship that Freud held to exist between psychoanalysis, art, and religion. In *The Future of an Illusion* Freud characterized religion as, among other things, a means of social control that monitored sexual and aggressive tendencies. It created a worldview that pretended to completeness and infallibility and protected its epistemological assertions from encroachments by science. Such a worldview magnified guilt and shame, promoted a childish orientation toward reality, and stunted the critical use of one's intellect and creativity. Furthermore, as we have seen, Freud was convinced that Christianity catered to intolerance and anti-Semitism. Art, on the other hand, never made epistemological assertions about reality, nor was it able to construct a worldview. It was an "illusion," but pretended to nothing more. Artists, moreover, existing at the margins of culture, seemed to have an unusual access to the unconscious and the talent to represent unconscious processes in symbolic, experience-distant ways. Art could be therapeutic in providing an outlet for instinctual gratification and edifying when it stirred the imagination and ignited introspection. Thus conceived, art had a special relationship to psychoanalysis. As we have previously seen, the great poets and philosophers hailed from that tradition whose adherents we have referred to as "intuitive psychologists." The latter embodied the dramatic themes and tendencies of human behavior, evinced in works like *Hamlet* and *Oedipus Rex*, from which Freud learned so much.

Rolland was a complex figure precisely in that he became associated in Freud's mind with both institutional religion and "intuitive psychologists," a fact that accounts for his role as "silent interlocutor," as well as for the varying evaluations offered of mysticism in *Civilization and Its Discontents*. Indeed, as we shall see in later chapters, even Freud's assessment of the value of mystical "intuition" varied according to whether the knowledge of the soul garnered through it was embodied in a "great man" and artist par excellence like Rolland or whether it was interpreted and represented through the auspices of a particular, institutionalized religious worldview. In other words, to find the considerable nuance of meaning here as elsewhere in Freud's writings one cannot dispense with the often laborious task of proper contextualization. Only then do Freud's seemingly contradictory or unorthodox statements on mysticism reveal their inner logic and true meaning.

Two models, then, for two different mystical phenomena, the meaning of which cannot be divorced from the social and developmental echoes of the Freud–Rolland correspondence—these are the essential conclusions of our analysis in this chapter. Clearly Freud's reflections on mysticism are considerably richer, less pejorative, and more suggestive than has been traditionally thought to be the case. So too is it apparent that our analysis, in deconstructing the received view, has served to raise new questions. Primary in this regard is the relation, if any, between transient mystical experiences and the oceanic feeling. If statelike mystical phenomena found in other mystics like Teresa and Ramana Maharshi are any indication, we can expect that there is in fact an important relation; that the oceanic feeling is a rather advanced or mature development in Rolland's spiritual journey. Again, the recourse to other mystics raises questions about Rolland's comparative pursuits: how he arrived at his perennialist conclusions and the precise relation between the oceanic feeling and other types of mysticism. In turn, the answer to such questions will provide us with a platform from which to assess the psychoanalytic theory of mysticism. These issues will be addressed in short order. Before we do, let us proceed to examine more closely Rolland's side of the story and the texts and letters which make up the last phase of the Freud–Rolland correspondence.

# THREE

# Rolland and the Emerging Psychology and Religion Movement

We have seen that Rolland, in his letter of December 5, 1927, indicated he was researching a book on the Hindu saints Ramakrishna and Vivekananda.[1] It has generally been assumed that the references to Freud and psychoanalysis in those books are a direct response to *Civilization and Its Discontents*, much as Rolland's description of the oceanic feeling has been presented as a reflex action to *The Future of an Illusion*.[2] This view is untenable because Rolland finished revising his biographies for publication almost two months before he learned of Freud's interest in analyzing the oceanic feeling. In fact, Rolland did not read *Civilization and Its Discontents* until late December of 1929, approximately a week before the last volume of his biography of Vivekananda was issued.[3] The primary motivations behind Rolland's biographies, then, were not in any way directly connected with *Civilization and Its Discontents*. Rather, they reflect Rolland's own cultural agenda. Like Freud, Rolland was convinced of the waning ability of Judeo–Christian culture to monitor man's antisocial proclivities. Like Freud, he turned to the intellectual elite, what Freud called the "brainworkers" of society, to help him promote a "universal science-religion," a veritable religio-mystical psychology. And, again like Freud, Rolland's biographies, his "cultural works," as it were, found their instigators in a definable sociocultural context—the emerging East–West dialogue and the traumatic social events surrounding the Great War—and had roots deep in his childhood. Accordingly, in this chapter we shall complete our analysis of the middle period of the Freud–Rolland correspondence by elucidating selected contents of the biographies, linking them with relevant aspects of Rolland's developmental past and sociohistorical milieu.

## Mysticism and the Mother

By 1913, with the publication of *Totem and Taboo* and the thesis of the "primal crime," Freud had pretty well ensured both the universality of the Oedipus complex and, with respect to other social sciences, the methodological primacy of psychoanalysis concerning self, culture, and society. In the last analysis, culture was shaped by psyche and psyche by Oedipus. The individual was seen as a discrete entity standing for the most part outside of and in opposition to civilization, and the phylogenetically based memory trace of the primal deed, existing in the deepest layers of the unconscious of all men, made its presence felt by constantly moving society toward a patriarchal organization and religion toward monotheism. Since that time, Freud's views on the relation between self and society have undergone significant criticism and revision. Sociologists and anthropologists have relativized Freud's findings by questioning the accuracy of his views on the origins of civilization while documenting cross-culturally the existence of several "complexes" aside from the Oedipal.[4] Indeed, from this perspective, classic psychoanalysis has been cast as a Western-bound ethnoscience and Freud revisioned as a psychologically gifted ethnographer of his culture. While debates rage on, many in the psychoanalytic study of religion influenced by cross-cultural studies and psychoanalytic anthropology have come to favor more "contextual" and "configurational" approaches. These approaches emphasize an adaptive, relativistic view of the relation between self and society and a "fit" or mutual interplay between cultural expressions, family configurations, and various "developmental lines."[5]

Given Freud's religious background and sociohistorical reality, particularly the fact of German patriarchy and the impact of nineteenth-century industrialized capitalism on father–son relationships, such revisionist views see it as more than understandable that Freud was predisposed to finding Oedipus everywhere. Didn't he state in the preface to *The Interpretation of Dreams*, a work which introduced Oedipus and is in some sense a psychoanalytic autobiography, that his most important relationship was with his father? So too does this perspective find little wonder that Freud's psychological battles were with Jewish Fathers like Jacob, Joseph, and Moses, that his primary conception of religion was one based on obsessional neurosis and the *uber-ich*, and that his attitude toward the East ranged from disinterest to perplexity to "Orientalism." These studies, following in the tradition of Weber, Rieff, and the general, ideal-typical thought endemic to sociology, find it logical that among the major participants of the psychology–theology debate of the 50s were classic psychoanalysis and Protestantism and that the major issues were those concerning the superego, the nature of belief, and ethics. So too would they understand why the adherents of Catholicism and Hinduism, who have internalized a more maternal worldview, seem to favor mysticism and object-relations theory.[6]

However individual exceptions may escape general sociological expectations, Rolland is one case that fits the bill. At the center of his autobiography, *Journey Within*, is not the Father but the Mother. "She made me," he states, "not only on the day of my birth; but to the day of her death, she nourished the life within me."[7] Even a cursory perusal of *Journey Within* reveals that his musical under-standing and gravitation towards the maternal in both religion and psychoanaly-sis had complex roots in his childhood. I say "complex" because Rolland really had two "religions" in his youth.[8] The first was more orthodox and institutional-ized, his native Christianity. His mother was a devout if simple-minded Catholic who indoctrinated him into the faith through pilgrimages to St. Martin's, the old cathedral church that overlooked their house and the canal on which it rested. Rolland characterized her as "a true Christian, who in early childhood inspired me with a passion for the eternal."[9] He recalls seeing in her prayer book a note reminding her of the day "her dear little Romain" was born: "She must have read and reread it in church along with the mass."[10] As expected of him, the young Romain dutifully participated in organized Catholicism for the greater period of his youth, later claiming that in such a "stifling atmosphere" it was lit-erally impossible to do otherwise.[11] Indeed, the time (Rolland was born in 1866), place (Clamency, a small French town in western Burgundy on the Yonne River), and relative lack of social stratification virtually ensured the hegemonic character of Clamency's sacred canopy. As Rolland put it, he was "born Catholic, in a Catholic family, in a Catholic town."[12]

At the same time, Rolland created a private "religion" whose reigning deity was Nature. Clamency was an area replete with a natural aroma and beauty as yet untouched by the ravages of industrialism and capitalism. Rolland later re-counted the almost unconscious feeling of fusion and delight he felt in Her arms: "Even today, I know no other place so satisfying to all my physical needs. . . . I should never tire of drinking in the perfect symmetry of its contours. . . . My flesh is impregnated with it for all time."[13] The natural impulse of his youth was not to observe nature but to flow into it: "The passing glance of a dog, a cat, of cattle . . . was enough for me to descend into the depths of their cavern . . . for all is of one substance; everything comes from it, everything returns to it."[14] This Nature God inspired Rolland and proved to be the reliable compan-ion he could commune with and depend on:

> The bells of St. Martin!. . . . Their music is engraved on my unawakened heart. They pealed forth from the open tower of the old cathedral above my house. But it was not the church that these ecclesiastical songsters called forth in me. . . . The God who heard me—The God whom I created so that he would listen to me, and in whom I have confided all my life—was in the hovering song-birds: the bells, and in the air. Not the Lord of St. Martin's, hidden in his retreat above the sculpture arches.[15]

What these two religions had in common was their deep maternal matrix. As indicated above, Rolland, in speaking of his mother, often fused her with Catholicism: "I am on the threshold of the church. My heart is overflowing with piety, pain and love, as I kneel on entering the sanctuary of the soul that was the dearest to me of all the living . . . my mother."[16] But so too did he associate her with the natural surroundings of his childhood. In his autobiography Rol-land revealed his mother's love of nature and the excitement she would convey to him in their frequent forays into the surrounding countryside. "Face to face with nature" and "with deeply moved heart" she would endeavor to "miss nothing of the glorious summer nights, and, bare-footed, look out of the window hour after hour, drinking in the coolness of the air."[17] Again, in a letter to his mother from his school in Paris, the young Romain urges his mother to go to the Swiss Alps. "It is there where I left most of myself . . . mixed with the infinite soul of Divine Nature," he tells her, and more: "(it is that Divinity) who I am, who in spite of yourself you are, and in whose bosom we will all be united."[18]

Where these two religions parted was in their intellectual content. On the one hand, as we shall catalog momentarily, Rolland's love for Nature became allied with his later pursuit of an unchurched, mystical religion. On the other, by early adolescence, after Romain's family moved to Paris to further his education, he had firmly renounced his membership in the Catholic church, a decision he termed his "first act of strength" and "most religious act."[19] In his autobiography Rolland speaks of emotionally railing against a God who had been presented to him as a "monarque étranger" while becoming increasingly suspect about Christian tenets: "I was most distressed that I couldn't bring myself to believe in the religious mysteries which were taught to me; I saw the others believing and I couldn't imagine that they were lying."[20] Ritualistic activity, he once noted, failed to engage his unconscious or elicit emotional response. He felt that the confessional and communion opened the door to moral hypocrisy, that "trickery of the lying slave" wherein sins can be committed at leisure and salvation bought for a price.[21]

Throughout his life Rolland repeated his suspicions in more theologically informed ways, citing his aversion to the ritualized accoutrements of organized religion and intellectual objections to revealed religion, the divinity of Christ, and the doctrine of Original Sin.[22] He was adamant in his distaste for the anti-intellectualism and absolutism that pervaded the office of the Pope, once referring to Pius X as the "unworthy vicar of the Prince of Peace" who led an "odious church" which leveled all individuality, stifled freedom of thought, and demanded blind obedience.[23] As a social institution, Rolland saw the church catering to class ideology and nationalistic fervor, an opinion impressed on him during the Great War and expressed in *Liluli*. "Christians of this war," he declared, "have distanced me from Christianity forever. No possible reparation in the future will wash the Gospel clean of the blood with which it has been stained by its faithful congregation."[24]

However, despite Rolland's often harsh statements about Christianity, he was never an out-and-out enemy of the church. Indeed, Rolland maintained an ambivalent relationship with Catholicism throughout his life. He admitted to an "instinctive preference" for it, never ceased to promote dialogue with Catholic friends like Paul Claudel and Louis Gillet, had favorable opinions of Catholic thinkers like Teilhard de Chardin and Henri de Lubac, and, despite his avowed anticlericalism, once referred to the papacy as a bastion of idealism and a moral force.[25] Catholics like Claudel have seized these remarks as an indication that Rolland was "really" a theologian of sorts who constantly tried to instill "le vrai, le grand" Catholicism back into the church.[26] This attempt is unconvincing, as

Rolland explicitly stated that he did not consider himself, nor did he want to be considered, a "Christian Thinker."[27] Indeed, undoubtedly with those like Claudel in mind, Rolland suspected any Catholic who attempted to judge his thought, for he knew that they would forever try to find parallels with Catholic ideology—parallels which did not exist.[28] Late in life, in a document entitled "My Confession," Rolland reiterated his aversion to the revealed basis of Christianity.[29] As Rolland put it: "I am not a Christian. . . . I am not a believer in a revealed religion. I am a man of the Occident who, in all love and in all sincerity, searches for the truth."[30] It was to the light of reason and freedom of thought that Rolland remained eternally loyal. He described this loyalty as a "perpetual drive for truth," a drive which corresponded to a "religious instinct."[31]

The nature religion of his childhood received formal expression in Rolland's late adolescence. Once in Paris and bereft of traditional ways of expressing his religious needs, the young Romain, relying on the mélange of cultural materials afforded him by an increasingly secular and pluralistic society, created his own religion. Although Rolland's general aversion to systematization rendered the content of this personal religion somewhat vague and idiosyncratic, one can unequivocally state that its initial expression can be found in his first philosophical statement, a late-adolescence document he entitled the *Credo quia verum*. At the heart of this religion lay a number of mystical experiences Rolland identified as feelings of communion or identity with Nature. Ineffable and transformative, Rolland gave form to these experiences by combining the philosophies of Spinoza, Leibnitz, and the pre-Socratics, Eastern religion, the ethics of Tolstoy, and his native Christianity. The result was an unchurched, highly eclectic, mystical philosophy of life. Later, during the 1920s and 1930s, Rolland turned to psychology and India, intellectual pursuits which led him from an unchurched mysticism to the advocacy of a mystical psychology. Although we shall have occasion later to delve further into the evolution of this trend, what is relevant at present is the ubiquitous maternal presence one finds in these formulations. For example, Spinoza's formula *Deus sive natura* was central to Rolland's *Credo* and a mystical perennialism was the animating feature of his biographies of Ramakrishna and Vivekananda. Surely this shows a continuity with the religion(s) of his childhood.

The depth and significance of Rolland's unconscious bond with a maternal matrix as well as his insistence on a life based on reason can be gauged by recounting an episode which occurred in 1943, a year before his death. During a particularly bad illness, Rolland recorded a series of "visions" with a revealing religious content. In perhaps the most important of these visions, Rolland, suffering from insomnia as a result of a nagging cough, saw a little chapel with a bell on the edge of a great expanse of water. From this chapel he spied a swallow which he felt symbolized the union of Mother Mary with his own mother. As he watched the flight of the swallow, he felt soothed, and his cough disappeared, enabling him to sleep.[32] Treating this vision as one would a dream, one does not have to look far to see the connection between a "cough" and a "swallow." Interestingly enough, the determining factor in the vision evokes an overwhelming maternal presence and, insofar as it led to a "cure," clearly served what Winnicott would call a "transitional" function. Most important, the maternal imagery recalls Rolland's past in Clamency: the Mother, Catholicism, and particularly St. Martin's—its bells and the canal that it overlooked. Paul Claudel attached great religious importance to this vision, seeing in it a sign from God and urging Rolland to return to Catholicism. Rolland discounted Claudel's interpretation and ignored his advice. However, the vision did move him to observe a peculiarity:

> Strange duality of my nature! A reason, firm, composed, and inflexible, which does not believe, and on which no argument of faith takes hold. An instinct of the heart that abandons itself to flights of prayer, and perhaps especially to the mighty current of the invisible river that flows underground from centuries of believing souls who preceded me and gave me birth. Thus we go on two parallel roads, without being able to do anything for each other, but without collision.[33]

Rolland, like Freud, certainly had a loyalty to the light of the intellect. However, unlike Freud, whose psyche was primarily structured along Oedipal lines, Rolland's "instinct of the heart" predisposed him to pre-Oedipal issues, to mysticism, perennialism, and, as we shall see, the advocacy of a maternally based psychology.[34]

## The Turn East

By his own admission, Rolland's exposure to Indian culture at the École Normal Supérieure had been real but cursory. He read some of Eugene Burnouf's studies on Indian philosophy and translation of the Bhagavad Gita and composed a notebook on "le Bouddha Siddhartha." Some of these influences found expression in his *Credo quia verum*, where one finds sporadic references to Eastern doctrines like "nirvana" and "maya."[35] But even this minimal exposure, associated as it was with the emotional impact of his mystical experiences and childhood religion, played no small part in his later, more extensive engagement with the East. As we shall see in chapter 5, Rolland's mystical experiences and formation of his *Credo* were directly associated with, and became the eventual solution of, an adolescent crisis that betrayed identity and self-esteem issues. Faced in his later life with what he perceived to be an imminent Western cultural crisis, it is little wonder he turned back to the crisis of his adolescence, as well as the Eastern and Western mystical past, to help him fashion a new prescription, a mystical psychoanalysis, for the malaise at hand. Thus it is that one finds in Rolland's biographies of the Hindu saints, his journal *Inde,* and in letters to Indian correspondents like D. K. Roy several references to how the mystical experiences and philosophy contained in his *Credo* predisposed him to resonating with the mysticism of India.[36] It is here, then, that one finds general affinities between Freud's cultural works and Rolland's biographies. Both advocated prescriptions for culture based on institutionalizing psychological modes of introspection. Both were the direct result of social events that recalled formative experiences and ignited powerful developmental forces.

Rolland's eventual advocacy of a mystical psychology was part of a much more extensive, inclusive interest in the East. Unlike Freud, who approached Indian culture as an unavoidable consequence of the "Oriental renaissance," or even Jung, whose interest in India and the Orient was limited to his psychological pursuits, Rolland's relations with the East took place in a number of cultural arenas and engaged its most formidable representatives. Certainly the Great War was the initial catalyst behind his turn to Asia. Yet Rolland also intimated that the war merely dramatized an ongoing social dislocation in the West. He bemoaned the inability of Western cultural expressions, particularly religion, to provide adequate cultural containers for monitoring man's more irrational needs, pursuits, and tendencies. At the same time, he warned of the dangers that could accrue from a technologically advanced civilization subject to the excesses of rationalism. Although a strong promoter of science and technology, Rolland warned of their consequences in a socioeconomic system dominated by a materialistic capitalism, a violent imperialism, and a culture that had demonstrated, in the drastic form of a war, its inability to tolerate the social other both within and without.[37] Science could well end up promoting logic and the intellect at the cost of creativity, sensual joy, intuition, and spontaneity.[38] Further, the ethic espoused by the imperialistic and capitalistic West promoted egoism, greed, and the acquisition of wealth at the cost of humanistic values. "In Europe," Rolland stated to Tagore, "we feel we are imprisoned in a cage. . . . There is a tendency for our whole life to degenerate into a huge mechanical organization."[39]

Rolland's first important contact with a representative of India came, he informs us in his journal *Inde*, in 1915, by way of an article entitled "A New World Policy for India." The author, Ananda Coomaraswamy, dedicated the essay to Rolland and argued that East and West, each of which had developed different but beneficial cultural assets, needed to become equal partners and contributors in the creation of a new humanity. Upon reading the article, Rolland noted in his journal that if he were granted ten or twenty more years to live, he would like to play a part in leading Europe to the "high plateaus" Coomaraswamy dreamed about. "There are a number of us in Europe," he was later to write in the foreword to Coomaraswamy's *The Dance of Shiva*, "for whom European civilization no longer suffices . . . (we) have had to confess its inadequacies and its limited arrogance. We few look towards Asia!"[40] The following year, a lecture given in Tokyo by Rabindranath Tagore had a similar effect on Rolland. Like Coomaraswamy, Tagore noted the importance and inevitability of the coming East–West dialogue. While applauding the scientific genius of the West, he warned of its materialism, militarism, and imperialism and urged Japan, as a representative of the East, to keep its independence, integrity, and humanism intact. With his inimitable dramatic flair, Rolland characterized the lecture as "a turning point in the history of the world."[41] By the end of the decade, Rolland had established correspondences with both Coomaraswamy and Tagore. In the following decade, Rolland was to further his contacts with a variety of representatives of the East, including the biologist J. C. Bose, Professor Radhakrishnan, various disciples of Aurobindo and Ramakrishna, and, of course, a notable correspondence with Mahatma Gandhi.[42] "The Unity of Europe and Asia," he wrote, "must be, in the coming centuries, the most noble task of mankind."[43]

For the better part of two decades, Rolland engaged in a sustained effort to expose the riches of Indian culture to the West. The biographies of the Hindu saints belong to this period, as does Rolland's biography of Gandhi, his numerous articles and reviews extolling the culture and religious tradition of the East, and his attempts to establish an international university. Rolland held up the best of India's religious intellectuals and sociopolitical figures as models for the reeducation of the West. A spirit of internationalism, not nationalism, was the path the future must take. Rolland put into operation in a number of cultural arenas his plan to promote international dialogue and cooperation. His attempt to create an "intellectual's international" (a voluntary association of the intellectual elite that was apolitical and free from the machinations of nationalism and would promote cooperation and equality between nations), the dissemination of Esperanto, and the establishment of an international review dedicated to East–West issues were all examples of Rolland's universalistic and humanistic agenda.[44] In this Rolland was surely a man of his times, as is exemplified in the emergence of a host of social institutions from the League of Nations to the Olympics.

Rolland's infatuation with India also took place at a particularly sensitive time for East–West relations in France. Edward Said's well-known thesis bears directly on our study in his characterization of Oriental studies in France during the 1920s. As reflective of the "cultural ambiance" of this period, Said adduces a survey initiated by the French periodical *Les Cahiers des mois*, which, in 1925, surveyed prominent French intellectuals in an effort to gain their views on the status of East–West relations. Each of the participants was asked five questions, all of which Said thinks contained gross assumptions and prejudices about the "nature" of "East" and "West." For example, one question asked whether there existed Oriental and Occidental lobes in the brain and whether the interpenetration of the two cultures was possible. A second question inquired as to whether Henri Massis was correct in his assertion that the East presented a "grave menace" to the West, and a third asked which Western values showed the superiority of the Occident.[45] A few of the participants argued that interpenetration was for the good, whereas others, like Massis, argued in favor of French nationalism and eschewed the effort at cross-cultural synthesis. Most exemplified a distinct prejudice in favor of Western values and exhibited a resistance toward granting full and equal status to the East. For example, the writer Paul Valéry, while noting the value of the Orient as a past source of art and science, extolled the superior ability of the Occident to extract and transform whatever the East had to offer through analysis and lucid reason. Although the West had little to fear from the East now, it must continue to analyze, extract, and "selectively disorganize" lest the East organize materially and militarily.[46]

As Fisher has noted, Rolland was a staunch critic of Eurocentric superiority, militarism, and imperialism vis-à-vis the Orient. He adopted and popularized Gandhi's political philosophy, which called for national independence, pacifistic resistance, equal relations between nations devoid of racial or religious prejudice, and the promotion of democratic methods.[47] Both civilizations could benefit from such a free and mutually respectful dialogue. Rolland's stance combined with his stature as a social figure invariably brought him into conflict with many French intellectuals. Massis, as one would expect, characterized Rolland as an "Asian ideologue" who undermined French culture.[48] The renowned scholar Sylvian Levi had this to say of Rolland: "From East to West, from West to East, let us try to know each other just as we are, loyally without being either favorably biased or blindly prejudiced. Romain Rolland, who depicts the India of Gandhi as Philostrates depicted the India of the Gymnosophists, does an ill turn to India which he pretends to glorify."[49] Levi's critique was more subtle than that of Massis, for while the latter's criticism merely reflected the prejudices of his own French nationalistic credo, Levi implied that Rolland's cultural agenda undermined his attempts at objective scholarship.

## Rolland's Perennialism

Levi did have a point. Rolland's biographies can be read as simply informative, chronicling the events and describing the worldview that animated the lives of Ramakrishna and Vivekananda. But at times they resembled hagiographies fit for missionary activity. No detailed psychological analyses of these saints, as can be found in recent works by Sil, Kakar, and Kripal, can be found.[50] Indeed, one can discern Rolland's moral and sociopolitical message seeping in throughout the biographies. In the preface to the biography of Ramakrishna, Rolland recalled his past accomplishments as a social reformer: "I have dedicated my whole life to the reconciliation of mankind. I have striven to bring it about among the peoples of Europe. . . . For the last ten years I have been attempting the same task for the West and the East."[51] In his biography of Vivekananda, Rolland emphasized the need to reject Western imperialism and the "pre-eminence of one incomplete and partial civilization" in favor of the creation of a new humanity in which Asia and Europe, standing "face to face as equals" could be fellow collaborators.[52] Each civilization should learn to educate the other. Again, in his biography of Ramakrishna, Rolland emphasized how his researches revealed a "lofty system of thought, at once religious and philosophic, moral and social, with its message for modern humanity from the depths of India's past."[53] Europe could learn the virtues of "quietness, patience, virile hope, serene joy."[54] The East, on the other hand, could learn from the scientific and technological advances of the West and its proclivity to "action."[55] Rolland did not, however, fall prey to the claim that one civilization was accorded exclusive rights to certain aspects of human behavior. At the bottom of all civilizations was Man: "There is neither East or West for the naked soul."[56] Particular facets of human potential were developed over others in different lands due to varying geographic, socioeconomic, and political conditions. Europe, feeling the spiritual consequences of an all-too-rapid growth of industry and technology in an imperialistic, capitalistic society, had simply lost touch with virtues buried in its past but presently thriving in the East.

It is also noteworthy that Rolland's conclusions concerning the nature of the mystical element in religion (which is to say his perennialism) fit hand in glove with his cultural agenda. Whereas Rolland's schoolboy knowledge of Indian mysticism had been rudimentary, his reacquaintance with the East after the Great War afforded him a new opportunity to become conversant with India's primary mystical texts, as well as with important comparativist and interpretative studies.[57] In his attempt to synthesize mysticism East and West, he took as his starting point the two principal ideas behind Vedantic philosophy: the essential spirituality of life and the divinity of man.[58] He did not, to the chagrin of his Indian contacts, conceive of these ideas as the exclusive property of Indian philosophy or even give India primacy in their dissemination. Rather, the essential ideas of Vedantic philosophy could be found in others areas of the world, for example, in the pre-Socratic philosophy of Empedocles, the mysticism of Plotinus, Philo, Denis, and Eckhart, the poetry of Whitman, and the transcendental movement initiated in early-twentieth-century New England by Thoreau and Emerson.[59] Vedantic philosophy merely cataloged what was a universal, innate feature of consciousness. The fundamental source of religion was dynamic in character, a free and vital becoming that, given the proper individual and social conditions, "spontaneously" manifested itself and eventually solidified into discernible religious forms. As Rolland put it: "mysticism is always and everywhere the same."[60]

Rolland's promotion of a version of the perennial philosophy was combined with what Schwab refers to as an essentially Unitarian outlook, that is, a respect for and acceptance of individual freedom of belief, the attempt to reconcile religion with science, a unified world community, and humanistic social action.[61] Rolland was adamant about an individual's or a culture's need to accept other religions on an equal footing: "every faith has an equal right to live, and . . . there is an equal duty incumbent upon every man to respect that which his neighbor respects."[62] Rolland distinguished the word "acceptance" from "tolerance," which implied a hidden sense of superiority. An attitude of "protective tolerance" implied that, although one had a fellowship with others, it was one which secretly prayed: "God! give them the light Thou hast given me!" True acceptance, however, eschewed any kind of religious propaganda or attempts at conversion. The attitude espoused toward other religions was: "Give them all the light and truth they need for their highest development!"[63] However, although allowing for individual freedom of belief, nowhere does Rolland ever indicate that he believed in or favored a religion of revelation. What Rolland promoted was a mystical but rational religion that was highly moral and universalistic yet tolerant of individual differences.[64]

We have seen some of these ideas before in Rolland's letters to Freud, especially that of December 5, 1927. Indeed, Rolland, in describing the source of all religions in his biographies, uses metaphors and imagery that make the continuities quite obvious:

> Now of all rivers the most sacred is that which gushes out eternally from the depths of the soul, from its rocks and sands and glaciers. Therein lies primeval Force and that is what I call religion. Everything belongs to this river of the Soul, flowing

from the dark unplumbed reservoir of our being down the inevitable slope to the Ocean of the conscious, realized and mastered Being. . . . From the source to the Sea, from the sea to the source, everything consists of the same Energy, of the Being without beginning and without end. It matters not to me whether the Being be called God (and which God?) or Force. . . . Words, words, nothing but words! Unity, living and not abstract, is the essence of it all.[65]

In all this Rolland was following a pattern endemic to many religious intellectuals of the twentieth century who sought a solution to the collapse of Western culture in other cultures and in the religious past of their own culture. Rolland's inquiry into Eastern civilization led him to their religion and mystics, back into his own personal past, to the Greek and Christian mystics of Western culture, and finally to the conclusion that there existed a deep, universal dimension of the human soul which, as part of a mystical psychoanalysis, could be an invaluable source for the regeneration of a decaying Europe.

## Therapy East and West

Rolland's call for a scientific analysis of mysticism fit in well with his advocacy of the perennial philosophy and Unitarianism and his attempts at an East–West synthesis. Rolland considered science to be the most international of creeds. Insofar as it searched for truth, cut through illusions, and promoted unity and justice, science could also be conceived of as "religious." On more than one occasion, Rolland referred to science as "one of the ways to God," as "the living spirit of God."[66] In his biographies of the Hindu saints, Rolland elaborated on this claim:

> If it turns fearlessly towards the search for truth at all costs with single-minded sincerity prepared for any sacrifice, I should call it religious. . . . Skepticism itself, when it proceeds from vigorous natures true to the core, when it is an expression of strength and not of weakness, joins in the march of the Grand Army of the religious soul.[67]

On the social level, anything that led to greater harmony, unity, tolerance, and brotherhood could be seen as "religious." On the individual level, having faith or being religious was never defined solely or even necessarily in terms of assent to religious propositions and doctrine. Rather, the emphasis lay on a set of attitudes and capacities through which one exhibited a devotion to the truth and to the creation of unity and put into practice an ethical code general enough to be called humanistic or religious. For Freud such characteristics clearly lay outside the parameters of what could properly be termed "religious." For Rolland, however, Freud too was "religious," for although he was an avowed atheistic Jew, his researches were driven by humanistic considerations, the promotion of tolerance, and above all the destruction of illusion and attainment of truth at any cost.

Given Rolland's characterization of science and advocacy of a generic and dynamically conceived religious a priori, it should come as no surprise that he was more than open to a psychological investigation into mysticism. Indeed, in his biographies of the Hindu saints Rolland essentially repeated the views he expressed to Freud in his letter of December 5, 1927. First, he denied religious status to the "common-man," to those "cowardly believers, clerical and lay" who gave blind acceptance to sterile beliefs. This "religion" lacked strength of character and was determined by "obedience . . . interested or indolent motives."[68] Then, Rolland defined true religion as proceeding from religious experience, from mysticism.[69] Finally, Rolland called for a scientific investigation of mysticism. Institutionalized Christianity had created and defended the age-old dichotomy between faith and reason in order to offset scientific inquiry into its epistemological claims. The mystical traditions of India, according to Rolland, followed scientific methods, invited scientific scrutiny, and comprised psychophysiological methods like Yoga. Throughout the biographies, Rolland appealed to psychologists to take more interest in these methods. Citing various scientific forays into the religious subconscious, Rolland stated: "I do not know whether any modern psycho-physiologist, armed with all the latest instruments of the new sciences of the soul, will be able to attain to a full knowledge of them one day, but I am willing to believe it."[70] Rolland acknowledged that he conjoined "scientific skepticism to spiritual faith" and approved of Vivekananda's call for a "rationalistic religion," one which was universal and in which science and religion could meet and unite. Such a religion would be the "religion of the future," one on which "the salvation of Europe depends."[71]

In calling for a psychological inquiry into mysticism, Rolland was merely one of many who were participating in the spirit that animated the meeting of science and religion at the turn of the century. Beginning in the 1890s, a discernible subset within the field of psychology, the psychology of religion, emerged as, depending on one's perspective, heir, competitor, or supplement to the more traditionally grounded philosophical and theological modes of analyzing religious behavior. Most studies of the formative period of this movement (1880–1930) have identified the leadership and pioneering studies as coming from three generations of scholars based in the United States.[72] These studies, based in Protestant New England, were led by William James and G. S. Hall, their students Edwin Starbuck and James Leuba, and the researches of W. E. Hocking, George Coe, James Pratt and others. In the main, they utilized the methodological framework of a functional and pragmatic psychology and evinced a healthy respect for the adaptive benefits of religion.[73] The studies centered around many aspects of religion, from prayer and revivalism to conversion and studies of religious leaders. Within this broad range, mysticism hardly drew a dearth of interest. Indeed, the certified classics from the psychology of religion of this period, such as James's *The Varieties of Religious Experience*, Leuba's *The Psychology of Religious Mysticism*, and Hocking's *The Meaning of God in Human Experience*, were essentially studies on mysticism. Interestingly enough, psychoanalysis, while hailed, at least by James, as the psychology of the future, was notably absent from the American classics. Rather, it was the researches of

Janet and Myers that formed the substance of the European influence on the Americans.[74]

If the birth and leadership of this movement evolved in the United States, it is equally clear that a strong interest in and effect on the movement came from the continent, particularly France. Pratt and Schaub, noted for their surveys of this period, pointed to France as the leader of the psychology of religion in Europe.[75] So too was France, perhaps as a result of its Catholic past, known for its leadership in the psychological study of mysticism. The first such product of what can be called the "French School," Ernst Murisier's *Les Maladies du sentiment religieux* (1901), was followed by a host of influential studies, including those of Delacroix, Pacheu, and Maréchal.[76] Although psychoanalytic studies of mysticism on the continent were few, they had lasting impact, as is exemplified in the studies by Alexander and Morel.[77] In general, however, the studies of the French School, despite their almost exclusive reliance on some form of the conception of the "subconscious," preferred to pay their debts to Janet, Myers, and even the American theorists over Freud and psychoanalysis.[78] Indeed, even a cursory glance at the major books and articles of this period demonstrates how closely the American and French scholars followed each other's work.[79]

In attempting to account for the interest in the psychology of religion in France, Pratt, citing the conclusions of studies in the *Mercue de France* and in M. Arreat's *Le sentiment religieux en France*, suggested that something in the religio-cultural makeup of France was, like that of the United States, particularly susceptible to the effects of secularization. Many people in France had lost their enthusiasm for institutional religion, but considered themselves "religious" in an undefined sense: "France has ceased to be passionately Catholic. . . . The Frenchman gives up the religion of his fathers to turn to skepticism or some philosophy."[80] Pratt saw the emerging field of the psychology of religion on the continent and in the United States as able to fulfill the function, formerly the sole province of the church, of helping man come to grips with his religious feelings.[81] Certainly Rolland's distaste for institutional Catholicism and his call for a "psychological" religion fits hand in glove with this cultural trend and its dominant social type. Indeed, given Rolland's interest in promoting a mystical psychoanalysis, one could consider him a heretofore unacknowledged figure of this period.

The extent of Rolland's knowledge of studies in the psychology of mysticism is uncertain, although it does appear from the works cited in his biographies to be adequate. Within the confines of his biographies, Rolland makes explicit reference to Starbuck, Frederic Myers, and James.[82] He also makes an unspecified reference to a work by Flournoy, which was undoubtedly one of his studies in the *Archives de Psychologie*, perhaps his classic study of the modern Protestant mystic, Mlle Cecile Vé.[83] If so, Rolland was, at least in a cursory and second-hand way, exposed to the works of Leuba, Hocking, and Delacroix, all of whom Flournoy cited and used. Unfortunately, with the exception of James, Rolland had little to say about these studies. James was depicted as a model in methodological humility; as an example of how psychologists should position themselves with respect to mystical phenomena. In the first volume of his biographies, Rolland had stressed how the first prerequisite for "knowing, judging . . . and condemning a religion" was to have experimented with mystical experiences.[84] He was thus deeply impressed with James, who, despite what he called a constitutional intolerance to mystical experience, was able through "the scrupulous honesty of his intellect alone . . . (to) have arrived at the positive statement of the objective existence of these very realities."[85] Rolland also followed James's "modern" approach to mysticism, which stressed the personal, subjective, and experiential over and against "secondhand" institutional religion and its accoutrements. Furthermore, James supplied the theoretical basis which enabled Rolland to move easily between comparative–theological and psychological studies of mysticism. By stressing the role of the subconscious in explaining mystical experience, James undoubtedly fostered Rolland's view that a common-core of mysticism could be found deep within the psyche. Historically, one could cite these early theorists as providing the conceptual basis for the beginning of a shift from the perennial philosophy to what Wilber has called the perennial psychology: "a universal view as to the nature of human consiousness, which expresses the very same insights as the perennial philosophy but in more decidedly psychological language."[86] Finally, Rolland's conception of the unconscious as housing the germs of artistic and scientific productions, so evident, as we shall see momentarily, in his critique of Morel, owes something to the "subliminal self" of James and Myers.

At the same time, Rolland made a concerted effort to dialogue with studies championing psychoanalytic modes of interpretation. For example, one can discern throughout the biographies Rolland's unsystematic attempt to revision Yoga as a therapeutic technique akin, at least in some respects, to psychoanalysis.[87] Yoga, he correctly related, was derived from the same Sanskrit root as the English "yoke," which meant "to join," and implied union with the divine. As a technique, it was bound up with a specific worldview that saw ultimate reality as essentially spiritual or mental and held that in the final analysis subject and object, inner and outer, were transcended and united in primal Being.[88] Yoga, then, aimed at inducing religious experience, the realization that one was identical with the universe and its laws, with Being itself. However, the purpose of Yoga consisted in far more than the inducement of mystical feelings of unity. It consisted in a path or process that aimed at inner transformation in which the intellect, will, and feeling played independent but inexorably allied roles. Mysticism as evinced in the practice of Yoga was a true therapy, an existential becoming, a process of individuation in which one freed oneself from the illusions which bound one to the world. Yoga was a "science of the soul," a psychophysiological method that was experimentally and scientifically verifiable. Yoga adopted the introspective-empathic mode of observation with the aim of coming to "know the laws that govern the passions, the feelings, the will of mankind."[89] Yogic techniques enabled the ego to gain access to and hence mastery of unconscious contents.[90] Its goal, like that of psychoanalysis, was freedom. The characteristic of mystical introversion was not weakness and "flight," that is, the employment of any number of defense mechanisms against repressed contents, as many in the West had taken it to be, but strength and combat. "The ancient Yogis," states Rolland, "did not wait for Dr. Freud to teach them that the best cure for the mind is to make it look its deeply hidden monsters straight in the face."[91] Strength and the will to arrive were essential to undertake the rigors of Yogic training.[92] The practical results of this psychic surgery were insight, renunciation of instinct, freedom from the return of the repressed, and a strengthening of individuality.[93] Yoga was also seen as conducive to the generation of creativity—great artists had "instinctively" and "subconsciously" practiced it.[94]

Rolland further indicated that Yoga was a moral psychology the practice of which resulted in a host of moral and civic virtues.[95] Yoga increased alloplastic adaptation to social reality and provided the ego strength necessary for individuals to engage in the regeneration of a society beset with moral malaise.[96] Yoga was touted as at the heart of a "universal science–religion" that would promote social action aimed at spiritual brotherhood. Freedom, fraternity, and a universalism that acknowledged and valued individual religious and cultural differences would reign. One can readily see Rolland's cultural agenda at work here. It was this agenda he had in mind when he wrote to Freud to enlist his help in analyzing mysticism. This was the "rationalistic" religion that Rolland hoped would be "the religion of the future," a religion on which he said "the salvation of Europe depends."

Rolland became more specific about the relation of mysticism to psychoanalytic psychology in the appendix to his biography of Vivekananda, entitled "Concerning Mystic Introversion and its Scientific Value for the Knowledge of the Real." As we have indicated, the arguments contained in this appendix were not a direct reply to *Civilization and Its Discontents*. Rather, Rolland built his critique around another formidable if not paradigmatic study of this genre, Ferdinand Morel's *Essai sur l'introversion mystique*.[97] Morel, who was a professor of psychiatry at the University of Geneva, eschewed the transcendental epistemological claims of the mystics and applied the central psychological theories and concepts of his day—Pierre Janet's hierarchical conception of the mind, Freud's psychosexual developmental theory, Eugen Bleuler's study of autism, and Jung's concepts of "introversion" and "extraversion"—to some of the leading mystical texts and authors from various religious and philosophical traditions.[98] Dividing his study into two parts, Morel devoted the entirety of the first part to a detailed examination of Pseudo-Dionysius, his mystical experiences and theology, while examining more briefly in the second part "speculative mysticism" (e.g., Plotinus, Eckhart, Tauler), "Oriental mysticism" (Buddhist, Taoist, and Hindu mysticism) and various men (Suso, Bernard of Clairvaux, Francis de Sales) and women (Madame Guyon, A. Bourignon, Catherine de Sienne, M. Ebner) of the Christian mystical tradition.

While allowing for individual differences between mystics within a specific religious tradition, as well as between traditions, Morel posited certain general conclusions that applied across the board. First and foremost, Morel classified all mystics as "introverts." Morel took this from Jung's earliest use of the term, which the latter arrived at through his observation of mental patients. It did not, then, carry the connotation of a tendency to reflect, analytic introspection, fantasizing, daydreaming, or even indulging nostalgically in the past. Rather, it designated the characteristic tendency of neurotics and psychotics to turn away from reality, regress to earlier developmental stages, engage infantile imagos, and live in a fantasy world divorced from the common social reality of everyday life.[99] Mystics, as a special case of introverts, were sexually maladjusted and weak-willed and had difficulty in adjusting to social reality. In playing out their repressed desires, mystics regressed to narcissistic and autoerotic stages of development, spinning out fantasies in various forms, for example, elaborate metaphysical systems and erotically tinged hallucinated encounters with religious archetypes. Deep ecstatic experiences, such as those of a Pseudo-Dionysius, were interpreted as a longing for the security and quietude of the intrauterine state. Directly opposed to mystical introversion were the extraverts, those freed from the nostalgic desire for the mother, able to surmount the pull of fantasy and combine thought and action in a healthy adaptation to society. It would perhaps be redundant, then, to state that Morel's interpretation of mysticism, from the religious perspective, was both reductionistic and pejorative.[100]

Despite referring to Morel's study as "one of the best works devoted to this subject" and praising his thorough command of psychological method, Rolland had few positive things to say about it. With regard to his primary source material, Rolland thought Morel's treatment of Dionysius to be adequate but observed that the treatment of mysticism in part 2 of his work contained numerous inaccuracies. Morel relied for his depiction of Eastern mysticism on "third-hand information," and his selection of the men and women mystics of the Christian tradition was "arbitrary and inadequate." Like the Catholic psychologists of his time, Rolland made a distinction between grades or levels of mystics and objected to Morel's classifying mystics such as St. Bernard and Francis de Sales, whom Rolland thought to have "superior and complete personalities," with "definitely diseased" mystics such as Madame Guyon and Antoinette Bourignon.[101]

Rolland reserved his most constructive criticism for Morel's methodology and conclusions. In order to facilitate his critique, Rolland differentiated between "introversion" in its "mitigated" and "unmitigated" forms. Rolland defined the mitigated form of introversion as engaging "normal" contents of the imagination: fantasy, reverie, and its products.[102] This category, then, referred to art and the creative process, not to the unitive encounters of religious mystics. That was reserved for the "complete, absolute, unmitigated" form of introversion "as we have been studying it in these volumes in the case of the highest mystics."[103]

Rolland aimed two general critiques that cut through Morel's analysis of both of these forms of introversion. First, Morel had equated mystical introversion with pathological regression and concluded that the fantasies, reveries, and metaphysical systems created by the mystics reflected their withdrawal from reality and subsequent regression to primitive modes of the developmental cycle. Rolland did not object to the conclusions psychologists had come to concerning the state of mind of neurotics and psychotics. Such people were mentally ill and seriously regressed, and to speak of self-absorption or to say that fantasy and reverie took the place of reality in their case seemed a matter of course. On the other hand, Rolland thought that many mystics were also examples of the best humanity had to offer. So Rolland offered a constructive proposal for the emendation of psychological theory. Citing an article by the Swiss psychologist Charles Baudouin, Rolland proposed distinguishing between "regression" and "introversion." The former would denote "a step backwards in the line of evolution . . . a retreat without any idea of regaining lost ground and advancing again," whereas introversion would characterize the process which "is the indispensable condition of evolution and if it is a recoil, it is one of those recoils that render a forward thrust possible."[104] This achieved, the psychological gulf between introversion and extraversion could be bridged. Citing the heroic, socially regenerative actions of great mystics like Vivekananda, St. Bernard, and St. Ignatius as empirical evidence for such an emendation, Rolland posited an indispensable and mutually complimentary relationship between the tendencies of introversion and extraversion: "A great 'Introvert' will know at the same time how to be a great 'Extrovert.' Here the example of Vivekananda seems to me to be conclusive. Interiorization has never led in principle to diminution of action."[105]

In all this, Rolland was prefiguring revisions of psychoanalytic metapsychology.[106] Rolland's observation that a distinction was needed between introversion and regression was the same kind of problem the artist and ego psychologist Ernst Kris attempted to circumvent through his formulation of "regression in the service of the ego."[107] Rolland would have also agreed with Heinz Hartmann's portrait of art and science set in the context of his distinction between progressive and regressive adaptation:

> The term progressive adaptation is self-explanatory. . . . But there are adaptations—successful ones, and not mere unsuccessful attempts—which use pathways of regression. . . . The reason for this is that the function of the most highly differentiated organ of reality adaptation cannot alone guarantee an optimal total adaptation of the organism. . . . There is, for example, the detour through fantasy. Though fantasy is always rooted in the past, it can, by connecting past and future, become the basis for realistic goals. There are the symbolic images familiar in productive scientific thinking; and there are poetry and all the other forms of artistic activity and experience.[108]

Further, Rolland's claim that India's "science of the soul" prefigured the insights and method of psychoanalysis and his "empirical" finding that the mystical religion of a Vivekananda not only accommodated the individual to society (autoplastic adaptation) but proved to be a means for the regeneration of culture (alloplastic adaptation) anticipates some of Erikson's conclusions concerning the therapeutic value and regenerative effects of Luther's Protestant revival.[109]

Rolland's second criticism was a cousin of the first. He claimed that the psychological models utilized by Morel contained value-laden cultural assumptions concerning the nature of the mind and reality. For example, Rolland noted that Janet had created a normative hierarchy of functions of the mind. The ideal norm Janet called the "supreme function" of the mind, the "function of the real," defined as an "awareness of the present, of present action, the enjoyment of the present." Next on the hierarchical scale came "disinterested action and thought, which does not keep an exact account of present reality," and at the bottom level "imaginary representation . . . the whole world of imagination and fancy." Various psychologists had conjoined to this hierarchical view a number of supposedly value-neutral descriptive terms like regression, the pleasure principle, and narcissism. Finally, the entire hierarchy was set in the context of evolutionary theory. The highest functions in the hierarchy were acquired through species adaptation and were historically the most recent. They must, therefore, be the most complex and evolutionarily advanced functions. Thus, psychologists were all too ready to see fantasy, reverie, and the like as primitive functions with little progressive value. Freud, noted Rolland, had asserted that "reverie and all that emerges from it, is nothing but the debris of the first stage of evolution."[110]

For Rolland, this was a deep and insidious problem. Even if mystical introversion were to be deemed nonpathological, it would still carry the stigma of primitivity, a charge that affirmed the common Western perception of the East as composed of an inferior people and way of life. Psychologists were often less servants of the "real" than of "a proud and Puritanical faith, whose prejudices they no longer see because those prejudices have become their second nature."[111] The devaluation of fantasy, reverie, and mystical introversion betrayed "a kind of perverted asceticism and religious renunciation."[112] Rolland implied that there existed a cultural fit between the capitalistic and industrial West and a psychology that stressed the value of extraversion, asceticism, work, and technological reason while devaluing fantasy and introversion. From such a perspective, thought Rolland, a mystic like Ramakrishna would be as a matter of course "placed in a lunatic asylum under a daily douche of psycho-therapy."[113]

Rolland took these observations and conjoined them to another left specifically for Morel's analysis of mysticism in its "unmitigated" form. Morel, as we saw earlier, concluded that the unitive experiences of deep mystical introversion signified "a return to a primary stage, an intra-uterine state." Rolland took this opportunity to address the psychoanalytic conception of the unconscious. Surprisingly enough, he agreed that the maternal imagery and symbols pervading mystical texts and the "curious instinct" that gave rise to the worship of the "Mother" lent strength to Morel's interpretation.[114] However, he insisted that there lay something beyond the pre-Oedipal; that the kind of awareness the mystic had attained demanded epistemological analysis and a richer view of the unconscious. He then went on to describe the essential characteristic of this layer of the unconscious: Unity. Unity was the most archaic dimension of the unconscious, the very foundation of one's Being and the source of the most Real.

This new conception of the unconscious clearly differed from that advocated by Freud. As important, Rolland thought knowledge of this Unity was attained not only through introspection and mystical exercises but also through the awakening and cultivation of that faculty he called intuition. It is here that Rolland went beyond developmental hypotheses to engage the philosophical problem of the epistemology of mystical experience. In the text of his *The Life of Vivekananda*, Rolland, speaking of the relation between mysticism and science, drew upon Kant's epistemology, the foundational theory of knowledge that grounds the limits of thought and hence what we can — and cannot — know. Rolland noted that, according to Kant, the structure of the mind precluded the kind of direct, unmediated contact with the noumenal realm the mystics often claimed to intuit. But Rolland stated that "Kant's analysis was familiar to Vivekananda" and that "centuries before Kant" various Vedantic philosophers "had already predicated and even surpassed it."[115] Thus implicit in Jnana Yoga was an understanding of Kantian notions of the conditions of knowledge. Through an intuitive faculty that bypassed the more ordinary channels of reason and the senses, its adepts came into contact with the Unity that lay beyond the otherwise conditioning, a priori structures of the mind. Subject and object, inner and outer were transcended and united in a primal reality. One literally "merged" one's being with the universal consciousness buried deep in one's unconscious, returning with a new impression about the true nature of self and universe.[116]

In developing this concept of intuition Rolland played with the distinction between art, science, and mysticism. He drew attention to several notable figures in the West, particularly Henri Bergson and his disciple Edouard Le Roy, as well as those in the East, such as the Hindu philosopher and mystic Sri Aurobindo Ghose, whose studies on intuition he thought helpful in bridging the gap between intuition and reason, religion, art, and science.[117] For example, treading into dubious territory, Rolland posited an isomorphic relation between the external and internal world:

> What is the "function of the real" of which scientific psychology claims to be the standard-bearer? . . . is it what can be observed by extrospection or by introspection. . . . There are not two realities. That which exists in one exists equally in the other. The laws of the inner psychic substance are of necessity themselves those of outside reality. And if you succeed in reading one properly, the chances are that you will find confirmation and, if not, the presentiment of what you have read or will read in the other.[118]

Rolland adduced Lao-tzu's metaphysical insight, expressed in the form of a metaphor and concerning the nature of the relationship between the Tao and the created world (all the spokes of a wheel lead to and are dependent on "the central non-perceptible void of the nave") as an illustration of the formal relation between the intuitions of mystics and those of science. Corresponding to Lao-tzu's intuition, then, would be the hypotheses of astronomy, which postulated enormous "gulfs of cosmic emptiness" as the source of the matter that composed the universe.[119] This being the case, scientists should avail themselves of a method, approximating the Plotinian unity of the seer with the thing seen, which could facilitate the production of testable hypotheses.[120] Here Rolland cited the plant biologist J. C. Bose, with whom he had corresponded on the topic and who synthesized "the severest observation and experimentation of western science with the Asian faculties of concentration."[121] Bose had related to Rolland that before performing an experiment, he preconceived the reactions of the plants within himself:

When I study a tree, a plant, while observing them in a rigorously objective manner (or better, while letting them trace, by themselves, the graphs of their reactions
through the recording instruments invented by me), I *am* the tree or the plant, and
I myself become their recording instrument.[122]

Rolland promoted Sri Aurobindo's model of the relation of reason to intuition
as laid out in the latter's pivotal essay, "The Life Divine."[123] In Aurobindo's account, intuition played the part of the "quartermaster and intelligence of the
mind" and operated as "advance guard of the army of the spirit marching forward to the scientific conquest of the universe."[124] Reason, then, was "the rank
and file of the army bringing up the rear," which sifted the wheat from the chaff,
refined and gave empirical legitimacy to the more general insights given to it by
intuition.[125] In order to insure the veracity of one's intuition, Rolland recommended following the procedures laid out by ascetic mystical regimes such as
Yoga or those advocated by Western promoters of the intuitive method like
Edouard LeRoy. These procedures purified one's mental faculties of unseen intellectual and emotional prejudices so that intuition could be truly impartial and
objective.[126] This did not, of course, exempt the content of intuition from being
subjected to the rigors of empirical scientific verification. In fact, Rolland insisted that such verification was necessary: "By all means let us continue to
doubt, even after having proof!"[127]

Unfortunately, Rolland's description of this deeper, universal dimension of
the unconscious, the faculty of intuition and its method of operation, received
little more nuance than what we have detailed above. Rolland never clarified his
position beyond his sweeping statements or acknowledged the complex logical
and philosophical difficulties his views entailed. There is a general dearth of
specificity with regard to parameters for distinguishing various forms of intuition
and its precise relation to art, science, and mysticism. Indeed, Rolland often
blurred the distinction between unmitigated and mitigated forms of intuition.
Moreover, the authors Rolland cited in support of his effort to rehabilitate intuition confused the issue, for they formulated their views on that faculty in diverse
and not easily reconcilable ways.[128] Yet while it would be correct to conclude
that Rolland suffered from a hazy eclecticism, it would also be accurate to note
that he aimed less at exact philosophical statement than at the promotion
of a general orientation that he hoped the West would explore and integrate
into its culture. In other words, his was an appeal for East–West synthesis—an
appeal which presented various areas that scientists and scholars of the West
should take more interest in, perhaps even completing a task he could only
begin to undertake.

To sum up, one could say that the biographies of the Hindu saints were to
Rolland what *The Future of an Illusion* was to Freud. In light of the rise of science and the failure of traditional forms of belief to engender authentic human
beings, Rolland called for the creation of a religious psychology that was scientific and could revitalize a continent beset with moral malaise. This cultural
agenda could not be seen by Freud as anything less than a competitor to a psychoanalysis envisioned as the "secular cure of souls." While Freud sought to dis-

place religion, psychoanalysis was still quite Western, carrying the values of his humanism, religious upbringing, and scientific training. Rolland's "psychology" was far more maternal, based in his Catholic past, mystical experiences, and turn to India. He proposed nothing less than the emendation of the psychoanalytic conception of the unconscious, a displacement of sexuality as a primary force in the motivation of individuals, a new developmental schema, and a new therapeutic technique. Moreover, while not devaluing reason, he sought to validate seemingly "primitive" modes of cognition such as intuition. These emendations in technique and metapsychology were promoted to cultivate a new kind of subjectivity, one envisioned as the prerequisite for understanding the true, essential, mystical meaning of religion. In short, to Freud, Rolland was beginning to sound like Jung. And, like Jung, he had thrown down the gauntlet by unceremoniously attacking psychoanalysis. This clearly called for a rebuttal. Needless to say, Freud wasted little time in letting Rolland know what he thought of his proposals.

# The Debate Continued

After Rolland sent Freud a copy of his biographies of the Hindu saints, each man now had the other's views on the psychology of mysticism firmly in hand, a state of affairs that led to the debate carrying over into a new phase of their correspondence.[1] The essential letters of the latter are but two in number: Freud's letter of January 19, 1930, and Rolland's of May 3, 1931. Although Rolland's letter was a response to both Freud's analysis in *Civilization and Its Discontents* and his letter of January 19, 1930, it evoked no immediate counter from Freud. In fact, Freud never directly responded to the content of Rolland's letter. However he did, with Rolland in mind, continue his reflections on mysticism in his *New Introductory Lectures on Psychoanalysis* (1933) and in his essay, dedicated to Rolland, entitled "A Disturbance of Memory on the Acropolis" (1936). Since there is no indication that Rolland ever responded to these texts, our exegesis of the late period will be very much a Freudian affair. We will find that the bulk of Freud's reflections can be considered as a direct response to the arguments Rolland put forward in his biographies. Indeed, if one had to characterize Freud's position of this period it would revolve around the theme of psychoanalytic perspectives on mystical intuition in art and religion, what Rolland in his critique of Morel referred to as the "mitigated" and "unmitigated" forms of mystical introversion. However, now that Rolland had unambiguously promoted a religious worldview, so too would Freud respond in kind. We may expect, then, not only continuities with his more positive assessment of poetic-mystical "intuition" but evaluations commensurate with the more reserved posture always taken by Freud when confronted with the claims and interpretations of institutional religion.

## The Late Period: Final Letters

Freud received Rolland's biographies at the outset of 1930. He must have also read them at once, for just past the middle of January he replied to Rolland's views on mysticism and psychoanalysis found therein:

> My warm thanks for the gift of your twin-headed, three-volume work! Contrary to my calculation, my "discontented" little book preceded yours by several weeks. I shall now try with your guidance to penetrate into the Indian jungle from which until now an uncertain blending of Hellenic love of proportion (σωφροσύνη) Jewish sobriety, and philistine timidity have kept me away. I really ought to have tackled it earlier, for the plants of this soil shouldn't be alien to me; I have dug to certain depths for their roots. But it isn't easy to pass beyond the limits of one's nature.
>
> Of course I soon discovered the section of the book most interesting to me—the beginning, in which you come to grips with us extreme rationalists. That you call me "grand" here I have taken quite well; I cannot object to your irony when it is mixed with so much amiability.
>
> Concerning the criticism of psychoanalysis, you will permit me a few remarks: the distinction between *extrovert* and *introvert* derives from C. G. Jung, who is a bit of a mystic himself and hasn't belonged to us for years. We don't attach any great importance to the distinction and are well aware that people can be both at the same time, and usually are. Furthermore, our terms such as *regression, narcissism, pleasure principle* are of a purely descriptive nature and don't carry within themselves any valuation. The mental processes may change direction or combine forces with each other; for instance, even reflecting is a regressive process without losing any of its dignity or importance in being so. Finally, psychoanalysis also has its scale of values, but its sole aim is the enhanced harmony of the ego, which is expected successfully to mediate between the claims of the instinctual life (the "id") and those of the external world; thus between inner and outer reality.
>
> We seem to diverge rather far in the role we assign to intuition. Your mystics rely on it to teach them how to solve the riddle of the universe; we believe that it cannot reveal to us anything but primitive, instinctual impulses and attitudes—highly valuable for an embryology of the soul when correctly interpreted, but worthless for orientation in the alien, external world.
>
> Should our paths cross once more in life, it would be pleasant to discuss all this. From a distance a cordial salutation is better than polemics. Just one more thing: I am not an out-and-out skeptic. Of one thing I am absolutely positive: there are certain things we cannot know now.

Freud had accentuated his differences with Rolland in past letters, but here the language of warmth, longing, and idealization through which those differences had been expressed were replaced by a more sober, distancing tone. One does not have to search too far to find the reasons for this. In the beginning of the letter Freud emphasizes his cultural upbringing and orientation toward reality by referring to his humanistic Jewish past and the classical education he had received at the gymnasium. Although also nurtured on the classics, Rolland had been brought up Catholic and was at least unconsciously predisposed to accepting the maternally based mystical worldview. These cultural roots found expression in the psychological theory each championed. Rolland was associated with Jung in Freud's mind in this sense; both were "mystics" in that they had denied the fundamental tenets of psychoanalysis in order to postulate a deeper, religious layer to the unconscious.[2] Like Jung, Rolland could no longer be thought of as a member of the band of brothers. Rather, he had become the European social other who posed an obstacle to Freud's efforts to install psychoanalysis as a secular cure of souls.

Freud then addressed Rolland's critique of psychoanalytic theory. Turning to Rolland's discussion of artistic intuition, Freud undermined Rolland's objections by reiterating a position he had established long before. As we saw earlier, Freud characterized artists as having a special access to the contents of the unconscious and the talent to parlay intuitive insights into creative works. The same intuitive insights, when interpreted "correctly," that is, psychoanalytically, aided in the scientific task of helping to create a metapsychology and the therapeutic techniques needed for healing. If Rolland had read more closely his copy of *Introductory Lectures on Psychoanalysis*, he would have noted that in speaking of the artist Freud made an explicit point of distinguishing his own use of the terms *introversion* and *extroversion* from that of the early Jung.[3] The more positive assessment Freud had rendered of the distinction between the two terms enabled him to speak of the artist as reconciling the inner and the outer, the pleasure and reality principles. The artistic process could help solve inner conflict and fulfill wishes, hence being of personal value, yet also modify external reality, hence contributing to social welfare. This brought him closer to Rolland's position, at least as regards the "mitigated" form of mysticism, than the latter had given him credit for.[4]

In his biographies, Rolland had also claimed that knowledge of inner as well as outer reality was not wholly mediated through the senses, reason, and the ego but "intuited" by the mystic in the deepest layers of the unconscious. This threatened central tenets of psychoanalytic metapsychology, for it undermined the latter's conception of the unconscious and bypassed the need for those ego processes associated with the "sole aim" of psychoanalysis. Freud's response reaffirms views on this "unmitigated" form of intuition that we have seen before: caution ("there are certain things we cannot know now"), an affirmation that it unearthed psychological insight about the personal unconscious ("valuable for an embryology of the soul"), and warnings with regard to its proper interpretation. It may now be added that these thoughts are continuous with another neglected text in which Freud addressed the problem of mystical intuition. In Chapter 5 of *The Future of an Illusion*, Freud speaks to what he calls one of the "desperate efforts" of philosophers to defend the legitimacy of religion:

> the 'Credo quia absurdum' of the early Father of the Church . . . maintains that religious doctrines are outside the jurisdiction of reason—are above reason. Their truth must be felt inwardly, and they need not be comprehended. But this *Credo* is

only of interest as a self-confession. As an authoritative statement it has no binding force. Am I to be obligated to believe *every* absurdity? And if not, why this one in particular? There is no appeal to a court above that of reason. If the truth of religious doctrines is dependent on an inner experience which bears witness to that truth, what is one to do about the many people who do not have this rare experience? One may require every man to use the gift of reason which he possesses, but one cannot erect, on the basis of a motive that exists only for a very few, an obligation that shall apply to everyone. If one man has gained an unshakable conviction of the true reality of religious doctrines from a state of ecstasy which has deeply moved him, of what significance is that to others?[5]

The defensive rationalizations and rhetorical questions that litter this passage can be read as a tacit admission that there may be some religious validity to the mystical experience. At the same time, Freud clearly indicates that such experiences are far too rare, subjective, and inaccessible to reason to serve as a basis for the defense of institutional religion. In other words, mysticism was not the "common-man"'s religion. The meaning of this tacit admission becomes more evident in the next chapter, where Freud, returning to religious assertions about the epistemological status of mystical intuition, comments that although intuition cannot verify the existence of an ontological realm, it could provide insight into the personal unconscious: "(it is) an illusion to expect anything from intuition . . . (it) can give us nothing but particulars about our own mental life, which are hard to interpret."[6] Intuition, in and of itself, could not effect an automatic orientation to the external world. Rather, some mediating (interpretative) framework was needed, of which religion was one and psychoanalysis another. Here, of course, lay the problem, since Freud thought philosophers and theologians would always interpret mystical intuition in ways which would legitimate a particular religious worldview. For Freud, that meant circumventing ego functions such as reality testing and adaptation in favor of appeals to wish fulfillment and regression. The result was a faulty adaptation to reality and the continued legitimation of religious institutions, both of which heightened the *Unbehagen* in society and men.[7]

Over a year later, in the spring of 1931, Freud sent Rolland an edition of *Civilization and Its Discontents* with the dedication "The Landtier to his great oceanic Friend."[8] Then, on May 3, 1931, Rolland, writing in order to congratulate Freud on his seventy-fifth birthday, used the opportunity to respond to some of Freud's criticisms of mysticism:

Dear Great Friend,

Permit me to add my wishes to all those that will be addressed to you, on this day, your 75th birthday! I offer them with all my heart. May you continue to pursue your intrepid work for a long time to come, work that only passion for the search of truth can guide—without desire, without hope, and without fear!

And allow me to say (in thanking you for having wanted to associate my name with your recent book: *Civilization and Its Discontents*), that it is by these last words ("*without desire, without hope, and without fear*") that I feel morally the closest to you! Your kind dedication juxtaposes with an affectionate irony, the "Landtier" with the "Oceanic" friend. This opposition does not materialize, (not) only between two men, but neither in one man, in me. I also am a *Landtier* from the French countryside, from the core of old France, who seems best protected from the ocean breezes! And I am also an old Frenchman who is able to see through illusions, who is able to bear life without them, who no longer needs them. If you would allow me, for documentary purposes, to expound on the psychological curiosity in my case, I distinguish very clearly in myself:

1. What I *feel*;
2. What I *know*;
3. What I *desire*.

What I *feel*, I have told you it, and I have explained it in the introduction to the *Ramakrishna*: it is the *Oceanic*. What I *know*, it is the: "What do I know?" of Montaigne. And what I *desire*, is: *Nothing* . . . (Nothing, *for me*). As for others, may their desires be fulfilled! But I do not aspire to anything more, for myself, other than repose and effacement, unlimited and total. I have labored enough in my life. . . . But I add that, whatever can become of it, I am prepared for all that may come. I would not be French, if it were not inscribed in my character: "*Do what you must*" (or, more accurately: "*Be what you must*"), "*come what may!*"

I am therefore telling you that my feeling—or intuition—(or whatever one calls it)—"*Oceanic*"—is absolutely disinterested! I state it, but I am not particular about it. It (the feeling) is a psychological fact, a vital trait of my character. But the curious thing is that this vital trait is imprinted on the brow of thousands of these European and earthly "*Landtier*" who for the most part know nothing about Asia—or even about any Ocean! Since the appearance of my "*Oceanic*" works, letters have come forth from all corners of the earth (including your Austria), like a gushing of waters that had been suppressed. I have amassed a complete file of these letters. And that is why I think that, in history and in action, one must always take into account these invisible forces that act in secret when they are not made manifest by explosions in broad daylight. They are not born of a particular period of time. They go as far back as I can drive my borer into the past centuries of Europe and Asia. It would be dangerous for the philosopher and man of action to ignore them.

Moreover, their existence does not establish, to any great degree (in my eyes), their *truth*. It only establishes their *reality*.

Please believe, dear great friend, in my respectful and affectionate devotion.

Freud responded immediately, thanking Rolland for the "precious information" about his innermost self and adding:

Approaching life's inevitable end, reminded of it by yet another operation and aware that I am unlikely to see you again, I may confess to you that I have rarely experienced that mysterious attraction of one human being for another as vividly as I have with you; it is somehow bound up, perhaps, with the awareness of our being so different.

## Eastern Oceans, Western Rivers

From this point on direct communication between the two figures was sporadic, brief, and lacking in any reference to mysticism. However, Freud did refer to Rolland and mysticism a year later, in his *New Introductory Lectures on Psycho-analysis*, a text he sent to Rolland in 1933, and then again in 1936, in his "open letter" to Rolland concerning his "mystical experience" on the Acropolis.[9] The reference to mysticism in the former text is of especial interest insofar as it occurs as part of one of the most quoted passages within the Freudian corpus. It appears at the end of Lecture 31, where Freud, by way of summing up his discussion of the division of the psyche into the ego, id and superego, states:

> It is easy to imagine, too, that certain mystical practices may succeed in upsetting the normal relations between the different regions of the mind, so that, for in-stance, perception may be able to grasp happenings in the depths of the ego and in the id which were otherwise inaccessible to it. It may safely be doubted, however, whether this road will lead us to the ultimate truths from which salvation is to be expected. Nevertheless it may be admitted that the therapeutic efforts of psycho-analysis have chosen a similar line of approach. Its intention is, indeed, to strengthen the ego, to make it more independent of the super-ego, to widen its field of perception and enlarge its organization, so that it can appropriate fresh por-tions of the id. Where id was, there ego shall be. It is a work of culture— not unlike the draining of the Zuider Zee.[10]

On the face of it this text is an obvious reflection and confirmation of Freud's previous statements on mystical intuition and practices. The latter, like psycho-analysis, can indeed be utilized in the service of insight, although, given that there is no "religious" dimension to the unconscious, intuition is not privy to salvific truth. However, if one looks closer, one finds that the grammatical struc-ture of the psychoanalytic "motto" ("where id was, there ego shall be") and its qualification with respect to the "draining of the Zuider Zee" indicate that Freud intended it to carry a deeper meaning, one which was directed to Rolland and displays his thorough command of the written word and broad humanistic training.

With respect to the qualification, Bettelheim has pointed out that although the draining of the Zuider Zee was a technical achievement, Freud chose to re-fer to it not as *Urbarmachung*, which is the proper German term to denote the reclamation of land for agriculture, but as *Kulturarbeit*, that is, a work of culture or "labor to achieve culture." He adds that Freud's choice of this metaphor is sig-nificant, for it recalls the last two acts of Goethe's *Faust*.[11] Briefly put, the essence of the latter consists in Faust's renouncing his more youthful and grandiose attempts at harnessing the meaning of the universe and his place in it in favor of the seemingly more limited goal of the reclamation of land from the sea for the purpose of creating a working community beneficial to himself and humankind as a whole. It is this more limited and Faustian sense of "reclaiming the soul" that Freud wished to convey in his qualification of the psychoanalytic motto. Now we have already alluded to Freud's condensation of Oedipal and oceanic imagery as well as the figures of Rolland and Goethe in his remarks on Schiller's *The Diver*. Further, we have seen that Freud sent a copy of *Civilization and Its Discontents* to Rolland with the dedication, "from the Landtier to his great Oceanic Friend." These terms, which can be viewed as metaphors for the position each took with regard to the issue of mysticism, recall, as does *The Diver*, the imagery from Faust. Freud undoubtedly equated Rolland's promotion of mystical intuition with Faust's striving for the meaning of all things. Psychoanalysis, like the more mature Faust, promoted the value of the more limited but practical and attainable task of reclaiming land from the sea, of helping the ego in its attempt to mediate between the id and the external world. What psychoanalysis strove for was not simply insight, but renunciation, sublimation, structure building. In short, psychoanalysis was that interpretative and cultural science which endeavored to make people more civilized and civilization more human. In contrast, mystical practices may be able to grasp deep "happenings" in the ego and id, but this did not necessarily translate into enlarging the organization of the ego or appropriating portions of the id. On the contrary, in the interpretative hands of religion, mystical insight served merely to heighten individual and social disease.

The subtle meaning behind Freud's alteration of the grammatical structure of the psychoanalytic motto fits hand in glove with the above analysis. In the German, the motto reads *Wo Es war, soll Ich werden*. Missing from *Es* and *Ich* are the definite articles. Rhetorically, this has the effect of elevating *Es* and *Ich* into archetypes. The use of *werden* (to become) and *soll* (must, shall be) now become tinged with a definite and deliberate religious meaning. Indeed, it recalls the creation imagery of Genesis and the imperative language of Exodus. By intentionally using religious language in a ironic way and in referring to Faust and Rolland, Freud was once again juxtaposing the contrasting agendas of psychoanalysis and religion.[12] In this, then, the most famous of psychoanalytic one-liners, Freud had in mind not simply a generalized audience. He was thinking of and speaking directly to Romain Rolland.

### Freud and Hinduism

Freud returned to the problem of mysticism in his 1936 paper "A Disturbance of Memory on the Acropolis."[13] The product of Freud's effort, which consists of a piece of self-analysis, has been characterized as consisting of multiple layers and multiple meanings, like "a crystal which refracts at different angles" the entire range of Freud's fantasy life.[14] Given this, the Acropolis essay has understandably been the object of many psychoanalytic studies that have treated it as an entry into the deeper recesses of Freud's unconscious.[15] Though not disputing the value of these studies, our emphasis will not be so much on Freud's developmental vicissitudes as on analyzing how his experience on the Acropolis was part and parcel of his general reflections on mysticism and, more specifically, its status as a direct response to Rolland's biographies of the Hindu saints.[16]

Before we proceed to an analysis of this essay, we might note that this was not the first time Freud had referred to his experience on the Acropolis. The first reference occurs in chapter 5 of *The Future of an Illusion,* in the midst of a discussion on the contrasting epistemological claims of religion and science. Freud begins the passage by observing that whereas both religion and science initially require belief in their assertions about the nature of reality, only science gives us the means to confirm that belief for ourselves. The simplest of these "means" is the "self-evident" truth of our senses:

> Let us take geography. We are told that the town of Constance lies on the Bodensee. A student song adds: "if you don't believe it, go and see." I happen to have been there and can confirm the fact that that lovely town lies on the shore of a wide stretch of water which all those who live around it call the Bodensee; and I am now completely convinced of this geographical assertion.[17]

Freud then goes on to relate an unusual experience the above example "reminded" him of that had occurred a generation earlier:

> In this connection I am reminded of another, very remarkable, experience. I was already a man of mature years when I stood for the first time on the hill of the Acropolis in Athens, between the temple ruins, looking out over the blue sea. A feeling of astonishment mingled with my joy. It seemed to say: "So it really *is* true, just as we learnt at school!" How shallow and weak must have been the belief I then acquired in the real truth of what I heard, if I could be so astonished now! But I will not lay too much stress on the significance of this experience; for my astonishment could have had another explanation, which did not occur to me at the time and which is of a wholly subjective nature and has to do with the special character of the place.[18]

Two observations can be made about this passage that are directly relevant to our analysis of Freud's "open letter" to Rolland. First, one cannot help noting the resemblance between the language Freud employs in describing his experience on the Acropolis and that which pervades phenomenological descriptions of mystical experiences. Freud states it is not an ordinary but a "remarkable" experience in which preponderated elements of "joy," "astonishment," and a sense of reality. Jones reports that soon after his visit to the Acropolis Freud related to Marie Bonaparte that the experience on the Acropolis "had surpassed anything he had ever seen or imagined" and that "the amber-colored columns of the Acropolis were the most beautiful things he had ever seen in his life."[19] So too are the images of water and maternal warmth reminiscent of the images and symbols utilized by mystics. Surely these associations reveal why it is Freud picked this particular experience to analyze for Rolland. It was, in effect, the closest analogy to mysticism he could find within the realm of his experience. In this respect one should not overlook the fact that Freud's depiction of his "geographical location" — in the domain of Athena overlooking the blue sea — bears a striking thematic resemblance to the pre-Oedipal imagery and analysis he was to render of Rolland's "oceanic feeling" three years later.[20]

We might also note the intriguing reference to the "another explanation . . . of a wholly subjective nature" which would have to take into account the "special character of the place." Here Freud's use of the word "reminded" takes on new meaning, for it suggests that we treat it as a free association or fantasy. The question, then, is what the content of that fantasy is and its significance for Freud's analysis of mysticism. This question can only fully be answered during the course of our analysis of Freud's "open letter" to Rolland. For the moment, we need only to point out that Athens was not the only city that evoked religious feelings in Freud. Writing from Paris in 1885 to his fiancée, Freud spoke of his feelings upon entering the Cathedral at Notre Dame: "This is a Church . . . I have never seen anything so seriously moving and somber."[21] Gedo compares this "sensation" to the one Freud experienced on the Acropolis: "So it really is true!"[22] Again, when in Rome, the visits to which Jones states brought Freud "great happiness and exaltation," Freud had an irresistible desire to worship at the temple of Minerva, an event directly related to the Acropolis episode in that Minerva is the Roman counterpart of Athena. It seems there was something about Rome, Paris, and Athens that engendered in Freud associations and feelings of a similar nature. We have seen this before, and it suggests a certain avenue of exploration, one which we shall attend to momentarily.

Turning now to Freud's "open letter" to Rolland in 1936, the major aim of this self-analytic session was to explain what he called a "feeling of derealization," a feeling that led to a disturbance or falsification of memory. Freud prefaced his remarks by stating how every year during his vacation he was in the habit of traveling with his brother Alexander to some location on the Mediterranean Seaboard. In 1904, Freud planned on visiting Corfu, a Greek island, by way of the Italian port of Trieste. Upon arriving in Trieste, however, they were advised, on account of the bad weather in Corfu, to visit Athens. Freud remarks that this possibility, which opened the way for the fulfillment of a long-standing wish, should have brought feelings of pleasure. Instead, it caused a depressive and irresolute frame of mind that continually cast doubts on the feasibility of such a trip.

Once on the Acropolis, a feeling came over Freud that moved him to exclaim: "So all this really does exist, just as we learnt at school!" In contrast to his analysis of this utterance in *The Future of an Illusion*, Freud then goes on to posit that the utterance involved a "splitting of the ego" between the "person" who made the remark and the "person" who took cognizance of the remark. Whereas the first person was astonished at the actual existence of the Acropolis, the second person was astonished that the existence of the Acropolis had ever been the subject of doubt. Freud notes that in his schoolboy days doubt had indeed been associated with the Acropolis. That doubt, however, pertained not to the existence of the Acropolis but to whether he would ever have the opportunity to see it with his own eyes. Somehow a disturbance or falsification of memory had taken place. Freud reasons that such a disturbance could have taken place only if while on the Acropolis he had had a "feeling of derealization"; that upon arriving on the Acropolis a momentary and not altogether conscious feeling had been engendered that, had it been translated into conscious thought, would have been expressed as follows: "What I see here is not real." It was the attempt to keep this thought from coming into conscious awareness through repression that accounted for the falsification of memory—the displacement of doubt from seeing the Acropolis on to its actual existence.

This analysis, of course, left unexplained the unconscious forces that provoked the feeling of derealization. To this explanation we will momentarily attend. First, however, let us note the significant alterations between Freud's account of the Acropolis episode above and that given in *The Future of an Illusion*. Most crucial in this regard is why it is that Freud changed his emphasis from joy, astonishment, and a sense of "reality" to "derealization" and "unreality." A clue to the answer can be gleaned from Freud's isolation of another set of mental phenomena, the most prominent being "deja vu," which he regards as the positive counterpart of derealizations. Freud then goes on to state: "A naively mystical and unpsychological attempt at explaining the phenomena of deja vu endeavors to find evidence in it of a former existence of our mental self." The reference is, quite clearly, to the Indian doctrine of reincarnation. Similarly, to make explicit what is implied in the text, the phenomena of derealization, the sense of the unreality of the world, would become the experiential basis for the essentially mystical doctrine of maya. Significantly, both of these doctrines received play in Rolland's biographies of the Hindu saints. It is here, then, that we arrive at the true motive behind Freud's emendation of his account of the episode on the Acropolis. Freud wished to emphasize, as he had in *The Future of an Illusion* with respect to Western religion, the psychoanalytic understanding of the origin of some of the cardinal tenets of Eastern religion and the value of such a worldview for adaptation or "orientation" to the external world.

Freud characterized a derealization with the German word *Empfindung* (sensation, feeling), which is the same German term he had used to characterize the "oceanic feeling." And, like the oceanic feeling, Freud sought a psychoanalytic explanation for this "mystical experience" and indicated how the latter became connected with religious doctrine. Emphasizing the Oedipal, Freud argued that his fervent wish to see the Acropolis was tied in with the wish to overcome his father—a wish that invariably brought with it feelings of guilt:

> But here we come upon the solution to the little problem of why it was that already at Trieste we interfered with our enjoyment of the voyage to Athens. It must be that a sense of guilt was attached to the satisfaction of having got so far: there was something about it that was wrong, that was from the earliest times forbidden. . . . It seems as though the essence of success were to have got further than one's father, and as though to excel one's father were something still forbidden.[23]

At Trieste, the fulfillment of the wish was still only a possibility and the depression a symptom of the unconscious Oedipal conflict. On the Acropolis, possibility had become actuality, and the reality of success, which brought with it intense conflict and guilt, was overwhelming. An equal attempt had to be made to defend against the reality of success, namely, that of derealization—"what I see here is not real." Thus it is that Freud endeavored to show the superior interpretative power of psychoanalysis and the danger in mistaking a feeling of derealization, or a déjà vu for that matter, as an indicator concerning the true nature of Reality. The "oceanic feeling" was "used" by religion as a means of consolation and a way of seeking to restore a sense of limitless narcissism. Derealizations, however, became the experiential basis for the doctrine of maya, a doctrine which, if taken as an accurate account of the nature of reality, could justify passivity, fatalism, self-absorption, and withdrawal from the world.

This was not Freud's only foray into the psychological dis-ease created by Eastern religious worldviews. In a rumination that was at least in part inspired by Rolland, Freud, in the second chapter of *Civilization and Its Discontents*, drops his supposedly value-neutral clinical stance in order to address the philosophical problem of the purpose and meaning of life. This, he states, stands and falls with the problem of happiness. The question is how, given the tendencies, capacities, and limits of man's nature, we can best fulfill the program of the pleasure principle. Freud eventually argued for a general position that stressed the value of work, being loved, and loving others. Indeed, "to love and to work," like the psychoanalytic motto, has become but another famous one-liner representing accumulated Freudian wisdom. However, along the way to his conclusion Freud considered and then dismissed a number of other "prescriptions," many of them religious, for Freud thought that religion stood and fell with the question of happiness. It is in this context that his reflections on what he referred to as the "wisdom of the East" can be found.

Freud begins the passage under consideration by noting that because of the diverse internal and external circumstances of individuals, there is no one particular path that can be prescribed for all. Indeed, one can find a variety of paths offered by diverse schools of thought. Many schools, in acknowledgment of the limits and suffering imposed on us by biology, psychological constitution, relations with others, and external nature, define happiness less in positive terms than in the modified and negative sense of avoidance of pain, pleasurelessness, suffering, and unhappiness. A good example of such a path is that of the hermit who, finding his greatest source of suffering in his dealings with others, adopts the plan of "voluntary isolation." Other schools point to our internal life as the origin of our suffering and seek to master or control the instincts. The path "prescribed by the worldly wisdom of the East" combines these latter two "schools" of thought. It recommends that one "kill off the instincts" and withdraw from active social life and the community of men. Its ideal, then, is that of the religious ascetic, and the "technique" in its service is Yoga. Like psychoanalysis, then, the "therapeutic" technique of Yoga was inexorably bound up with culture, in this case the mystical Eastern religious worldview. However, in contrast to Rolland's assertions, Freud thought that any psychological insight garnered through Yoga would not result in greater social adaptation or individuality but in something like a permanent "liminal" state, an erasure of personal and social history. As such, Yoga, inexorably bound up with the "worldly wisdom of the East," was really in the service of the "death instinct," of quiescence and simplicity, a state Freud would correlate with his term the "nirvana principle."[24]

Finally, returning once again to the Acropolis paper, it is worth noting that the latter also contains traces of Freud's Hannibal Complex. It is here, I think, that one finds the meaning of the other "explanation" Freud referred to in *The Future of an Illusion* and why it was he was "reminded" of his trip to Athens while writing a book on religion. This becomes evident when Freud, in characterizing his wish to see the Acropolis, allows himself a memory—a memory which led to a fantasy:

> When first one catches sight of the sea, crosses the ocean and experiences as realities cities and lands which for so long had been distant, unattainable things of desire—one feels oneself like a hero who has performed deeds of improbable greatness. I might that day on the Acropolis have said to my brother: "Do you still remember how, when we were young, we used day after day to walk along the same streets on our way to school, and how every Sunday we used to go to the Prater or on some excursion we knew so well? And now, here we are in Athens, and standing on the Acropolis! We really *have* gone a long way!" So too, if I may compare such a small event with a greater one, Napoleon, during his coronation as Emperor in Notre Dame, turned to one of his brothers—it must no doubt have been the eldest one, Joseph—and remarked: "What would *Monsieur notre Père* have said to this, if he could have been here today?"[25]

The memory of walks Freud took with his brother, which, considering the age difference between the two (they were ten years apart), could never have occurred in the form Freud relates, has been interpreted by Kanzer and Masson with respect to Freud's autobiographical account, found in *The Interpretation of Dreams*, of the anti-Semitic incident that had afflicted his father.[26] It was this memory, as we saw earlier, that Freud cited as giving rise to his Hannibal Complex and wish to conquer Catholicism. It is, then, of all the more interest that Freud goes on to associate to this memory a fantasy in which he identifies himself with Napoleon, whom Freud associated with Hannibal, being crowned emperor in that bastion of French Catholicism, Notre Dame. Of course, Rolland was associated with French Catholicism and it was in Notre Dame that Freud experienced a "mystical" feeling akin to his experience on the Acropolis. Significantly, Napoleon was not, in fact, crowned in Notre Dame but in Milan. The wish operating behind Freud's displacement, then, was the same as that which motivated the writing of the text as a whole—the desire to "displace" Rolland's mystical religion.

PART II

# The Oceanic Feeling Revisited

FIVE

# A Congregation of One

Our efforts up to this point have aimed at elucidating the issues entertained and perspectives offered by Freud and Rolland during the course of their debate on mysticism. The result has been the deconstruction of the common understanding of Freud's views on mysticism. Certainly the latter were more subtle, complex, and interesting than has been acknowledged. At the same time attention can be drawn to the disjointed and "unfinished" character of the Freud–Rolland debate. Our analysis seems to have raised as many new questions as it dispensed with misleading interpretations. The debate could well have used a mediator who could have clarified muddled issues, adjudicated misunderstandings, and attempted to further the cause of a series of highly interesting but ultimately unresolved conversations. On the other hand, it is here where opportunity lies for anyone pursuing a revisionist agenda.

It is undoubtedly the case that more than one entry exists in the debate for those seeking to pursue constructive proposals. Our entry takes its cue from Rolland's pivotal letter to Freud of December 5, 1927. In that letter, as we saw in chapter 2, Rolland, in describing the oceanic feeling, stated that it reflected both his own personal mysticism and mysticism everywhere. In other words, his letter contained both personal confession and scholarly statement. This observation leads us to question whether Rolland's letter contained an adequate description of his own mysticism. Given his vague and cursory description of the oceanic feeling to Freud, it is more than likely that there exist other texts in the Rolland corpus that will enable us to reconstruct in a more detailed way the precise nature of his mysticism. In turn, this reconstruction will enable us to critically examine his perennialism. Once accomplished, these tasks will afford us a more secure basis on which to develop a critique of Freud's interpretation as found in

*Civilization and Its Discontents*, as well as provide avenues for readdressing the role psychoanalysis should play in an interdisciplinary approach to mysticism.

## Rolland's Early Mysticism: The Credo Quia Verum

To briefly review the salient points of our summary of Rolland's religion in chapter 3, two developments of Romain's boyhood were instrumental in preparing the psychic soil for his relatively early entry into the mystical life. The first was the dysfunctional nature of the Catholicism into which he was socialized. In his autobiography, Rolland relates how his encounters with the "Lord of St. Martin's," referring to the old cathedral church which overlooked his household in Clamency, were essentially ceremonious and experience-distant: "In spite of my honest efforts, I never succeeded in getting in touch with him."[1] Unfortunately, the characteristics of the Christian God mediated to him consisted in an unholy mix of arbitrariness and power: "He is most powerful, that's his definition. All the catechism of the Catholic church and the home boils down to that definition."[2] In the young Rolland, such a conception translated into feelings of oppression. God was a tyrant who abused his power. This God, thought Rolland, should not gain entry into his heart: "Be true! Do you believe in the Person of a God, distinct from you, unique and all powerful? And I answer: No . . . everything within me protests against this foreign monarch."[3]

The second was a life change which occurred during early adolescence. In 1880 Rolland's parents, realizing the intellectual gifts of their only son, spirited the entire family off to Paris to further the aim of creating a scholar of the young Romain. The move paid off, for, after studying for the next nine years at three schools—the Lycée Saint-Louis, the Lycée Louis-le-Grand and the prestigious Ecole Normale Supérieure—Rolland went on to a doctorate and then, in 1895, was offered a position at the Sorbonne. However, on another level the effect of the move was to disappoint both of his parents. In the throes of adolescence, in a city far removed from the maternal serenity of the Clamency countryside, and in an intellectual and moral atmosphere he later referred to as "deicidal," Romain found it imperative to formally renounce his ties to the church. In its stead, Rolland found himself privy to a number of mystical experiences that had a profound and formative impact on his life. This is evident from any number of Rolland's letters, not the least of which is his letter of December 5, 1927, to Freud. In his essay "Romain Rolland, Les dernières etapes du voyage intérieur," Louis Beirnaert relates that Rolland, even at sixty-three years of age, did not waver in stressing to him the importance of his early mystical experiences for the course of his life:

I had, between the ages of 15 and 20 . . . several brief and staggering contacts with the Unity. These obscure illuminations were the key to the spiritual world where I lived for the next forty years. I passionately explored this world among the trials and torments of my life of flesh and blood, here and there visited by new revelations (éclairs).[4]

It is unfortunate, given the importance Rolland ascribed to these early experiences, that he left us few detailed autobiographical descriptions of these "éclairs" or revelations. The two richest sources for such accounts are Rolland's autobiography, *Journey Within*, and his *Mémoires*. Writing in the former, he informs us that his very first mystical encounter occurred during the summer of 1882.[5] He relates that as a lad, experiencing the trials and tribulations of his new life in Paris, he was taken by his mother to Allevard, just over the French border, as part of a therapeutic regimen for a resurgence of bronchial problems he had experienced since infancy. On the way home they stopped at Ferney, which had been the home of Voltaire for many years. On emerging from Voltaire's house, Rolland took one look at the landscape ahead of him and "the thunder roared":

> I see! At last I see! What did I see? The countryside, very beautiful but not unusual. From there the distant mountains do not overwhelm by their gigantic vastness. . . . Not a trace of Romanticism. This is the great pre-Rousseau classic landscape: full, tranquil harmony, with consonant chords, superbly orchestrated. . . . Why, then, did the revelation come to me here, rather than elsewhere? I do not know. But it was like the rending of a veil. The spirit, a desecrated virgin unfolding under the embrace, felt stirring within it the virile ecstasy of nature . . . suddenly everything took on meaning; everything was explained. And in that moment, when I beheld Nature in all her nakedness, and went in to her, I loved her in my past, for it was there that I knew her. . . . Then the veil descended, and I returned to Paris.[6]

One must remember that this autobiographical account was penned in 1924, over forty years after the fact. Moreover Rolland, now an internationally acclaimed writer, was less interested in delineating a precise descriptive account of his mystical experience than in exhibiting his ample rhetorical skills. The reference to the "rending of a veil" is biblical, symbolizing access to God, while Rolland's reference to loving Nature "in my past" establishes continuity between his "éclairs" and childhood love of the Clamency countryside.[7] One assumes that something significant took place, but Rolland does not give us any further hint as to its true identity.

We get a better idea of what occurred in Rolland's *Mémoires*, which he wrote in 1939. In the latter, Rolland recalls once again his years as a student in Paris, the hardships and the suffering he had to endure. It was his trips back to the French and Swiss countryside, he stated, that saved his soul: "I will never be able to adequately convey what Nature meant to me during the years of troubled adolescence."[8] For Rolland Nature was "the Book of Books . . . the living God."[9] What broke the seal of the Book of Nature was a series of mystical communions, of which Rolland specifically mentions the revelation at Ferney. However, he goes on to state that there were others of a like kind. Citing directly from his notes taken during September of 1889, he describes what he experienced while hiking in the Alps:

> I feel faint under the pressure. . . . [I]f I had been alone, I would have thrown myself to the ground, I would have bitten the stones, the beautiful, shining, green

and garnet-red stones, and the dust with its sparks of gold. . . . I was possessed by nature like a violated virgin. For a moment my soul left me to melt into the luminous mass of the Breithorn. . . . Yes, extravagant as it may sound, for some moments I *was* the Breithorn.[10]

Of course the "Breithorn" and "Ferney" experiences were not the only contact with Unity Rolland enjoyed. In his letter to Beirnaert, Rolland refers to "several brief and staggering" mystical experiences. He reiterates this in his *Mémoires:* "My notes are full (throughout 1888–1889) . . . of these spasms of a female lover in the arms of a giant."[11] In his autobiography yet another description of one of these communions can be found. Rolland recalls how in the fall of 1886, just before he was to enter the Ecole Normale Supérieure, a train he was traveling on suddenly stopped in a tunnel near Paris. Passengers began to panic as all power failed and the lights went out. However, Rolland, who was meditating at the time, did not feel fear or restlessness. Rather, he felt a "veil" being rendered asunder in his mind and a calm, joyous mood descended on him. An absolute certainty enveloped him that his "true" self, as opposed to his material body, was utterly incapable of being harmed. Rolland knew that in his deepest core he was Unity: "All that is mine. It is me." In describing the impact of this revelation, Rolland drew a parallel with that experienced by the character of Pierre Bezuhov in Tolstoy's *War and Peace.* A prisoner of the French awaiting execution, Pierre suddenly bursts out laughing:

> They have captured and imprisoned me. . . . Me? My immortal soul? . . . The full moon was at its zenith. The woods and the fields were outlined around him; and beyond those fields and woods flooded with night, the view stretched out far as eye could reach towards a boundless horizon. Pierre gazed intently at the night sky. "And all that is mine," he thought. "All that is in me; all that is me! And that is what they have captured; that is what they have shut up in prison!" He smiled, and went to lie down by his comrades.[12]

Two decades later, in his novel *Jean-Christophe,* one finds an echo of these many mystical mergings with nature occurring in the character of Christophe. In the first and most significant of these, Rolland depicts Christophe, in the throes of adolescence, as being possessed by "a furious wind in the desert," as in the midst of growing a "new skin." Suddenly, the "veil was rent," and Christophe saw:

> By a flash of lightning, he saw . . . he was God. God was in himself; He burst the ceiling of the room, the walls of the house; He cracked the very bounds of existence. He filled the sky, the universe, space. The world coursed through Him, like a cataract. In the horror and ecstasy of that cataclysm, Christophe fell too, swept along by the whirlwind which brushed away and crushed like straws the laws of nature. He was breathless: he was drunk with the swift hurtling down into God . . . God-abyss! God-gulf! Fire of Being! Hurricane of life! Madness of living,—aimless, uncontrolled, beyond reason,—for the fury of living! . . . He rediscov-

ered the world, as though he had never seen it. It was a new childhood. It was as though a magic word had been uttered. An "Open Sesame!" Nature flamed with gladness. The sun boiled. The liquid sky ran like a clear river. The earth steamed and cried aloud in delight. The plants, the trees, the insects, all the innumerable creatures were like dazzling tongues of flame in the fire of life writhing upwards. Everything sang aloud in joy.[13]

Although it is fictional, surely Rolland was drawing in part on his own adolescent mystical experiences in writing this passage. The imagery and feeling of expansion to include nature recall the Ferney and Breithorn experiences, whereas the terminology employed (the biblical "rending of the veil") can be found in the Ferny experience as well as in the "train episode." From the information at our disposal, then, we can conclude that, starting with the first experience with Nature in 1882, Rolland had several similar episodes during the decade of the 1880s and perhaps even more in later years.

If the precise phenomenological accounts of Rolland's early mystical experiences are important, then no less so is the fact that these experiences formed the existential basis for Rolland's first philosophical statement, his *Credo quia verum*. As a prelude to our analysis of the *Credo*, we should note that Rolland's descriptions and references to his "éclairs" were never entirely devoid of intellectual influences. Although much of the above reflects Rolland's background in literature, other descriptions are firmly indebted to philosophical and religious sources. For example, in describing his experiences in his journal, written while at the Ecole Normale, Rolland states:

> Movement is attributed to the sea, and is opposed to the immobile mountain. . . . Error! there is more movement in the mountain. On the one hand, the momentum from low to high, an aspiration more powerful than that of the cathedrals. On the other hand, the fall into the abyss . . . the silence of an underground stone cave, is it more profound, and by how much, than that of a prairie. . . . ? The grass and the plants emit a harmony that our body unconsciously drinks and perceives, as the millions of waves separated from the ocean, which Leibnitz talks about. . . . The entire universe is one unique, immense sound from which burst, like a ripe pomegranate, billions of harmonics, all composing one same oceanic harmony.[14]

Further perusal of his journal confirms the influence Leibnitz had on Rolland.[15] Indeed, there were many such intellectual influences that aided Rolland in his attempt to make sense of the profound but ineffable experiences of his youth. Without any question, the earliest and most important of these was Spinoza. Writing in his autobiography, Rolland relates that just after his initial contact with Unity at Ferney "my mind was still closed to abstract ideas."[16] However, during the winter of 1885–1886 the situation changed. Rolland was preparing for his entrance exams to the Ecole Normale Supérieure (which he attended from 1886–1889). Sitting at his desk in the family apartment on the rue Michelet, Rolland embarked on a reading of Spinoza's *Ethics*. "One page was enough," he said, to strike "sparks of fire."[17] What did he find? "'Natura naturans' and 'natura naturata' are one and the same."[18] That is, God and Nature are one. Rolland found extraordinary comfort in this insight: "Everything that is, exists in God.[19] . . . And I too, am in God![20] . . . I can fall only in Him. I am at peace; all is peace."[21] The net effect of a universe conceived of as a Unity was joy: "Joy is a passion that increases and stimulates the power of the body. . . . Gaiety can never be in excess, for it is always good. . . . Make use of everything in life and enjoy it as much as possible."[22] This joy, found Rolland, contained a social imperative: "Unite with others and try to unite them one to the other—for everything that tends to unite them is good . . . Unite oneself, consciously, with all nature."[23] For Rolland, then, Nature was not an abstract, amoral entity. On the contrary, it was a "living presence," the fundamental matrix through which all beings were interconnected. As he later put it, "at bottom each mind and what is convenient to call nature share the same reality, have the same origin, are the issue of the same cosmic energy."[24]

Rolland intimated that his reading of Spinoza was not approached with scholarly intent. Rather, in reading the texts of Spinoza, he discovered himself:

> I shall not here try to explain the liberating significance of Spinoza's philosophy, but what I myself found in it.[25] . . . I discovered not him but my unknown self. . . . I read not what he had said, but what I wanted to say—the words that my own childish thoughts were trying to stutter with my inarticulate tongue. No one ever reads a book. He reads himself through books, either to discover or to control himself.[26]

Indeed, Rolland's equation of Nature with "the living God" and his notion of being "one" with the Breithorn seem to reflect the influence of Spinoza. This gives us a clue as to why Spinoza remained so important to him forty years later. Although it was not, like the experience at Ferney or in the Alps, a merging or communion with Nature, it was nevertheless classified by Rolland as a "revelation." Recall that at Ferney Rolland's mind was, as he tells us, "still closed to abstract ideas." He did not have, then, an appropriate language to convey what must have been, as James informs us and as Rolland confirms in the above ("my inarticulate tongue"), an "ineffable" experience. This may be why we have no immediate account of what was a life-changing experience (and thus certainly deserved some account) at Ferney. Indeed, the first written account we have of Rolland's mystical experiences cannot be found until after Rolland read Spinoza. It was, then, Rolland's exposure to Spinoza and other philosophers that provided him the needed language through which to express the "ineffable" experience. This process was not a simple transposition from experience to text. Rolland informs us of the difficult process of reworking and integrating ineffable experience into a wide-ranging philosophical credo in *Journey Within*:

> I applied myself doggedly during my years at the Ecole Normale. . . . [I]t was necessary for me to incorporate the revealing Word of Spinoza. . . . The long daily account of my struggles at the Ecole Normale between 1886 and 1888 can be

found in my notes. By remodeling, building up, and tearing down Spinoza's formula, I tried to make it my rule of life, until the date of victory, April 11, 1887 . . .
when at last I caught hold of Spinoza's God, duly taken apart and put together
again to suit my tastes and my needs.[27]

What seems to have happened, then, is a slow working and reworking of ineffable experiences through an intellectual medium into a bona fide mystical philosophy. April 11, 1887, is, as one might suspect, the date that marks the (conceptual) completion of Rolland's *Credo quia verum*.[28] The finished product, a
twenty-seven-page document, was put down in essay form on May 24, 1888.[29] It
is without question the most crucial document of Rolland's early mysticism.
Consisting of several sections, each ranging from a paragraph to a few pages, its
content revolves around religio-philosophical issues concerning the nature of
God and the self and portrays the attempt to map out guiding ideals upon which
a young person can orient a life. The difference between it and Rolland's communions with Nature, then, is all the difference between experience per se and a
worldview. In effect, the *Credo*, as "ideology," depicts that process whereby Rolland transformed episodic experience into permanent psychological and ethical
structure.

As with most philosophical discourses, the driving force behind Rolland's
*Credo* is the search for truth, the "one unassailable point," as he puts it, upon
which a life can be built. The method for arriving at the truth is twofold. First,
Rolland reasons, truth can only be found within: "If the world has an explanation, it is inside of us that we must search."[30] Second, following Descartes, Rolland searches for the (inward) truth through doubt: "to engage in the search for
truth, one must begin like Descartes . . . doubt everything . . . all one needs
is one solid unassailable point."[31] The "unassailable point" Rolland found was
formulated as follows: "I feel, therefore It is." The It, as one may surmise, is Being or God, the bedrock of Reality. Turning within, Rolland concluded that only
the present sensation can be designated as truly "real." Sensation, defined widely
as including the immediate content of consciousness—"ideas of reason, volition,
desire, tendencies, all that is immediate"[32]—is particular, that is, a sensation of
something (heat, cold, whiteness, etc.), and as such can be doubted. However,
while a particular sensation can be doubted, the fact of Sensation cannot:

> Sensation, both present and fleeting, has led me to discover Being. Yet Being is not
> the sensation that passes and that one cannot establish. In each sensation Being af-
> firms itself, without limits. . . . When I say: "I feel, therefore there is something," I
> don't place emphasis on the word "something" but rather on the fact of existence,
> which is simple and without restriction. . . . It is. It is any sensation. No sensation
> is truly It; no sensation Is, since we can always doubt. . . . One can contest the re-
> ality of hotness, coldness . . . anything that is particular or relative. It is absolutely
> necessary, however, that Being be—not this or that—but anything (all things). . . .
> [P]articular existence must perpetually pass into the unchanging Being.
>     In this sensation, past and future meld into one, as into an eternal present. Bil-
> lions of sensations, little droplets that grow, come closer together, and disappear in

order to come back again to the Ocean of Being. . . . It is these infinite waves of the Divine Sea whose slow palpitation I feel in my heart.[33]

It is "intuition" (the same "intuition" Spinoza spoke of in the *Ethic*)[34] that disclosed to Rolland the true Being through particular, fleeting sensation: "It is Intuition that discovers for me the absolute Being. But what is intuition? The present sensation (therefore a real one), but profound, eternal (therefore certain), of the One."[35] Intuition is distinct but related to Reason. The time will come, says Rolland, when the "simple discovery will be made that intuition can be a scientific method, no less rigorous, but fertile in a different way than . . . dry Deduction."[36]

However philosophically wanting Rolland's position might be, he had satisfied himself that he had formulated a working theory or doctrine of God. This formulation clearly shows the influence of both his mystical experiences and of many intellectual influences. To Andre Suàres, his closest friend at the Ecole Normale Supérieure, Rolland confided that his breakthrough consisted in conceiving of Spinoza's "substance" not as an idea of Reason but as sensation: "I define the Being: that which is everything . . . the feeling of being everything, of being complete, of being free.[37] . . . God is all sensation and the sum of all sensations."[38] This was what Rolland called a "Spinozism of sensation,"[39] so conveniently expressed through a Cartesian formula. Rolland conceived of this God as a Nature-God, pantheistic and impersonal, the Divine ground of one's own self and all other selves.[40]

Aside from the dominant figure of Spinoza, one can discern several other intellectual influences in Rolland's characterization of "Being." Most obviously, Rolland's reference to the "Ocean of Being" and the "infinite waves" seems to recall the influence of Leibnitz. It may be the case, however, that Rolland's reading of Tolstoy was even more determinative. This becomes quite apparent in an entry in 1887 from his journal at the Ecole Normale Supérieure where Rolland, in jotting down preparatory notes for the writing of his *Credo*, cited the following passage from Tolstoy's *War and Peace* to illustrate his emerging conception of self in relation to God:

> All that lives, is God. . . . Animated sphere, trembling, without clearly defined contours, whose surface is composed of drops of water (gouttes d'eau) squeezed into a compact mass, that slides in all directions . . . that is the image of life. . . . God is at the center. Each one of these drops tries to stretch out in order to better reflect him. It gets larger, makes itself smaller, disappears, in order to come back again at the surface.[41]

This sounds similar to Rolland's description cited above ( "Billions of sensations, little droplets [gouttelettes] that grow, come closer together, and disappear in order to come back again to the Ocean of Being"). So too have we seen Rolland using Tolstoy to convey the meaning of the "train episode." Given these observations, one is justified, I think, in casting Rolland in his all-too-familiar role as a master of eclecticism, this time mixing the thought of Spinoza, Leibnitz, and Tolstoy in order to arrive at a personally acceptable representation of God.[42]

There also may have been some influence from India and the philosopher Empedocles. As mentioned in chapter 3, we know that around this time Rolland read some of the famous Oriental scholar Eugene Burnouf's studies on Indian philosophy, as well as his translation of the Bhagavad Gita, and composed a notebook on "le Bouddha Siddhartha."[43] As we shall see momentarily, Rolland characterized the moment of mystical ecstasy in terms of "nirvana" and refers to the "illusion" of individuality in terms of "maya," facts which clearly demonstrate an Eastern influence. However, there is no direct evidence that Rolland utilized images from these sources in characterizing Being or God, although they could well have been seen by Rolland as reinforcing a general sense of Being as the "oceanic." This point becomes especially important in light of Masson's conclusion in his *The Oceanic Feeling*, arrived at through a close and laborious reading of Hindu texts, that Rolland coined the term "oceanic feeling" during his research on his biography of Ramakrishna.[44] Masson's conclusion, followed by Kakar, are the only published attempts to establish the intellectual influences of Rolland's use of oceanic imagery in speaking of mysticism.[45] Their conclusions, however, cannot be substantiated, as Rolland did not know of Ramakrishna's existence before 1926 and yet in 1888 spoke of the "Ocean of Being" and referred to an "oceanic feeling."[46] As for Empedocles, Rolland was in fact introduced to his thought before he read Spinoza.[47] In his biography of Empedocles, written in 1918, Rolland clearly identifies him with mysticism and refers to how Empedocles, the "poet, visionary, forerunner," opened up the Mediterranean mind "to the oceanic perspectives of the infinite God."[48] Nevertheless, there is no indication that Empedocles had the effect Spinoza did on mediating the meaning of Rolland's mystical experiences. Thus Empedocles deserves to be seen, along with the other intellectual influences, as a background source rather than primary instigator in the expression of mysticism in Rolland's *Credo*.

Rolland's conception of God also became the basis for his characterization of individual existence. If God or Being was defined in terms of the totality of sensations, then each individual became a relative manifestation of Being, a grouping of sensations that were attached to the divine center yet self-conscious of a unique and separate existence: "Each group of sensations has its own consciousness and this I . . . is what we commonly call the me, the personal life."[49] The individual, as a unique group of sensations, is one of an infinite number of forms in which Being manifests itself. The individual is a "role" that God plays:

> I believe in and conceive of human existence exactly in the same way that I believe in the roles that flutter about on the great stage.[50] My divine Self plays out an infinite number of performances of which I am but a small actor—immense symphonies of which I am but a chord. . . . Everything is at once an individual soul, and a role in the Divine Tragedy.[51] . . . Each of us is God, that is to say, eternal Unity, but in a relative and individual form. Every person is a group of sensations and of potential sensations, each attached to the divine center.[52]

Rolland held that in individual life one was privy to four qualitatively different apprehensions of Sensation. The first was everyday normal life, which Rolland referred to as "the normal maya state" and defined as "the (illusive) feeling of an individual state closed off from other beings."[53] While in this state, one had recourse to another state, that of "maya suggestion," which was the goal and function of art and allowed oneself to become, through one's imagination and deep empathy, another of the "roles" God plays.[54] A third "sensation" occurred only at death and allowed one to enjoy the dual perspective of being God in his eternal totality yet also each individual manifestation of God, each "role," in its minutest detail.[55] The fourth sensation, which could occur during this life, was that of the "vague, formless, oceanic feeling" of being the totality. This experience, which Rolland referred to as that of "ecstasy" and "nirvana," contrasted with what was experienced at death in two ways. First, one could only apprehend the totality and not the dual perspective of both totality and its infinite roles. Even one's own role, in the moment of ecstasy, was obliterated and forgotten. Second, one's apprehension of the totality of Being was somewhat obscure, a "vague sensation" as Rolland put it, as opposed to the "clear" and "full" sensation of Being and of infinite roles one gained at death.[56] In ecstasy, one became aware that one played but a role and that in one's essence one was Being itself. It was the task of religion, thought Rolland, to take us to this state of awareness.[57]

The ordinary person unacquainted with religious experience lived his life unaware that it was but a role, suffering needlessly in his ignorance.[58] For the person like Rolland who had experienced the momentary shattering of his role in ecstasy, other options were available. One such option, advocated by Spinoza, consisted in living by reason and in reason, renouncing individuality and becoming the universal.[59] Living from the perspective of the whole, one was truly free from the suffering imposed by limiting one's self within the confines of a role. Free from the illusion of separate, individual existence, one would see the entire melody of existence, appreciating each part in the whole. This Spinozistic option, however, was rejected by Rolland as being too passive, an "inferior state" because it requires the sacrifice of developing one's unique individual existence.[60] Instead, one should passionately embrace one's role in all of its pain, joy, nuance, and detail:

> Wouldn't it be better . . . to live as Spinoza would wish us to live, by reason and in reason? What happens? One renounces one's self in order to be God . . . I would have sacrificed the direct vision of my own existence. . . . Let us therefore live our lives knowing who we are. Let us place ourselves entirely into our ephemeral role, in the subtlety of its nuances, as well as in the fits of fury that sweeps it away. Let us feel, think and act with all our energy. . . . We must be ourselves, but our whole selves, and (this is the hardest part) without ever becoming the dupe of our selves.[61]

Thus it is that we have come across Rolland's parameters for living, a set of guiding principles that he used to orient his life and thought. The first of these parameters, as seen above, was Rolland's dictum to "live irony," that is, to live life with the whole of one's self without becoming the "dupe" of it. By this dictum, Rolland was attempting to draw attention to the existential paradox created by living the life of the particular and the universal at the same time. "Living irony" meant striking a balance between detachment and passionate involvement.[62] Rolland found this life exemplified in the works of Plato, in Goethe, and in Renan.[63] In striving to hold the two opposed tendencies together, "an ironic smile transfigures happiness and illumines our pain."[64] One had the "wondrous calm" of the Greek gods which allowed one to "master life."[65] Rolland cited with approval Renan's injunction to "make room for the smile" and his claim that the "old Gallic gaiety is the most profound of philosophies."[66] Such a life, thought Rolland, was one of a "noble egoism."

Living with irony was not the only existential parameter Rolland thought essential to a valued life. Indeed, Rolland claimed that the human ideal consisted in synthesizing "ironic peace" with the "ardor of passion" and "charity." If one could actualize such an ideal, concluded Rolland, "that would be truly living."[67] For Rolland, the term "passion" referred to a wide range of behavioral propensities: the exaltation of life in all of its joys and sufferings, a heroic and courageous spirit, the conscious establishment of a goal for oneself and the will to see it through, the capacity to tolerate perpetual becoming, the insistence on absolute liberty of thought, and the continuous and unremitting search for truth.[68] For our purposes, these can be condensed to three interrelated elements: the emphasis on heroism, the injunction to seek the truth, and the demand for absolute liberty.

The themes of heroism, of heroic action and thought, of an idealism based on truth and rooted in the power of the will to overcome any obstacle, are omnipresent in Rolland's life and thought. In his *Mémoires* and *Journey Within*, he saw his contacts with Nature as contributing to this dynamic conception of life. "One should not think that in the embrace of Nature I was a mere passive voluptuary," he states, for "the lesson taught me by the mountain was not forgetfulness of the world and action. It was a lesson of energy and combat."[69] Indeed, in the *Credo* Rolland advocated a life of "perpetual becoming."[70] This "great school of heroism," a spirit of action and thought, of victory even through defeat, of the power of the will to overcome historical contingency and material circumstance, was impressed on him through the various characters in Shakespeare's plays and in the spirit that animated the Italian Renaissance.[71] He found the same themes in the *Stirb und Werde* of Goethe and in Nietzsche's *Übermensch*.[72] Later, during the Great War, despite bouts of pessimism with respect to the performance of his fellow men and nations, Rolland never gave up this optimism of the will.[73] For Rolland, true idealism always took into account the reality of the horrors and evil manifested in the world.[74] Heroic action and a virile will were the prerequisites of success in any undertaking.[75] Spurring on his own desire for heroic action, a role he was destined later to fulfill, Rolland endeavored to portray such heroism in his early unpublished plays and then later in his biographies of great men like Beethoven, Michelangelo, and Tolstoy.[76] The general set of traits and ideals that became associated with the heroic life and that ran through the biographies like a red thread—the defense of liberty, equality, and justice, the search for beauty, the power of the will, purity of soul, sincerity and truth and the sacrifice of self for the sake of a worthy ideal—were meant to restore hope and instill ideals in a society Rolland thought overcome by pessimism and material-ism.[77] The same intent animated many of Rolland's other works, such as his plays on the French Revolution, the "Tragedies of Faith" (*Aërt, Saint-Louis, The Triumph of Reason*), and *Jean-Christophe*.

An essential part of the passionate life that Rolland embodied and tried to in-culcate in others was his stress on absolute liberty. "I have many Gods in my Pantheon," he stated in an article to Ellen Key in 1914, but "my first goddess is Liberty."[78] One can profitably view Rolland's embrace of freedom in two senses, existential and intellectual. With respect to the former, Rolland's position was straightforward if unsophisticated. In the *Credo* he concluded that only in Being was there absolute freedom. Whatever issues forth from Him is determined, for it is bound by laws. However, this did not imply, at least according to Rolland, a thoroughgoing determinism or fatalism for individual selves. Rather, Rolland thought the question did not make sense or apply to the particular. To take an ex-ample, whether one sings a song or not involves free will. But once the decision is made, the song simply "is." To ask whether a song is free or not is absurd. It ap-plies only to the singer, not to that which is sung. The analogy holds for the rela-tion between Absolute and relative Being. Thus "liberty has no meaning for the relative self, and only holds meaning for the Absolute self."[79] As a man, one could be free by raising oneself to the level of the universal. Curiously enough, Rolland stated that one could also be free by being "that which I am, without worrying about other things, to believe in what I am, in what I want, in what I do."[80] Thus it is that, despite the logical conclusion of determinism his "system" implied, Rolland insisted, without philosophically justifying it, on the feeling of free will for the particular individual. One should act and act with conviction and passion. Because we have the conscious feeling of freedom in thought and deed, for all intents and practical purposes we do have free will. Thus, while granting a determining role to historical, social, and psychological circum-stances, Rolland stressed that in the last analysis the tragic as well as divine ele-ment in the universe consisted in the fact that nothing was preordained. Man was free to overcome and even shape his circumstances, a fact which freed up the will to act passionately while obliging one to work for the good.[81]

Rolland's demand for intellectual freedom was equally as prevalent in his life and thought. In the *Credo*, this is apparent in his adoption of Cartesian doubt as a method of finding "truth." As Rolland's thought evolved, his stress on the pur-suit of truth at any cost became more pronounced. He espoused the "pessimism of the intelligence" whose task was to unveil every illusion and subscribed to a "School of Doubt," among whom he included Renan, Shakespeare, and Mon-taigne: "My attitude is always one of profound Doubt, which is to be kept hid-den in my cave like a strong, bitter, but health-giving tonic, for the use of the strong."[82] Much like Nietzsche, whom Rolland called "the freest man to have existed for centuries" and "the greatest philosopher of the second half of the 19th century,"[83] Rolland hated hypocrisy, endeavored to expose mendacity in the so-cial arena, toppled idols, and advocated the pursuit of truth even at the cost of disillusionment and unhappiness. He yearned for the "free spirit," one who was free "from prejudices, free from every idol; free from every dogma, whether of class, caste, or nation; free from every religion."[84] Such a soul was a true man, one able to "love with its own heart, to judge with its own reason," to be "l'un contre tous" if need be.[85] Indeed, we saw in Rolland's letters to Freud the same emphasis on a life of critical reason that endeavored to see without illusion.[86] One can readily see why Rolland agreed with Freud's assessment of the "common-man"'s religion in *The Future of an Illusion*. As we saw earlier, it was the stress on reason and freedom of thought that was the primary barrier in keeping him from the Catholic Church. So too did he emphasize the sure and certain steps of science over belief. One should not believe out of desire or seek happiness if it goes against the truth, which for Rolland was dependent on the light of the intellect. Even mystical revelations, however powerful their authority might be for the recipient, did not have the right to overturn reason or impede the freedom of scientific inquiry.[87]

Rolland's insistence on the life of freedom and truth must be qualified, however, with respect to the last parameter for living the good life stressed in the *Credo*, that of charity. The ontological base of the injunction to love others derived from Rolland's mystical experiences as mediated through the thought of Spinoza. In Spinoza's *Ethics*, Rolland had found the injunction to share truth and joy with others. Thus every effort must be made to create a basis for fraternity, tolerance, equality, and harmony. In the *Credo*, Rolland added to Spinoza the voice of Tolstoy and echoed the Christian ethos of his childhood: "This continual celebration of all my being, is it not sad if others do not share it with me? . . . This God that is in me, I find him in all my sensations, as well as in the sensations of others. To love God is therefore to love others."[88] Eschewing diluting one's charity into "vague sentimentality," Rolland stressed the need for specific acts directed to specific people: "Make yourself useful in a concrete, active way. Without ever neglecting the general opportunities to do good that present themselves. . . . [C]onsecrate the work of your life to the well being of another, or of others."[89] One hears echoes of this ethic in Rolland's later researches into Indian mysticism. As he states in the preface to his biography of Ramakrishna: "I have dedicated my whole life to the reconciliation of mankind."[90] Indeed, if Freud's attempts to create a "secular cure of souls" was in part motivated by his Hannibal Complex, surely the seeds of the ethic contained in Rolland's early mystical experiences were similarly determinative of his later attempt to promote a mystically based religious psychology.

In sum, with respect to Rolland's early mysticism, three points deserve to be emphasized. First, Rolland's mystical experiences were spontaneous, sporadic, and transient. Thus despite the reference to the "oceanic" in the *Credo* we have yet to come across that statelike mystical phenomenon Rolland described to Freud in his letter of December 5, 1927. Second, it is clear that the meaning of these mystical experiences cannot be wholly divorced from the *Credo*. The latter gave intellectual content to ineffable experience, thereby transforming seminal insight into meaningful psychological and ethical structure. Finally, it is clear that Rolland constructed his mystical philosophy from bits and pieces of religious ideation extant in pluralistic fin-de-siècle Parisian culture. While this culture was still in general Catholic, Rolland firmly repudiated the central tenets of the latter, synthesizing much of its ethic with a variety of personally acceptable philosophies into a "religion" all his own.

## Rolland's Mature Mysticism: The Oceanic Feeling Defined

Although one can find brief allusions to mysticism in Rolland's written corpus after the *Credo*, it is not until the Great War that one finds him once again engaging in a systematic study and interpretation of mystical texts and experiences. Rolland's biographies of the Hindu saints belong to this period, as does his debate with Freud. Under the duress of a war and fully aware of the weight of responsibility brought him by his international fame as a French writer, Rolland looked back into the past, to the *Credo* of his youth and the Greek and Christian mystics of Europe, and across cultures, to the mystics of the East, in order to find an answer to the malaise affecting Western civilization. As we cataloged in chapter 3, Rolland's exposure to the psychology of religion and the comparative study of mysticism during this period resulted in a significant shift in his conceptualization of mystical experience and the mystical "path." General yet essential elements of his early mysticism, such as the stress on a dynamic mysticism of becoming and social action and the postulation of a creative (mitigated) and religious (unmitigated) intuitive faculty, remained intact. On the other hand, Rolland moved from a philosophical–poetic conception of mysticism to a position close to that of what I earlier referred to as the "perennial psychology." We will return to a consideration of these conceptual revisions in later chapters. For the present, assuming that a complete understanding of Rolland's mature mysticism includes these significant theoretical shifts, we will proceed by focusing exclusively on the matter of whether the texts of this period reveal significant changes in Rolland's mystical subjectivity and, if so, whether these changes enable us to ascertain with greater precision the identity of the statelike "oceanic feeling" he described to Freud.

Once again the most fruitful place to begin lies with Rolland's autobiography. Of particular interest is Rolland's chapter entitled "The Three Revelations." There he describes two of the mystical experiences of his youth, what I have referred to as the "Ferney experience" and the "train episode," as well as the influence of Spinoza. However, now, on the doorstep of his sixth decade of life, Rolland contextualized those "éclairs" within the broad expanse of his life. First, he speaks of having lived two lives simultaneously: the first being material, finite, that determined through heredity and the familial-social circumstance, and the second infinite, spiritual, "a formless Being, nameless, homeless, timeless, the very substance and breath of all life."[91] He then goes on to state that the first concealed the second for the greater portion of his life. When it did reveal itself, it did so through "spiritual outbursts," the reference being, of course, to the "éclairs" or mystical experiences of his youth:

But of those two essences . . . the first, quite naturally, concealed the second during the greater part of my childhood, my youth, and even my active and emotional
life. It is only by sudden explosions that the hidden consciousness succeeds in
piercing the surface of our days, gushing up like the boiling stream of an artesian
well, for a few moments only, and then again disappearing. . . . Up to the time of
full maturity, when the repeated blows and wounds of life have widened the cracks
of the surface, the subconscious struggles to open up a river-bed leading toward the
unrevealed Being.

   Before reaching the state I now enjoy, of immediate communion with universal
Life, I lived apart from her, yet ever near, listening to her traveling by my side under the rock—and suddenly, in the far distance, at moments when I least expected
it, she was quickened by the upsurge of artesian springs. . . . I have noted three
of those spiritual outbursts. . . . The terrace at Ferney. The passionate words of
Spinoza. And the revelation of Tolstoy in the darkness of the tunnel.[92]

This passage is relevant to our search for the identity of the oceanic feeling as
a state in several respects. Rolland clearly distinguishes between the relationship
he had with the "formless" Being in his maturity and that of his youth. In the latter, Rolland lived apart from Being and came in touch with it "for a few moments only" in the form of spiritual "éclairs." In his maturity, however, Rolland
enjoyed a *state*, that of "immediate communion with universal Life." The passage between youthful and mature relation with Being is depicted in poetic but
decidedly existential terms. It is the "repeated blows and wounds of life" that, in
accordance with the purposeful (teleological) nature of the "subconscious,"
eventually "widen the cracks of the surface" and "open up a river-bed leading toward the unrevealed Being."[93]

The existential process that connects mystical experience with mystical
state is given more detail, albeit once again poetically, later in the same chapter
of *Journey Within*. Having finished describing the various spiritual experiences
of his youth, Rolland then pauses and continues with the following commentary:

For one ray of sunlight to split asunder the protective covering of the clouds is not
enough to keep the fields bathed in light. . . . Nevertheless, the mind has won a
great victory . . . it must now redouble its efforts to find the weak points, so that it
may, at last, remove every obstacle.

   But it is one thing to know, another to be able. Our power is weak, confused
and contradictory. It has not had the time to learn, by long discipline, the great art
of concentration. . . . Many people lose it along the way. Few have the patience
to unwind it persistently and tirelessly . . . the essential thing, for one who wishes
to emerge from the chaos of his days, is to tie the guiding thread of the spirit to that
blind mass joined to his being; to let into its darkness a tiny ray of sunlight, com-
mingling them, until the ray is reflected in each of the cells, as the dawn on the
dew of the meadows. That is the work of a lifetime. No one accomplishes it in one
attempt.[94]

Here again Rolland distinguishes between momentary mystical experience ("one ray of sunlight") and the existential task of reflecting each ray so that the "fields are bathed in light." It begins to sound like the oceanic feeling as a state is the existential denouement of a mystical and psychological process of becoming.

Rolland's attraction to the psychology of religion, his interest in Eastern mysticism and attempt to revision Yoga along therapeutic lines buttress this emerging thesis. With respect to Rolland's biographies, we have seen that, although ostensibly objective treatments of Indian spirituality, they were shot through with his social agenda. We may now elaborate on the further claim that they were reflections of Rolland's personal mysticism. In a letter of June 3, 1930, to his Indian friend D. K. Roy, Rolland explicitly states the similarity between the experiences and philosophy contained in his *Credo* and that which he found in India:

> Now listen to my personal experiences. I find in Sri Aurobindo's Ishopanishad . . . just what I myself had found, unaided, at the age of twenty, when I wrote the same thing in my Credo Quia Verum. Only the names of the Hindus were naturally absent from my thought, since I did not even know then that such thoughts existed in India. . . . I had no knowledge of the religions and philosophies of India. I had not even read the rare philosophers like Schopenhauer who had contacted them.[95]

Rolland is overstating the case, for clearly he knew *something* about Indian religion and its mysticism when he wrote his *Credo*. Nevertheless, to continue the point, in his biographies Rolland confirmed the above by stating that he was not a novice in the field of comparative mysticism; that nothing he saw in Indian mysticism was existentially alien, for the spiritual experiences outlined in *Journey Within* brought him "singularly near to the spirit of India when I later came to know it."[96] Spinoza was but the "European Krishna."

If one finds Rolland reading his transient nature mystical experiences into Indian mysticism, then one might expect to see in his biographies some evidence of the oceanic feeling as well. Searching through *The Life of Vivekananda*, one is not disappointed. Commenting on the mysticism of Walt Whitman, Rolland calls attention to two forms of mysticism apparent in Whitman's works. The first, which came to Whitman in his early thirties, Rolland characterizes as an "éclair" and "ecstatic blow," as the more familiar transient mystical experience whose content consisted of an "immediate perception of Unity." The second type of mysticism, however, he depicted as consisting in the awareness of the "permanence of the Self (Moi)" and the latter's identity with the All. Rolland thought this state preponderated late in Whitman's life, after the "blows of life" had taken their toll.[97] In other words, Rolland was distinguishing between a mysticism of youth, whose main characteristic consisted of transient experiences of unity, with a later or mature mysticism that was the result of an existential process and whose defining characteristic consisted of a mystical state. Indeed, one cannot help but note the striking similarity between the terms Rolland uses in this "commentary" on Whitman's mature mysticism ("éclairs," "blows of life") and that found in Rolland's poetic, autobiographical description of the existential "process" involved in his coming to the state of "immediate communion with universal life." It does seem that Rolland's treatment of mysticism in these volumes is as reflective of his own as it was an objective description of that of others.

A similar personally based mode of inquiry animates Rolland's depiction of Yoga as a therapeutic regimen. Recall that Rolland envisioned Yoga not only as a means of inducing transient mystical experience but also as a path or process in which the contents of the unconscious were unearthed, "worked-through," and sublimated for use in art, science, and social service. Its ultimate goal, according to Rolland, was the gradual elimination of illusion, of maya: "the very object of life, of individual life . . . is the gradual elimination of the Screen (of Maya)."[98] For Rolland, this meant a process that induced becoming or individuation, involved the interplay of intellect, will, and emotion, and resulted in freedom. Rolland eschewed the Western prejudice that characterized doctrines such as maya and techniques such as Yoga as world-denying and escapist.[99] On the contrary, Rolland characterized the process of Yoga as the existential correlate of the scientific search for truth.[100] Existential truth meant freedom and individuation. Through Yoga one did not "lose oneself" but fully became that unique individual one was meant to be.[101] Mystical experience played an important role in this process, for it enabled one to experience for a moment that Unity in which one saw through maya and felt the most authentic part of one's self. In the biographies, Rolland described this process poetically: "The very first illumination of the mind makes a tiny hole, through which the glance of the absolute filters. As the mind grows, the hole grows larger . . . each day a wider surface is covered until the whole screen is lost."[102] Becoming autobiographical, he relates how he was familiar with this process; that the mystical experiences of his youth enabled him to see through maya and spring, if but momentarily, to freedom.[103] Since that time, he continues, he had endeavored to make "the hole of light bigger with my fingers."[104] Again, the use of imagery to describe the mystical "process" is strikingly reminiscent of the passages quoted above in *Journey Within* and denotes that a dialectical relation existed between transient mystical experience and mystical state.

One also finds the notion of a mystical process of becoming central to the leading protagonist of Rolland's novel *L'Âme enchantée* (*The Soul Enchanted*). The latter, best read as a document revealing Rolland's personality, consists of five volumes and was written during the years 1922–1933, right in the middle of Rolland's infatuation with the East. Like *Jean Christophe*, it is an epic, tracing the trials, tribulations, suffering, and victories of a soul, one Annette Rivière, during the course of a lifetime.[105] The first volume, *Annette and Sylvie*, begins with the death of Annette's father and then goes on to chronicle, appropriately enough, her subsequent discovery of and relations with her half-sister Sylvie. As the volumes proceed, numerous new characters and subplots are introduced. Although the last three volumes in particular reflect Rolland's engagement as an intellectual committed to international cooperation, antifascism, and Marxist thought,[106] *L'Âme enchantée* as a whole reflects Rolland's turn to the East and the evolution of his personal mysticism. Here the question regards not nuance of plot but basic structure and overall intent. Behind the details of Annette's trials and tribulations lies a basic psychoreligious theme, one Rolland derived from his own personal experience and guised in terms taken from the East. In a letter written soon after the publication of *Annette and Sylvie* to Herman Hesse, the famous European intellectual and writer who had befriended Rolland and shared a keen interest in Eastern religions, Rolland described the guiding intent behind *The Soul Enchanted* as follows:

> You realize, of course, that it is a question of "enchantment" in the sense of "magic," of "illusion," of "Maya." The soul forsakes its masks one by one. With every disguise that falls, it discovers yet another. Gradually, however, the soul progresses to deliverance. In short, the continuance of the work is the story of the long "disenchantment," of deliverance from the bonds of Maya.[107]

As Starr has noted, the animating theme of *The Soul Enchanted* is "the history of the progressive disillusionment of a human soul. . . . [T]he gradual freeing of the body and soul of all the bonds and clinging vines of the past."[108] Rolland likened this process to the "maternity" of the "buried soul." As one disenchants the world, one frees oneself from a "chain of servitudes." The soul grows in a spiral fashion: "One returns on the spiral above the past; one does not descend to it again." In order to start the process of disillusionment, one must begin life in a state of ignorance about self, world, and other. Rolland depicts this stage of life in the beginning of *Annette and Sylvie*, where we find a slumbering Annette dreaming of bathing in a pool in the midst of a forest. She contemplates her nudity, feels shame, and, in trying to free herself from the pool, sinks further into it, becoming caught up in the vines and mud. The religious and psychological imagery is quite intentional. The pool is a metaphor for the unconscious, and the vines and mud the atavisms of the past. Rolland depicts Annette as "an Eve in the garden. . . . [H]er true nature still remained unknown to her. . . . She had not yet become aware of the desires that were within her; nothing had awakened her . . . [S]he preferred to ignore that interior sea."[109]

If the adolescent Annette could ignore her inner being, the ripening of her spirit in conjunction with the vicissitudes encountered upon her entrance into the world of enchantment would force her to introspect, reflect, grow. In *The Soul Enchanted*, Rolland never depicted the world of maya, of illusion, in wholly negative or pejorative terms. Broadly speaking, it referred to all the passions and ideals that bind one to others and society. Illusion in this broad sense is the very stuff of life, every bit as "real" as the Being behind the world of appearances. Indeed, to carry some illusions was seen as a necessary part of being a living, acting person. Disenchantment, then, did not refer to the withdrawal from life but signified the ongoing process of formulating, discarding, and reformulating the illusions by which one lived. This process was engendered in Annette through the existential impact of life's exigencies, monitored by an intellect that sought to pierce every illusion and spurred on by a will able to withstand the emotional strain of disenchantment and self-overcoming. The result was an ever-increasing sense of freedom and knowledge. Although the genre employed precluded any significant theoretical references to psychological theory, Rolland does refer explicitly to psychoanalysis. As Georges Buraud has pointed out, *The Soul Enchanted* is a poetic rendering of the best psychology had to offer about the nature and function of the human spirit. In this regard, we should not forget the value Rolland attached to Freud's approval of the first few volumes.[110]

In the last volume, near the end of her life, Annette becomes fully disenchanted. Starr has characterized this stage of Annette's life as one in which Annette is "completely free. The last veil of illusion has fallen and she stands within the threshold of universal life. She lives in a state of hyperesthesia of sight, in a condition of continuing consciousness, a state of continual and intimate contact with the world and the life forces."[111] This sounds like Rolland's description of the oceanic feeling, and indeed Rolland ushers in this last stage of Annette's life with recourse to Hindu mysticism and numerous references to the "Ocean of Being."[112] However, the statelike oceanic feeling is not the only defining characteristic of Annette's disenchanted being. Alongside the feeling of the "oceanic," Rolland depicts Annette's intellect as holding fast to Montaigne's "What do I know?" and her will as being cohesive enough to play out her destiny, her "role" in the world.[113] Of course, we have seen this before, both in the *Credo* and in Rolland's letter to Freud in May of 1931. Recall that in that letter Rolland distinguished between three dimensions of his spirit: what he felt, knew, and desired. What he felt was the mystical, oceanic communion with the all. What he knew he characterized by referring to Montaigne's "What do I know?" and by claiming to resonate with Freud's attempt to penetrate all illusions and pursue truth without want, hope, or fear. What he desired was nothing but "total self-effacement," adding that he was prepared to be and to do what his conscience dictated. Seen against the background of the disenchanted Annette, we can appreciate the existential message Rolland was trying to communicate to Freud. One could say that in the figure of the fully liberated Annette one finds the meaning and identity of the mature mysticism of Romain Rolland.

## The Oceanic Feeling Reconsidered

Our reconstruction of the mysticism of Rolland's maturity reveals that the "oceanic feeling" was nothing less than the existential denouement of a mystical process of becoming. In his youth Rolland made sense of his transient mystical experiences by creating a worldview from a variety of literary, philosophical, and religious sources. From the perspective of his mature mysticism, Rolland suggests that these early experiences seemed to contain a teleology all their own, one which demanded introspection and eventuated in the statelike phenomenon he called the oceanic feeling. Then, drawing on a lifetime of introspection, renunciation, and the psychological structure-building process of disillusionment ("disenchantment"), the mature Rolland endeavored to make sense out of this mystical process of becoming with recourse to not only scholarly researches in the comparative study of mysticism but also the psychology of religion. One could say that as Rolland progressed from transient mystical experiences to the statelike oceanic feeling, so too did he move from Spinoza to a position close to Jung, from a "Spinozism of Sensation" to a mystical psychoanalysis and "perennial psychology" complete with a purposeful and religiously toned unconscious. Truly he was a congregation of one.

One can further conclude that Freud both misunderstood and misinterpreted the nature of Rolland's mysticism. The oceanic feeling was not an aesthetic phenomenon, a benign vestige of an early phase of pre-Oedipal life, nor was it the basis for withdrawal from reality into an illusory maternal matrix. Rather, it was an existential achievement, a fact that gives it ethical and developmental depth. Clearly, Freud's model fails to address these dimensions of the oceanic feeling. The letters he had from Rolland concerning his personal mysticism were simply too few and vague for him to do the topic justice. Of course, it may well be that Freud's lack of personal and scholarly acquaintance with mysticism in conjunction with a rather narrow metapsychology doomed his analysis from the outset. In any case, now that we have reconstructed Rolland's mysticism, the interpretative task confronts us anew.

# Mysticism East and West

In order to do interpretative justice to the reconstructed version of Rolland's mysticism, it is clear that the two avenues of analysis suggested by Freud—one championing a view of mysticism as regressive and defensive; the other as therapeutic and adaptive—need to be expanded and developed, if not altogether superseded. New resources must be found to not only ground a fresh interpretation of Rolland's mysticism but to help rethink the relationship between psychoanalysis and the interdisciplinary study of mysticism as a whole.

Such resources can be found if one proceeds historically. During Freud's time, and certainly after his correspondence with Rolland, there have been numerous interpretations of mysticism utilizing psychoanalytic models. In previous chapters I have referred to them as falling into one of three approaches or schools: classic, adaptive, and transformational. These schools can be seen as rooted in the Freud–Rolland correspondence. For example, Freud's reflections on mysticism fall into the classic-adaptive category; Rolland's in the adaptive-transformational.

There are, of course, dangers inherent in generalizing about any aspect of a discipline that has proved to be as diverse as psychoanalysis. Theorists who are typically lumped together within a school, such as D. W. Winnicott and Melanie Klein (object relations) or Erikson and Heinz Hartmann (ego psychology), have made clincial and metapsychological contributions that distinguish them as originative psychologists who merit individual treatment. In the final analysis, such treatment is both desirable and warranted. At the same time, generalizations provide an indispensable organizing function. They serve to highlight similarities between individual theorists and help distinguish groups of theorists from each other. If properly defined and qualified, such generalizations have proved useful for promoting analysis and dialogue.

Certainly, psychoanalytic studies of mysticism are in need of organization. The threefold typology presented here can be seen in part as furthering the need for historical and conceptual clarity. As we proceed, what can be called primary and secondary criteria for distinguishing between schools will become apparent. For example, the primary criteria used to define each school will be seen to revolve around the legitimacy and value each approach ascribes to mystical modes of knowing. Thus, classic school studies interpret mysticism as solely regressive, defensive, and pathological. Adaptive studies may admit that pathological elements can be found in some mystics. However, while bracketing the issue of transcendence, they ultimately see mysticism as a healing, therapeutic endeavor. Transformational school studies may, like adaptive studies, admit to seeing pathological and adaptive elements in mysticism. However, these studies also provide models that allow for dialogue with the transcendent, noetic claims of the mystics.

While simple and general, primary criteria afford us the most reliable basis on which to classify individual studies. Studies within each school vary little with respect to primary criteria. Secondary criteria, on the other hand, are more complex. They seek to catalogue the nature, extent, and sophistication of engagement with those fields usually associated with the psychology–comparativist dialogue: relevant philosophical and theological reflection, comparativist literature, and textual and culture studies. As one might expect, individual studies within schools exhibit a much greater variation with respect to interdisciplinary engagement. As a result, secondary criteria make evaluation of the schools more difficult, creating the need for attention to individual studies and careful qualifications.

While I do catalogue many important studies within each school, the overview presented here is not meant to be exhaustive. Again, although primary criteria are definitive enough to anchor my typology, the attention needed to evaluate individual studies with respect to secondary criteria is beyond the scope of the general, programmatic aims of this chapter. In other words, I endeavor to do justice to the general orientation exhibited by each school, but my overview will be in some sense selective. I use my typology to highlight those studies that best illustrate my programmatic agenda, which consists of promoting a general shift or reorientation in the relationship between psychoanalysis and the interdisciplinary study of mysticism.

For the sake of clarity, a final word concerning organization and procedure in this chapter is in order. In arguing my case, I begin the chapter with an analysis of Rolland's comparativist conclusions. Rolland can be considered to be a relatively obscure figure in comparativist studies. His researches, however, had considerable impact on east-west relations in general and psychoanalysis in particular. Presenting his comparativist conclusions in context, then, is of interest on purely historical grounds. More important, Rolland was a perennialist who helped form the initial relationship between psychoanalysis and mysticism. A critique of his position, then, enables me to bring in the constructivist response. The result is the conclusion that there exist many "mysticisms," a variety of different expressions of the mystical life of which Rolland's was but one.

While I find the constructivist critique of Rolland helpful, I also find it lacking in important respects, including the fact that it has yet to incorporate depth-psychological perspectives or any meaningful cross-cultural studies in the area of psychoanalytic anthropology. This gives me an opportunity to stress the depth-psychological process dimension of mysticism, an opening for a historical overview of the three schools mentioned, and the articulation of the shift for the psychoanalytic theory of mysticism I have in mind. The resources unearthed through this overview will, in the next chapter, prove to be useful in undertaking a fresh analysis of Rolland's mysticism.

## The Quest for Unity: Rolland as Comparativist

Rolland's active engagement with comparativists during the 1920s and 1930s mirrored a preoccupation with mysticism throughout Europe, particularly in France. With regard to the latter, the majority of the studies were penned by Catholic theologians and philosophers. The rise in neoscholasticism during the end of the nineteenth century coincided with the emergence of a controversy within Catholic theology over the nature of mysticism. By 1901 the writings of Abbe August Sandreau and Augustin-François Poulain had drawn the battle lines over what was to be a forty-year debate. The general issues concerned the accessibility and desirability of the mystical life to the everyday Christian and the precise nature of the various states and stages of prayer. More specifically, one finds debates over the contrast between "acquired" and "infused" contemplation, the relation between prayer, faith, and grace, the goal of the Christian life, and the definition of Christian "perfection." Although the nuances of this debate are beyond the scope of this study, it is of more than passing interest that Rolland, who despite having renounced Catholicism gives clear indications of having closely followed its movements, had little to say about either the issues or participants. The significant exception to this is Rolland's infatuation with Henri Bremond's monumental work, *A Literary History of Religious Thought in France*. Bremond's study, which canvassed the major French mystics of the seventeenth century, was hailed by Rolland as the greatest work on Catholic mysticism of his time. He exchanged letters with Bremond and sent him a copy of his biographies of the Hindu mystics. However, what Rolland conveys to us by way of summarizing his exchange with Bremond once again reveals an absence of concern with specifically theological issues. Rather, Rolland's interest lay in eliciting Bremond's response to Indian mysticism.[1]

A similar observation can be made with respect to the philosophical studies on mysticism that pervaded Rolland's intellectual milieu. Of the major theorists of his day—Joseph Maréchal, Maurice Blondel, Henri Bergson, and Jacques Maritain—Rolland mentions only Bergson and his disciple Edouard Le Roy. Even here the intent was comparativist, for Rolland evoked the Bergsonian concept of "intuition" (as elaborated by Le Roy) for the purpose of noting its affinity to that espoused by Indian philosophers. It seems, then, that Rolland's unchurched status, personal mysticism, and cultural agenda predisposed him to being more conversant with comparativist and psychological perspectives—perspectives which, as we endeavored to show in chapter 3, were closely linked in his mind.[2]

Rolland did not possess the academic training required to be classified as a true comparativist. However, even a cursory survey of texts such as his journal *Inde*, his biographies of the Hindu saints, and his correspondence with European intellectuals and Indian friends indicates that Rolland was at least minimally prepared to take on his comparativist agenda. He was familiar with a variety of primary source material, ranging from the scriptural basis for mystical inspiration and commentary to works by mystic figures East and West.[3] So too was he informed with respect to important secondary literature. Rolland was aware of the central studies of his day, Orientalists such as Eugène Burnouf, Hermann Oldenberg, Max Müller, and Paul Deussen, and exchanged ideas with two leading scholars in France, Sylvian Levi and Paul Masson-Oursel.[4] Although Rolland's comparativist interest can be found laced through his journals, letters, novels, and biographies, his comparativist conclusions found their fullest and clearest expression in the long appendix at the end of *The Life of Vivekananda* entitled "On The Hellenic-Christian Mysticism of the First Centuries and its Relationship to Hindu Mysticism."[5] Here, as in his correspondence with Freud, Rolland assumed mystical experience to be an extraordinary kind of perception that bypassed ordinary modes of knowing, required a corresponding faculty ("intuition"), and resulted in a radically new kind of subjectivity. Emphasizing the subject and his "religious consciousness," Rolland posited that mystical experience found its source deep within the soul or subconscious, spontaneously manifesting itself under conditions that could be scientifically studied. Further, Rolland affirmed the independence and primacy of mysticism vis-à-vis "secondary" institutional manifestations of religion:

> Religions are not ordinary matter of intellectual dialectic, but facts of experience. . . . [A]lthough reason steps in afterwards to construct systems upon the facts, such systems would not hold good for an hour, if they were not based upon the solid foundation of experience. . . . [S]uch simple observation . . . leads us to recognize *the same religious facts* as the foundations of all the great organized religions. . . . [T]heir uprising is spontaneous, it grows from the soil under certain influences in the life of humanity almost "seasonal" in their recurrence.[6] (Italics in the original)

Rolland thought that generic mystical "facts" of experience could be distinguished in the phenomenological reports of the mystics, a claim which allowed for access to the pure, unmediated "experience" behind the "interpretation" invariably present in the text. This assumption, alongside Rolland's claim that "mysticism is always and everywhere the same," brought him in line with that theory of mysticism that champions what is commonly referred to as the "perennial philosophy." Popularized in the book by Aldous Huxley of the same name, these thinkers claim to have isolated a common-core of mystical experience that transcends ideology and unites all religions.[7] However, within the perennialist camp one can ascertain at least three subtypes, distinguished as a result of recent critical surveys of the perennialist movement, that can aid us in circumscribing Rolland's position more precisely. These subtypes can be categorized with respect to how they characterize the "core" of mysticism and the degree of distortion they accord to sociocultural factors.

The first subtype, most readily associated with Aldous Huxley, is what I call the "perennial invariant" model of mysticism. It posits that all mystical experience is composed of the same core characteristics and that their formal expression in mystical texts is so similar as to transcend religio-cultural influences. A second model, which I call "perennial variant," argues, like the first, that the core of mystical experience is universally the same. However, it acknowledges in a more explicit fashion that tradition exercises an influence on the mode or form in which that experience is expressed. An underlying similarity of content is posited alongside an acknowledgment of the diversity of form. A good early example of this can be found in the works of the Indian philosopher Radhikrishnan and in various works of Ninian Smart.[8] A third model, which I dub the "typological variant" model, argues, like the second model, that the forms in which mystical experiences are expressed admit of variation and that those variations are attributable to the religio-cultural surround. However, unlike the first two models, variation in the *content* of mystical experience is also posited. Thus, according to R. C. Zaehner, there exist three universal "core" mystical experiences (nature or "panenhenic," monistic, and theistic).[9]

Rolland's position is best characterized as an example of the perennial variant model. This is evident in Rolland's depiction of what he promoted as "Lectureships of Comparative Eastern and Western Metaphysics and Mysticism" in both India and Europe.[10] Rolland conceived of the cross-cultural study of religion as having two separate but equal parts: the study of mystical experiences and the study of "systems" or worldviews.[11] The "first result" of comparing and classifying mystical experience would be to "demonstrate the universality and perennial occurrence of the great facts of religious experience" and to show that the ecstasies of the Greek, Christian, and Indian mystics were "identical experiences."[12] Only then should one proceed to the study of the comparative value of ideological structures. Rolland thought metaphysics differed from mystical experience in that the former synthesized the claims of "intuition" alongside those of reason and the senses into a coordinated whole, an ideology or worldview. Furthermore, worldviews also reflected cultural and historical determinants.[13] Ideally, worldviews would change and evolve, incorporating new information brought about through the various modes of knowing.[14] Rolland agreed that worldviews differed and intimated that they channeled the energy of mysticism in various directions. As a result, one could find broad, general distinctions between European mysticism and Indian mysticism. For example, Hellenic-Christian mysticism tended to stress a superior "architectural" metaphysics, a nuanced psychology, and a stress on action.[15] However, these attributes were by no means seen as absent from Indian mysticism, but rather as existing as undeveloped seeds that could flower with prolonged exposure to the sun of the West.[16] In any case, however a worldview might develop the seeds of intuition and regardless of the similarity or diversity in expression, the underlying *experience*, that of *Unity*, was always the same.[17]

Rolland's own attempts at the interpretation of mystical texts confirms that he advocated the perennial variant model. Thus in *The Life of Ramakrishna* Rolland adduces the famous passage found in biographies of Ramakrishna in which the latter, longing for a vision of the Divine Mother Kali, impulsively seizes a sword in order to end his life. However, upon reaching the sword Ramakrishna entered into an altered state:

> Lo! the whole scene, doors, windows, the temple itself vanished. . . . Instead I saw an ocean of the Spirit, boundless, dazzling. In whatever direction I turned, great luminous waves were rising. They bore down upon me with a loud roar, as if to swallow me up. . . . Round me rolled an ocean of ineffable joy. And in the depths of my being I was conscious of the presence of the Divine Mother.[18]

Rolland interpreted this "text" in the following manner:

> It is noticeable that in this beautiful description there is no mention of the Divine Mother until the end; She was merged in the Ocean. . . . My own view, if I may be pardoned the presumption, is that he *saw* nothing, but that he was *aware* of Her all-permeating presence. He called the Ocean by her name. His experience was like a dream, to give a lesser example, wherein without the slightest feeling of incongruity, the mind attaches the name of the being filling its thoughts to quite a different form; the object of our love is in everything; all forms are but its cloak. On the shores of that sea which rolled down upon Ramakrishna, I see immediately the form of St. Teresa of Avila. She also felt herself engulfed in the infinite until the scruples of her Christian faith and the stern admonitions of her watchful directors led her against her own convictions to confine God within the form of the Son of Man.[19]

In this analysis, Rolland clearly distinguishes the actual "experience," the feeling of Unity and Eternity, from the "interpretation," the figure of Kali in the case of Ramakrishna and of Christ in that of St. Teresa. As Rolland puts it in a similar context, "Hindus fetch the water they call Brahman . . . Christians draw the water they call Christ. But it is always the same water."[20] Rolland intimates that the essentially conservative bent of religious tradition and the ecclesiastical hierarchy which oversees it keeps a more generic account of religious experience from prevailing cross-culturally.

In adopting this view, Rolland may have been influenced by several intellectual sources, prominent of whom are James and Otto.[21] As argued in chapter 3, the major contribution of James to the development of Rolland's thought was in providing him with the theoretical lens necessary to facilitate an easy conceptual transition between the "perennial philosophy" and the "perennial psychology." We can now add that James, read as a comparativist, can be, and certainly has been, read as advocating a perennial variant perspective. His enumeration of core characteristics (ineffability, noesis, passivity, transiency, unity) that could be married to diverse worldviews undoubtedly buttressed Rolland's way of thinking about mysticism.[22] With regard to Otto, we know that Rolland not only read Otto's works but apparently corresponded with him and cited him as backing for his own claim that "mysticism is always and everywhere the same."[23] In the work which influenced Rolland, *Mysticism East and West*, Otto had taken two mystics, Meister Eckhart and the arch proponent of Advaita Vedanta, Sankara, and attempted to delineate the similarities and differences between them.[24] During the course of his work Otto distinguished between two basic "types" of mysticism, the "inward way" and the "way of unity," which he thought to be irreducible and cross-culturally valid. He characterized the "inward way" or "mysticism of introspection" as rejecting the outward world for the search inwards, there to find the deepest essence of the soul (*Atman* for Sankara, *das Gemüte* for Eckhart).[25] The "way of unity" or of "unifying vision," on the other hand, looked outward upon the world, there to perceive in ascending degrees a Unity that started with the apprehension of oneness in the external world and culminated in the realization of the sole existent One, Brahman, or Godhead.[26] Otto thought that these "types" were played out in Eckhart and Sankara and could be found in some sense in all mystics. So too did Otto indicate that the full existential impact of mystical experience could not be wholly divorced from the "soil" of sociohistorical and ideological factors. Thus it is that one could isolate similarities and differences between mysticism East and West.

Given Otto's typology, one could classify him as advocating a perennial typological model. However, Rolland never delineated anything like a typology of mystical experience (or distinguished between extrovertive and introvertive mysticism) and apparently took the differences that Otto noted in the mystical experiences of the "inward" and "outward" ways as signifying that there were but degrees or variations of a single defining characteristic: Unity. This led him to violate Otto's typology and gloss over what are substantial differences in the phenomenological descriptions of mystical experience. Thus it is that on the one hand Rolland, like Radhikrishnan and most perennialists, seemed to point to the "contentless" mystical experience often associated with Advaita Vedanta, Plotinus, Eckhart's "Godhead," Pseudo-Dionysius, and others as the normative "core" upon which a perennialism could be built. Texts were adduced from the fifth and sixth Enneads and from the fifth chapter of *The Mystical Theology* for the purpose of showing the great tradition of the "path of negation" the West had mastered.[27] Plotinus was described as a "great fellow Yogi," while the negative language used by him and Dionysius was viewed as "equal and parallel to Vedantic language" and identical to the "Advaitic teaching of the absolute Jnana-Yoga."[28] Because according to Rolland there was no evidence to justify the view that these thinkers from the West were influenced by the East, he concluded that "they both came from a common quarry" and that Vedantism merely described a universal dimension of the soul.[29]

On the other hand, it becomes clear that Rolland thought such experiences to be essentially similar in kind to texts which, phenomenologically speaking, exhibited pantheistic and "panenhenic" tendencies. For example, Rolland, in order to show that a predisposition to Vedantism existed in America before Vivekananda's pilgrimage to it, devotes a long analysis to figures in New England (Emerson, Thoreau, Whitman). Thus Whitman, who "immediately perceived, embraced, espoused, and became at one and the same time each distinct object and their mighty totality, the unrolling and the fusion of the whole Cosmos realized in each morsel of the atom and of life," is portrayed as reaching states identical to the Indian samādhi.[30] Again, referring to the reports in *The Varieties of Religious Experience* of Tennyson, Charles Kingsley, John Symonds, and Bucke, Rolland remarks that "they realized states identical with the characteristic Samadhis of India" and the ecstasy attained in the Plotinian flight to the "One."[31] One cannot unequivocally state, then, that Rolland built his perennialism around the contentless mystical experience associated with the apophatic tradition. Rather, Rolland's advocacy of a generic, vague core characteristic of "unity" suggests another conclusion: that the normative core of Rolland's perennialism was a pantheistic nature mysticism which he was personally acquainted with and thought was similar in degree and kind to mystical experience of all types. Textual and scholarly resources, it seems, were in the service of a hermeneutic strategy based on personal experience. Recall that for Rolland, because mysticism pointed beyond the horizon of ordinary experience, personal mystical encounters were a prerequisite for entry to the field ("The first qualification for knowing (and) judging . . . a religion . . . is to have made experiments for oneself in the fact of religious consciousness"[32]). Recall, as well, how Rolland related, in his biographies and letters to Indian friends, that he found an identity between his own mystical experiences and those found in Indian mysticism.[33] But Rolland's own experiences were, phenomenologically speaking, far closer to Whitman's pantheism than Sankara's unqualified monism. Thus, although appealing for a detailed comparative study of mysticism, Rolland cut short what it would reveal by indicating what its conclusion would be: "mysticism is always and everywhere the same"—a conclusion which went so well with the "morality" of religious and cultural equality that pervaded his social agenda.[34]

## Perennialism Reconsidered

Rolland's comparativist conclusions were not wholly lost on his contemporaries. Although criticisms were sparse, two in particular, coming as they did from practitioners of Indian mysticism, are especially relevant. The first came from the pen of Swami Ashokananda, a Rolland correspondent and revered disciple of Ramakrishna and Vivekananda. As seen earlier, Rolland had canvassed a variety of mystics both East and West to buttress his claim that mysticism arose naturally, spontaneously. Such an assertion allowed Rolland to promote his call for a universal "science–religion," for it displaced primacy from adherence to the beliefs of any one religion or dogma to psychological notions of the workings of the unconscious. Mysticism was thus everywhere the same, finding its source in an innate feature of Man. Ashokananda's primary objection concerned the implications of this assertion. He agreed that Man's essential nature was divine, but only in potentia. Because access to the experience of the divine was so very difficult, one needed recourse to dogma, mystical techniques, and a guru to awaken what was innate and gain realization. These things, argued Ashokananda, all found their home in India. Although Ashokananda agreed that such ideas and practices could be found elsewhere, he maintained, by undertaking a laborious review of studies on "The Influence of Indian Thought on the Thought of the West," that India was the historic source of the dissemination of Vedantic ideas. By arguing for the primacy of India and need for a guru, Ashokananda seemed bent on undermining Rolland's social agenda.[35]

Yogi Sri Krishnaprem, another mystic who had a long correspondence with one of Rolland's pivotal Indian contacts, D. K. Roy, was even less decorous. Roy had urged Krishnaprem to take note of Rolland's efforts to spread Indian mysticism. In response, Krishnaprem questioned the depth of Rolland's understanding of Indian mysticism:

> You talk again of Romain Rolland. . . . [M]y chief objection to him is that I suspect him of using the words and expressions coined by yogis and rishis in their efforts to set forth their experiences—of using, I say, these expressions to lend a sort of borrowed grandeur to the pale experiences of "Art" which . . . are to the former as the moon is to the sun. He is thus helping to debase the currency as it were. . . . These moderns, when they do believe in religious experience, can think of it only in terms of a sort of vague Wordsworthian "Spirit divine which rolls through all things," or "something far more deeply interfused" . . . [T]hey think that these vague poetic intuitions are the same thing as the living experience of the mystics. . . . [T]he majesty of the ocean may be a great thing, but it was not that which intoxicated Sri Gauranga, but the infinitely more maddening sense-destroying beauty of Sri Krishna whom he saw standing in front of him.[36]

Since Krishnaprem never had access to Rolland's mysticism apart from Roy, it is doubtful he knew the true nature of Rolland's mysticism. Nevertheless, the essential point, which is Krishnaprem's denial of a common-core and privileging of Indian mysticism, remains intact. Mystical experiences of merging with external nature were surely different in degree, if not in kind, from that of the Indian theistic tradition.

Ashokananda and Krishnaprem's criticisms, cursory though they were, bring up the general question of the adequacy of Rolland's comparativist conclusions. This is a crucial issue, for although it can be rightly claimed that Rolland was more interested observer than bona fide comparativist, his scholarly forays are neither without merit nor importance. The issues he unearthed and evaluated are central to historical debates in the study of mysticism. So too has his example exerted a formative and in many ways continuing influence on the psychoanalytic theory of mysticism. All the more reason, then, to note that, at least as far as recent advances in the field are concerned, his perennialism is problematic on epistemological and textual grounds. An examination of these problems from a contemporary perspective can but help us to begin rethinking the relation between psychoanalysis and the interdisciplinary study of mysticism.

The most trenchant critique of Rolland's comparativist conclusions is best articulated by that school of thought that has come to be known as "constructivism" or "contextualism." This school, organized around a critique of the kind of secondary literature Rolland relied on, argues against the project of isolating a common-core of mystical experience by drawing attention to the mediated nature of all experience:

> *There are* NO *pure (i.e. unmediated) experiences*. Neither mystical experience nor more ordinary forms of experience give any indication, or any grounds for believing, that they are unmediated. That is to say, *all* experience is processed through, organized by, and makes itself available to us in extremely complex epistemological ways.[37] (Italics in the original)

The levels at which mediation occur are many. The most fundamental of these levels engages the epistemological grounds of conceptual knowing. As Perovitch has pointed out, members of the constructivist school such as Bruce Garside, H. P. Owens, Rufus Jones, and Katz implicitly or explicitly adopt a Kantian epistemology.[38] The "content" that is harnessed through mystical intuition is given organizational form by the a priori structures or categories of the mind. Katz speaks to this subtle and basic level of epistemological mediation in the following:

> Allied to the erroneous contention that we can achieve a state of pure consciousness is the oft used notion of the "given" or the "suchness" or the "real" to describe the pure state of mystical experience which transcends all contextual epistemological coloring. But what sense do these terms have? . . . It can fairly be said that no attempt to state clearly or individuate the "given" has succeeded. . . . All "givens" are also the product of the processes of "choosing", "shaping", and "receiving". That is, the "given" is appropriated through acts which shape it into forms which we can make intelligible to ourselves given our conceptual constitution, and which structure it in order to respond to the specific contextual needs and mechanisms of consciousness of the receiver . . . (the mystic) is not a tabula rasa on which the "ultimate" or the "given" simply impinges itself—whatever ultimate he happens to be seeking and happens to find. This much is certain: the mystical experience must be mediated by the kind of beings we are.[39]

In Katz's view, the adoption of a Kantian epistemology does not affirm or deny the ontological assertions of mystics but brackets them on philosophical grounds as inaccessible. There are simply no philosophical or hermeneutical means for getting behind the text or establishing the veracity of the ontological claims, where made, of mystics. In order to establish the meaning of mystical experience and states, then, one must examine a second level of conditioning, the religio-cultural surround, which further shapes the mystical experience. For the constructivists, mystical experience, like all experience, is not only subject to the a priori structures of the understanding but is also influenced by one's immersion in the language, concepts, beliefs, worldview, and values of a specific culture and religious tradition. Rufus Jones put the point well when he said:

> There are no 'pure experiences', i.e., no experiences which come wholly from beyond the person who has them. . . . The most refined mysticism, the most exalted spiritual experience is partly a product of the social and intellectual environment in which the personal life of the mystic has formed and matured. There are

no experiences of any sort which are independent of preformed expectations or unaffected by the prevailing beliefs of the time. . . . Mystical experiences will be, perforce, saturated with the dominant ideas of the group to which the mystic belongs, and they will reflect the expectations of that group and that period.[40]

As Katz emphasizes, the conditions of knowing are operative before the actual "experience" (in the sense of conditioning the recipient as to how to interpret what is intuited), during the actual experience, and after it.[41] Because the terms used to describe the experience vary even within a religious tradition, as well as between them and from culture to culture, the words used in describing the mystical experience, such as "self," "God," "nirvana," "nothingness," "sunyata," and even "unity," do not have an essential, invariant, and cross-cultural core of meaning. Instead, they are defined with respect to the problems, the proscribed path, the metaphysical superstructure, and the expected solution generated by the specific religio-cultural tradition through which the mystic seeks deliverance.[42] Thus, the constructivist argues for the acknowledgment of difference, a plea which calls for the phenomenological mapping of a variety of "incorporated interpretations" of mystical phenomena.[43] The thrust of this school, then, is pluralistic and favors the particularity of traditional religions.

Applied to Rolland, the constructivist critique would make the following observations. First, we have seen that Rolland emphasized the extraordinary character of mystical experience, what James calls the mark of *noesis*. This is the sine qua non of mysticism, without which it ceases to exist as a category sui generis. In Rolland's case, the content gleaned through mystical intuition was described, using Spinoza, as the felt union with nature. He then posited an essence to all mysticism, a "common-core" of experience "behind" the text, which he based on the evidence of his personal mystical experiences and tried to ground with respect to emerging philosophical studies of intuition and psychological views of the nature of the psyche. Now, contextualists rule out the veracity of a perennialism based on such grounds. Drawing on Kant, they undercut the possibility of identifying an ontological core or source of any mystical experience. There is no philosophical way to verify that mystics of different traditions glimpse the same noumenal realm. Indeed, the content of Rolland's mystical intuition was shaped before, during, and after the momentary encounter with the transcendent by the extant philosophical, religious, and literary symbols of his day. The meaning of Rolland's mysticism, then, is relegated to the "text," that is, the *Credo quia verum*. However, on the textual level, the contextualist would find significant differences between Rolland's "experiences" and those of a Dionysius, Ramakrishna, Teresa, and so forth. In other words, Rolland's mysticism is but one of many "mysticisms." The legitimacy of Rolland's arguments for a common-core, undermined on the epistemological and textual levels, is relegated to the more dubious grounds of his personal mystical experiences and the compelling nature of his social agenda. The latter, however, are insufficient to ground his advocacy of perennialism. Rather, they force the conclusion that Rolland's cross-cultural pursuits were colored by personal and cultural projection. He attempted to universalize a mysticism which, in actuality, reflected his own.

## Toward Reorientation: Psychoanalysis and Constructivism

The general claims of constructivism—that the arguments of perennialism are suspect on epistemological and textual grounds—seem reasonable enough to hold as valid. That Rolland's arguments were additionally swayed by personal experience and social agenda also rings true. Certainly, the constructivist plea for attention to the text and religious context should be part of any interdisciplinary approach to mysticism.[44] On the other hand, recalling our analysis in chapter 3, Rolland's comparativist agenda called for the adoption of a dialogue with non-Kantian epistemologies and depth psychology. The kind of dialogue promoted by Rolland should not go unheeded. In other words, this study cannot promote a wholesale adoption of constructivism. Rather, the constructivist understanding of mysticism needs to be amended on two fronts: that concerning mystical noesis (the matter of Kantian bracketing) and the complex cultural and psychological issues associated with mysticism as process.

Beginning with the first issue, the sine qua non of mysticism, as stated above, consists in its claim to alternate modes of cognition. John E. Smith, in his commentary on James's discussion of noesis, puts it well:

> [T]he point I want to underscore for future reference is the idea, *and it expresses one of the truly universal features of all mysticism,* that day-to-day consciousness, shaped by ordinary needs, accompanied by habitual and familiar ways of responding to the world, has in some way to be suspended if some special insight into the nature of things, the true self, the purpose of life is to be gained. In short, there is the belief that the mystical truth is always there, but that ordinary experience stands in the way and must be put aside just as one removes a veil to reveal a treasure which existed all along. One key to unlocking the secrets of the many different forms of mysticism is an understanding of the various modes of preparation or discipline whereby the "eye of the soul"—to use a favorite mystical image—is cleansed and attains the proper vantage point from which to see. (Italics in the original)[45]

The notion that certain forms of mystical experience utilize a special faculty or eye that grants one access to transcendent truths goes to the heart of mysticism. For example, in speaking of samādhi, Ramakrishna's major disciple Vivekananda states how the mind arrives at "a higher state of existence, beyond reason," and that once attained, "this knowledge beyond reasoning comes."[46] The Sufi al-Ghazali, describing the highest levels of the states and stages of the mystical life, echoes: "just as the understanding is a stage of human life in which an eye opens to discern various intellectual objects uncomprehended by sensation; just so in the prophetic the sight is illumined by a light which uncovers hidden things and objects the intellect fails to reach."[47] One finds similar statements coming from Christian mystics. St. Teresa, reflecting on her "intellectual visions," voices her inability to articulate the channels through which such lofty modes of noesis take place: "I confess that is all a mystery in which I am lost."[48]

As Rolland noted, the mystic testimony of a direct, immediate encounter with or intuition of the divine argues for a need to go beyond Kant. Many contemporary philosophers would agree. Louis Dupré, in his survey of the Christian category of "intellectual visions," certainly the highest, most trustworthy of all Christian mystical experiences, notes that such visions bypass the everyday channels of sensation, judgment, and rational thought through which we attain our normal awareness of self, world, and other. According to Dupré, "while many epistemologists have followed Kant in denying that the human mind ever attains such a direct insight into the presence of the real as such. . . . [E]ven Kantian students of the mystical experience are forced to admit that no other explanation remains."[49] Anthony Perovitch, in his critique of Katzian constructivism, sets the problem:

> Mystical experiences . . . are not human experiences which seem to employ typically human faculties in typically human ways. Consequently, no presuppositions about the mediated, shaped, conceptualized character of "human experience" . . . are relevant to the sorts of "nonhuman experience" being reported by such mystics. "Kantian" epistemological assumptions may extend as far as the "human experience" . . . but the experience being reported by many mystics demands a suspension of our assumptions not only of a uniformity in the experience had by humans, but also of a uniform epistemological apparatus for handling that experience. . . . The results achieved here are, I believe, of some help in providing further direction for the study of mysticism. They show that an important area for investigation . . . is the area of "mystical epistemology."[50]

One may hold that Rolland's efforts to go beyond Kant were too cursory to be convincing. However, this still leaves open the possibility that one could develop a cogent enough post-Kantian epistemology to ground claims concerning mystical forms of noesis. Moreover, such an epistemology would not necessarily lead to verifying the perennialist claim that there exists a common-core. Certainly a number of philosophical avenues could be taken to further this project. I only add that any attempt to do so must take into account the fact that philosophers and mystics in various religious traditions have formulated positions on mystical epistemology in different and not always commensurate ways. We have seen that Rolland's attempt to counter Kant's view of the limits of the mind led him to synthesize comparativist, philosophical, and psychological perspectives: how emerging philosophical studies of intuition by Le Roy and Aurobindo and views of the subconscious, unconscious, and developmental theory in the works of James and Freud could unite in the formulation of a mystical epistemology. In turn, these formulations promoted the rather modern view of all mysticism as innate psychological potential waiting to be accessed, developed, and mapped.

A typical Christian such as St. Augustine, however, would have reservations about such a conclusion. Like Rolland, Augustine undoubtedly based his attempts at formulating a mystical epistemology on the personal mystical experiences at Milan and Ostia so well described in Books 7 and 9 of *The Confessions*. In distinguishing between intellectual, corporeal, and spiritual (imaginary) visions, he endeavored to provide an epistemology for these experiences, as well as those of other religious figures like Paul and Moses, in noted works such as *The Literal Meaning of Genesis, On the Greatness of the Soul, De Trinitate,* and various letters and homilies. However, even a cursory glance at these mystical visions reveals significant differences from those described by Rolland. More important to the discussion at hand, in formulating a position on mystical epistemology, Augustine, in contrast to Rolland, was indebted to the Greek philosophical matrix, particularly Plotinus, as well as to specifically Christian notions of grace, love, and the imago Dei. Mystics in other religious traditions, from Buddhist analyses of the epistemology of the self to Muslim philosophers like Alfarabi and Avicenna's meditations on the Active Intellect, buttress the point: The attempt to arrive at a satisfactory understanding of mystical modes of knowing will be a laborious enterprise requiring analyses of individual cases in context. It will require a bona fide dialogue between philosophy, psychology, textual studies, and religious conceptions of mystical faculties and their operation. The complexity of this issue deserves a philosophical prolegomenon beyond the scope of this study. However, in the next chapter, we will contribute to this project by showing how such a dialogue might proceed in the case of one mystic, namely, Romain Rolland.[51]

This leads us to the second critique of constructivism, referred to earlier, which concerns what in the introduction I called the process nature of mysticism. The latter is generally compatible with what James calls the methodical cultivation of mysticism. Here the noetic dimension of singular mystical experience cannot be divorced from the mystical life. The transformative effects of mystical experience, seen as part of the total response of an individual to moments of intuitive contact with the divine, is prepared for and integrated into a mystical life as defined by a particular religious tradition. The term "process," then, shifts the criteria for evaluating mysticism from mystical experience per se to the cultivation of a specific set of dispositions, capacities, virtues, states of consciousness, and patterns of behavior. Mystical experiences are seen as part of this process, receiving from it their meaning and identity. Because the perennialist-constructivist debate on mysticism has centered on mystical experience and its epistemology, it has neglected to engage the more profound and complex depth-psychological issues associated with the process nature of mysticism.

One might note that the process view tends to give mysticism a therapeutic aura. But the meaning of terms like "therapy" or "development" are laden with western understandings of health and self, psyche and maturity. Furthermore, mystical traditions have an explicit soteriological aim absent from psychological metapsychology. One could rightly say that psychological therapeutic systems and mystical traditions East and West are introspective paths aiming at individual transformation. They share general, underlying themes apparent in any introspective endeavor: models of the mind, introspective techniques of transformation, markers or aims of development, solutions to existential dilemmas, definitions of the life cycle, constructions of gender, and prescriptions for organizing one's sexuality. Yet it is clear that there exist significant and perhaps incommensurate variations between (as well as within) Western and Eastern introspective—transformative traditions as to how such themes are defined and elaborated. In sum, while a psychoanalytic perspective might frame mystical traditions, when healing and adaptive, as "therapies," it is more accurate, given the many associations linked with the meaning and use of the term "therapy," to say that both psychology and mystical traditions are introspective disciplines containing healing, transformative practices.

Put in the context of the psychology-comparativist dialogue, these observations lead to the question of how psychoanalysis can engage in the cross-cultural interpretation of mystical paths of tranformation without falling prey to unwarranted reductionism. If, as we have seen, concerns over the possible validity of mystical forms of noesis challenge the existing parameters of psychoanalytic metapsychology, then culture studies, particularly those that address the multiple issues surrounding the hazards involved in the cross-cultural study of healing traditions, ask us to reflect further. To what extent is psychoanalysis to be considered an ethnoscience, containing models of self, health, and maturity reflecting unacknowledged normative values that would undermine a bona fide cross-cultural dialogue? If cultural elements and "orientalist" tendencies are accounted for, can psychoanalytic models be successfully adapted to apply to the healing traditions of other religio-cultural contexts? If so, does psychoanalytic metapsychology harness enough explanatory power to account for the deepest forms of mystical subjectivity? Are mystical traditions to be seen as speaking a mythical and symbolic language that contain psychological truths (which are more precisely articulated in psychoanalytic metapsychology), providing transformation and healing insofar as those truths — in conjunction with the personality of healers and introspective techniques — engage developmental conflicts in a culturally appropriate and hence therapeutically effective manner? Or is it the case that the transformative techniques and religious ideation associated with mystical traditions speak to a realm of subjectivity wholly alien to, and perhaps incommensurate with, forms of subjectivity mapped by extant forms of metapsychology? If so, how might one construct a dialogue to bridge these differences?

Historically speaking, there has been a long line of psychoanalytic studies of mysticism emerging from the Freud–Rolland debate that have considered these issues. An evaluation of those studies and recommendations as to how psychoanalytic models might investigate such issues in a convincing manner can be facilitated through an overview of the three basic schools of psychoanalytic theorizing about mysticism: classic, adaptive, and transformational. In what follows I will first sketch a brief history of studies animating each school. Then, in order to best illustrate how each has addressed the issues under consideration, I will adduce representative studies. In particular, to provide continuity with the Freud–Rolland correspondence, I will highlight three recent psychobiographies of Ramakrishna, each of which reflects the general orientation of the three schools in question. Through elaboration and critique of studies within these schools, I will distill conclusions definitive enough for reorientation yet general and flexible enough to both accommodate and promote, within the suggested broad parameters, more nuanced theoretical debate.

The classic school is reflected in what I have referred to as the "received view" and its historical roots in Freud's more pejorative comments on Yoga and

Hinduism as found in *Civilization and Its Discontents* and "A Disturbance of Memory on the Acropolis." Other studies that were undertaken during this formative era of the psychology of religion, all of which emphasize regression and pathology and interpret mysticism with respect to prenatal consciousness, archaic pre-Oedipal modes of unity, hysteria, and psychotic states, have been similarly cited by contemporary members of this school. Morel's *Essai sur l'introversion mystique* belongs here, as do the early studies by Moxon and Schroeder.[52] Among the established psychoanalysts of this era, both Jones and Federn identified mystical experience with primitive narcissistic states, whereas Franz Alexander, in his famous study "Buddhistic Training as an Artificial Catatonia," concludes that the Buddhist meditator, motivated by the need to return to the womb, engages, through various stages of meditation, pathological states from melancholia to schizophrenic dementia.[53] This trend was continued into the 50s and beyond by Lewin (who elaborated these hypotheses in terms of manic denial), Sterba (who noted the mystic's need to defend against the threat of mortality), and studies of saintly figures such as Scharfstein's interpretation of Patanjali (which stresses the relation between Yoga and the death instinct) and Kligerman's reduction of Augustine's famous vision at Ostia to an incest fantasy.[54]

In general, these studies do not directly deal with philosophical controversies over the nature of the epistemology of mystical experience. However, a recent representative view that explicitly states what is implicit throughout these studies can be found in the works of the psychoanalyst and Sanskrit scholar Jeffrey Masson. In his critical review of Stace's famous *Mysticism and Philosophy*, Masson centers his analysis on what he thinks is Stace's major assumption about mystical texts: that they reveal a form of consciousness that enables mystics to grasp valid, objective truths about the nature of self and the universe that are inaccessible through science and the logical intellect.[55] Masson never directly challenges the possibility of such knowledge. Rather, drawing attention to Stace's many assumptions and prejudices and circular reasoning, Masson concludes that Stace never proves the mystic claim to extraordinary insight. Although this hardly negates the validity of the transcendent claims of mystical noesis (only Stace's failure to prove it), Masson goes on to champion an assumption of his own: that only truths discerned by the rational intellect and scientific method should be deemed admissible as knowledge. Masson then promotes his own view of how mystical noesis should be interpreted, namely, with respect to developmental issues. As is typical of the classic approach, Masson, following theorists like Lewin and Morel and case studies of psychotics like Freud's Schreber (branded "a mystic"), views mysticism East and West as regressive, defensive, and indicative of pathology.[56] Thus Indian mysticism reveals states of derealization and depersonalization; the content of the vision found at the apex of the ascent of Eros, from boys to the Form of the Good, in Plato's *Symposium* is rendered but "an intellectually sublimated reversal of the homosexual relationship."[57]

In moving across cultures, the sociohistorical issues endemic to any psychological endeavor become pointed and explicit. To what extent can a metapsychology and therapeutic technique born from the matrix of late industrial capitalistic culture be said to harness psychological universals? In what ways does culture shape universals and does psychoanalysis contain hidden cultural assumptions about health and maturity that invariably play a distorting role in cross-cultural analysis? As may be gleaned from the above, proponents of the classic approach give little credence to arguments from cultural relativists concerning the ambiguity of concepts like gender, sexuality, value, reality, health, or development.[58] Following the lead of Freud and Jones, universal themes emerging from all cultures are evaluated with respect to Western (psychoanalytic) norms of sexuality and maturity.

An apt illustration of this, one which has the advantage of illustrating the classic-school approach to mystical process, can be found in Masson's analysis of Buddha's four noble truths and eightfold path. Masson views the religious reflection that accompanies this "therapy" as a higher form of repression that betrays a misguided attempt to understand and heal psychic disturbances. For example, the first noble truth of Buddhism (*dukkha*, life is suffering) becomes symptomatic: Gotama Buddha suffered from depression. Early in life he must have been abandoned by loved ones, a deep wound that led to a recurrent depressive state as an adult and the need for a cure. He found that cure in meditative activity, which facilitated regression and the preconscious awareness of childhood trauma. In order to ease painful memories, the Buddha resorted to a manic defense, the blissful state of nirvana. Detachment, eradication of passion, and quiescence in the bliss of union was hailed as the cure of existence. States of derealization (the world is an illusion) and of depersonalization (I am but an observer) were inevitable concomitants of this process and signify aggressive annihilation fantasies. The dim, repressed need for love and affection found expression in the creation of mythological worlds filled with imaginary beings.[59]

Another good illustration of the tenets of the classic approach can be found in Narasingha Sil's recent psychobiographic study of Ramakrishna.[60] Ramakrishna (1836–1886) was semiliterate and left no written corpus. What we know of him comes from the many biographies and hagiographies manufactured by disciples and scholars. Rolland's biography is, of course, to be included in this group, as are the famous biographies by Ramakrishna's disciples Mahendranath Gupta (or "M") and Swami Saradananda.[61] Taken together, these biographies catalog details of his upbringing (family and sociocultural considerations) that are essential for reconstructing his developmental years, his pivotal relationships and events of his adult years (particularly those with his various gurus and his disciples), and his emergence as a saint who, through his major disciple Vivekananda and the establishment of the Ramakrishna movement, ended up championing social reform and charitable works. Most important, these biographies catalog his many mystical visions and associated practices (sadhanas). Until recently, Ramakrishna has been cast as an avatar and proponent of those Vedantic practices that culminate in the worldview associated with Advaita Vedanta, that philosophic form of Upanishadic spirituality made famous by Sankara and promoted by Ramakrishna's disciples. However, it is also the case that Ramakrishna engaged in other practices, most notably those according to the Tantras, the mystical and erotic spirituality often downplayed because of its potentially scandalous, socially subversive implications.

Sil is, as he notes, the first to probe Ramakrishna's developmental past. For Sil, it is beyond a reasonable doubt that Ramakrishna was seduced in his childhood by the village women, wandering monks, and neighbors. Those facts, alongside the death of his father (in childhood) and his brother (in adolescence) and his gravitation toward identification with women (his cross-dressing started early), accounts for Ramakrishna's asceticism and what Sil frames as misogynistic acts and expressions of gender confusion. To buttress his case, Sil uncovers distortions in the two major biographies available to English readers: Nikhilananda's bowdlerized translation of Gupta's *Kathamrta* and Jagananda's faithful rendering of Saradananda's hagiographic, revisionist portrait of the paramahamsa. When the original Bengali text is reinstated, the vulgar and sexual connotations of Ramakrishna's utterances become indisputable. With respect to Sarada, Ramakrishna's wife, Sil describes episodes that parallel Gandhi's cruelty toward Kasturba. The humanitarian objectives of the Ramakrishna Movement, inaugurated after the master's death by Vivekananda, "were something the master would never have understood or endorsed."[62] Uneducated and ignorant, Ramakrishna's spirituality was hardly based on a deep understanding of scripture, much less born of reflection on the intractability of suffering and evil.

Sil links this developmental portrait to Ramakrishna's mysticism: "it is necessary to understand the origins and nature of Ramakrishna's psychosis . . . in order to make any sense of his theosis."[63] In making explicit his desire to follow up on Masson's pathologizing of Indian mysticism, Sil depicts Ramakrishna's trances as betraying a host of psychic mechanisms at work: regression, manic denial, reaction formation, hypnotic evasion, and a constitutional psychasthenia, all spurred on by a family history of madness and mystical practices. In Sil's estimation, Ramakrishna's pivotal first vision of Kali, acknowledged by most commentators as the beginning of his spiritual path, is "hardly the *facies Dei revelata*" but rather a simple hallucination, "possibly the outcome of his depression and aggression towards the most important object (the Mother Goddess) in his life . . . and thus, in Freudian terms . . . a classic case of the shadow of the object falling upon the ego."[64] Sil would agree with Masson's claim that Ramakrishna was a psychotic who "had delusions and hallucinations at least equal to if not greater than those of Schreber".[65] Indeed, Ramakrishna's *madhurya bhava*, that devotional practice associated with romantic love, linked to Krishna's lover Radha and, in males, to cross-dressing, is seen as nothing but the cultural justification for "a public release of his feminine urge."[66] Ramakrishna was a "happy pervert" who found a home in a culture that legitimated, if not cultivated, such behavior.[67]

The classic-school approach is suspect from the vantage point of those who are sympathetic to the epistemological claims of mysticism and seek to promote a bona fide dialogue between psychology, religion, and culture studies. Historically, one virtue of both the psychology–theology and psychology–comparativist dialogues has been a serious engagement with religious models of transcendence and the attempt to articulate metapsychological grounds for a deeper form of religious subjectivity. With respect to mysticism, this translates as an active involvement with the problem of mystical noesis. But classic-school studies do not allow other perspectives on mystical intuition to gain entry into the debate over how to interpret the deepest form of mystical subjectivity. Mystical noesis becomes explained in terms of developmentally archaic modes of apprehension and branded as primitive and defensive. All mysticism becomes but instances of the "common-man's mysticism."

The minimal engagement with contested issues in psychoanalytic anthropology also undercuts any significant role culture might play in the hermeneutic enterprise. It is well known that Freud, in *Totem and Taboo*, assumed a host of universal psychological actualities that ranged from the primacy of Oedipus to the notion of an autonomous individual, all of which are seen as shaping, not shaped by, the sociohistorical process. It never occurred to Freud to conceive of his contribution as that of a psychologically gifted ethnographer who unearthed possible psychological conflicts that, under the proper sociohistorical circumstances, could become psychological actuality. Masson and Sil never seriously entertain the notion that metapsychology might be an ethnoscience that, applied cross-culturally, harbors a form of Orientalism that reflects the norms and values of Western society.[68] There is no real need for ethnographic mediation or thick description. What constitutes a wink, much less perversion, is readily ascertained. Because the often bizarre behavior of mystics is never relativized with respect to religio-cultural considerations but is seen as outright symptomatic behavior, it can but reveal perversion and pathology. Thus Ramakrishna's *bhavas* and mystical sadhanas become nothing but the social justification for the expression of gender confusion, infantility, autoeroticism, and voyeurism. Indeed, from the perspective of the work-and-love ethic that pervades classic psychoanalytic models of health, how can the hermetic, meditational lifestyle of a Theravadin forest monk like Adjun Mun, who seeks the eradication of all defilements and release from the cycle of rebirths, be indicative of anything but escapism and regression?[69]

The above is not meant to suggest that the contributions of the classic school are to be rendered null and void. Properly qualified, such constructs can have a place in the proposed reorientation. With respect to Sil's work, one can hardly ignore his fine textual work and his convincing treatment of the developmental infrastructure of Ramakrishna's misogyny, asceticism, and gender confusion. Indeed, it stands to reason that any therapeutic endeavor inevitably provokes or uncovers mental abnormalities of the kind noted by the classic school. Clinical studies like those by Engler confirm the suspicion that the kind of introspective probes and regressive movement facilitated by Buddhist forms of meditation can expose and exacerbate underlying neurotic and even psychotic tendencies.[70] Studies by Kohut and Lasch, which conclude that shifts in family and social structure have resulted in a generation characterized more by self-pathology than Oedipal distress, suggest that pre-Oedipal issues have played a significant role in the emergence of interest among contemporary Western youths in mysticism.[71] In sum, to say mystics and their practices are able to circumvent developmental conflict is to ignore the complexity of the psyche and the power of sexuality and the unconscious. Classic-school models may be reductionistic, but they do illuminate common human foibles endemic to even the saint.

On the other hand, from the perspective of the wider, interdisciplinary study of mysticism, studies in this genre are more likely to be dismissed as lacking in dialogical sophistication. Early studies, such as Alexander's study of Buddhist meditation, are understandably superficial, being ruled by the state of comparative studies of the day. Unfortunately, many recent studies are similarly suspect. For example, Gombrich and Halbfass have provided definitive critiques of Masson's selective, misleading appropriation of Eastern scriptures, including his misunderstanding of the function of Sanskrit in priestly writings.[72] In light of recent studies by Roland, Kakar, and Kurtz, which convincingly argue for the ways in which culture shapes developmental conflict and cast doubt on an unnuanced view of psychoanalysis as a value-free social science, classic-school understandings of the cross-cultural application of psychoanalytic methodology are in need of new scholarly justification.[73] Again, with respect to the utilization of psychoanalytic models, it is one thing, as has been attempted in studies by Meissner, Rubin, Engler, Kakar, and Kripal, to allow space for pathological, adaptive, and even transformational elements in mysticism.[74] It is quite another to reduce all mysticism to pathology. By undercutting the legitimacy of extraordinary mystical modes of knowing, devaluing the need for ethnographic activity and the task of thick description, classic theorists like Sil and Masson find the mystical subjectivity of men like Ramakrishna and the Buddha all too easy to understand and, once understood, easy to dismiss. The lack of interdisciplinary sophistication combined with the utilization of models designed to perceive pathology and the seeming unwillingness to entertain the possibility that mysticism incorporates a variety of experiences that reflect varying degrees of subjective depth and psychological maturity have rendered proponents of the classic approach bystanders in the contemporary study of mysticism. If the psychoanalytic theory of mysticism continues to be viewed as synonymous with the classic school (as it historically has been), then one can only conclude that as far as the broader interdisciplinary study of mysticism is concerned, psychoanalysis will remain marginalized as a methodological tool for the interpretation of mysticism.

Proponents of the adaptive school can find their canonical source and justification in Freud's analysis of mystical intuition in *Civilization and Its Discontents*, the "Goetz Letters," *New Introductory Lectures*, and various letters to Rolland. This scriptural foundation, elaborated through the formulations of ego psychology and object-relations theory and, in some studies, extensive dialogue with culture studies, has provided an extensive basis for revisioning mystical experience and process as healing and therapeutic. Several sociohistorical factors (including a growing sense of disillusionment with Western culture and its championing of a moral, heteronomous God; the influx of and interest in Eastern religions and subsequent dialogue with Hindu and Buddhist religious intellectuals; and the search for authentic experience through drugs and meditation and reformulations of religious subjectivity as evinced in the fruitful debates of the psychology–theology dialogue) created an atmosphere favorable to the emergence of the adaptive school.

During the 40s and 50s, Karen Horney was an early proponent of the adaptive approach. In works such as *Our Inner Conflicts* and *Final Lectures*, influenced by D. T. Suzuki, James's writings on spiritual training, and Aldous Huxley's writings on the perennial philosophy, Horney sought to integrate psychoanalysis with Zen and Morita therapy through her conception of "wholeheartedness."[75] Erikson, influenced in his youth by German mystics, was also sympathetic to the therapeutic potential of mysticism. His psychobiography of Luther contains ego-adaptive views of intuition (seen as relaying normally inaccessible information from the depths of the id and hence central to existential development), monasticism ("true monasticism is a late development . . . possible only to a mature ego"), and meditative techniques (in contrast to the classic school's widely held view of them as diminishing one's sense of identity, Erikson sees them as "a supreme test of having a pretty firm one").[76]

The explosion of interest in Eastern religions during the 60s gave rise to numerous attempts at dialogue. Fromm's collaborative effort with D. T. Suzuki, *Zen Buddhism and Psychoanalysis*, is one of the more successful results of this renewed interest in mysticism.[77] Fromm argued that although the methods of psychoanalysis and Zen differed, there were substantial similarities between the goal of Zen (enlightenment) and that of psychoanalysis (making the unconscious conscious, "where id was there ego shall be"). Both "therapies" resulted in increased insight, ego-syntonic behavior, freedom, and the ability to love and work.[78] Herbert Fingarette, a philosopher fond of psychoanalysis, utilized the models of ego psychology and a series of clinical vignettes to demonstrate that the terminology of Zen (e.g., "selflessness," "emptiness") had been wholly misunderstood by Westerners to refer to an absence of passion and wish to escape reality. The nature of self "lost" through Zen was the "transference" self, the neurotic self. In its stead a cohesive self was created that integrated infantile residue and promoted freedom and individuality.[79] Another pivotal study of this period, Prince and Savage's "Mystical States and the Concept of Regression," utilized Kris's famous formulation "regression in the service of the ego" to argue that mystical experience was a controlled regression that enabled the practitioner to return from the depths of the unconscious with new insight and will to live.[80] Studies in recent decades by Horton, Shafii, Milner, and Fateaux belong here as well.[81]

These models relegate mystical noesis to various lines of development, particularly that of the pre-Oedipal, to interactions between structural components of the psyche, and to "intuitive" modes of apprehending messages arising from the more diffuse, loosely organized energies of the id. To be sure, there are many interpretative variations within this general framework. Many of these studies also make a concerted effort to address philosophical, theological, and comparativist views on the epistemology of mystical experience. For example, Merkur, who links mystical union with access to the depths of the superego, prefaces his interpretation with a historical survey that places psychoanalytic theorizing about mysticism with respect to the debate between common-core and constructivist perspectives on mystical union.[82] Meissner, who interprets the visions of St. Ignatius as transitional phenomena that reflect libidinal and narcissistic content, includes a spirited dialogue with theological literature on the nature of infused visions.[83] At best, however, studies of this genre bracket the thorny question of a transcendent source to mystical forms of noesis. Kakar exemplifies the spirit of the most charitable of these studies when he comments: "I have approached the mystic . . . with empathy, respect, and a sense of the complexity and wonder of human life. My intention has not been to pursue any reductionistic agenda, to 'shrink' the mystic. . . . The psychological understanding, I hope, complements other kinds of understanding; it does not replace them."[84] While acknowledging the possible and, in some cases, actual pathology of mystical states, the proponents of this school see mystical modes of cognition as ultimately valuable and adaptive. As Merkur puts it, mystical experiences "can be used as a source of emotional and religious renewal when they are integrated within a responsible, socially active, practical, productive, moral, and empathetic way of life."[85]

These studies also display a range of engagement with textual and culture studies. At one end of the spectrum are studies like those of Fromm and Fingarette, who view Buddhism as a healing enterprise commensurate with the aims and ideals of psychoanalysis. In effect, Buddhism becomes but a cultural variant of psychoanalysis. Through the long, arduous commitment to monastic living, the adherent accomplishes therapeutic goals similar if not identical to those of the Western analysand. Scant attention is paid to observations such as those of Edward Conze, who stated that psychoanalysis and Buddhism "differ profoundly in their theoretical assumptions about the structure of the mind and the purpose of human existence, and in the methods which they prescribe for the attainment of mental health."[86] Western psychological conceptions of self, development, health, and maturity become unquestioned assumptions that rule cross-cultural discourse. Combined with the seeming sympathy these theorists have toward mysticism, one wonders whether their conclusions harbor a more insidious form of Orientalism than the overt one exemplified in classic-school studies.

At the other end are those theorists like Kakar and Rolland, who have promoted dialogue between psychoanalysis and anthropology and argued persuasively for the need to mediate between the extremes of psychological universalism and cultural relativism. In so doing, they follow in a long tradition, spurred on by the famous Bronislaw Malinowski–Ernest Jones debate over the universality of the Oedipus complex and given nuance by contributions from Erikson, Ann Parsons, Obeyesekere, and Kurtz. These theorists have formulated the relation between psychoanalysis and culture in diverse ways. However, specific differences, although crucial in laying the theoretical groundwork for individual analyses, are not of concern at this juncture. What is of concern to the reorientation championed by this study is the general agreement between these theorists with respect to two pivotal issues that affect the adequacy of cross-cultural psychoanalytic forays into mysticism.

First, they agree that psychoanalysis needs to be seen not simply as another chapter in the history of science, born from empirical observation, testing, and verification, but as an ethnoscience, a "theodicy-turned-poetics" which betrays continuities with the Western religio-cultural past.[87] Underlying psychoanalytic discourse and the healing encounter are narrative structures that promote the virtues of autonomy and individualism and culturally specific conceptions of love, work, intimacy, gender identity, and understandings of the life-cycle. As Kakar observes in his critique of Masson, it is precisely such unexamined values within psychoanalysis that are complicit in the depiction of non-Western cultures and their mystics as inferior and pathological.[88] Although this does not amount to a wholesale condemnation of psychoanalytic cross-cultural pursuits, it does prescribe a certain form of cultural self-reflection. Suzanne Kirschner puts the point well:

> The recognition that our (psychological) categories may embody local values, assumptions, and prescriptions does not inevitably necessitate that we discard or delegitimatize them. But such enhanced self-consciousness does (or at any rate should) engender greater attentiveness to our theories' own sources and continuing situatedness, as well as to the ways in which our frameworks and categories may at times mitigate against the very understanding and illumination they are intended to promote.[89]

Second, sensitivity is demanded to how mystical therapies, similarly embedded in a culturally specific symbolic universe, contain potentially radically different views of self, health, and development. Kurtz, for example, has distinguished between the Western developmental norm, *separation–individuation*, and that of India, which highlights group participation in facilitating a distinct developmental line he calls *separation–integration*.[90] Roland has similarly elaborated on the Indian focus on the group as found in what he calls the we-self and the spiritual self.[91] Kakar has written at length on how different visions of self, other, and reality animate Western psychoanalytic therapies and Eastern mystical ones and on how Hindu Tantric practices facilitate solutions to universal dilemmas concerning gender conflict (the notion of a "divine bisexuality") and orientation toward reality (a state of psychic preparedness that he calls "focused receptivity") that are in stark contrast to the solutions of the same dilemmas mediated through the Western psychoanalytic encounter.[92] These developmental lines and therapeutic solutions are seen as different but, insofar as each is defined as legitimate and adaptive by its cultural context, equally valid.

Again, one can find differences in this group of theorists concerning precisely how culture shapes psyche and guides developmental aims. Although such differences are important for individual analyses, as far as our programmatic agenda is concerned, we can rest content by adopting the above-cited two points of general agreement, for these are sufficient to separate a culturally sensitive adaptive reading of mysticism from that advocated by the classic approach. In order to illustrate this, I choose to highlight Kakar's work on Ramakrishna in his *The Analyst and the Mystic*.

In contrast with Sil, Kakar is convinced that a simple reading of Ramakrishna's mysticism as pathological or his sexuality as hopelessly conflicted betrays the prejudices of a culture-bound ethnoscience. As a result, he calls for a "radical revision" of the psychoanalytic theory of mysticism. First and foremost, this demands ethnographic sensitivity, the ability to take the "native's point of view." Only then can one set aside cultural prejudices and empathize with the inner world of the Indian mystic and thus have some hope of utilizing an appropriate psychological framework for analysis.

After providing a brief summary of Ramakrishna's biography and overview of his sadhanas and visions, Kakar proceeds to his interpretation. Although he emphasizes the multiple determinants of mystical intentionality and vision, Kakar's primary aim is to counter psychoanalytic pathologizing by granting metapsychological legitimacy to Ramakrishna's quest for eternity. So Kakar turns to Jacques Lacan, whom he refers to as one of the "mystics" of psychoanalysis. Lacan posits that humans exist in relation to a primordial reality he called "the Real." Separated from the unknowable Real and possessed of a seemingly incurable sense of incompletion, life becomes a history of the search for unity. The problem for Lacan is that most seek fulfillment in what he calls "The Imaginary and, with the advent of language, in The Symbolic order."[93] So conceived, human desire is essentially misdirected and perverse, for it seeks the eternal in *maya*: a realm defined by transiency. The mystic claim to uniqueness and true sanity lies in the seeking of fulfillment in the Real:

> Born of rupture, desire's fate is an endless quest for the lost object; all real objects merely interrupt the search. As the Barandes put it, "It is the task of the *neotenique* [i.e., immature, even fetalized being] being separated from its original union by its fall into life and into time, to invent detours for itself, deviations of object and as well as means and aims. Its condition is inexorably perverse—if perversions must be." The mystic quest seeks to rescue from primal repression the constantly lived contrast between an original interlocking and a radical rupture. The mystic, unlike most others, does not mistake his hunger for its fulfillment. If we are all fundamentally perverse in the play of our desire, then the mystic is the only one who seeks to go beyond the illusion of The Imaginary and, yes, also the *maya* of The Symbolic register.[94]

Kakar then gives psychosocial depth to the mystic's metaphysical intent by embarking on an analysis of the Hindu concept of *bhava*. For Kakar, the psychosocial significance of *bhava* lies in its ability to produce a passionate form of devotion done with "all of one's heart . . . soul . . . might," thus engendering an intense form of experiencing akin to extreme forms of love, grief, and fear.[95] Kakar characterizes it as the structural component that links Ramakrishna's various sadhanas and categorizes its product, mystical visions, under three headings: simple hallucinations or nightmarish visions (seen as nonpathological and indicative of "thin boundaries" and artistic sensibility); conscious visions (culturally specific symbolic representations of psychic processes), and unconscious visions. The latter, consisting of Ramakrishna's experiments with Vedanta and Tantric visions (including the pivotal first vision of Kali), are especially interesting because it is here that Kakar's departure from classic psychoanalytic pathography is abundantly evident. Kakar does see pre-Oedipal issues (particularly Mahler's rapprochement phase) represented in these visions. Further, following the researches of Nathaniel Ross, Kakar relegates mystical noesis to that symbiotic state where affect is synonymous with knowing. However, Kakar goes beyond the traditional regressive emphasis by creating a metapsychological space for linking mysticism with creativity. *Bhava* becomes "the ground for all creativity," a culturally specific defense mechanism that plays an indispensable role in igniting mystical experiences. Insofar as it engenders extreme emotional states, it sets the stage for "ideal experiencing," the essence of the creative approach to life. Thus Kakar sees in Ramakrishna's visions not simply the Freudian emphasis on parental images and functions in disguise but, in following Winnicott's view of symbols, as a spontaneous capacity for creative experiencing:

> The primary object of creative experiencing is not mother or father but the unknowable ground of creativeness as such. . . . What we should then pay equal attention to is not only the conflicts of the mystic that threaten to deform or disperse his creative experiencing, but the experiencing itself—its content, context, and evolution. . . . Mystical experience, then, is one and—in some cultures and at certain historical periods—the preeminent way of uncovering the vein of creativity that runs deep in all of us.[96]

Like art and science, mysticism is an adaptive phenomenon, being but one more culturally honored and favored mode of access to the wellsprings of imagination.

Extending his analysis to Ramakrishna's eroticism, Kakar admits that developmental factors (a traumatic "bath episode," the loss of paternal figures, and the subsequent identification with women) played a significant role in Ramakrishna's celibacy and symbolic expressions of homosexual libido. However, Kakar shows how physiological and cultural factors relativize the complex issue of saintly eroticism. Touching on the important topic of Tantric conceptions of bodily energies, Kakar intimates that the motivational skein of celibacy is complex, being in the case of the mystic an indispensable technique for achieving mystical insight and ecstasy. Again, properly contextualized as commensurate with the Indian construction of gender, Ramakrishna's seemingly bizarre acts, such as his cross-dressing (*madhurya bhava*), hardly reveals, as Masson and Sil would have it, a culture that spawns and protects happy perverts. On the contrary, it is part and parcel of a bhakti path to God that engages and develops what Winnicott called the "pure female element," revealing a culture that promotes males' experiencing their femininity while prescribing the virtues of "being" and "receptive absorption" over "doing" and "active opposition."[97]

The adaptive school's manner of engagement with culture studies alongside their ability to integrate and supersede the view of mysticism as harboring pathology is a step forward in the attempt to empathize with mystical forms of subjectivity. Indeed, it may be that this approach is sufficient to explain certain forms of mysticism. But in the matter of the higher forms of mystical encounters (the Christian category of intellectual visions, Ramakrishna's *nirvikalpa samadhi*, Plotinus's flight to the One, etc.), it is arguable whether the models favored by adaptive studies, with respect to both mystical experience per se and the kind of mystical subjectivity cultivated through mystical process, are adequate.[98]

Kakar is certainly correct in drawing attention to theorists, broadly classified as within the psychoanalytic tradition, who have endeavored to articulate a metapsychological basis for a truly transcendent, mystical dimension to the personality. Most associate this kind of theorizing with the Jungian tradition: its notions of the collective unconscious and archetypes. Within the psychoanalytic tradition, such theorizing belongs to the transformative school. The latter has its roots in the Freud–Rolland correspondence, specifically Rolland's call for the creation of a mystical psychoanalysis. Other pivotal theorists have followed in Rolland's footsteps. Erikson's reference in his book on Luther to the "unborn core of creation" (*ein lauter Nichts*)–a phrase indebted to Angelus Silesius and elaborated in later works in terms of the numinosity of the "I"–certainly suggest a bona fide mystical dimension to the human personality.[99] Bion refers to his concept of "O," the actualization of which is the ideal aim of the therapeutic encounter, in explicit religio-mystical terms as "the absolute truth, the godhead, the infinite, the thing-in-itself . . . it can 'become,' but it cannot be 'known.'"[100] Lacan's notions of *jouissance* and the Real are similarly mystical. Lacan was influenced by mystics like Plotinus and Teresa and objected, in his inimitable way, to Freud's reduction of mysticism "to questions of fucking." He thought mystical utterances were the "best thing you can read," adding that his own work should be regarded as essentially "of the same order" as mysticism.[101] It may well be, as Webb and Sells have noted, that Lacan and Bion have shifted psychoanalytic conceptions of language, the unconscious, truth, and healing toward a perspective commensurate with the apophatic mystics.[102] Certainly Julia Kristeva's examination of the jouissance she hears in the mystical utterances of Eckhart and St. Bernard belong here, as does Michel de Certeau's exploration of the similarities between psychoanalysis and mystical traditions.[103] One can also include as part of the metapsychological arsenal of the transformative school Kohut's concept of "cosmic narcissism," a rare developmental achievement beyond the bounds of typical therapeutic intervention that symbolizes the religio-ethical goal of Kohut's psychology, and Arthur Deikman's innovative use of ego-psychology's concept of "deautomatization" to create a metapsychological space for the noetic claims of meditators.[104]

Psychoanalytic models have been utilized in studies by Wolfson, Ewing, and Frohlich to create non-reductive dialogue between the developmental and transcendent dimensions of mysticism in the Jewish, Islamic, and Christian traditions.[105] With respect to Buddhism, perhaps the most sophisticated, nonreductive attempt to illumine the relevant application and limits of psychoanalytic metapsychology to the various stages of Buddhist mystical subjectivity (as catalogued in Buddhist texts and Abhidhamma and realized through meditation) lies in the closely argued series of studies by Jack Engler.[106] Engler proposes that psychoanalysis and Buddhist psychology map discrete states of a single developmental sequence, the former describing the lower stages of "conventional" development, the latter the more subtle, spiritual stage of "contemplative" development. In describing the relation between the two stages of development, Engler agrees that mystical/contemplative forms of therapy can attract and exacerbate the condition of those with self-disorders. Such persons are not yet fit for the rigors of the meditational life. Rather, their task is not to "lose" a self but grow one—a task best treated with psychodynamic or object-relational forms of therapy and not meditation. However, once a cohesive self is attained, the doors to meditation and Buddhist ideas of health and maturity beckon. These are seen as contrary to the goals of psychoanalysis. Paradoxically, from the Buddhist perspective, once one has a cohesive self, one is ready to see that this very "self" is an illusion of sorts. As Engler succinctly puts it: "You have to be somebody before you can be nobody."[107]

According to Engler, Buddhist psychology has little to say about the vicissitudes of conventional development. Rather, its goal is to arrive, in a phase-appropriate developmental sequence, at a new form of awareness that completely overcomes the illusion that there is a self, hence dispelling dukkha: a state of psychological well-being that some Buddhists have described as "sa-upadi-sesa Nibbana" (the total "extinguishing" of defilements) and Freud an "ideal fiction."[108] This goal, then, is not within the purview of western-based psychoanalytic understandings of the psyche. Rather, it is part of that psychic kingdom explored and mapped by Buddhist texts. As Engler shows, the two opposed systems are, from the Buddhist perspective, capable of being reconciled as part of a single developmental sequence. However, from a strictly psychoanalytic standpoint, this is far from being the case, since the final aims of the two psychological systems are entirely different. Not "to work and to love" in Freud's sense of the words but total freedom from suffering and, ultimately, from rebirth is the attainment sought by the Buddhist adept. In mapping Buddhist psychology, then, Engler is pointing to a radically different dimension of subjectivity that validates Buddhist reflections on the doctrine of *anatta* and meditative states, that cannot be described as defensive or accounted for by the models utilized by the classic (Alexander-Masson) or adaptive (Fromm-Fingarette) schools, and that can only be attained through the healing insight which accrues through a long period of meditative process. In this sense he belongs to those studies animating the transformative school.

Another good example of a study championing the transformative approach can be found in Jeffrey Kripal's psychobiography of Ramakrishna, *Kali's Child*. Kripal's study is a model of interdisciplinary sophistication, applying classic, adaptive, and transformational models with an appropriate nod to textual studies, comparativist literature, culture studies, and philosophical reflections on mystical epistemology. Kripal's initial project is the restoration of the text. Going well beyond Sil, Kripal unearths what he refers to as Ramakrishna's "secret talk": highly erotic and homoerotic accounts of mystical practices and visions found in the original Bengali texts but absent from bowdlerized translations. Kripal plays off the multiple and often conflicting versions of Ramakrishna's visions, practices, and teachings in the disciples' biographies, contextualizing them with respect to socioreligious typologies (the renouncer/householder and inner/outer groupings) and comparativist issues (the precise nature of Ramakrishna's complex sadhanas). Along the way Kripal inserts his central comparativist claim: Ramakrishna rejected an absolute nondualism, associated with Advaita Vedanta, that posits the world as a "framework of illusion," in favor of a Tantric worldview that posits a dialectic between form and void while emphasizing the ascendancy of *lila* and the world as a "mansion of fun." The net result is an accurate descriptive and historical account of Ramakrishna's mystical practices, revealing insights into the social construction of sainthood and, most important, the unraveling of apologetic concerns, so evident in Saradananda's biography, which seeks to cast Ramakrishna as a proponent of Advaita Vedanta.

The text reinstated, Kripal sets his sights on doing interpretative justice to the relation between sexuality, mysticism, and significant others in Ramakrishna's life and thought. Kripal's interpretative forays reveal that his hermeneutic strategy is multidisciplinary. First and foremost, he is wedded to psychoanalytic theory in the widest sense of the disparate and often conflicting schools of thought it has become. When appropriate, building on Sil and Masson, Kripal champions the approach and conclusions of the "classic" school. He interprets crucial elements of Ramakrishna's religious life with respect to the return of the repressed, cultural norms (its complicity in the shame the young Gadadhar felt over his homoerotic feelings) and pivotal relationships. For example, Kripal fully accepts the notion that Ramakrishna was subject to childhood sexual trauma, which, combined with paternal loss, constituted the developmental infrastructure of his homoeroticism, misogyny, and asceticism. Some of Ramakrishna's visionary experiences, such as those associated with the Bhairavi and heterosexual Tantric practices, are designated as defensive trances. Others, notably the "fog of bliss" vision and those associated with "Handmaid state" and "Tantric latrine," are seen as unconsciously structured along homoerotic and Tantric thematic lines and linked to pivotal figures like Mathur (the temple manager), Tota Puri (Ramakrishna's Vedantic guru), and the disciples.

On the other hand, reacting to Masson's "dogmatic, universalizing rhetoric" and the "ontological reductionism it implies," Kripal insists that Ramakrishna's sadhanas were at times adaptive and revelatory.[109] Here Kripal promotes a reading of Ramakrishna's mystical eroticism that (and here he draws analogies with Plato) accounts for "a homoerotic infatuation harnessed and 'winged' for ecstatic flight."[110] His aim is to relate mystical experience to both "the physical and emotional experience of sexuality and . . . the deepest ontological levels of religious experience."[111] In so doing, Kripal builds a psychology–comparativist dialogue that includes a new cross-cultural category he dubs "the erotic," as well as Lacan and the "mystics" of psychoanalysis, the anthropologist Gananath Obeyesekere's view of "personal symbols," and a stand on contemporary debates in mystical epistemology (drawing on the contributions of Robert Forman, Frederick Streng, and Michael Sells) that promotes a dialectical Tantric worldview.

The best example of this lies in Kripal's thorough textual and interpretative study of Ramakrishna's first vision of Kali. Sifting through the multiple versions of this pivotal vision, Kripal isolates two significant psychosocial facts: (1) the culturally shared, tradition-based drama where Kali's sword demands one's severed head in return for mystic vision and (2) Ramakrishna's personal, idiosyncratic, homoerotic "vocabulary of desire." Interpreting the former with respect to Hindu iconography and rooting the latter in Ramakrishna's developmental past and homoerotic longing for his boy disciples, Kripal concludes it was the shame

Gadadhar felt over illicit homoerotic desires that ignited his first vision of Kali. Left here, Kripal would be but another instance of the classic school. However, by locating the meaning of Ramakrishna's mystico-erotic energies in a Tantric worldview and by utilizing Obeysekere and Lacan, Kripal argues that Ramakrishna's mystical experiences engaged both divine ground and sexual conflict.

In articulating this specifically mystical dimension to the personality, Kripal draws attention to Lacan's reading of Teresa's mystico-eroticism. Noting Lacan's commentary on Bernini's statue, "Teresa in Ecstasy," Kripal unpacks Lacan's question "And what is her *jouissance*, her *coming* from?":

> This, it seems to me, is as important a question as any, and I doubt very much that questions of pathology or the dynamics of psycho-social processes, however crucial such issues might be, have anything to do with its answer. It is simply a different type of question. Lacan was clear enough about his own answer to where Teresa was "coming from." He rejected the notion that the mystical can be reduced to sexuality and instead speculated that such ecstatic experiences of a *"jouissance which goes beyond"* issue forth from our own ontological ground. . . . Ramakrishna in *samadhi*, not unlike Bernini's "Teresa in Ecstasy," is obviously "coming." But "what is his *jouissance*, his *coming* from"? . . . I have respected the religious world of Tantra and have chosen to interpret Ramakrishna's mystico-erotic experiences within that universe. I would argue, then, that the saint's experiences were "coming from" the ontological ground of his Tantric world. . . . I would insist, moreover, that such a realization be understood on its own terms, as a genuine religious experience.[112]

In bridging psychoanalytic and Tantric notions of sexuality and vision, Kripal sees in the symbols and acts of Ramakrishna's homoerotic mysticism a progressive (cultural-mystical) as well as regressive (psychoanalytic) meaning. It is Obeyesekere's anthropological take on Paul Ricoeur's dialectic between *arche* and *telos* that paves the way for providing a relation between the two:

> Sometimes, in exceptional cases, we find genuine two-way "symbols" that function *both* as symptoms, hearkening back to the original crisis, *and* as numinous symbols, pointing to a resolution of the crisis, greater meaning, and what Obeyesekere calls a "radical transformation of one's being." Obeyesekere identifies Ramakrishna as one of those "exceptional cases" in which the symptom became a symbol and turned a crisis into an experience of the sacred: "Ramakrishna's Hinduism permits the progressive development of the personal symbol. . . . To Ramakrishna his own mother is mother Kali who is *the* Mother and the guiding principle of cosmic creativity. Through Kali, Ramakrishna has achieved trance and knowledge of a radically different order from the others, and he can progress to the heart of a specifically Hindu reality that is essentially salvific."
>
> Here, then, is where I would locate the meaning of Ramakrishna's *eros* — *both* in his obvious infatuation with his boy disciples, an infatuation somehow connected with the archaic "regressive" motivations of his own personal history . . . *and* in a "progressive," essentially mystical, order of rapture and vision. . . .

[W]hat was once a crisis became the secret, not only of his mystical and charismatic success, but of his very divinity.[113]

This progressive movement, however, cannot be accounted for by simple sublimation but only through an alchemical transformation of bodily energies that necessitates a move to a specifically Tantric worldview, one in which libido receives its definition in relation to the erotic-mystical energy known as *shakti*. So too must one note the very different view of development inherent in such a worldview. It is the opening of those psychophysiological structures known as *cakras* and the mystical understanding they bequeath that become the markers of development. From this perspective, libido-based notions of development are relativized and turned on their heads. As Kripal points out, from the standpoint of the successful Tantric, "Freud only got to the third Cakra."[114]

While providing path-breaking analyses that illustrate the transformative orientation toward mysticism, the above theorists and studies are hardly beyond reproach. For example, originative psychologists like Lacan, Bion, and Kohut tend to articulate a generic psychological conception of the divine that needs to be qualified and refined when applied to a particular religious worldview and mystic in question. Simply pointing to a generic category of the transcendent, as these psychologies do, leaves out important issues in mystical epistemology that separate "mysticisms." In the case of Engler, a variation of this theme can be isolated. Engler's study aims at establishing a universally valid stage approach to mysticism—one informed primarily by eastern meditational texts, amounting to a form of "process perennialism" that ignores the very different goals and vicissitudes of development found in the mystical paths of the world's religious traditions. Indeed, the conceptualization of his stage approach is itself problematic. While privileging contemplative modes of development as higher, Engler acknowledges that some tradition-sanctioned Buddhist masters suffer from what appears to be unintegrated aspects of self-pathology. Engler is thus forced to admit that there exists a more complex relation between conventional and contemplative lines of development than he initially lets on. However, that complexity is never fully addressed. The admission that the developmental ascent upward is less than linear leaves many questions unresolved.[115]

Although Kripal's study manifests a more thorough interdisciplinary and dialogical treatment of Ramakrishna's mystical life, his seductive rhetoric does not always suffice to hide the theoretical problems inevitable in any attempt to integrate conflicting perspectives through a "both/and" approach. For example, with respect to his cross-cultural psychobiographical forays into Ramakrishna's childhood, Kripal, citing the ethnographically sensitive psychoanalytic agenda of Stanley Kurtz, suggests that psychoanalysis must be "reshaped" to fit any cultural context it purports to investigate.[116] Yet Kurtz is never alluded to after the single reference in the introduction. Indeed, where issues of seduction and asceticism are concerned, Kripal's analysis draws more on the reductive psychoanalytic universalism of Masson. While this does not necessarily imply theoretical inconsistency, sustained reflection on the tension between the two camps is needed. Furthermore, although Kripal utilizes the transformative model of Lacan to account for the properly religious dimension of Ramakrishna's mysticism, one wishes for more on the precise psychological processes involved in sadhanas that led not to the bliss of manic denial but to the insight of alchemical transformation. An attempt to sound out the important issues surrounding the relation between the therapeutic effects of psychoanalysis and meditation is needed. Although Kripal does, however briefly, attempt to integrate the philosophical studies of Forman, Sells, and Streng, further dividends would have accrued had he undertaken a more thorough dialogue between Lacan's concept of the Real and Vedantic and Tantric understandings of the epistemology of mystical forms of noesis.

At the same time, one does not have to endorse every nuance of these theorists and studies to applaud the perspective on mysticism they exemplify. Indeed, given the general dearth and relatively recent onset of studies from this perspective, it is fair to say that a promising start has been made. Our historical survey has contributed to this project by revealing the very real differences in approach offered by theorists like Sil, Kakar, and Kripal on Ramakrishna and Alexander-Masson, Fromm-Fingarette, and Engler on Buddhism. Such differences serve to illustrate the contrasting perspectives of the classic, adaptive, and transformational schools and have helped to articulate the general reorientation for the psychoanalytic theory of mysticism advocated in this study. That shift acknowledges, along with the constructivists, the existence of many "mysticisms" and the need to restore and contextualize each with respect to relevant theological and comparativist literature. In promoting the ability of psychoanalytic models to engage in cross-cultural analysis and to contribute to the task of illuminating the subtleties of mystical subjectivity, the proposed reorientation asks those utilizing psychoanalytic models to reflect on the cultural situatedness of such models and to respect the different views of process and development of mystical "therapies." It calls for a dialogue between transformative models and philosophical and tradition-based reflection on the epistemology of insights garnered in mystical experience and, in acknowledging the complexity of the psyche and the power of sexuality and the unconscious, the judicious application of the insights afforded by classic and adaptive models. Once again, it is acknowledged that the variety of mysticisms and mystical paths insures that the reorientation proposed here must remain programmatic. As new cases are investigated, new issues and debates will be unearthed and addressed, adding specificity to an admittedly general framework. To illustrate this, we return to the mysticism of Romain Rolland.

# The Oceanic Feeling Interpreted

D rawing on the multiple resources unearthed in the last chapter, we are now in a position to offer a fresh interpretation of Rolland's mysticism. The latter presents interesting peculiarities: Rolland was an unchurched Western mystic deracinated from traditional religious modes of expressing religious sentiments, a recipient of unchurched mystical experiences, and an advocate of the creation of a "mystical psychoanalysis." As such, a psychoanalytic analysis of his mysticism does not encounter the more difficult sociohistorical and comparativist problems presented by tradition-bound mystics. On the other hand, I do think Rolland belongs to what can loosely be called a "tradition." I begin, then, by situating Rolland's mysticism with respect to extant comparativist literature, focusing at first on what has been termed "nature mysticism." Here I appropriate the writings of R. C. Zaehner, for only Zaehner has suggested a conception of nature mysticism fruitful enough to begin to account for the experiential, sociohistorical, and theoretical dimensions of Rolland's mysticism. As important, Zaehner's rubric provides convenient theoretical bridges to psychoanalytic studies that allow me to implement the dialogical position advocated in the last chapter. Building on Zaehner, then, I devote the rest of the chapter to creating a dialogue between Rolland's mysticism, culture studies, psychoanalysis, and issues in mystical epistemology.

### Revisioning Zaehner: Rolland and Unchurched Mysticism

Zaehner's conception of nature mysticism, best elaborated in his classic *Mysticism Sacred and Profane*, is inextricably bound up with his comparativist agenda.

Simply put, Zaehner argues for the existence of three universal, cross-culturally valid types of mysticism (nature or panenhenic, monistic, and theistic). These types are then evaluated and placed in a hierarchical order, with theism placed in a position of primacy over monism and nature mysticism. As one might expect, Zaehner's thesis has evoked numerous criticisms, ranging from his misappropriation of texts and the unwarranted narrowness of his typological schema to his admitted Catholic bias and stage approach to mysticism.[1] Let me state unequivocally that I accept these criticisms. One does not, however, need to accept his typology or hierarchy to acknowledge that his observations concerning nature mysticism have merit. At the same time, in order to appropriate Zaehner's rubric for application to Rolland, it must be revised. In so doing I will highlight, with certain qualifications, two central characteristics of nature mysticism. First, following the lead of Zaehner's critics, I omit the attempt to read nature mysticism into Vedanta and Buddhism. We are then left with a rubric that comprises Western nonconfessional mystical texts, all evincing a kind of generic religious consciousness. This new rubric is to be understood as a singular category divorced from Zaehner's value-laden typological schema, free from his comparativist intents and hence its problematic implications. Second, in contrast to the almost exclusive emphasis that has been placed on the phenomenological characteristics of nature mystical experiences, I will unpack and expand on his suggestive observations concerning its sociohistorical and psychological dimensions. Thus revised, this rubric offers unparalleled insights to illuminate the task at hand.

The revised version of nature mysticism I am advocating is best rendered "unchurched mysticism." Having so dubbed it, let us first proceed to an examination of its existential component. There are essentially four kinds of experience that I find admissible as unchurched mystical phenomena. The most defining is the ineffable, transient experience of unity with the external world. Paradigmatic in this regard is Malwida von Meysenbug's report, which Zaehner takes from James's *The Varieties of Religious Experience:*

> I was alone upon the seashore as all these thoughts flowed over me, liberating and reconciling; and now again, as once before in distant days in the Alps of Dauphiné, I was impelled to kneel down, this time before the illimitable ocean, symbol of the Infinite. I felt that I prayed as I had never prayed before, and knew now what prayer really is: to return from the solitude of individuation into the consciousness of unity with all that is, to kneel down as one that passes away, and to rise up as one imperishable. Earth, heaven, and sea resounded as in one vast world-encircling harmony.[2]

The above report is of especial interest, for Meysenbug was a close friend and confidant of Rolland.[3] A second kind of "experience" comes from the pen of the Irish novelist Forrest Reid, who, upon lying down in the countryside, was the recipient of the following:

> It was as if everything that had seemed to be external and around me were suddenly within me. The whole world seemed to be within me. It was within me that

. . . the skylark was singing, it was within me that the hot sun shone, and that the shade was cool. A cloud rose in the sky, and passed in a light shower that pattered on the leaves, and I felt its freshness dropping into my soul, and I felt in all my being the delicious fragrance of the earth and the grass and the plants and the rich brown soil. I could have sobbed with joy.[4]

The distinction between this experience and that of von Meysenbug is subtle but real. In the latter, the experience is of a felt merging with a greater whole external to oneself; in the former, the expansion of self to include all of Nature within oneself. In a third example Zaehner adduces, this time from the philosopher Karl Joel, one finds both the sense of merging with external nature and of feeling nature within oneself combined.[5] Finally, in describing the experiences of Aldous Huxley, Zaehner points to yet a fourth kind of nature-based mysticism:

Everything shone with the Inner Light, and was infinite in its significance. The legs, for example of that chair—how miraculous their tubularity, how supernatural their polished smoothness! I spent several minutes—or was it several centuries?—not merely gazing at those bamboo legs, but actually *being* them—or rather being myself in them; or, to be still more accurate (for "I" was not involved in the case, nor in a certain sense were "they") being my Not-self in the Not-self which was the chair.[6]

Huxley's experience is distinct from the others insofar as it is clothed in the terminology of Vedanta and Buddhism. The actual union is in the land of the "Not-self." Nevertheless, these variations on a theme all fall under the same rubric, for they are united by the more general and hence inclusive criteria of nature mysticism: "without and within are one."[7] Such experiences are usually spontaneous, although they can be artificially induced through drugs, asceticism, and meditative techniques like Yoga.[8] Zaehner also finds "panenhenic" experiences operative in the psychobiological aberrations found in manic-depressive psychosis, so well exemplified in the case of John Custance.[9] In addition to the above reports, there is a qualitatively distinct kind of experience that I also subsume under the category of unchurched mysticism. In contrast to the first, that is, the felt merging with nature, the second kind of natural mystical experience reveals another "self" aside from the ego. One momentarily apprehends a self outside time, apart from one's ordinary conscious everyday "ego," which is felt to be deeper and more "real." One feels immortal, death being a "laughable impossibility."[10] This experience Zaehner finds best exemplified by Marcel Proust, who cataloged them in his classic *Remembrance of Things Past*.[11] In the latter, Proust speaks of seemingly insignificant events—the taste of a bun soaked in tea, the gazing at some church spires, the sight of a few trees, the stumbling over some paving stones—that became the occasions for a sudden, momentary, and wholly unexpected glimpse of an eternal self:

[T]he permanent essence of things which is usually hidden, is set free, and our real self, which often had seemed dead for a long time yet was not dead altogether, awakes and comes to life as it receives the heavenly food now proffered to it. . . .

How easy to understand that this man should be confident in his joy, even if the mere taste of a bun may not seem, logically, to contain within itself the reasons for that joy. It is understandable that the word "death" can have no meaning for him: situated as he is, outside time, what could he fear from the future?[12]

Like the first kind of mystical experience, this second kind can be either "spontaneous" or induced through meditative exercises. So too can it be evoked through drugs, and here Zaehner calls our attention to the famous experience, cataloged in the *Varieties of Mystical Experience*, which James had under nitrous oxide.[13] All unchurched mystical phenomena, then, are conceived of as innate potential lying dormant deep in man's psyche.

The above accounts closely resemble those of Rolland. Like the poets and philosophers cited by Zaehner, Rolland's mystical experiences were spontaneous, seen as innate potential that excluded any dependence on a traditionally conceived transcendent Other. On the textual level, the unitive experiences with the Breithorn and at Ferney recall the unitive consciousness of both Meysenbug and Huxley, whereas the "train episode," emphasizing as it did an immortal self beyond the touch of death, and Rolland's distinction, in his *Journey Within*, between two "selves," the everyday self and the deeper, timeless Self, recalls the experiences of his compatriot and fellow novelist Proust.

Rolland's unchurched status also has affinities with these mystics on sociohistorical grounds. Pivotal in this regard are Zaehner's suggestive observations concerning the connection between the nonconfessional character of nature mysticism, the deracinated status of the recipients of nature mystical experiences, the subsequent attempts of many of its proponents to formulate a quasi-religious and psychological theory of the mind, and a pluralized, secularized Western culture.

The best example of this is found in Zaehner's critique of Huxley's attempt to formulate his perennial philosophy. The latter, Zaehner tells us, shared the culturally popular view of the 1950s that came to view Christianity as synonymous with a heteronomous ethical code. For Huxley and others of his generation, that code was sexually, politically, and economically oppressive.[14] Disillusioned, Huxley found readily available in the pluralistic culture of the West other ways of expressing his religious needs: the classic texts of Buddhism and Hinduism, which emphasized experience over ethics, authenticity over convention, introspection over belief. So too did he find attractive the turn to mystical experience via mescaline. The latter then became the existential basis for his perennialism, which was formulated from multiple religious sources and culminated in the concept of "Mind at Large." As Zaehner points out, "Mind at Large" is heavily psychological, a rudimentary version of Jung's concept of the "collective unconscious."[15] In other words, Huxley, far from promoting a doctrinaire Hindu or Buddhist agenda, presented an individually specific, quite modern, Westernized version of the perennial philosophy. Disillusioned with traditional religion, Huxley took his own mystical experiences, ran them through the concepts available to him in his culture, created a rudimentary religio-psychological theory to explain mysticism and religion in general, then offered it to a generation disillusioned by traditional, institutionalized religion.

Zaehner does not analyze other nature mystics in quite the depth he reserves for Huxley. Nevertheless, many of the same characteristics can be found in what he does say of them. Both Richard Jefferies and Arthur Rimbaud, for example, broke with institutional religion before they became full-fledged nature mystics.[16] Rimbaud went on to develop a theory, based on his mystical experiences, of something he called the "universal mind," which drew from alchemical doctrine and aspects of the Christian faith and which Zaehner thinks is a rudimentary version of Jung's collective unconscious.[17] In endeavoring to make sense of his nature mystical experiences, John Custance's formulations were also heavily indebted to Jung.[18] In all these cases, then, nature mystical experience becomes the basis for a new theory of the mind, one which draws in various ways from culturally available religious and psychological materials. Rolland too belongs in this group, for he, like the above, became disillusioned with his native Christianity, moved to an unchurched mysticism based on Spinoza (who Zaehner sees as providing a philosophical rationalization of nature mysticism), and then to a perennialism based on psychology.[19]

Interesting in this regard is Zaehner's view of Jung. Like Rolland, Jung broke from his native Christian faith and was privy to a number of what he called, following Otto, "numinous" religious experiences, including at least one drug-induced experience that involved a feeling of oneness with external reality and another experience of the "Self" that he characterized as nontemporal and an integral part of the individuation process.[20] Jung used such experiences, along with clinical data and the resources of numerous religious traditions, to formulate a religio-psychological theory of the mind. In so doing, Jung also turned to the mysticism of the East, a fact especially evident in his metapsychological concept of the Self archetype.[21] He is, in Zaehner's view, the paradigmatic example of a *rationalized* nature mysticism, of a "perennial psychology," of psychology *as* a "religion." At the same time, Jung's psychology, viewed in the classic sense as a psychology *of* religion, also becomes the interpretative lens through which Zaehner evaluates the various cases of nature mysticism.[22]

This last point has been similarly glossed over by most of Zaehner's critics. Underneath the high visibility of Zaehner's stress on mysticism as experience—even despite his definition of mysticism in terms of experience[23]—lies a view of mysticism as "process" that is far closer to the true aim and spirit of his inquiry. It is to this end that he employs Jung's psychology. In other words, not nature mystical experience per se but the Jungian psychoethical task of individuation is the final concern of Zaehner. Thus the unitive experience with all of creation or nature signifies "inflation," in this case the effect of an archetype of the "Great Mother" at work.[24] Similarly, the apprehension of the deeper "Self," the momentary glimpse and felt wholeness of all the components of the self outside time, is the experience of the Self archetype and the foretaste of the more permanent state that the ego is privy to when fully individuated.[25] It is the felt glimpse of what such a psychologically integrated state would be like—a state in which the ego does not cease to exist but is displaced from its central position by the timeless, deeper Self.[26] Zaehner's stress on the individuation process over against the episodic nature of experience connects the two types of nature mystical experience, thus giving the rubric psychological coherence. Both types of experience are valued only if they result in individuation, a result which by no means follows necessarily. In this regard, Zaehner favors Proust and James over Huxley, Custance, and Rimbaud. Huxley's mergings with nature are viewed as not only episodic and drug-induced but due to the neurotic need to escape by merging with a higher Other. James's experience under nitrous oxide, on the other hand, was part and parcel of his "healthy-minded" approach to life, where as Proust's experience of an integrated Self outside time was the occasion for the cure of his neurosis, the restoration of purpose, and the enlargement of his personality.[27] Rolland belongs with James and Proust, for, as we have noted, the mystical process described in *The Soul Enchanted* and *Journey Within* and in his comments on Yoga in the biographies of the Hindu saints approximates the Jungian task of individuation.

In sum, the category "unchurched mysticism" as delineated here speaks to the accounts of mystical experience found in Rolland's corpus while its instances reveal an affinity between a secularized, pluralized culture and the emergence of a nonconfessional mysticism. Here one can almost speak of a "tradition" all its own: a specifically modern one which, in its most rationalized form, the perennial psychology, seeks to organize, express, and interpret mystical phenomena in a psychological manner. The comparativist attempts of Rolland, and perhaps others, reveal perennialist leanings reflective of the aims, self-understanding, and sociohistorical locale of that tradition. So too do the implications of individuation, with its inclusion of mystical experience in the developmental process, come closer to capturing the existential and ethical dimension of Rolland's mysticism than does Freud's recourse to primary narcissism. Despite all this, I am not advocating that we rest with these cursory observations on the sociohistorical locale or adopt a Jungian interpretation of unchurched mysticism. Resources exist within the psychoanalytic tradition to further what is a useful first approximation.

## Psychoanalysis and Rolland's Mysticism: Theoretical Considerations

Within the broad expanse of resources found in the psychoanalytic study of religion and culture, two interrelated arenas of dialogue, each representing major approaches in the field, are especially conducive to adding nuance and precision to the conclusions arrived at thus far. First, with respect to the traditional data allotted to the psychology *of* religion, we have suggested that the concept of individuation offers a better developmental portrait of the "process" nature of Rolland's mysticism than does Freud's recourse to the preservation of primary narcissism. However, historically speaking, psychoanalysis has found Jungian metapsychology anathema, as is so well captured in the title of Edward Glover's classic and polemic work *Freud or Jung*. In order to bridge this impasse, I will follow the lead of those clinicians and scholars from both camps who have sought a basis for rapprochement in the form of object-relations theory. These studies have revisioned Jung as an originative psychologist whose own psyche, as well as those of his patients, was, due to the collusion between sociostructural shifts and family constellations, organized along the pre-Oedipal or narcissistic line of development. Central concepts like the collective unconscious, archetypes, and individuation are metapsychologically recast as engaging the developmental line of narcissism: issues of self-esteem, cohesion, and the task of becoming an autonomous self.[28] In accordance with this agenda, then, I will utilize the ideas of the originative theorists Heinz Kohut and D.W. Winnicott, especially as they have been modified by those psychoanalysts and comparativists who seek their maximal use in the interpretation of religious phenomena.

Although object-relations theory and Kohut's self psychology avoid the problematic implications of the notion of a collective unconscious populated by archetypes, it is unable to account for Rolland's mystical experiences without reducing the epistemological to the developmental. I find the standard recourse to reducing mystical experiences to early phases of the mother–infant relationship inadequate. Similarly, I find the notion of archetypes inadequate for explaining the epistemology of mystical experience. This is true in the general sense, for Jungian psychology, applied to mystical experience, is commensurate with a psychological form of perennialism and cuts short the need for contextualization and dialogue with philosophical and religious views on mystical epistemology. It is also true in the specific case of Rolland. Rolland's approach to mysticism was certainly more like Jung's than Freud's, an observation that justifies those who wish to further Zaehner's initial Jungian probes into unchurched mystics. However, just as I will show that Rolland's oceanic feeling is better conceptualized with respect to the developmental line of narcissism, so too will I show that the dialogical position concerning mystical epistemology articulated in the last chapter can be applied in the case of Rolland. In so doing, I will take the opportunity to elaborate further on what I have referred to as the classic, adaptive, and transformational schools. Although I will argue that all three can be used to illuminate various facets of Rolland's mysticism, my emphasis will be on the adaptive–transformational.

The second forum of engagement concerns those biographical and sociohistorical conditions that gave birth to Rolland's "tradition," his unchurched mysticism. What is interesting about Rolland is his move from Catholicism to an unchurched mysticism based initially on Spinoza (the *Credo quia verum*) and then to a "perennial psychology" or "mystical psychoanalysis." In one sense Rolland was like Freud. Due to secularization and other social and personal forces, he became disillusioned with institutionalized religion and convinced of the need to replace it with psychology. In another sense, however, he was more like Jung, for his psychology housed an explicit religious dimension. Thus, despite his renunciation of Catholicism, in a very real sense religion lived on in his mystical psychology. It is this sense of historical continuity which is responsible for the oft-repeated apprehension of psychology "as" a religion. Because the issue here concerns the sociohistorical and cultural continuities between psychology and religion, the approach does not warrant a psychological analysis "of" religious accoutrements and ideation, as in Freud's attempt to seek its origins in development and projection, or the attempt to facilitate "dialogue" between religious intellectuals and psychologists. It demands a more inclusive, integrated social scientific approach—one in which psychology and social theory unite in an attempt to unpack the complex historical relation between religion and the emergence of specifically psychological modes of introspection and theorizing. In particular, it demands what has been called the "psychology *and* religion" approach, which, as Homans, Van Herik, and Henking have pointed out, is neither primarily reductive nor dialogical because it stresses historical relation, viewing both religion and psychology as products of culture.[29]

A psychology *and* religion approach seizes on biography, focusing on the complex interplay in individuals between religion (culture), secularization (sociohistorical factors), and development (psychology). Homans has noted that the key to linking psychological processes (the developmental notion of individuation) with sociohistorical processes is a "double" ideal-type, which he refers to as "the tension between analytic access and a common-culture." Analytic access simply refers to an individual's introspective activity and depth-psychological probes. It is in "tension" with what Talcott Parsons refers to as a "common-culture," for, sociologically speaking, analytic access always takes place at the margins of culture. The double ideal-type presupposes an inclusive concept of mourning, one which depends on the psychological concept of disillusionment or deidealization and extends what is mourned to social and cultural "objects" such as values, ideals, and symbols. In an ideal-typical sense, the process is envisioned as starting when the power of a religious worldview or common-culture to command allegiance wanes and symbols "die" (disenchantment, as Weber would have it). What was previously idealized, and hence believed or given allegiance to, becomes deidealized. This loss leads to mourning, a regressive process that involves, to various degrees depending on the person, an introspective engagement with unconscious contents. This is so because the unconscious, previously worn "on the outside"—that is, projected onto, hence contained and monitored by, religious ideation and hence dealt with in what Kohut has described as an "experience-distant" manner—no longer finds nourishment on the collective level. Such loss thus loosens unconscious contents, turns one back in on oneself and may result in breakdown, despair, or cynicism. However, it also provides an opportunity for individuation, which is to say the process of growing out of the social womb and the integration of previously unmonitored unconscious contents. This process can result in a response to the loss of religion in the form of the creation of new ideals and symbols. The latter, in turn, usually display some form of connection with the religious past. Although deidealized and in some sense rejected, religion is never wholly left behind but rather is repudiated and assimilated in varying degrees and proportions.[30]

This approach has been shown to be useful for understanding the psychosocial matrix that gave rise to the creative activity of originative psychologists, particularly the early psychologists of religion. Certainly it is clear that in developing their respective psychologies both Freud and Jung grappled with and wrote extensively on religion, explaining its psychological power by rooting it in developmental theory and processes like identification, internalization, and projection. Yet although both rejected the irrational, revealed, projected aspects of religion, one can tease out in their psychology the echoes of transformed religious elements. This is particularly evident in Jung's method of "amplification," theory of the collective unconscious, and archetypes, all of which point to an archaic dimension in man and the connection we all have to the religious traditions of the past. I think Rolland belongs in this group, for although his creative response never gave rise to a full-blown psychology of religion, it did display that process of mourning that eventually led to his attraction to psychology and offered a creative response to the loss of his native Catholicism, a response that contains elements of both the repudiated and assimilated religious past.

The above suggests that although it is helpful and necessary to distinguish the psychology "of" from the psychology "and" approach to religion, in the final analysis the two are complementary and inexorably interwoven. In order to best illustrate the approaches advanced in a way consistent with the narrative of Rolland's mysticism weaved in previous chapters, I offer in what follows three short vignettes, each corresponding to a significant period in Rolland's life: his childhood in Clamency, his youth in Paris, and his adult engagement with psychology and mysticism. Each vignette utilizes, appropriate to the material at hand and in varying degrees, both the psychology "of" and psychology "and" approaches to religion. The aim is to provide windows into the evolution of the existential and theoretical components of Rolland's mysticism: the development of a psychologically meaningful mystical consciousness, expressed in his move from Catholicism to an unchurched mysticism and then to a mystical psychoanalysis, framed by the dialectic between changing social conditions and the mourning process.

## Clamency and Catholicism

There is no evidence that Rolland was privy to what could even remotely be called mystical experiences in his childhood. Nevertheless, the years in Clamency are important, for here Rolland received his first exposure to religion. He was, as we have seen, "born Catholic, in a Catholic family, in a Catholic town."[31] Madame Rolland's strong Jansenist beliefs and the daunting presence of St. Martin's insured that, for the young Romain, Christianity was the only game around. However, alongside the public and the institutional, we have seen that Rolland also created an idiosyncratic, private nature religion which, like Catholicism, became associated with his mother. He speaks in several places of a symbiotic union with nature, of merging with and flowing into it to play and dream. In other places he explicitly identifies nature with his mother and, after one of his mystical experiences, writes to implore her to seek unity with him in the spirit that inhabited the countryside and mountains.[32] Yet while the maternal matrix afforded by the "good mother" and Nature became the developmental infrastructure of his *Credo*, Rolland maintained a lifelong ambivalence toward Catholicism. Certainly it maintained positive roots in his unconscious, as is evinced in our earlier analysis of the "Chapel vision," what he referred to as his "instinctive preference" for Catholicism, and his continued desire to promote dialogue with its proponents.[33] Yet Rolland eventually broke with the Church, continuing his criticisms of it in writings like *Liluli*. Our specific interest in this period, then, concerns not only the psychosocial matrix that gave birth to these "religions" but also the nature of their configuration in Romain's psyche and how the latter paved the way for Rolland's eventual break with Catholicism, development of an unchurched mysticism, and promotion of a mystical psycho-analysis.

As far as Catholicism is concerned, the fated event seems to have been the death of Rolland's younger sister Madeline in June of 1871. Madame Rolland, devoted to her children and by nature carefree and robust, became morbid, a seeming stranger buried in a perpetual state of mourning.[34] Relative to her relation with Romain, the net effect was an empathic absence manifested as suffocating presence. Her overprotectiveness toward her remaining child resulted in an emotional solicitude, what Rolland refers to as an "anxious surveillance."[35] A lack of empathic communication between the two rendered Romain a self-object used to fortify his mother's flagging, depressed sense of self:

> When my mother discovered in me a little companion for her lonely heart, she transferred to me all her determination to conquer life with which she had decided never to compromise. Elected by her, without being consulted, to become the champion of her ideas; her lieutenant, without the least idea what his mission was, *I was treated by her as another phase of her own being.*[36] (italics added)

Rolland came to identify this absent maternal presence with Catholicism: "she shut herself up in her dungeon of solitary and armed faith, and along with herself, imprisoned her son."[37] His mother's anxiety passed from Madeline to Romain, and Catholicism became permeated with an aura of death. The young Romain, already sickly due to a bout with bronchial problems in his infancy, became fearful of his own death. In his autobiography he relates how he would repeatedly proclaim "I don't want to die!," to which his mother would tearfully answer: "The good God will not want to take you away from me, too!"[38] Her strict Jansenism further extended to Romain's daily duties. He recalls how "under the reproachful glance of my severe judge," his mother, he

> suffered from my moral weaknesses, my little fears, my white lies, my low ranking, as from a disease, almost as though they were dishonorable. It was at that time that the uneasy conscience of the little communicant kept him from sleeping, and made him run tearfully to the church in the morning, to confess an innocent sin, forgotten in the list of those that had been washed out the previous night, before taking communion.[39]

No wonder Rolland came to have a critical view of the confessional![40] He wondered about a God whom he thought abused his power. His "most lucid thought" was "that of the Gardener for his Lord. . . . In appealing to Kings, you make great fools of yourselves. You must never let them enter your lands."[41] And indeed Rolland never did. His encounters with the Christian God were, despite what Rolland says were his honest efforts to get in touch with him, "cold, ceremonious and distant."[42] These reflections clearly reveal a disillusionment with Catholicism and its tenets. In Rolland's inner world, it became associated with death and an overbearing, suffocating maternality, what he referred to as the "stifling" atmosphere of Clamency. Surely it is no accident that central elements of his later criticisms of Christianity revolved around issues of freedom and autonomy.

Equally determinative seeds of Rolland's antipathy towards organized religion were sown by his "Fathers": Emile and Edme. Here the impact of social forces and secularization begins to make itself felt. Most important in this regard is the fact that both paternal figures were notaries. In the French countryside, the *notaire* exercised important economic and legislative duties. Halfway between a public official and the head of a private enterprise, the notary collected taxes, was a financial advisor and a source for loans and savings, and exercised the duties of a lawyer, judge, and mayor. He was also seen as a friend and protector of families, at times a moral exemplar. Influence on the family was initiated at the contractual proceedings of marriage and often extended to death, where the notary served a priestly function by being witness to the last wishes of the dying. Thus although reflecting the rationalized, bureaucratic mechanisms of the state and the secular capitalism of private enterprise, the notary had a generic aura of the religious and moral. He was not, however, beholden to any institutionalized religious tradition.[43]

Romain's father Emile was a good notary who commanded love and respect from the residents of Clamency: "My father held a privileged position in his little city. He directed the municipal affairs along with his notary's practice, the most successful in the district . . . (it) was a balm to my childish heart."[44] More important, Emile was a good man, one who exemplified and practiced the virtues of practicality, enthusiasm, optimism, joy, and the natural ability to reconcile men. As Rolland tells us: "I think that, if he were shut up in a room with his worst enemy, after five minutes they would be heard laughing uproariously . . . he . . . got along with everybody, and was loved by all."[45] Surely one sees these very same traits in the son, reconciler of Germans and French, Europe and the Orient. But Emile was not a strong supporter of institutional religion. He was, in fact, a nonbeliever, but one who thought it good and necessary for children to be indoctrinated into the faith. In one sense, then, he condoned his wife's efforts to instill religion in the young Romain. Nevertheless, even the least taint of hypocrisy is never lost on a child. Emile's personal example relayed another, more powerful message: a break with the faith was admissible if done at an appropriate point in time.[46]

A similar scenario animated Rolland's relationship with his maternal grandfather Edme. Nearing sixty years of age, retired from his duties as notary and having just lost his wife, Edme joined his daughter and her family in Clamency. Rolland recalls him with great fondness. In Clamency, says Rolland, where "everyone worshipped my father," it was Edme who struck him as possessing "much more real tenderness."[47] A lover of Montaigne and passionate devourer of ideas ("What an unquenchable fire!"), Edme founded in Clamency a "Scientific and Artistic Society" complete with a library, museum, and bulletins penned at times by "grandson Romain."[48] Indeed, more than anything else, it was Edme's love for learning that impressed the young Romain. He recalls with great delight the hours he spent from the ages of seven to fifteen in Edme's house library reading classical authors: "Shakespeare, Schiller, Chateaubriand, Byron, Lamartine . . . Herodotus, Plutarch, Seneca and Cicero. I found them all . . . in his big library with its many windows."[49] The young Romain's infatuation with books was not lost on his parents, who later moved to Paris for the sole pursuit of furthering his education.

Edme's impact is particularly significant in light of the role at least two of these classical authors, Montaigne and Shakespeare, were to play during the course of his life and thought. P. J. Jouvre has called attention to Rolland's repeated remark that of the two tendencies he had, to believe and to know, the latter was the stronger. Jouvre attributes this to a school of thinkers who professed a "science of doubt." For Rolland, Shakespeare and Montaigne belonged to this school, as did Renan, Nietzsche, and Freud.[50] Indeed, recall Rolland's letter of May 3, 1931, where, in professing a moral sympathy with Freud in their mutual search for Truth "without desire, without hope, and without fear," he associated this intellectual pursuit with Montaigne's "Que Sais Je?" Again, in his *Compagnons de route*, a book that expresses Rolland's intellectual debts, a third of the text is allotted to Shakespeare, cited for his love of Truth, his endeavor to expose individual and social illusions through art, and his contribution to social progress.[51] This "school of doubt" found its counterpart in Rolland's love for the "free spirit," that man he defined as free from constraint, prejudice, and idols, "free from every dogma, whether of class, caste or nation; free from every religion. A soul which has the courage of the straight-forwardness to look with its own eyes, to love with its own heart, to judge with its own reason; to be no shadow but a man."[52] The school of doubt and the free spirit: these were the intellectual cornerstones of Rolland's later criticisms of the irrational, revealed basis of Christianity.

It seems evident, then, that two psychological modes of orientation, each fueled and shaped by events to come, were mediated to Rolland in his childhood. One was maternal, associated with both institutional religion and a private, idiosyncratic one. It was complicit in his ambivalency towards Catholicism, "need to believe," and eventual search for a maternal, mystical core to religion and psychology. The other, based in paternal sources, was associated with more secular pursuits and a humanistic culture. It was aligned with his "need to know," passion for the truth, and membership in a school of doubt and contributed to Rolland's distaste for the irrational, revealed elements of Catholicism. These developmental roots are reflected in what Rolland later referred to as that "strange duality of my nature." On the one hand a Reason "on which no argument of faith takes hold," on the other an "instinct of the heart" that "abandons itself to flights of prayer," flowing "from centuries of believing souls."[53] And, like many other modern religious intellectuals, Rolland spent much of his life working out an equitable compromise between the two. His unchurched mysticism and advocacy of a mystical psychoanalysis were the eventual result.

Interesting in this regard is Rolland's portrait of a third paternal influence, his great-grandfather Boniard. Rolland never met Boniard but learned about him later in life through journals and family papers. Yet in his autobiography Rolland devotes to him over twenty pages, four times that reserved for his father and twice that for Edme. The question is why. The answer, I think, is that Boniard, like Beethoven, Tolstoy, and others who were the subjects of Rolland's biographies or "Vies," was one more figure through which he could, as Rolland once said of Spinoza, "read himself through" to "discover himself." Certainly Rolland found much in Boniard that was directly relevant to his life. Like Madame Rolland, Boniard was deeply religious. Like Rolland's "fathers," he was a notary, intensely curious, a "great devourer of books" who took an active interest in science (particularly astronomy and math), and a supporter of freedom of thought and speech. Indeed, Boniard defied the reigning political and religious institutions of his day, taking on priests and even the Vatican when he felt a religious principle was compromised. What was important for Rolland was how Boniard reconciled the "strange duality" of his nature. Like Rolland, Boniard attempted to "bring about the fusion between science and the free religious spirit." In so doing, he affirmed two ideas Rolland claimed he made his own: "the unity of man with the divine, in the immediate consciousness of his own existence . . . (and) the coexistence of two principles: God and Nature."[54] It is here, then, in his sixth decade of life, that Rolland finally found that Father of his past in whose image he could truly say he was created.

## "Deicidal" Paris: Epiphanies and the Credo

In 1880, when Rolland was fourteen, his family moved to Paris for the express intent of furthering his education and future career as an academic. The move clearly affected Rolland on several levels. The culture of Clamency and its bucolic surroundings provided that intimate, small-town atmosphere within which Romain could play and dream. His family was a cohesive unit that, due to Emile's prominent social position, received respect and even adulation from the townsfolk. Intellectually, Rolland grew in the confidence brought him by being at the top of his class. Finally, although he was unable to fully idealize and internalize Catholic tenets, the church, supplemented by Romain's bond with Nature, provided a good enough cultural container to house a nourishing maternal presence.

Paris was an altogether different story. The urban sprawl was anathema to the young Romain, who was "disgusted" by the "unhealthy fermentation" of the big city.[55] In his *Mémoires* Rolland recalls sighing for the country of Clamency and describes his move from Clamency as the destruction of his "nest in the province."[56] "I was gasping for ten months of the year," he writes, and the trips back home were breaths of fresh air: "I will never be able to adequately convey what nature meant to my life during the years of troubled adolescence."[57] Indeed, the "shock of adolescence," Rolland tells us, "increased the upheaval of the exodus."[58] In school Rolland disappeared in the mass of more than sixty bright young Parisians: "there was no longer any question of coming out first: I had scarcely room to exist at all."[59] Perhaps most important, the secular atmosphere of fin-de-siècle Paris fueled his developmentally based predisposition to break with the church:

> God was dead. . . . A few months in Paris opened all the doors. Behind them there was nothing. The Master had left the house in ruins and semi-darkness. . . . I cannot tell you how completely the minds of all about me: masters and comrades, the whole moral atmosphere of Paris around 1880, was *deicidal*.[60]

The degree to which the secular, humanistic education Rolland was exposed to facilitated his disillusionment with the church can be aptly gauged by contrasting his reaction to a pivotal French intellectual, Ernst Renan, with that of his schoolmate, the ardent lifelong Catholic Paul Claudel. Like both Claudel and Rolland, Renan had been raised Catholic and excelled in his studies as a youth. Although trained in the best seminaries in Paris, he became disillusioned with Christian tenets due to his inability to square his faith with his critical reading of the Bible and what he felt was the intellectually restrictive atmosphere of the priesthood. Embarking on a secular career, Renan was schooled in a variety of fields—the sciences, history, philology—and became particularly attracted to the idealistic philosophy of Hegel. In his attempt to synthesize religion and science and as a substitute for his lost Catholicism, Renan wrote, at the age of twenty-five, his pivotal work *The Future of Science*, the central theme of which consisted in replacing the dogmatic and irrational basis on which Catholicism rested with the critical spirit of science. Humanity was seen as progressing towards perfection and science was its beacon. Religion was not discarded but its truths rendered void of their supernatural dimension and transformed through rational, critical inquiry. The will of God, for example, could be seen in terms of natural forces; a personal and anthropomorphic conception of God the Creator in terms of a rationally ordered universe that is ever "becoming." For Renan, "religion" became defined in terms of the progress of reason and science.

Renan was appointed administrator at the Collège de France, which neighbored Rolland's Ecole Normale, in 1884. Rolland took the opportunity to seek an audience with the "great man," and, on December 26, 1886, the two had lunch together. Renan spoke to him about the decline of religion, its concepts, and God and the inevitable march of science. Rolland asked him whether he thought the masses could tolerate the loss of God. Renan replied that although the process of transition would be painful, progress was insured and truth would win out. Rolland came away impressed, struck by the Stoic yet Epicurean Renan, a "pessimist–optimist," "un vrai homme, un homme vrai," a man who believed yet doubted.[61]

The lasting impact on Rolland of reading and meeting with Renan is apparent in Rolland's continuing to cite him, as late as 1936 in *Compagnons de route*, as a pivotal figure of his youth. Claudel, on the other hand, who was a "true believer" in Freud's sense of the term, was similarly exposed to Renan yet had an altogether different reaction. In his late work *Ma Conversion*, Claudel recalls his youth in Paris, his days at the Ecole Normale, and the fascination with Renan that gripped schoolmates and intellectuals. He deplored the influence of Renan on French culture for the singular reason that he thought he personified hostility to the church. Claudel was especially enraged at Renan's "detestable remarks" such as the one made in the preface to his *The Priest of Nemi:* "Who knows whether the truth is not sad?"[62] In contrast, Rolland remained an admirer of Renan precisely because of his critical intellect and stress on complete freedom of thought, reason, and science. The search for Truth was valued above and beyond personal happiness.

The net effect of Rolland's move to Paris can thus be conceptualized under the general rubric of loss: that of his childhood and schoolboy friends, of his social position, the warmth of Nature, and, of course, religion, for it was in Paris that Rolland formally renounced his membership in the church. One could say that under the duress of the breakdown of attachments to his common culture, Rolland was thrown back in on himself and his unconscious. Such loss led to a predictable life crisis:

> It was only too natural that in these first years of brutal transplantation to Paris that, besides coinciding with the shock of a breaking of the voice of a particularly disturbing puberty, the equilibrium of the child was, for one or two years, broken. Too many new elements, for the body and the mind. The monstrous life, in a single blow, assaulted, violated the adolescent and left him outraged and crazed. . . .[63] I was going through a terrible crisis of personality disintegration. . . . Everything eluded me, all security in life; the good comfortable social position upset; mental equilibrium unbalanced; confidence in study lost. . . . I was a mountain of confused weaknesses and strengths; of attacks that blindfolded me; of giddy spells that sapped my strength; of desires, aversions, of fever, of debility of the flesh and of the spirit.[64]

Such a state, Rolland continues, predisposed him "to mystic agitations." Over the course of several years he was privy to, as he tells us, "several violent illuminations (I described three of them under the title 'The Three Illuminations' in my *Journey Within*). It was the only recourse. Fire shoots out. From two abysses of life: Nature and Music."[65] Along with his mystical experiences came a period of reading about and reflecting on the thought of such notable figures as Renan, Tolstoy, and Spinoza. Rolland's assimilation of the thought of these and other figures found expression in his *Credo quia verum.* The *Credo,* then, was the product of a long period of mourning that displays loss, deidealization, regression, and introspective probes. It was Rolland's first definitive creative response to the loss of his Catholicism. Truth for Rolland became based not on revealed scripture or on naive belief but on immediate mystical experience and introspective insight filtered through the tests of reason.

It is here that we arrive at the first real opportunity for a fresh psychoanalytic accounting of Rolland's mysticism. Generally speaking, proponents of the classic psychoanalytic approach would start by calling attention to Rolland's experience of loss. His mystical experiences would be seen as regressive and defensive, if not pathological, revealing defects in self-structure and the capacity for reality testing and adjustment. For example, Masson would see Rolland's mystical experiences as a manic denial of the abandoning mother. Depression, not joy and elation, is the unstated psychological reality. Although Masson never recognizes the existence of Rolland's *Credo*, he would undoubtedly see in it elements of depersonalization, derealization, aggressive annihilation fantasies, and other pathological, narcissistic phenomena.[66] David Fisher, following in the spirit of Masson, has this to say about Rolland's mysticism:

> I would like to extend the Freudian interpretation of the oceanic sensation by arguing that . . . it is actually a reaction-formation. That is to say, the limitless narcissism of the oceanic conceals or counters a feeling of universal hatred for humanity.
>
> I think that individuals who proclaim love for humanity secretly have powerful feelings of aggression and contempt for humanity, that feelings of eternity actively spring from unbounded feelings of repressed rage, of unsatisfied oral cravings. Rolland's oceanism conceals a strong sadistic impulse, a monumental fury against humanity, a drive to destroy civilization. . . . The oceanic sensation comforted Rolland by wiping out his recurring feelings of despair and loss of direction; monumental feelings of connection opposed his feelings of unconnectedness. The reactions took the form of omnipotence, grandiosity, optimism. . . . To defend himself against his own self-punishing conscience, Rolland emerged as a public man of virtue, self-sacrifice, and penance. . . . For Rolland, then, and by implication for all humanistic mystics, total love of humanity may be unconsciously fused with the impulse to annihilate humanity totally.[67]

Given the complex nature of the psyche, the possibility of overdetermination, and the diversity of unconscious impulses and motives, one can assume that Rolland's mysticism not only engaged archaic unconscious elements and early developmental issues but also served multiple functions, including defensive ones. To be sure, in light of Rolland's own testimony with regard to Clamency and the impact of Parisian culture, one can hardly dissociate the abstract formula "*Deus sive natura*" from pre-Oedipal elements. So too can one can spy elements of depersonalization and derealization in Rolland's identification of individuality with the ultimately illusory "role" an "actor" plays. Again, it would be unreasonable to altogether doubt a developmental contribution to his later humanitarian efforts, although I would be more inclined to link it to the feelings of guilt and need for reparation that must have surrounded the loss of his sister Madeline.

Yet interpretations of Rolland from Freud onward suffer from a serious misunderstanding of the complex nature of his mysticism. Our reconstruction of the latter does not lend support to the view that Rolland was psychotic or that his mysticism evinced a retreat from reality. On the contrary, his mystical experiences and writing of the *Credo* were ultimately adaptive, promoting self-cohesion and the passionate pursuit of goals. Recall his admonition that it would be a mistake to think that in the embrace of Nature he was a "mere passive voluptuary," for the "lesson" he learned was "not forgetfulness of the world and action. It was a lesson of energy and combat."[68] Again, one cannot divorce his recourse to mystical views of self and Reality, of being a actor in a divine play, from his overall parameters for living: the dictum to "live irony" and his call for a passionate life filled with charity. These reveal not pathology but, at the very least, the kind of typical internal struggles one would expect of an adolescent in search of an ideology.

Also relevant in this context is the fact that, in stark contrast to the deceased tradition-bound mystics who are usually the object of psychoanalytic studies of mysticism, Rolland understood and responded to an arch proponent of the classical approach, Ferdinand Morel. Although Rolland was hardly a sophisticated clinician, it would be unjust to accuse him of a lack of familiarity or active hostility toward psychoanalytic modes of investigation.[69] Here Masson's opinion, based on the erroneous assumption that Rolland never read Morel, that the latter's *Essai sur l'introversion mystique* was "too rich in psychological insight" to have "appealed to Rolland," does not give him due credit.[70] Although clearly critical of Morel, Rolland referred to it as "one of the best works devoted to this subject," granting his views credence in the case of certain mystics and offering just responses in others. Notably, Rolland guised his responses in psychoanalytic terminology, citing works by clinicians like Baudouin in his efforts to promote a progressive view of mysticism.

This brings us to what I have referred to as the adaptive school. Of the numerous studies during the sixties that championed this approach, Paul Horton's study of the mystical experiences of an adolescent girl is particularly suggestive in its use of Winnicott's notion of a "transitional object"—a concept wholly suitable for use in illustrating an adaptive reading of Rolland's mysticism.[71] Winnicott used the concept of a transitional object to explain what happens in the inner world of the infant while it begins to separate from the mother and faces the demands of external reality. The clinical fact that intrigued Winnicott was the emergence in the child's life of an object, such as a blanket or stuffed animal, to which the child developed an intense bond and from which it received nurturance. Winnicott hypothesized that transitional objects symbolized the absent mother and afforded the child an opportunity to creatively master external reality. The little boy's relationship with the alien in the movie *E.T.*, the tiger in the comic strip "Calvin and Hobbes," and Linus's attachment to his blanket in the comic strip "Peanuts" are all cultural examples and admissions of the power of transitional objects. The capacity and inner space denoted by the existence of transitional objects also led Winnicott to modify the sociological and epistemological implications of classical metapsychology. Sociologically, the transitional object denotes the child's first use of a symbol. It thus points to an area of experience to which both inner psychological and outer cultural reality contribute. Hobbes, insofar as he is an object of play given to, and not created by, Calvin, is constituted by culture. Yet Calvin also creates Hobbes, "breathes" life into him and invests him with meaning in an attempt to facilitate the transition from mother to reality. These observations led Winnicott to posit a "third" area of experiencing beyond Freud's simple opposition between inner–outer reality and the pleasure–reality principles that he refers to as the "substance of illusion." This area or capacity is illumined by the transitional object in infancy, play in childhood, and the arts, religion, and science in adulthood. "Illusion" is thus never equated with "delusion" or wish fulfillment, for it points to the necessary psychological conditions of man's being-in-the-world.[72]

No one has modified Winnicott's clinical formulations for application to religious phenomena more successfully than AnaMaria Rizzuto. In contrast to Freud, who saw religion as an "illusion" based on childish wishes, Rizzuto stresses the adaptive benefits of religion by envisaging the components of a religious worldview as a transitional object.[73] What she dubs the "God-Representation" is a "special" transitional object insofar as it is formed not from "plushy fabrics" but "representational materials" that find their source in the primary objects of infancy and childhood. The God-Representation is a representational collage, a "work of art" overdetermined on a variety of levels, being constructed from extant cultural materials, the full spectrum of developmental phases and abstract ideational components. Culture mediates the components of religion through family, church, and school. Clinical studies show that the God-Representation can be composed of paternal and maternal elements and reflect pre-Oedipal as well as Oedipal developmental configurations. Further, the God-Representation evolves throughout the life-cycle and is able to supersede the infantile past through the reworking of its representational elements. Crucial to this task is the integration of the "conceptual" aspects of the God-Representation, fabricated at the level of secondary-process thought, and the deeper, developmentally and interpersonally based "images" of God. A dialectical process between the two is posited as taking place through significant experiences, those idealized mentor figures who elicit transference, and the integrative psychical work of self-scrutiny and reflection. Through such auspices a process akin to the analytic session takes place, resulting in the integration and transformation of conceptual and image-based aspects of the God-Representation.[74]

Applied to Rolland, this formulation allows us to see Rolland's *Credo* as a transitional document. The initial components of Rolland's God-Representation consisted of the Catholic worldview mediated to him by culture and family. One can also discern rudiments of a Nature God here, although during his days in Clamency it was far from being articulated in any sophisticated way at the conceptual level. The young Romain's total rejection of Catholicism in Paris indicates that his God-Representation was no longer capable of engaging, monitoring, or nourishing his unconscious and hence unable to serve the adaptive task of meeting the exigencies of life. Given his life-stage, one could say that Rolland was undergoing an "identity crisis." In the throes of deidealization and loss, unconscious contents were unleashed, leading to Rolland's mystical experiences. In effect, Rolland had a series of conversion experiences that can be conceptualized as an adaptive, regressive reactivation of archaic structures of his personality. The sense of ineffability, affective-toned noesis, oneness, unity, and merger all indicate that what was derepressed was a maternal, pre-Oedipal parental representation. Rolland's introduction to Spinoza was crucial in that it enabled him to integrate the deeply buried "image" component of his God-Representation with an acceptable conceptual counterpart. Spinoza's formula *Deus sive Natura* suggests that it was Rolland's association of his mother with Nature that found expression. Despite its wealth of maternal ideation and imagery, Catholicism was no longer able to engage the deeper narcissistic structures of his personality. Rather, the less revealed, more rational philosophy of Spinoza, similarly imbued with a maternal presence, took its place.

Spinoza, of course, was but one figure who affected Rolland during this pivotal period in his life. We have seen how others, such as Leibnitz, Renan, Tolstoy, and the pre-Socratics were similarly complicit in the development of Rolland's *Credo*. What occurred during the years 1886–1888 was the tearing down and remolding of a wealth of disparate philosophies into an idiosyncratic whole. This process was composed of not only significant mystical experiences, self-scrutiny and reflection, but also the mediating presence of significant others. Renan is a case in point, as is Tolstoy, whom Rolland idealized, engaged in a long correspondence, and later cited as a pivotal influence of his youth, and whose ideas on an "oceanic" being were, like Spinoza, integrated into the *Credo*.[75] Renan and Tolstoy, then, acted as mentor figures who elicited enough transference to have a profound effect on mediating and helping Romain integrate the "image" and "conceptual" components of his evolving God-Representation. In this regard it is hard not to spy psychological continuity with Edme. In point of fact, in the 1880s both Renan and Tolstoy were old enough to be Rolland's grandfather. Indeed, it is hardly a coincidence that Rolland was to characterize Renan as a member of the "school of doubt" and Tolstoy a paradigmatic example of the "free spirit."

The *Credo* also reflects the impact of a pluralistic culture on the mourning process. Envisaged as a God-Representation, the *Credo* denotes that transitional space where inner psychological reality and outer cultural reality meet and merge. Loss due to the change in cultures (from Clamency to Paris) led to deidealization, repudiation of tradition, and a long process of mourning which eventuated in a creative response. And, as one might expect, the *Credo*, as a creative response to the definitive and irrevocable loss of Rolland's Catholicism, shows both continuities and discontinuities with his Christian past. On the one hand, Rolland firmly rejected the irrational, revealed element of Catholicism. Knowledge was based on the immediacy of experience and introspection and not on belief and assent to religious propositions. In this context one might note that the title of Rolland's work, *Credo quia verum*, literally "I believe because it is true," referring directly to his mystical experiences, must have been intended to stand in direct opposition to Tertullian's championing of proposition-based religiosity in his famous dictum *Credo quia absurdum*. On the other hand, the strong stress on charity and a maternal presence, firmly internalized through tradition and the Mother, was maintained through the auspices of an unchurched mysticism. The net result was the emergence of a God-Representation Rolland could live with: "Suffice it to say that to . . . (the Credo) I owe a new tranquillity . . . it was so much my own. . . . [I]t supplied me with a sufficient foundation, or at any rate a solid-enough platform on which to wait, while, comforted as to my doubts, I began to construct my life—my true creative life—my passions and my works."[76]

Certainly Rolland gives evidence that he would agree with much of what an adaptive reading has to offer. For example, recalling our discussion in chapter 3, one could link his admission that the maternal symbols used by mystics "adds weight" to Morel's "assumption" that mystical experience expresses various forms of the mother–infant dyadic relationship to his promotion of Baudouin's adaptive view of regression.[77] On the other hand, as we have seen, Rolland also insisted on a more archaic level of the unconscious which he correlated with the mystical faculty of intuition. Rolland claimed that "unmitigated" mystical intuition was radically different from the "confused pre-intuition of a child."[78] Over against Kant, Rolland thought intuition enabled the mystic to go beyond the a priori conditions of the mind in order to come into contact with that energetic Unity from which all minds issue.[79] In this Rolland was following in the footsteps of a long mystical tradition. Although religious traditions have conceptualized mystical faculties and the content of the knowledge they intuit in different ways, Rolland's general epistemological point, as well as his use of the latter to qualify a purely developmental perspective, is representative of the mystic position. The question is what resources within the psychoanalytic tradition exist to promote dialogue with Rolland's views. For this we will have to turn to the transformative school.

Initial help comes, surprisingly enough, from Freud. In an understandably neglected text in his corpus that lies outside his correspondence with Rolland, Freud gives evidence of accepting Rolland's views on archaic modes of knowing. In attempting to account for empirical riddles such as how "common purpose comes about in the great insect communities" and what he eventually came to accept as the very real phenomenon of "thought-transference" in dreams, Freud postulates that there exists a dimension of the unconscious, activated during states of altered consciousness such as sleep and the frenzied excitement created by mobs, that allows for a direct transference of psychical content. He further speculated that

> One is led to a suspicion that this is the original, archaic method of communication between individuals and that in the course of phylogenetic evolution it has been replaced by the better method of giving information with the help of signals which are picked up by the sense organs. But the older method might have persisted in the background and still be able to put itself into effect under certain conditions.[80]

This allows for a new understanding of "intuition" that goes beyond Freud's previous formulations. It is a metapsychological construct that legitimates direct psychic contact between minds, a form of knowing which, because it bypasses the senses and those linguistic-symbolic modes of communication fostered through culture, can be described as an unmediated immediacy.

The self psychologist Heinz Kohut, using this very passage from Freud as a starting point for his own observations, refers to a mode of knowing, primary empathy, which he thought had precursors in both the history of the race and the pre-Oedipal period. For Kohut, empathy is the essential mode of observation through which we obtain access to the complex psychological configurations in another's mind. This mode is innate but increasingly overlaid by other, nonempathic modes of cognition during the course of development. It can thus be lost but also regained under certain conditions, for example, in addition to the ones cited by Freud above, the "intentional curbing of the usual cognitive processes of the ego (such as is brought about in the analytic situation)."[81] It can also be cultivated to a point where, as Kakar reminds us in the case of the mystics, the "awareness of 'I' in a composite self" is expanded so that one "also has a similar feeling of 'I' in the selves of others, an empathy amplified to the point of complete identification."[82] One's own psychological configurations are left in abeyance and altered as one literally becomes the other. In other words, these theorists posit archaic modes of cognition that, although innate, uncultivated, and overlaid by other functions, are capable, under special conditions, of being reactivated and developed. One could further speculate, as did Rolland, that culture and the socialization process, particularly in a capitalistic culture dominated by a work ethic, have a good deal to do with whether such faculties become valued or not and hence cultivated or dismissed.

The furthest development along this avenue of thought is found in the work of Arthur Deikman. Relying on empirical data and utilizing the formulations of psychoanalytic ego psychology, specifically the concept of deautomatization (initially coined by Hartmann and elaborated by Gill and Brenman to account for the undoing of ego functions during hypnosis), Deikman theorized about the nature of the altered state induced through meditation.[83] Deautomatization holds that as development proceeds our perceptual, motor, and behavioral systems undergo a slow process of automatization until they operate on a "second-nature" or "automatic" level. For example, walking, talking, perceptual focusing, audio processing, and the like are all functions that adults take for granted and use with facility in a way infants do not. As one grows up, one invests less attentional energy on such functions, thus allowing for the allocation of energy saved to new and more complex tasks, such as abstract reasoning. The drawback of the process of automatization, according to Deikman, is that certain archaic modes of perceiving and relating to the world may be left in a nascent state or even abandoned in favor of an environment and socialization process that demands the cultivation of abstract reason. The techniques utilized in some forms of meditation "deautomatize" cognitive-perceptual processes, restoring and even cultivating archaic modes of apprehending the world and relating to others. One of these archaic modes of relating to the world, thinks Deikman, may well explain some mystic assertions that there exists an underlying unity between man and nature:

> Logically, there is also the possibility that the perception of unity does correctly evaluate the external world. Studies . . . suggest that development from infancy to adulthood is accompanied by an organization of the perceptual and cognitive world that has as its price the selection of some stimuli and stimulus qualities to the exclusion of others. If the automatization underlying that organization is reversed, or temporarily suspended, aspects of reality that were formerly unavailable might then enter awareness. Unity may in fact be a property of the real world that be-

comes perceptible via the technique of meditation and renunciation, or under special conditions, as yet unknown, that create the spontaneous, brief mystic experiences of untrained persons.[84]

The avenue of metapsychological reasoning promoted by Freud, Kohut, and Deikman can be brought to bear on Rolland's constructive criticisms of hierarchical views of the mind as they informed Morel's analysis of "unmitigated" introversion. As we saw in chapter 3, Rolland, like Freud and Kohut above, fully acknowledged the phylogenetic evolution of psychological functions during the course of the history of the race. And, again like these authors, he was willing to follow Janet and others in characterizing the mode of knowing associated with mysticism as primary and archaic. What he found troubling was psychology's ignorance and devaluation of these archaic layers of the unconscious and its modes of knowing—a value judgment he thought bound up with the industrial, capitalistic ethos of Europe. What the texts cited above do is provide metapsychological justification for Rolland's claims. In effect, one could entertain the possibility that in his youth Rolland was privy on several occasions to a spontaneous deautomatization that created the psychical conditions necessary for the cultivation of empathic states, identification with the other, and a unitive consciousness—one he later conceptualized as pointing to a deeper layer of the unconscious and the existence of mystical intuition.

The above metapsychological formulations cannot buttress religious, ontological claims nor do the epistemological work of ascertaining the precise nature of intuitive faculties. However, they do create the basis for dialogue between psychology (the *Credo* as a transitional document) and studies on mystical epistemology. It suggests the possibility that deautomatization or deconditioned modes of consciousness and the operation of intuitive faculties and deep empathic states are linked, and that the latter, once awakened and cultivated, grant one access to new modes of awareness.[85] If granted this (and here let me be clear: this is an "if" in need of further epistemological justification), one can then speak of a properly mystical level of the *Credo*, one which denotes a specifically mystical form of subjectivity that requires a corresponding hermeneutical strategy. When Rolland speaks of the ethic implicit in Spinoza's *Deus sive natura* ("Unite with others and try to unite them one to another") and its complicity in his later efforts to reconcile mankind, it reflects the operation of an empathy bordering on complete identification with the other—and the deautomatized states of consciousness operative in the mystical mergings of his youth. It was this kind of mystical insight and not, as the received view would have it, the primitive pre-Oedipal memory of unity or, as Fisher would have it, a massive reaction formation, that formed the primary experiential basis—albeit one given further structure and direction through the writing of the *Credo*—for the subsequent cultivation of that moral disposition and the issue of those acts which moved Freud to call Rolland "the apostle of love for mankind."

At the same time, being privy to such deep insight hardly renders moot the need to analyze the complicity of developmental issues in mystical experience or mystical process. Granting primacy to a mystical reading of the *Credo* does not abrogate or diminish the contributions of the classic and adaptive schools. In the case of Rolland, it does call for their analyses to be relativized with respect to those offered by the transformational school. The *Credo* can still be conceived of as a transitional document and overdetermined "work of art" — only one which now exhibits the dialectic between a regressive engagement with both developmental and mystical levels of consciousness and the progressive movement of such levels into symbolic forms. In turn, such forms signify psychical discontents and their integration; they point transparently to while participating in a mystical psychical reality.

## From Unchurched Mysticism to a Mystical Psychoanalysis

The most significant existential fact of Rolland's mature mysticism was the emergence of the oceanic feeling. In emphasizing the process nature of this aspect of his mysticism, Rolland posited a teleological dimension to his mystical experiences and a dialectical, psychological relation between them and the statelike oceanic feeling. Certainly Rolland's emphasis on the teleological dimension of mystical experiences has precedents in mystics of all traditions. Plato, for example, speaks of the "open sea of beauty" and the "wondrous vision which is the very soul of . . . beauty" which, once attained, casts a pall on the pursuit of fame, fortune, and sex and inspires a longing for the continued contemplation of that "eternal oneness."[86] Again, St. Augustine, after his visions at Milan and Ostia, speaks of the feeling of longing after being swept away from "That Which Is" due to earthly attachment.[87] So too does St. Teresa, in Mansion 5 of *The Interior Castle,* in describing her feelings of longing after transient, mystical feelings of unity, develop the metaphor of a butterfly that flutters about, seeking the rest of the statelike mystical marriage attained in Mansion 7. Of course, the descriptions of mystic visions and states in these and numerous other texts differ, as do the concepts used to describe the process of integration and enjoyment of such insight. Where they concur with Rolland is in the more general point that insists on the extraordinary nature of mystical experience and the imperative contained therein to undertake the hard psychical work necessary to realign one's inner life accordingly.[88]

Rolland's own efforts to conceptualize mystical process took a psychological turn — one which reflected a new creative response to a new phase of disillusionment, this time with religious and political leaders during the Great War. In *Above the Battle,* Rolland expressed his pain and outrage at the hypocrisy, baseness, and mendacity he saw at work in the church and religious intellectuals: "The love of God and the love of mankind have been invoked in order to burn, kill and pillage."[89] Rolland was disgusted by a Pope who could "hurl thunderbolts" at the "inoffensive priests who believed in the noble chimera of modernism" yet remain silent at the murderous acts of "criminal" political rulers.[90] *Liluli* directed enough bitterness and satire towards Christianity that one reviewer, J. R. Bloch, was moved to comment that it reflected "the spasm that seizes a man in the face of the ruins of his faith."[91] Indeed, the degree of Rolland's disillusionment can be gauged by a singular entry in his *Journal des an-*

*nées de guerre:* "Christians of this war have distanced me from Christianity forever."[92] As we have seen, it was this disillusionment which led him back to his *Credo,* to the East and mysticism in general, and to the promotion of a mystical psychoanalysis characterized as the universal science–religion of the future. The resulting reconceptualization of mysticism assimilated his lifelong stress on maternal inclusiveness and an ethic of love and unity. At the same time, metaphysics was repudiated and replaced by metapsychology. Spinoza gave way to a "universal science–religion." Mysticism was recast and evaluated in terms of developmental theory and the unconscious. A new chapter in the mourning process had begun.

In explaining the existential process involved in Rolland's attempt to actualize the teleological imperative contained in his mystical experiences, the classic and adaptive schools would seek its etiology in the pre-Oedipal. Generally put, the explanations would posit variations on a central theme: that the transient glimpse of the divine, explained in terms of the defensive or adaptive regression to the memory of maternal bliss, gives rise to the nostalgic longing for continued Presence. Drawing on our survey in the last chapter, I would say that Rolland's view of mystical process has more affinities with the psychology of Jung and Lacan than with that championed by the classic or adaptive school. However, it is in the transformative elements in the psychology of another theorist, Heinz Kohut, where one finds the most striking affinities with Rolland's mature mysticism. In his essays and books, Kohut gives no evidence, aside from the familiarity with *Civilization and Its Discontents* that he shared with all analysts, of acquaintance with the nuances of Rolland's mysticism. Again, along with Freud and many analysts, he interpreted the "oceanic feeling" as the fleeting regression to the stage of primary narcissism. At the same time, Kohut posited a related phenomenon, "cosmic narcissism," as the religio-ethical goal of his psychology. Cosmic narcissism is seen as a developmentally mature attainment indicative of ethical and existential achievement beyond the results of a successful analysis (the integration of archaic elements of grandiosity and the idealized parent imago into a cohesive self). It is characterized by its statelike character:

> The achievement . . . of a shift of the narcissistic cathexis from the self to a concept of participation in a supraindividual and timeless existence . . . (lies) in contrast to the oceanic feeling . . . which is experienced passively (and usually fleetingly). . . . The genuine shift toward a cosmic narcissism is the enduring, creative result of the steadfast activities of the autonomous ego, and only very few are able to attain it. . . .[93] I believe that this rare feat rests, not simply on a victory of autonomous reason and supreme objectivity over the claims of narcissism, but on the creation of a higher form of narcissism . . . a cosmic narcissism which has transcended the bounds of the individual.[94]

Kohut agreed that the mother–child relation genetically predetermined cosmic narcissism. However, he insisted that the latter was much more than the preservation of the pre-Oedipal feeling of unity. It signified the denouement of an existential process that consisted in a gradual decathexis of the individual self to participation in "supraindividual ideals and the world with which one identifies."[95] One lived *sub specie aeternitas* without elation or anxiety, bathed in a continual communion with a contentless and supraordinate Self.[96] This process of decathexis of the self cannot be branded as defensive. On the contrary, it demands not only engagement with and the transformation of archaic narcissistic structures into empathy, humor, wisdom, and creativity but also the acknowledgment and successful navigation of life's inevitable vicissitudes and disappointments—particularly the seemingly insurmountable fact of its transiency. In a general sense, this begins to sound very much like the process of "disenchantment," of the gradual detachment from maya which Rolland spoke of to Hesse and which he embodied in the figure of Annette. Through mystical experience, introspection, renunciation, and what Rolland called the "blows of life," one gradually decathects the self, displacing the locus of identity from self to a Self conceived of as supraordinate but contentless. Most important, this shift, signified by the presence of the oceanic feeling, also indicates the type of ethical and existential achievement stressed by Kohut.

If Kohut's citation of *Civilization and Its Discontents* and the oceanic feeling without foreknowledge of Rolland's mysticism is more than a striking coincidence, so too is it of interest to note what particular person or group of people he had in mind as exemplifying nonpathological forms of mysticism. Although in the above cited paper Kohut does not specify any singular individual, in his essay "On Leadership" he points to Dag Hammarskjöld, the former secretary-general of the United Nations, as a mystic worthy of emulation. Kohut seemed to idealize Hammarskjöld much as Freud did Rolland. Indeed, there exist similarities between the two men. Both were respected moral leaders who advocated and fought for principles upon which international peace, justice, and cooperation could be maintained. Kohut notes that Hammarskjöld spoke of a personal, mystical religion that made him an instance of someone who had attained the kind of transformation of narcissism indicative of mature mysticism. In so doing, Kohut made some observations on the relation between psychology and religion that are curiously reminiscent of Rolland's social agenda:

The survival of Western man, and perhaps of mankind altogether, will in all likelihood be neither safeguarded by "the voice of the intellect" alone, that great utopian hope of the Enlightenment and Rationalism of the 18th and 19th centuries; nor will it be secured through the influence of the teachings of the orthodox religions. Will a new religion arise which is capable of fortifying man's love for its old and new ideals? The transformation of narcissism into the spirit of religiosity, i.e., the tradition-bound communal amalgamation of nonrational elements to man's system of values, has often been capable of inspiring people to the heroic deeds on which at crucial junctures survival always depends. Could it be that a new, rational religion might arise, an as yet uncreated system of mystical rationality which could take the place of the religions of the past? Undoubtedly such a religion would initially have no appeal for the masses, but new religions are at first probably always only for the few (or even only for one?) who, thus inspired, are subsequently able to inspire others. There are, even in our time, instances of heroic men of constructive political action who have achieved a transformation of their narcissism into a contentless, inspiring personal religion. Is this the type which humanity will have to produce in greater numbers in order to survive? Dag Hammarskjöld . . . an example of this type, describes his contentless mysticism in the following words: "Faith is a state of mind and of the soul . . . the language of religion is (only) a set of formulas which register a basic religious experience."[97]

Unfortunately, Kohut's formulations on the religio-ethical goal of his psychology remained cursory. Most unfortunate is his failure to add conceptual sophistication to the relation between mystical experience and the achievement of cosmic narcissism. If Rolland and other mystics are taken at face value, such experiences are an indispensable prerequisite to arriving at the oceanic feeling. From the mystic's perspective, Freud's admission to Rolland that the oceanic feeling was not a feature of his inner world cannot be adequately accounted for by, as Freud would have it, the particular circumstances of his mental life that precluded the "preservation" of the primary narcissistic feeling of unity. On the contrary, if one takes seriously the ethical and therapeutic dimensions of Annette's (Rolland's) continuing process of disillusionment and mourning, Freud's perplexity signifies his inability to "breakthrough" to this deeper level of mystical subjectivity and "work it through" to the statelike oceanic feeling.

The extent to which the models used in explaining Rolland's mysticism can be fruitfully applied to other types of mysticism remains to be seen. Although the accumulation of case histories may well show that a radical conception of detachment or disillusionment is a universal aspect of mystical process, it is safe to say that the extraordinary diversity of mystical states and experiences extant in mystical traditions will require the creation of as yet unforeseeable advances in metapsychology. What one can unequivocally state is that in an age of postmodern confusion, psychological modes of thought, and the meeting of diverse cultures and religions, Rolland's stress on a mystical psychoanalysis, based on the felt inner certainty of interdependence, deep empathy, tolerance, and inclusion, is pregnant with potential.

# *Conclusion*

A scant year after Freud's death, W. H. Auden, in his "In Memory of Sigmund Freud," poetically expressed the impact of Freud on Western culture: "To us he is no more a person / Now, but a whole climate of opinion / Under whom we conduct our differing lives." Certainly Freud initiated a new form of self-reflection, subjectivity, and sociality that has both real continuities and significant differences with its religious counterparts. Safely behind the double doors of the psychoanalytic therapeutic encounter, one inhabits a liminal space which grants one access to the unconscious, leading to a qualitatively distinct self-relating activity. How that activity has altered the democratic West has been conceptualized and evaluated in diverse ways. Regardless of one's take on Freud, one must not forget that other figures deserve to be seen alongside him as, in Peter Homans's felicitous use of the phrase, "culture-makers": those originative psychologists and intellectuals who were complicit in helping to further psychological modes of thinking about self, culture, and society.[1] Of Freud's associates, Carl Jung, Otto Rank, and Alfred Adler readily come to mind. There was something about the culture of that time that led to a specific kind of mourning which fostered introspective probes and psychological analyses.

A good deal of this form of psychological creativity has been spent in analyzing as well as recreating religion. This study has sought to contribute to this specifically psychological tradition of "culture-analyzing" and "culture-making" by focusing on the correspondence between two men, Freud and Rolland, and their ruminations on psychology, culture, and mysticism. In so doing, we have achieved closure on some conversations and initiated the beginnings of others.

Most comprehensive in this regard has been our attempt to fill a gaping lacuna in the origins and development of the psychoanalytic study of mysticism.

Most studies on psychoanalysis and religion have traditionally, and quite justifiably, centered on Freud's engagement with Western religions and correspondences with men like Oskar Pfister and Ludwig Binswanger, now understood as being the figures behind the interlocutors of *The Future of an Illusion*. Freud's attempt to create a social space for a secular cure of souls gave rise to an equally fecund religious response. The emergence of pastoral care and the collusion between theology, ethics, and other extant psychologies joined in the effort to successfully articulate deep forms of the religious life. In contrast, this study, by analyzing the Freud–Rolland correspondence, has highlighted another kind of response to Freud's cultural works. In so doing we have noted the importance of other, neglected cultural texts and their role in revealing Freud's involvement with the East and of a different arena of dialogue and debates over a specifically mystical form of religious subjectivity. And, just as *the psychology–theology dialogue* of the 50s and 60s reflected the intellectual and social hegemony of a Protestant culture, the contemporary interest in mysticism and spirituality signifies the emergence of a genuinely pluralistic culture and a new social base, the members of which have embarked upon fresh, creative ways of articulating mystical subjectivity.

In furthering this endeavor, our analysis has contributed to a deeper understanding of those two aspects of the field of religion and psychological studies that I have referred to as *the psychology-comparativist dialogue* and psychology *as* a religion. With regard to the latter, we have seen that Freud's attempt to replace traditional forms of institutional religion with his secular cure of souls was countered by Rolland's equally adamant effort to enlist him in the creation of a social space for a distinctly religious psychology, a "mystical psychoanalysis." This psychology housed a form of perennialism that viewed mystical experience as innate potential, lying deep within a religious unconscious, waiting to be accessed. Moreover, it was motivated in large part by Rolland's own mystical experiences—experiences that gave him the utter certainty that here was a dimension of religion worth resurrecting and defending. Herein lies an important clinical point, for Freud's only existential apprehension of mysticism came in his disappointing experience of derealization on the Acropolis. On a personal and professional level (one must not forget Freud's patients were neurotics and psychotics) he remained clueless as to what the deeper meaning of mysticism might be.

While Freud remained undeterred, many psychologists of Rolland's generation were sympathetic to his agenda. Many were so as a result of their own mystical apprehensions. As we have seen, other researchers writing in the formative period of the field of religion and psychological studies like Jung, R. M. Bucke, and James had mystical experiences as a result of drugs (James), illness and near-death episodes (Jung), and a spontaneous happening (Bucke). Interesting enough, some of the avenues through which many of the early psychologists came to have mystical experiences have now become the clinical base for the emergence of an organized series of positive analyses of mysticism. Stanislav Grof, Robert Ornstein, Ralph Hood, Claudio Naranjo, and Michael Murphy are but a few of the recent many who have formulated new psychological theories promoting the value of mysticism as a result of clinical studies of meditation, drug research, and empirical analyses of spontaneous mystical experiences. Many of these theorists also share Rolland's penchant for perennialism, his technological construal of mysticism, and the institutionalization of an unchurched mystical psychology. Ken Wilber's ready use of the term "psychologia perennis" and Abraham Maslow's postulation of a core-transcendent experience demonstrate these tendencies, as does the attempt by some psychologists to translate the unarticulated psychological meaning of all tradition-bound mysticisms into the more progressive, enlightened language of modern, transpersonal metapsychology. And, following Bucke, there are modern attempts to link the institutionalization and dissemination of psychological techniques with evolutionary theory—one that sees the unfolding of man's psycho-mystical potential as the meaning of individual and collective history. Saints and avatars are but forerunners of the new species-consciousness now emerging. Once institutionalized and disseminated, psychological techniques can but help the process along.

An analysis and evaluation of the diverse figures, theories, and socio-historical context complicit in the origins and development of psychology *as* a religion would constitute an important chapter in religion and psychological studies. This study has contributed to such an enterprise by offering an analysis of Rolland's efforts to promote a religious psychology and a few general common characteristics, tendencies, and socio-historical coordinates applicable to Rolland, as well as others sharing his agenda, which may, if but in a preliminary manner, serve to help delineate the parameters of a twentieth-century form of psycho-mystical religiosity. A more precise mapping of the trajectory of this unchurched western form of psychological mysticism, as well as an evaluation of its central tenets and cultural impact, must be left for another time.

This brings us to a closely related rubric within religion and psychological studies we have touched on: *the psychology-comparativist dialogue.* In unearthing the problems inherent in Rolland's perennialism, we have advocated viewing mysticism in terms of a process constructivism. In providing a historical overview of psychoanalytic studies of mysticism and mystics, we have advocated the judicious, dialogical use of classic, adaptive, and transformative models in analyzing mystical subjectivity. Such a dialogue will inevitably change the self-understanding of mystical traditions. The profundity embodied in mystic writings must be tempered by the fact that they have not developed a map of how unconscious and early developmental factors determine behavior. Some mystics, like Sri Aurobindo, find psychoanalysis "inconsiderate, awkward, and rudimentary," deeming its province as separate from that of mysticism: "one cannot discover the meaning of the lotus by analyzing the secrets of the mud in which is grows."[2] But one need only to point to episodes of madness in someone like Ramakrishna (a fact Ramakrishna himself admitted to) as well as similar instances, including documented cases of power abuse, sexual and otherwise, recently displayed by tradition-sanctioned mystics in the west, which call attention to the need to utilize the insights of even the most "reductive" of psychoanalytic models in analyzing mysticism.[3]

At the same time, as a result of dialogue with mystical traditions and the increasing clinical evidence concerning mystical forms of subjectivity now being amassed, psychoanalytic models will similarly be subject to modification. Some advancements in this dialogue, illustrated in this study, can take place through the contextualization and analyses of traditional texts as found in psychobiographies. Indeed, although this study has concentrated more on the psychology-comparativist dialogue, on studies of Buddhism and Hinduism and Rolland's unchurched mysticism, many of the preoccupations, issues, and theoretical advances found in the psychology-comparativist dialogue can illuminate and help repair the shortcomings of other approaches and dialogues, particularly with respect to mysticism. This is in line with the view, presented in the introduction, which holds that although the dialogues which make up the field of religion and psychological studies have developed enough specialization that it is useful and necessary to award them separate designations, insofar as the various dialogues often draw on the same body of theory and engage different facets of the same issues, the boundary between them remains fluid.

These brief observations underscore the need for sustained interest in this area of inquiry. Questions abound concerning issues such as the varieties of mystical noesis, their effect on subjectivity, and the precise relation and interaction between what appear to be the co-existence in some mystics of both pathological and transformative elements. Although this and other studies have touched on a number of traditions, mystics, and studies of both in an effort to map an avenue of research, many other related studies are needed to provoke compelling and sustained discussions of mysticism. What William James once said about mysticism still holds true today: "We had better keep an open mind and collect facts sympathetically for a long time to come. We shall not understand these alterations of consciousness either in this generation or the next."[4]

# *Appendix*

## The Letters of Sigmund Freud and Romain Rolland

### The Letters of the Early Period

Dear Mr. Freud                                                February 22, 1923

Edouard Monod-Hertzen has forwarded your letter to me and I am very touched by it.[1]

Allow me to take this opportunity to tell you that if your name is now among the most illustrious in France, I was among the first Frenchmen to know you and read your work. It was about twenty years ago that I found one of your books in a Zurich bookstore (*The Interpretation of Dreams*), and I was fascinated by your subliminal visions which articulated several of my intuitions. You were the Christopher Columbus of a new continent of the spirit. As it had happened for the other America, more than one navigator of art and of thought have since reached its shores, pushed by perilous winds. But you were the first to recognize it and open it to all subsequent explorers. Medicine is not the only discipline to benefit from your discoveries; psychology in all its forms has also profited from them. And today more than one in the field of literature benefit from your conquests without explicitly saying so and without even realizing it.

I have spoken of you twice with my friend Stefan Zweig who admires you greatly. Your letter reveals a great melancholy of today's miseries. If it is sad to be, as you are, in a country that has been ravaged by war, it is no less sad, believe me, to be, as I, in a victorious country and to feel disconnected from it: for I have always preferred to be among those who suffer rather than among those who cause suffering. Time, alas! (and the lunacy of people), takes it upon itself to render everything equal: each victory ruins the victor, and the wheel of misfortune never ceases to turn. Yet I do not give up hope, even if the political ruin of western Europe seems to me to be inevitable. But humanity has a hard life, and

I am convinced that from these convulsions the spirit will renew itself. It is a heavy price to pay for renewal. But you know that nature is not economical and it is pitiless.

Please accept, dear Mr. Freud, my feelings of respect and admiration.

Romain Rolland


Dear Sir                                                March 4, 1923[2]

That I have been allowed to exchange a greeting with you will remain a happy memory to the end of my days. Because for us your name has been associated with the most precious of beautiful illusions, that of love extended to all mankind.

I, of course, belong to a race which in the Middle Ages was held responsible for all epidemics and which today is blamed for the disintegration of the Austrian Empire and the German defeat. Such experiences have a sobering effect and are not conducive to make one believe in illusions. A great part of my life's work (I am ten years older than you) has been spent [trying to] destroy illusions of my own and those of mankind. But if this one hope cannot be at least partly realized, if in the course of evolution we don't learn to divert our instincts from destroying our own kind, if we continue to hate one another for minor differences and kill each other for petty gain, if we go on exploiting the great progress made in the control of natural resources for our mutual destruction, what kind of future lies in store for us? It is surely hard enough to ensure the perpetuation of our species in the conflict between our instinctual nature and the demands made upon us by civilization.

My writings cannot be what yours are: comfort and refreshment for the reader. But if I may believe that they have aroused your interest, I shall permit myself to send you a small book which is sure to be unknown to you: *Group Psychology and the Analysis of the Ego*, published in 1921. Not that I consider this work to be particularly successful, but it shows a way from the analysis of the individual to an understanding of society.

Sincerely yours

Freud


Dear Friend                                            March 12, 1923

Thank you very much for the small book.[3] I have of course been long familiar with its terrible beauty. I find the subtle irony of your dedication well deserved since I had completely forgotten Liluli when I wrote the silly passage in question in my letter, and obviously one ought not to do that.[4]

Across all boundaries and bridges, I would like to press your hand.

Freud

Dearest Friend                                              June 15, 1924[5]

Mahatma Gandhi will accompany me on my vacation which will begin shortly.[6]

When I am alone in my study, I often think of the hour that you gave me and my daughter here, and I imagine you again in the red chair which we set out for you.[7] I am not well. I would gladly end my life, but I must wait for it to unravel.

My cordial wishes for you and your work.

Yours

Freud


January 29, 1926[8]

Unforgettable man, to have soared to such heights of humanity through so much hardship and suffering!

I revered you as an artist and apostle of love for mankind many years before I saw you. I myself have always advocated the love for mankind not out of sentimentality or idealism but for sober, economic reasons: because in the face of our instinctual drives and the world as it is I was compelled to consider this love as indispensable for the preservation of the human species as, say, technology.

When I finally came to know you personally I was surprised to find that you hold strength and energy in such high esteem, and that you yourself embody so much will power.

May the next decade bring you nothing but fulfillment.

Most cordially

Your

Sigm. Freud, *aetat.* seventy


Dear Friend                                                  May 6, 1926[9]

With all my heart I share with those who celebrate your birthday. May the power of your mind pierce the night of life for a long time to come! and for you, peace of the body and joy of thought!

Please give my respectful remembrance to your daughter, and believe in my affectionate admiration.

Romain Rolland


Dear Friend                                                 May 13, 1926[10]

Your lines are among the most precious things which these days have brought me. Let me thank you for their content and your manner of address.

Unlike you, I cannot count on the love of many people. I have not pleased, comforted, edified them. Nor was this my intention; I only wanted to explore, solve riddles, uncover a little of the truth. This may have given pain to many, benefited a few, neither of which I consider my fault or my merit. It seems to me a surprising accident that apart from my doctrines my person should attract any attention at all. But when men like you whom I have loved from afar express their friendship for me, then a particular ambition of mine is gratified. I enjoy it without questioning whether or not I deserve it, I relish it as a gift. You belong to those who know how to give presents.

With my warmest wishes for your well-being

Your devoted

Freud

## The Letters of the Middle Period

Dear and Respected Friend                               Dec. 5, 1927[11]

I thank you for being so kind as to send me your lucid and spirited little book.[12] With a calm good sense, and in a moderate tone, it pulls off the blindfolding bandage of the eternal adolescents, which we all are, whose amphibian spirit floats between the illusion of yesterday and  .  .  .  the illusion of tomorrow.

Your analysis of religions is a just one. But I would have liked to see you doing an analysis of *spontaneous religious sentiment* or, more exactly, of religious *feeling*, which is wholly different from *religions* in the strict sense of the word, and much more durable.

What I mean is: totally independent of all dogma, all credo, all Church organization, all Sacred Books, all hope in a personal survival, etc., the simple and direct fact of *the feeling of the 'eternal'* (which can very well not be eternal, but simply without perceptible limits, and like oceanic, as it were).

This sensation, admittedly, is of a subjective character. But as it is common to thousands (millions) of men actually existing, with its thousands (millions) of individual nuances, it is possible to subject it to analysis, with an approximate exactitude.

I think that you will classify it also under the *Zwangsneurosen*. But I have often had occasion to observe its rich and beneficent power, be it among the religious souls of the West, Christians or non-Christians, or among those great minds of Asia who have become familiar to me and some of whom I count as friends. Of these latter, I am going to study, in a future book, two personalities who were almost our contemporaries (the first one belonged to the late nineteenth century, the second died in the early years of the twentieth) and who revealed an aptitude for thought and action which proved strongly regenerating for their country and for the world.[13]

I myself am familiar with this sensation. All through my life, it has never failed me; and I have always found in it a source of vital renewal. In that sense, I can say that I am profoundly 'religious'—without this constant state (like a sheet of water which I feel flushing under the bark) affecting in any way my critical faculties and my freedom to exercise them—even if that goes against the immediacy of the interior experience. In this way, without discomfort or contradiction, I can lead a 'religious' life (in the sense of that prolonged feeling) and a life of critical reason (which is without illusion). . . .

I may add that this 'oceanic' sentiment has nothing to do with my personal yearnings. Personally, I yearn for eternal rest; survival has no attraction for me at all. But the sentiment I experience is imposed on me as a fact. It is a *contact*. And as I have recognized it to be identical (with multiple nuances) in a large number of living souls, it has helped me to understand that that was the true subterranean source of *religious energy* which, subsequently, has been collected, canalized and *dried up by the Churches*, to the extent that one could say that it is inside the Churches (whichever they may be) that true 'religious' sentiment is least available.

What eternal confusion is caused by words, of which the same one here sometimes means: *allegiance* to or *faith* in a dogma, or a word of god (or a tradition); and sometimes: a free *vital upsurge*.

Please believe, dear friend, in my affectionate respect.

Romain Rolland


My dear Friend                                              July 14, 1929[14]

Your letter of Dec. 5, 1927, containing your remarks about a feeling you describe as "oceanic" has left me no peace. It happens that in a new work which lies before me still uncompleted I am making a starting point of this remark; I mention this "oceanic" feeling and am trying to interpret it from the point of view of our psychology.[15] The essay moves on to other subjects, deals with happiness, civilization and the sense of guilt; I don't mention your name but nevertheless drop a hint that points toward you.

And now I am beset with doubts whether I am justified in using your private remark for publication in this way. I would not be surprised if this were to be contrary to your wishes, and if it is, even in the slightest degree, I should certainly refrain from using it. My essay could be given another introduction without any loss; perhaps it is altogether not indispensable.

So if you have any compunction about my quoting this remark I ask you to prevent me from abusing it by dropping me a friendly line.

Please bear in mind that I always think of you with feelings of most respectful friendship.

Very sincerely yours

Freud

Dear Great Friend                                                July 17, 1929[16]

I am much honored to learn that the letter I wrote to you at the end of 1927 has prompted you to new researches, and that in a new work you will reply to the questions I had posed you. You have the full right to bring them before the wider public; and I would not wish to evade responsibility for them in any way.

I should only acknowledge that being at a distance of one year and a half, I no longer remember very exactly the text of my letter. I was then no doubt at the beginning of my long studies on the Hindu mind, which I am going to publish in a few months, in three volumes devoted to 'Mysticism and action in living India.' Since 1927 I have been able to delve deeply into that 'oceanic' sentiment, innumerable examples of which I find not only among hundreds of our contemporary Asians, but also in what I might call the ritualistic and multi-secular physiology which is codified in treatises on *yoga*. . . .

At the end of my work, while reading, for comparison, some of the great mystics of Europe and particularly those of the Alexandrian epoch, those who lived in the West during the 14th century—not to speak of the considerable work of Abbé Brémond on French mysticism during the 16th and 17th centuries[17]—I was surprised to observe once again, that it is not at all true that the East and the West are two worlds separated from each other, but that both are the branches of the same river of thought. And I have recognized in both the same 'river ocean'. . . .

It would be a pleasure to offer you my work when it is published: (the first volume next October; the second and the third in January).

Pray believe, dear great friend, in my affectionate respect.

                                                                Romain Rolland


Dear Friend                                                      July 20, 1929[18]

My best thanks for your permission! But I cannot accept it before you have reread your letter of the year 1927 which I enclose herewith. I possess so few letters from you that I do not like the idea of renouncing the return of this, your first one. I am not normally a hunter of relics, so please forgive this weakness.

I was glad to hear that your book will appear before my small effort, which is unlikely to be in print before February or March. But please don't expect from it any evaluation of the "oceanic" feeling; I am experimenting only with an analytical version of it; I am clearing it out of the way, so to speak.

How remote from me are the worlds in which you move! To me mysticism is just as closed a book as music. I cannot imagine reading all the literature which, according to your letter, you have studied. And yet it is easier for you than for us to read the human soul!

        With warm wishes for your well-being

                        Very sincerely yours

                                Freud

Dear Great Friend                                                    July 24, 1929[19]

I am returning the letter that you so wanted to communicate to me. It conveys very accurately my present feelings, and I have nothing that I wish to change or add to it.

I can hardly believe that mysticism and music are unknown to you. Because "nothing human is unknown to you". Rather, I think that you distrust them, because you uphold the integrity of critical reason, with which you control the instrument.

As for me, since birth I have taken part in both the intuitive and the critical natures, I do not suffer from a conflict between their opposing tendencies, and I can adapt myself very well to at once "seeing, believing and doubting" (to parody irrespectively some famous words of Corneille). It is in this that the musician makes harmony with the enemy forces, and at the same time finds in it his greatest joy:

"The harmony between the opposing forces is that which is the most beautiful."[20]

The great words of Heraclitus that I have made mine.

Please believe, dear great friend, in my respectful devotion.

Romain Rolland


## The Letters of the Late Period

Dear Friend                                                         January 19, 1930[21]

My warm thanks for the gift of your twin-headed, three-volume work![22] Contrary to my calculation, my "discontented" little book preceded yours by several weeks. I shall now try with your guidance to penetrate into the Indian jungle from which until now an uncertain blending of Hellenic love of proportion (σωφροδύνη), Jewish sobriety, and philistine timidity have kept me away. I really ought to have tackled it earlier, for the plants of this soil shouldn't be alien to me; I have dug to certain depths for their roots. But it isn't easy to pass beyond the limits of one's nature.

Of course I soon discovered the section of the book most interesting to me — the beginning, in which you come to grips with us extreme rationalists. That you call me "grand" here I have taken quite well; I cannot object to your irony when it is mixed with so much amiability.

Concerning the criticism of psychoanalysis, you will permit me a few remarks: the distinction between *extrovert* and *introvert* derives from C. G. Jung, who is a bit of a mystic himself and hasn't belonged to us for years. We don't attach any great importance to the distinction and are well aware that people can be both at the same time, and usually are. Furthermore, our terms such as *regression, narcissism, pleasure principle* are of a purely descriptive nature and don't carry within themselves any valuation. The mental processes may change direction or combine forces with each other; for instance, even reflecting is a regressive process without losing any of its dignity or importance in being so. Finally, psychoanalysis also has its scale of values, but its sole aim is the enhanced harmony of the ego, which is expected successfully to mediate between the claims of the instinctual life (the "id") and those of the external world; thus between inner and outer reality.

We seem to diverge rather far in the role we assign to intuition. Your mystics rely on it to teach them how to solve the riddle of the universe; we believe that it cannot reveal to us anything but primitive, instinctual impulses and attitudes — highly valuable for an embryology of the soul when correctly interpreted, but worthless for orientation in the alien, external world.

Should our paths cross once more in life, it would be pleasant to discuss all this. From a distance a cordial salutation is better than polemics. Just one more thing: I am not an out-and-out skeptic. Of one thing I am absolutely positive: there are certain things we cannot know now.

With my warmest wishes for your well-being

Your devoted

Freud


Dear Great Friend                                        May 3, 1931[23]

Permit me to add my wishes to all those that will be addressed to you, on this day, your 75th birthday! I offer them with all my heart. May you continue to pursue your intrepid work for a long time to come, work that only passion for the search of truth can guide — without desire, without hope, and without fear!

And allow me to say (in thanking you for having wanted to associate my name with your recent book: *Civilization and Its Discontents*), that it is by these last words (*"without desire, without hope, and without fear"*) that I feel morally the closest to you! Your kind dedication juxtaposes with an affectionate irony, the "Landtier" with the "Oceanic" friend.[24] This opposition does not materialize, (not) only between two men, but neither in one man, in me. I also am a *Landtier* from the French countryside, from the core of old France, who seems best protected from the ocean breezes! And I am also an old Frenchman who is able to see through illusions, who is able to bear life without them, who no longer needs them. If you would allow me, for documentary purposes, to expound on the psychological curiosity in my case, I distinguish very clearly in myself:

(1) what I *feel*;
(2) what I *know*;
(3) what I *desire*.

What I *feel*, I have told you, and I have explained it in the introduction to the *Ramakrishna*: it is the *Oceanic*. What I *know*, it is the: "What do I know?" of

Montaigne. And what I *desire*, is: *Nothing* . . . (Nothing, *for me*). As for others, may their desires be fulfilled! But I do not aspire to anything more, for myself, other than repose and effacement, unlimited and total. I have labored enough in my life . . . But I add that, whatever can become of it, I am prepared for all that may come. I would not be French, if it were not inscribed in my character: *"Do what you must"* (or, more accurately: *"Be what you must"*) *"come what may!"*.

I am therefore telling you that my feeling—or intuition—(or whatever one calls it)—*"Oceanic"*—is absolutely disinterested! I state it, but I am not particular about it. It (the feeling) is a psychological fact, a vital trait of my character. But the curious thing is that this vital trait is, imprinted on the brow of thousands of these Europeans and earthly *"Landtier,"* who for the most part know nothing about Asia—or even about any Ocean! Since the appearance of my *"Oceanic"* works, letters have come forth from all corners of the earth (including your Austria), like a gushing of waters that had been suppressed. I have amassed a complete file of these letters. And that is why I think that, in history and in action, one must always take into account these invisible forces that act in secret when they are not made manifest by explosions in broad daylight. They are not born of a particular period of time. They go as far back as I can drive my borer into the the past centuries of Europe and Asia. It would be dangerous for the philosopher and man of action to ignore them.

Moreover, their existence does not establish, to any great degree (in my eyes), their *truth*. It only establishes their *reality*.

Please believe, dear great friend, in my respectful and affectionate devotion.

Romain Rolland

Dear Friend                                                                May 1931[25]

You answered my pleasantry with the most precious information about your own person. My profound thanks for it.

Approaching life's inevitable end, reminded of it by yet another operation and aware that I am unlikely to see you again, I may confess to you that I have rarely experienced that mysterious attraction of one human being for another as vividly as I have with you; it is somehow bound up, perhaps, with the awareness of our being so different.

Farewell!

Your

Freud

Best wishes from your faithful friend.          Vienna, January 29, 1936[26]

Sigmund Freud

Dear Friend,                                        Villeneuve villa Olga
                                                    February 8, 1936[27]

I cannot tell you how much I was touched by your participation on the occasion of my birthday.

Of all the reasons I have to be grateful to Stefan Zweig, the least of them is not for having introduced us, for it was from this meeting ten years ago that our friendship was born.

You know what respect I have for the man I have admired for so long, whose fearless glance is able to penetrate into the depths of the interior abyss. I am happy and proud to have his friendship.

Please believe me to be your affectionately devoted friend.

Romain Rolland


                                                    May 1936[28]

I want to thank you cordially for the part you played in the celebration of my eightieth birthday.

                                        Yours

                                            Freud

# Notes

Introduction

1. Ernest Jones, *The Life and Work of Sigmund Freud* (New York: Basic Books, 1953), 3:349.

2. The full range of studies that make up the psychology of religion in general and psychoanalytic interpretations of religion in particular is vast. Good bibliographies can be found in: W. W. Meissner, *Annotated Bibliography in Religion and Psychology* (New York: Academy of Religion and Mental Health, 1961); Don Capps, Lewis Rambo and Paul Ransohoff, eds., *Psychology of Religion: A Guide to Information Sources* (Detroit: Gail, 1976); Benjamin Beit-Hallahmi, *Psychoanalysis and Religion: A Bibliography* (Norwood: Norwood Editions, 1978). An extensive historical overview of the essays, books, and authors involved in the psychology of religion as a whole can be found in David M. Wulff, *Psychology of Religion: Classic and Contemporary Views* (New York: Wiley, 1991).

3. In using the phrase "psychoanalytic theory of mysticism," I do not mean to suggest that psychoanalysis boasts a unified ideology. The term is meant to cover those who have been designated as originative theorists within psychoanalysis (from Freud to Kohut and beyond), as well as those scholars (from Rolland to de Certeau and beyond) who have utilized psychoanalytic models to interpret mysticism. These models reflect varying sociocultural, historical, and gendered perspectives. The term "psychoanalytic theory of mysticism," then, should be understood as a loose designation, covering a disparate, conflicting spectrum of models of the psyche and therapeutic practices. Again, in chapter 6, I group such originative theorists and scholars as members of the classic, adaptive, or transformational schools. The grounds for such a grouping is general: that they all hold in common a view of mysticism as regressive, defensive, and pathological (classic); adaptive and healing (adaptive); or as indicative of contact with a religious dimension (transformational) and that each displays specific strengths and weaknesses with respect to interdisciplinary awareness (theological/philosophical reflection, textual, comparative, and culture

studies) and dialogue. Let me also note that I am not unaware of the problems associated with using generalizing terms like "schools." Ultimately, I acknowledge that each theorist is unique enough to merit individual attention. Nevertheless, I believe the delineation of these schools will be useful, if even in a preliminary sense, for rethinking the relation between psychoanalysis and mysticism.

4. For survey literature on mysticism see: F. C. Happold, *Mysticism: A Study and an Anthology* (Harmondsworth, England: Penguin Books, 1963); Sidney Spencer, *Mysticism in World Religion* (Baltimore: Penguin Books, 1963); Geoffrey Parrinder, *Mysticism in the World's Religions* (New York: Oxford University Press, 1976); Denise and John Carmody, *Mysticism: Holiness East and West* (New York: Oxford University Press, 1996). A useful anthology of essays introducing the study of mysticism from a variety of methodological perspectives can be found in Richard Woods, ed., *Understanding Mysticism* (Garden City, N.Y.: Image, 1980). The appendix to Bernard McGinn's *The Foundations of Mysticism: Origins to the Fifth Century* (New York: Crossroad, 1991) contains an excellent historical summary of the major theoretical approaches to mysticism found in this century.

5. William James, *The Varieties of Religious Experience* (New York: Modern Library, 1936, p. 29.

6. Ibid.

7. R. C. Zaehner, *Mysticism Sacred and Profane* (New York: Oxford University Press, 1961), pp. 32, 198–9.

8. See James, *The Varieties of Religious Experience*, p. 410.

9. Ibid., p. 371.

10. See William T. Stace, *Mysticism and Philosophy* (London: Macmillan, 1960), p. 44ff.

11. See Carmody, *Mysticism: Holiness East and West*, p. 10.

12. See G. Scholem, *Major Trends in Jewish Mysticism* (New York: Schocken Books, 1961), pp. 3–10. Current assessments of the role unitive experiences have played in Jewish mysticism have rendered Scholem's views problematic. See Moshe Idel, *Kabbalah: New Perspectives* (New Haven: Yale University Press, 1988), as well as his "Universalization and Integration: Two Conceptions of Mystical Union in Jewish Mysticism," in M. Idel and B. McGinn, eds., *Mystical Union and Monotheistic Faith* (New York: Macmillan, 1989), pp. 27–55.

13. See, for example, the introduction to McGinn's *The Foundations of Mysticism*.

14. See Louis Bouyer, "Mysticism: An Essay on the History of the Word," in *Understanding Mysticism*, pp. 42–56; Michel de Certeau, "'Mystique' au XVII$^e$ siècle: Le problème du langage 'mystique,'" in *L'Homme devant Dieu: Mélanges offerts au Père Henri de Lebac* (Paris: Aubier, 1964), 2:267–91.

15. R. Gimello, "Mysticism and Meditation," in S. Katz, ed., *Mysticism and Philosophical Analysis* (New York: Oxford University Press, 1978), p. 173. Despite this, most scholars, including Gimello, would agree with McGinn's assertion that words like *mysticism* and *union* are helpful "terms of art" (see *Mystical Union and Monotheistic Faith*, p. 186). This study utilizes such terms with the same understanding.

16. For example, Smart, in his famous reply to Zaehner's attempt to delineate three types of mystical encounters in his *Mysticism Sacred and Profane*, promotes the perennialist view that "phenomenologically, mysticism is everywhere the same." This conclusion, however, is prefaced by a definition of mysticism sympathetic to a perennialist conclusion: "[Mysticism is] an interior or introvertive quest, culminating in certain interior experiences which are not described in terms of sense-experience or of mental images." (See N. Smart, "Interpretation and Mystical Experience" in *Understanding Mysticism*, pp. 78–91.) Compare as well how the definition of mysticism is linked to theoretical

agenda in the following: Robert K. C. Forman's introductory essay in *The Problem of Pure Consciousness* (New York: Oxford University Press, 1990); Rowan Williams' comments on mysticism in chapter 5 of his *Teresa of Avila* (Harrisburg, Pa.: Morehouse Publishing, 1991); Scholem's comments in his *Major Trends in Jewish Mysticism*, pp. 5ff.; McGinn's introduction to his *The Foundations of Mysticism*; Kripal's attempt to delineate a definition more sympathetic to a Tantric worldview in the introduction to his *Kali's Child: The Mystical and the Erotic in the Life and Teachings of Ramakrishna* (Chicago: University of Chicago Press, 1995).

17. For a history of the major studies, figures, and arguments in this debate, see Robert K. C. Forman's introductory essay in *The Problem of Pure Consciousness* and the essay by Steven Katz in *Mysticism and Philosophical Analysis*.

18. See St. Teresa of Avila, *The Interior Castle* (New York: Paulist Press, 1979); St. John of the Cross, *Selected Writings* (New York: Paulist Press, 1987); A. Osborne, *Ramana Maharshi and the Path of Self-Knowledge* (New York: Samuel Weiser, 1973); A. Schimmel, *Mystical Dimensions of Islam* (Chapel Hill: University of North Carolina Press, 1975).

19. For an overview of this period, see Peter Homans, "The Psychology and Religion Movement," in Mircea Eliade, ed., *The Encyclopedia of Religion* (New York: Macmillan, 1987) 12:66–74; Benjamin Beit-Hallahmi, "Psychology of Religion 1880–1930: The Rise and Fall of a Psychological Movement," in *Journal of the History of Behavioral Sciences* 10 (1974):84–90.

20. Bouyer, "Mysticism: An Essay on the History of the Term," pp. 52–3.

21. See Michel de Certeau, "'Mystique' au XVII$^e$ siècle: Le problème du langage 'mystique'"; McGinn, *The Foundations of Mysticism*, pp. 311 ff.

22. James, *The Varieties of Religious Experience*, pp. 32–3, 370ff.

23. Ibid., p. 32.

24. See Wulff, *The Psychology of Religion*, pp. 473–5.

25. See James, *The Varieties of Religious Experience*, pp. 390–1; R. M. Bucke, *Cosmic Consciousness* (New York: Citadel Press, 1993).

26. See Jung, *Psychology and Religion* (New Haven, Conn.: Yale University Press, 1977), p. 6; *Memories, Dreams, Reflections* (New York: Vintage, 1963).

27. See J. Maréchal, *Studies in the Psychology of the Mystics* (Albany, N.Y.: Magi Books, 1964); J. Leuba, *The Psychology of Religious Mysticism* (New York: Harcourt, Brace, 1926); T. Flournoy, "Une Mystique moderne," in *Archives de Psychologie* 15 (1928) 1–224; P. Janet, *De l'Angoisse à l'extase*. 2 vols. (Paris: Félix Alcan, 1926–1928).

28. D. Mekur, "Unitive Experiences and the State of Trance," in *Mystical Union and Monotheistic Faith*, pp. 129–30.

29. Zaehner, *Mysticism Sacred and Profane*, p. 39.

30. R. Hood, Jr., "Conceptual Criticisms of Regressive Explanations of Mysticism," in *Review of Religious Research*, vol. 17, no. 3, 1976, p. 184.

31. Franz Alexander, "Buddhistic Training as an Artificial Catatonia," in *The Psychoanalytic Review* 18, no. 2 (1931):129–41; Jeffrey M. Masson, *The Oceanic Feeling: The Origins of the Religious Sentiment in Ancient India* (Dordrecht, Netherlands: D. Reidel, 1980); N. Sil, *Ramakrishna Paramahamsa: A Psychological Profile* (Leiden, Netherlands: E. J. Brill, 1991).

32. See Herbert Fingarette, "Mystic Selflessness," in *The Self in Transformation* (New York: Harper and Row, 1965); Erich Fromm, D. T. Suzuki, and Richard De Martino, eds., *Zen Buddhism and Psychoanalysis* (New York: Harper and Row, 1960); Raymond Prince and Charles Savage, "Mystical States and the Concept of Regression," in John White, ed., *The Highest State of Consciousness* (Garden City, N.Y.: Doubleday An-

chor Books, 1972), pp. 114–34; Paul Horton, "The Mystical Experience: Substance of an Illusion," in *Journal of the American Psychoanalytic Association* 22 (1974): 364–80; W. W. Meissner, *Ignatius of Loyola: The Psychology of a Saint* (New Haven, Conn.: Yale University Press, 1992); Sudhir Kakar, *The Analyst and the Mystic* (Chicago: University of Chicago Press, 1991).

33. Ken Wilber, Jack Engler, and Dan Brown, eds., *Transformations of Consciousness* (Boston: Shambhala, 1986); J. Kripal, *Kali's Child.*

34. For studies and figures in the formative period of religion and psychological studies see, in addition to the article by Beit-Hallahmi cited above, D. Wulff, *Psychology of Religion*, chapter 1.

35. See D. Wulff, *Psychology of Religion.*

36. See Peter Homans, *Jung in Context* (Chicago: The University of Chicago Press, 1979); *The Ability to Mourn* (Chicago: The University of Chicago Press, 1989). Homans focuses on the historical, social, and psychological dimensions of the process of mourning in an attempt to analyze value change and the emergence of creative social-scientific theorizing about religion in originative figures like Freud and Jung. Further illustrations of the inclusive social-scientific approach can be found particularly in works from theorists championing psychoanalytic anthropology and psychoanalytic sociology. Again, while paradigmatic studies in this area abound, see Michael Carroll, *The Cult of the Virgin Mary: Psychological Origins* (Princeton N.J.: Princeton University Press, 1986); William Beers, *Women and Sacrifice: Male Narcissism and the Psychology of Religion* (Detroit: Wayne State Press, 1992); Gananath Obeyesekere, *The Work of Culture: Symbolic Transformation in Psychoanalysis and Anthropology* (Chicago: The University of Chicago Press, 1990); Robert A. Paul, *Moses and Civilization: The Meaning Behind Freud's Myth* (New Haven, Conn.: Yale University Press, 1996). More on this approach can be found in Susan Henking, "Placing the Social Sciences: Cases at the Intersection of the Histories of Disciplines and Religions," in *Religious Studies Review*, 19 (1993):116–26. Let me note that while I distinguish between several approaches and dialogues in this section, it needs to be emphasized that they are hardly mutually exclusive. They often draw on the same body of theory, engage common issues, and overlap to the extent that sharp distinctions between them are blurred. At the same time, insofar as these dialogues and approaches also adopt different theoretical premises, engage different interdisciplinary strategies, and address different facets of issues germane to the field, they merit separate designations.

37. D. Browning, *Religious Thought and the Modern Psychologies* (Philadelphia: Fortress Press, 1987); J. Fowler, *Stages of Faith* (San Francisco: Harper and Row, 1981). For an overview of this period, see Peter Homans, "The Psychology and Religion Movement"; *Theology After Freud* (Indianapolis: Bobbs-Merrill, 1970). I am not claiming that Catholic, Jewish, Evangelical, or African theological perspectives are absent from this dialogue (for example, see D. Browning, T. Jobe, I. Evison, eds., *Religious and Ethical Factors in Psychiatric Practice.* Chicago: Nelson-Hall, 1990). Nevertheless, historically speaking, the psychology-theology dialogue has been ruled in the main by a Protestant mentality.

38. For a definitive overview of the figures and issues animating this dialogue, see Diane Jonte-Pace, "Feminist Transformations in the Psychology of Religion: New Developments in Method and Theory," in *Method and Theory in the Study of Religion* (forthcoming).

39. Eliade, Doniger (who specializes in Hinduism), and Campbell prefer Jung while Kakar (a psychoanalyst) uses psychoanalytic method in his comparative pursuits. Gómez specializes in Buddhism and has critiqued Jung's understanding and interpreta-

tion of Buddhist texts and practices. See M. Eliade, *Myths, Dreams and Mysteries* (New York: Harper and Row, 1960); J. Campbell, *The Hero with a Thousand Faces* (Princeton, N.J.: Princeton University Press, 1972); W. Doniger O'Flaherty, *Women, Androgynes and Other Mythical Beasts* (Chicago: The University of Chicago Press, 1980); Sudhir Kakar, *The Analyst and the Mystic* (Chicago: The University of Chicago Press, 1991); Luis Gómez, "Oriental Wisdom and the Cure of Souls: Jung and the Indian East," in Donald S. Lopez, Jr., ed., *Curators of the Buddha: The Study of Buddhism under Colonialism* (Chicago: The University of Chicago Press, 1995), pp. 197–250.

40. R. Schwab, *The Oriental Renaissance: Europe's Rediscovery of India and the East, 1680–1880.* Translated by Gene Patterson-Black and Victor Reinking (New York: Columbia University Press, 1984); A. Versluis, *American Transcendentalism and Asian Religions* (New York: Oxford University Press, 1993): G. Welbon, *The Buddhist Nirvana and Its Western Interpreters* (Chicago: University of Chicago Press, 1968); R. Fields, *How the Swans Came to the Lake* (Boston: Shambhala, 1992); T. Tweed, *The American Encounter with Buddhism* (Bloomington: Indiana University Press, 1992).

## Chapter 1

1. *The Letters of Sigmund Freud*, ed. Ernst Freud (New York: Basic Books, 1960), p. 341.
2. The complete letters of the Freud–Rolland correspondence and their grouping into the "early," "middle," and "late" periods can be found in the appendix of this study. Ernst Freud was the first to edit and publish the most crucial of his father's letters to Rolland (in his *Letters*). Colette Cornubert's doctoral thesis, *Freud et Rolland: Essai sur la découverte de la pensée psychoanalytique par quelques écrivains Français* (Thèse No. 453 pour Le Doctorat en Médecine. Paris, Faculté de Médecine de Paris, 1966), although still unpublished, set the parameters for subsequent studies by reproducing in an historically correct fashion most of the correspondence (in French), alerting the reader to many of the important written works of both Rolland and Freud that entered into their debate and providing valuable commentary (my thanks to Jeffrey Masson for making a copy of it accessible to me). David Fisher, in his "Sigmund Freud and Romain Rolland: The Terrestrial Animal and His Great Oceanic Friend" (*American Imago* 33, 1976:1–59), has done the English reader a great service by translating or summarizing and publishing all of the letters E. Freud and Cornubert cite, adding a few more they missed, and providing suggestive commentary. Doré and Prévost, in their *Selected Letters of Romain Rolland* (Delhi: Oxford University Press, 1990) have translated two important letters from Rolland to Freud: those of December 5, 1927, and July 17, 1929. Most recently, Henri and Madeleine Vermorel, in their *Sigmund Freud et Romain Rolland Correspondance 1923–1936* (Paris: Presses Universitaires de France, 1993) have provided a definitive and massive study of the relationship between the two men, including all of their letters (in French, with an appendix reproducing only Freud's letters in the original German).

I am most indebted to the studies by Cornubert and Fisher. Their path-breaking historical work is in evidence throughout Part I, and I have, for the most part, followed their reconstruction of the correspondence between the two men. At the same time, I should note that although I draw on many of the same letters and texts cited by these authors, I have added several texts (most notably the "Goetz Letters," *The Future of an Illusion*, aspects of Freud's essay on the Acropolis which speak to the problem of mysticism, and passages in Freud's *New Introductory Lectures* and Rolland's commentary on the work of F. Morel) that change the nature of their debate. Moreover, my interpretation of these texts, which draws on secondary literature lacking in Cornubert and Fisher, differs considerably from theirs. The historical overview offered by Fisher and Cornubert tends to confirm the common understanding that Freud's views on mysticism were wholly pejorative. Fisher has gone further by offering an interpretation of the oceanic feeling as a reaction formation hiding an intense hatred of humanity. My historical reconstruction and interpretative forays, on the other hand, have unearthed a positive, adaptive stain in Freud's views on mysticism. In sum, then, my view is that the above historical studies have misunderstood Freud's position on mysticism, omitted subtleties necessary for defining the two men's positions in the debate, and wholly bypassed the proper reconstruction of Rolland's oceanic feeling. Because my reading of the debate is so different from theirs, I have found it necessary to devote the entirety of Part I to a proper exegesis of the Freud–Rolland correspondence as it affected the origins of the psychoanalytic theory of mysticism.

The argument of Part I is adapted from my doctoral dissertation, entitled "Psychoanalysis and Mysticism: The Freud–Rolland Correspondence," submitted to and accepted by the University of Chicago in March of 1993. I have not, then, integrated any material from the study by the Vermorels, whose work was published months after mine, with two exceptions: one quote that appears in chapter 2 (concerning a remark Freud made to Baudouin) and more precise reproductions of Rolland's letters as found in Cornubert (see the appendix). Although the Vermorels' work is detailed and exhaustive, I have seen nothing in their study that has made me alter in any significant way my understanding of the Freud–Rolland debate on mysticism. It does not aim, as does this study, at a critical appraisal of Freud's views on mysticism.

3. The bulk of studies on the relationship between the two men are from the psychoanalytic realm. Most of these studies utilize the two men's correspondence as a window into Freud's developmental vicissitudes. This is especially true of those studies that have "analyzed" Freud through his letter to Rolland concerning his experience on the Acropolis (see chapter 4 for citations). Although purely developmental issues are important, these studies often shade off into aspects of Freud's life that are of primary interest only to analysts. I make use of these studies, then, alongside others from psychologically informed sociological, historical, and anthropological perspectives, only insofar as I deem them to have a direct and pivotal bearing on Freud's understanding and interpretation of mysticism.

4. For all letters of the Freud–Rolland correspondence cited during the course of this study, the reader is referred to the appendix. Stefan Zweig was a mutual friend of Rolland and Freud and served as an intermediary during the course of their one and only luncheon meeting in Vienna in 1924.

5. See Freud's letter of January 20, 1936, to Arnold Zweig for evidence of deeper conflict in his relationship with Rolland (in *The Letters of Sigmund Freud and Arnold Zweig*, ed. E. Freud [New York: New York University Press, 1970]).

6. Jones, *The Life and Work of Sigmund Freud*, 3:97. No one has expanded on Jones's initial observation better than David Werman (see his "Sigmund Freud and Romain Rolland," in *International Review of Psychoanalysis* 4 [1977]:225–43). Although my interpretation of texts in this section differs from that of Werman, the general orientation is similar, and I am indebted to his work for suggesting this line of approach.

7. Jones, *The Life and Work of Sigmund Freud*, 2:171. Chapter 7 in the latter contains a good historical overview of Freud's activities during the war. For an overview of Rolland's wartime activities, see William Starr, *Romain Rolland and a World at War* (Evanston, Ill.: Northwestern University Press, 1956); René Cheval, *L'Allemagne et la guerre* (Paris: Presses Universitaires de France, 1963); Pierre-Jean Jouvre, *Romain Rolland vivant (1914–1919)* (Paris: Ollendorff, 1920).

8. Jones, *The Life and Work of Sigmund Freud*, 2:177.

9. See Peter Homans, *The Ability to Mourn*, especially pp. 195–96, and Dennis B.

Klein, *Jewish Origins of the Psychoanalytic Movement* (New York: Praeger Publishers, 1981).

10. See Freud, "Thoughts for the Times on War and Death," in *Standard Edition* 14:273–300. Other papers Freud wrote dealing explicitly with war include: "On Transience," in *Standard Edition* 14:303–08; "Why War?" in *Standard Edition* 22:195–218. Freud also wrote a letter to Frederick Van Eeden on the subject (see "Appendix: Letter to Frederik Van Eeden" in the section "Thoughts for the Times on War and Death" in *Standard Edition* 14:301–03). Throughout this work *Standard Edition* refers to *The Standard Edition of the Complete Psychological Works of Sigmund Freud*, James Strachey, trans. and ed., 24 vols. (New York and London: The Hogarth Press, 1964).

11. See David Werman, "Sigmund Freud and Romain Rolland," in *International Review of Psychoanalysis* 4 (1977):240.

12. It is not my intent to provide a detailed biography of Rolland in this work. There are, however, several good introductory studies that can be recommended for the interested reader: William Starr, *Romain Rolland: One Against All* (The Hague: Mouton, 1971); Stefan Zweig, *Romain Rolland: The Man and His Work* (New York: Thomas Seltzer, 1921); Marcel Doisey, *Romain Rolland* (Brussels: Editions La Boétie, 1945); Harold March, *Romain Rolland* (New York: Twayne Publishers, 1971); Paul Seippel, *Romain Rolland, l'homme et l'oeuvre* (Paris: Ollendorf, 1913); Christian Sénéchal, *Romain Rolland* (Paris: Éditions de la Caravelle, 1933). For a dated but still useful bibliography of Rolland's primary works and crucial secondary studies, see William Starr, *A Critical Bibliography of the Published Writings of Romain Rolland* (Evanston, Ill.: Northwestern University Press, 1950).

13. For a good analysis of Rolland's *Above the Battle* (translated by C. K. Ogden. Chicago: Open Court, 1916), see D. Fisher, *Romain Rolland and the Politics of Intellectual Engagement* (Berkeley: University of California Press, 1988), chapter 3. The Nobel Prize was in 1915 for literature (for his *Jean-Christophe)*, but, as Fisher has observed, it was widely thought to be a surrogate peace prize (p. 44). Although not psychoanalytic in any way, *Above the Battle* did incorporate many of the themes Freud emphasized in his essays on war. Like Freud, Rolland saw through the machinations of culture, its role in breeding divisiveness and catering to the worst in man. Moreover, he was not shy about attacking socially respected intellectuals and institutions, including the church, in exposing the dangers of hypocrisy, nationalism, and herd mentality. Rolland stressed humanism, reason, and individuality while arguing for the primacy of the intellect in offsetting aggressiveness and fermenting cultural adaptability. Rolland's trenchant observations combined with his display of humanity and tolerance—surely Freud found much to agree with in these essays.

14. Cited in Henri and Madeleine Vermorel, *Sigmund Freud and Romain Rolland Correspondence 1923–1936*, p. 178.

15. See Werman, "Sigmund Freud and Romain Rolland," pp. 240–1. Werman thinks Rolland played a pivotal role in "converting" Freud to pacifism. Freud publicly admitted he was a pacifist in his 1932 letter to Einstein ("Why War"). For Freud, pacifism was the logical outcome of the evolution of culture. It consisted in a constitutional intolerance for war and was a prerequisite for becoming "organically fitted" for civilization.

16. See Freud, "Dostoyevsky and Parricide," in *Standard Edition* 21:173–94.

17. See the Editor's Note to "Dostoyevsky and Parricide," in *Standard Edition* 21:176; Jones, *The Life and Work of Sigmund Freud*, 3:143.

18. Fisher, "Sigmund Freud and Romain Rolland: The Terrestrial Animal and His Great Oceanic Friend," pp. 9–10.

19. Homans, *The Ability to Mourn*, pp. 89–90. I am indebted to Homans for raising

this line of interpretation. However, integral to Homans' argument is the conclusion, and here he follows Masson, that Rolland was anti-Semitic—a conclusion I cannot follow.

20. In addition to the studies cited by Jones and Homans, see Carl Schorske, "Politics and Patricide in Freud's 'Interpretation of Dreams,'" in his *Fin-de Siècle Vienna: Politics and Culture* (New York: Vintage, 1981); William McGrath, "Freud as Hannibal: The Politics of the Brother Band," in *Central European History*, 7 (1974):31–57; D. Klein, *Jewish Origins of the Psychoanalytic Movement*.

21. See Klein, *Jewish Origins of the Psychoanalytic Movement*; Homans, *The Ability to Mourn*. See also McGrath, "Freud as Hannibal: The Politics of the Brother Band," p. 43.

22. The term *Rome Neurosis* was coined by Schorske, *Hannibal phantasy* by McGrath.

23. Both Schorske and McGrath have pointed to other dreams, most notably "The Uncle with the Yellow Beard" and "The Revolutionary Dream," as similarly containing important sociopolitical elements. Good overviews and interpretations of the "Rome Dreams" can be found in Didier Anzieu, *Freud's Self-Analysis* (London: The Hogarth Press and the Institute of Psycho-Analysis, 1986) and Alex Grinstein, *Sigmund Freud's Dreams* (New York: International Universities Press, 1980).

24. Freud, *The Interpretation of Dreams*, in *Standard Edition* 4:196–7.

25. Schorske, "Politics and Patricide in Freud's 'Interpretation of Dreams,'" p. 191.

26. See McGrath, "Freud as Hannibal: Politics of the Brother Band."

27. See Gregory Zilboorg, *Psychoanalysis and Religion* (New York: Farrar, Strauss and Co., 1962); Kenneth Grigg, "'All Roads Lead to Rome': The Role of the Nursemaid in Freud's Dreams," in *Journal of the American Psychoanalytic Association* 21 (1973): 108–26.

28. See Freud's letter to Fleiss of October 3 and 15, 1897, in *The Origins of Psychoanalysis: Letters to Wilhelm Fleiss Drafts and Notes, 1887–1902*, ed. Marie Bonaparte, Anna Freud and Ernst Kris, pp. 218–25 (New York: Basic Books, 1954).

29. For deeper analyses of Rolland's works and involvement in the sociopolitical arena during this time, see the studies cited by Starr and Fisher. I am indebted to their work for the more cursory summaries offered here.

30. Jones, *The Life and Thought of Sigmund Freud*, vol. 3, p. 182; Fisher, "Sigmund Freud and Romain Rolland: The Terrestrial Animal and His Great Oceanic Friend," p. 46.

31. Rolland, *I Will Not Rest* (New York: Liveright, 1937), pp. 293–4. See also Fisher, *Romain Rolland and the Politics of Intellectual Engagement*, part 3.

32. See *Selected Letters of Romain Rolland*, ed. F. Doré and M. Prévost, p. 113.

33. From the statements against Hitler, racism, and the persecution of the Jews in *I Will Not Rest* (New York: Liveright, 1937), entries of April 5th and 9th, 1933, pp. 293–4.

34. See D. Fisher, *Romain Rolland and the Politics of Intellectual Engagement*, p. 179.

35. E. Freud, *Letters*, pp. 426–7; D. Fisher, "Sigmund Freud and Romain Rolland: The Terrestrial Animal to His Great Oceanic Friend," pp. 47–8.

36. From Freud's letter to Rolland of March 12, 1923.

37. Freud, *The Future of an Illusion, Standard Edition* 21:39. In the discussion that follows I am indebted to Philip Rieff's work, which first introduced this line of interpretation. See *The Mind of the Moralist* (Chicago: University of Chicago, 1979), especially chapter 8; *The Triumph of the Therapeutic* (New York: Harper and Row, 1966).

38. See Homans, *The Ability to Mourn*, chapters 2–4, especially p. 91.

39. See Freud's letter to Jung of August 18, 1907, in *The Freud/Jung Letters*, ed.

William McGuire, trans. R. Manheim and R. F. C. Hull (Princeton, N.J.: Princeton University Press, 1979), pp. 76–7.

40. E. Freud, *Letters*, pp. 339–40.

41. In his letter to Rolland of May 13, 1926, Freud refers to how Rolland's writings, like those of all good artists, "pleased, comforted, edified" men.

42. Letter of February 22, 1923.

43. Freud to Rolland, July 20, 1929.

44. See Starr, *Romain Rolland: One Against All*, p. 195.

45. Jones, *The Life and Work of Sigmund Freud*, 3:97.

46. A good history of psychoanalysis in France can be found in Elisabeth Roudinesco, *Jacques Lacan & Co.: A History of Psychoanalysis in France, 1925–1985* (Chicago: University of Chicago Press, 1990).

47. See Freud's letter to Jung of June 14, 1907, in *The Freud/Jung Letters*, 65; Freud, "On the History of the Psychoanalytic Movement," in *Standard Edition* 14:32; Marion Oliner, *Cultivating Freud's Garden in France* (Northvale, N.J.: Jason Aronson, 1988).

48. Freud, *An Autobiographical Study, Standard Edition* 20:62; Oliner, *Cultivating Freud's Garden in France*, p. 22.

49. Rolland seems to have had only a general grasp of psychoanalytic theory. His criticisms of it to Baudouin (letter of January 19, 1922, in Cornubert, "Freud et Rolland," 48) reveal that he interpreted Freud's dream theory much too narrowly. Freud's letter of January 19, 1930, also indicates further misunderstandings Rolland had vis-à-vis psychoanalysis. For a full treatment of this issue, see Henri and Madeleine Vermorel, *Sigmund Freud et Romain Rolland Correspondence 1923–1936*.

50. See Rolland, *Above the Battle*, pp. 42, 48–9, 110.

51. For Rolland's renunciation of Catholicism, see the first few chapters of his autobiography *Journey Within* (New York: Philosophical Library, 1947).

52. Rolland, *Liluli* (New York: Boni and Liveright, 1920), p. 53. See also pp. 50–60 and 89–95; Fisher, "Sigmund Freud and Romain Rolland," pp. 8–9

53. Freud, *The Diary of Sigmund Freud* (New York: Scribner's, 1992). See the entry of May, 1923, p. 56.

54. Freud's reaction to *Liluli* and its "terrible beauty" was shared by many reviewers of *Liluli*. Some, like J. R. Bloch, saw it as so destructive of beliefs that he labeled it as essentially nihilistic (see Starr, *Romain Rolland and a World at War*, p. 176).

55. Baudouin had enormous respect for Rolland, and the two seemed to have corresponded fairly regularly. See Henri and Madeleine Vermorel, *Sigmund Freud and Romain Rolland Correspondence 1923–36*.

56. As we shall see in the chapters to come, many of Rolland's ideas on religion are remarkably similar to those of Jung. It is unfortunate that Rolland seems not to have read Jung more extensively, a surprising fact given the time he spent in Switzerland. We know that Rolland read F. Morel's study on mysticism, *Essai sur l'introversion mystique* (Geneva: Kundig, 1918), which used a few of Jung's terms and cited his early work *Symbols of Transformation*. According to Ellenberger *(The Discovery of the Unconscious* [New York: Basic Books, 1970], p. 739), Maeder claimed he was a disciple of Jung, but I have been unable to find that Jung had any significant influence on Rolland through Maeder.

57. See Freud's letter to Rolland of January 19, 1930. In citing this letter, David Fisher also briefly notes the affinity between Rolland and Jung, further stating that Rolland's "desire to integrate Freud's work on the unconscious with the discoveries of spontaneous religion and creative art paralleled the approach of Jung on a certain level" (Fisher, "Sigmund Freud and Romain Rolland: The Terrestrial Animal and His Great Oceanic Friend," p. 31). I will elaborate on this insight during the course of both Part 1 and 2.

58. While I arrived at this conclusion prior to and independent of the work by the Vermorels, I should note that they have also noted the status of Rolland as interlocuter, referring to him as the "interlocuteur imaginaire," although they do not elaborate on this notion in any significant way (see *Sigmund Freud et Romain Rolland Correspondance 1923–1936*, p. 345).

## Chapter 2

1. The fact that Freud is referring to Rolland in the first paragraph of *Civilization and Its Discontents* has been noted by many commentators. See, for example, Fisher, "Sigmund Freud and Romain Rolland: The Terrestrial Animal and His Great Oceanic Friend," p. 26; H. Vermorel and M. Vermorel, *Sigmund Freud et Romain Rolland Correspondance 1923–1936*, Part 3, chapters 9–10.

2. Freud, *Civilization and Its Discontents*, in *Standard Edition* 21:64.

3. See for example Prince and Savage, "Mystical States and the Concept of Regression," in J. White, ed., *The Highest State of Consciousness*; Ralph Hood, Jr., "Conceptual Criticisms of Regressive Explanations of Mysticism," p. 184.

4. The precise dates are: Rolland to Freud, December 5, 1927; Freud to Rolland, July 14, 1929; Rolland to Freud, July 17, 1929; Freud to Rolland, July 20, 1929; Rolland to Freud, July 24, 1929 (see the appendix for these letters).

5. Freud to Pfister, November 25, 1928, *Psychoanalysis and Faith: Dialogues with the Reverend Oskar Pfister*, ed. H. Meng and E. Freud (New York: Basic Books, 1963), pp. 125–6.

6. For Freud's views on mysticism in *The Future of an Illusion*, see chapter 4 of this work.

7. For example, Teresa's concept of a "spiritual marriage" in *The Interior Castle*, Vɪɪ:2; Sri Maharshi's concept of sahaja samādhi (see Osborne, *Ramana Maharshi and the Path of Self-Knowledge*, p. 204). Interestingly enough, these concepts are used to describe late or mature phases of the mystical life. As we shall argue in chapter 5, this is also true of Rolland's oceanic feeling. This fact has eluded psychoanalytic interpretations of the oceanic feeling from Freud onward and is one reason why such attempts can be said to be in error.

8. Freud, *Civilization and Its Discontents*, in *Standard Edition* 21:66–7.

9. Ibid., p. 68.

10. Ibid., p. 72.

11. Freud, *The Future of an Illusion*, in *Standard Edition* 21:23–4.

12. Freud, *Civilization and Its Discontents*, in *Standard Edition* 21:72.

13. An enlightening discussion of Freud's criticisms of the love-command can be found in Ernest Wallwork, "Thou Shalt Love Thy Neighbor as Thyself: The Freudian Critique," *Journal of Religious Ethics* 10 (1982): 264–308 and in chapter 9 of his *Psychoanalysis and Ethics* (New Haven, Conn.: Yale University Press, 1991). In the latter, Wallwork points out that Freud did in fact recognize the usefulness of the love-command and embraced it as a necessary "good illusion" for the cultural elite to propagate. However, it should be noted that Freud insisted that ultimately only a psychologically qualified version of the love-command was acceptable. As Wallwork puts it, Freud's "apparent repudiation of (the love-command) is actually a reinterpretation of it along more modest lines" (p. 207). There also exists evidence that Rolland inspired Freud to reflect on yet another philosopher and cultural theorist, Empedocles, and the role of the "heavenly" Eros and Thanatos in the evolution of civilization (see Fisher, "Sigmund Freud and Romain Rolland: The Terrestrial Animal and His Great Oceanic Friend," p. 42). Freud, of course,

acknowledged his debt to Empedocles in his "Analysis Terminable and Interminable" (*Standard Edition* 24:211–53) but never directly to Rolland.

14. Freud, *Civilization and Its Discontents*, in *Standard Edition* 21:65.

15. Letter to Fliess, September 19, 1901. In *The Origins of Psychoanalysis*, pp. 335–6.

16. Ibid.

17. Schorske, "Politics and Patricide in Freud's 'Interpretation of Dreams'," pp. 190–3.

18. Freud, *Civilization and Its Discontents*, in *Standard Edition* 21:102.

19. Fisher, in "Reading Freud's *Civilization and Its Discontents*" (in Dominick LaCapra and Stephen L. Kaplan, eds., *Modern European Intellectual History: Reappraisals and New Perspectives* [Ithaca, NY: Cornell University Press, 1982]: 251–79) has also noted the association of Rolland with the love-command and the pre-Oedipal base to which Freud traced its origin (pp. 265–67). Further, he has attempted to connect Freud's reference to Rome as well as the quote from Grabbe to Rolland. His interpretation of these associations, however, is radically different from my own. According to Fisher, the association of the "oceanic feeling" with Rome is due to Rolland's first name (Romain) and the association with Grabbe indicates Freud's desire to link the "oceanic feeling" with narcissistic rage and suicidal feelings (pp. 262–63). In this article Fisher also reveals that he thinks the "oceanic feeling" is a reaction formation against fantasies of world destruction and the "universal hatred of humanity" (p. 267).

In Freud's 1919 paper "The Uncanny," one also finds avenues of argument linking mystical themes (immortality, miracles, the double) with the preoedipal developmental period. Because it lies outside the parameters of Freud's correspondence with Rolland, I have omitted it from the present study. Nevertheless, an analysis of it in relation to the arguments unearthed here would pay dividends.

20. See Freud, *The Future of an Illusion*, *Standard Edition* 21:32–3.

21. See Freud, *Psychoanalysis and Faith*. For an analysis of Pfister's response, see W. W. Meissner, *Psychoanalysis and Religious Experience*.

22. Tillich, of course, was the major theological figure who engaged Freud's pejorative views on religion during the most fruitful period of the "psychology-and-religion" movement. See especially his *The Courage to Be* (New Haven, Conn.: Yale University Press, 1952) and *The Meaning of Health* (Chicago: Exploration Press, 1984).

23. Fisher, who has also noted these qualifications, thinks Freud's rhetoric is defensive. See his "Reading Freud's *Civilization and Its Discontents*," pp. 257–260.

24. Freud, *Civilization and Its Discontents*, in *Standard Edition* 21:72.

25. By this point in time, Rolland's claims surely reminded Freud of Jung. Rolland's reference to Heraclitus and his conception of "opposites" and the "intuitive" versus "critical" functions of the mind are cases in point. So too is Rolland's notion of a "subterranean source" of religion reminiscent of Jung's collective unconscious. Indeed, Jung would come to claim, in his Terry Lectures at Yale in 1937, that creeds were but codified and dogmatized forms of original religious experience (see Jung, *Psychology and Religion* [New Haven, Conn.: Yale University Press, 1977]). Both Jung and Rolland were also indebted to Otto for their approach to religious experience (see chapter 6 of this work).

26. According to the editor's introduction to *Civilization and Its Discontents*. David Fisher also thinks the "another friend" Freud mentions is Rolland but gives no compelling reason why this is so (see Fisher, "Sigmund Freud and Romain Rolland: The Terrestrial Animal and His Great Oceanic Friend," p. 27, ft. 52). The Vermorels think otherwise (*Sigmund Freud et Romain Rolland Correspondance 1923–1936*, p. 340).

27. See, for example, Fritz Wittels, "A Neglected Boundary of Psychoanalysis," *Psychoanalytic Quarterly* 18 (1949): 44–59; Fisher, "Sigmund Freud and Romain Rolland: The

Terrestrial Animal and His Great Oceanic Friend," 27, ft. 52; James DiCenso, "Religion as Illusion: Reversing the Freudian Hermeneutic," in *Journal of Religion* 71 (1991):174.

28. Freud, *Civilization and Its Discontents, Standard Edition* 21:122.

29. As cataloged in S. Guttman, R. L. Jones, S. M. Parish, eds., *The Concordance to The Standard Edition of the Complete Psychological Works of Sigmund Freud* (New York: International Universities Press, 1984).

30. Ernst Kris, *Psychoanalytic Explorations in Art* (New York: Schocken Books, 1952), pp. 22–3.

31. To note just a few of these, Freud cites Schiller as prefiguring his early instinct theory (in his 1910 paper "The Psychoanalytic View of Psychogenic Disturbance of Vision," [*Standard Edition*] 11:209–18] and in connection with his theory of free association (see *Interpretation of Dreams*); Empedocles and his later instinct theory (in the 1937 paper "Analysis Terminable and Interminable"); the strong similarity between the ideas of psychoanalysis and those of Schopenhauer and Nietzsche (in his *An Autobiographical Study* and also in *On the History of the Psychoanalytic Movement* [*Standard Edition* 14:1–66], where Freud confesses that "I had therefore to be prepared . . . to forgo all claims to priority in the many instances in which laborious psychoanalytic investigation can merely confirm the truths which the philosopher recognized by intuition" [*Standard Edition* 14:16]). In his acceptance speech for the Goethe Prize, Freud commented on how Goethe had "approached (psychoanalysis) at a number of points" and "recognized much through his own insight that we have since been able to confirm" (see *Standard Edition* 21:208–12). In a short essay entitled "A Visit to Freud" (in *Review of Existential Psychology and Psychiatry* 9, no. 2 [1969]:130–4), Giovanni Papini, an Italian philosopher and writer, relates that Freud stated the following: "Psychoanalysis is no more than the interpretation of a literary vocation in terms of psychology and pathology. . . . [P]sychoanalysis was born . . . as a result of the scientific transposition of the literary schools I like the best. . . . In psychoanalysis you may find fused together though changed into specific jargon, the three greatest literary schools of the 19th century: Heine, Zola and Mallarmé are united in me under the patronage of my old master, Goethe." According to Ellenberger, Freud confided a similar sentiment to the playwright Lenormand in saying that "the essential themes of his theory were based on the intuitions of the poets" (see *The Discovery of the Unconscious*, pp. 460, 467).

32. The German original appeared as "Erinnerungen an Sigmund Freud," in *Neue Schweitzer Rundschau* 20 (1952):3–11. I have used an English translation: "That Is All I Have to Say About Freud: Bruno Goetz's Reminiscences of Sigmund Freud," translated by Shirley E. Jones in *International Review of Psychoanalysis* 2 (1975):139–43. Another translation (by Martin Grotjahn and Ernest S. Wolf) can be found in *Annual of Psychoanalysis* 10 (1982):281–91.

33. Goetz, "That Is All I Have to Say About Freud: Bruno Goetz's Reminiscences of Sigmund Freud," p. 139.

34. Ibid, pp. 141–42

35. See Raymond Schwab, *The Oriental Renaissance*. The term "Oriental renaissance" was the title of a chapter in Edgar Quintet's work *Le génie des religions: De l'origine des dieux* (Paris: Pagnerre, 1857). Schwab (chapter 10) traces the origin of the term back to Ferdinand Eckstewin and, before him, Friedrick Schlegel.

Guy Welbon, in his *The Buddhist Nirvana and Its Western Interpreters* has detailed the emergence and parameters of the debate over the term *nirvana* with great clarity. Following Schwab, Welbon points out that in contrast to the varying and often fantastic reports conveyed through the channels of missionaries, ambassadors, and travelers, the beginning of the nineteenth century saw the birth in universities across Europe of a scholarly and scientific study of Eastern mysticism. Many philosophers and scholars, including Henry Colebrooke, Eugene Burnouf, Hermann Oldenberg, Schopenhauer, Nietzsche, and, above all, Max Müller, contributed to what became a sustained debate over what was meant by the term *nirvana*. Indeed, Goetz's teacher Leopold von Schroeder's translations became part of this debate, being cited by Burnouf in favor of his arguments (p. 59). Most were content with the etymological researches of Colebrooke, who, for all intents and purposes, set the agenda for the study of nirvana early in the nineteenth century when he concluded: "In its ordinary acceptation, as an adjective, it signifies extinct, as a fire which has gone out; set, as a luminary which has gone down; defunct, as a saint who has passed away: its etymology is from *va*, to blow as wind, with the preposition *nir* used in a negative sense: it means calm and unruffled" (p. 27). Not as clear, however, were the ontological and psychological implications of such a definition. As might be expected, the matter resolved itself into a spectrum of diverse and often competing interpretations, all of which had some basis in the complex, subtle, and voluminous scriptures from the East. These arguments ranged from thoroughly negative views of nirvana as signifying an extinction or annihilation of the self and hence nihilism, apathy, and atheism to more positive assessments advocating world affirmation and bliss (see chapters 2 and 7). Of particular interest to us is Welbon's distinction between soteriological and metaphysical explanations of nirvana. The former holds that nirvana, as a thing-in-itself, is simply beyond the ability of the mind or language to grasp. As such, endless speculation on what metaphysical reality one is delivered into is set aside in favor of a practical therapeutic system whose aim is deliverance out of suffering. This approach is consonant with the kind of pragmatic, therapeutic interpretation championed by Paul Masson-Oursell, who concluded that the psychological effects of nirvana included those of enhanced creativity, freedom, and a "fecund autonomy" (pp. 59, 190–1). Freud's comments, we might add, gravitate toward the pragmatic and therapeutic as well, albeit psychoanalytically rendered.

36. Actually Rolland, as we shall see in part II, had been introduced to Buddhist and Hindu texts as early as the 1880s during his school days in Paris. Other texts in the Freudian corpus support the view that Freud was familiar with Indian sources before his debate with Rolland. For example, in 1920, in *Beyond the Pleasure Principle* (*Standard Edition* 18:3–64) Freud refers to the Upanishads and a conversation he had had with an academic colleague concerning another heated debate of this period: the Indian influence on Plato.

The passage in question (see *Standard Edition* 18:58) reveals Freud citing Plato's myth of the origin of sexuality as found in *The Symposium*. Following "the hint given us by the poet-philosopher," Freud argues for the revisioning of psychoanalytic instinct theory. In the footnote to this passage, he goes on to address the debate over the Indian influence on Plato's thought. Citing his conversations with Heinrich Gomperz and Max Müller's translation of the Brihadaranyaka-Upanishad, Freud, in contrast to "the prevailing opinion," hesitates to "give an unqualified denial to the possibility of Plato's myth being derived from the Indian source," because he thought a similar possibility could not be excluded with respect to the doctrine of transmigration. Indeed, Freud goes further, lending credibility to the Upanishadic insight: "Plato would not have adopted a story of this kind . . . unless it had struck him as containing an element of truth." The reference to Plato should come as no surprise. It is simply another instance of Freud being edified by someone he considered to be an "intuitive psychologist." More important is Freud's added reference to the Upanishads, Müller, and Gomperz. The reference to Müller is, quite obviously, to his monumental *Sacred Books of the East*, a series which contained the translation of the Upanishad in question. As for Heinrich Gomperz, Freud had a long-standing relationship with the Gomperz family. Theodor Gomperz, a famous professor of Classics and historian of Greek thought at the University of Vienna, had enlisted Freud as a translator for the works of John Stuart Mill in 1879–1880. Years later Freud would admit that it was then he had encountered Mill's essay on Plato and how deeply Plato's theory of reminiscence had affected him. Gomperz's wife Elise was both friend and patient and his son Heinrich, who became a correspondent of Freud's, was a professor of philosophy at the University of Vienna. Gomperz was conversant with Freud's work on dreams and had written on the influence of Indian thought on Plato (see P. Gay, *Freud: A Life for Our Times* [New York: W.W. Norton, 1988] pp. 36, 137, 166–7; E. Jones, *The Life and Work of Sigmund Freud* 1:55, 340). These observations suggest the channels through which Freud was influenced by the Oriental renaissance and suggests, along with the "Goetz Letters," that the classic works of the East, as well as those of the West, influenced his thought.

Jones has also noted Freud's contacts with Rabindranath Tagore and an unnamed Indian philosopher from Calcutta in 1926. Apparently neither impressed Freud, who was reputed to have said: "My need of Indians is for the present fully satisfied" (Jones, *The Life and Work of Sigmund Freud* 3:128). Freud also engaged in correspondences with Indian psychoanalysts in the 1920s (see T. C. Sinha, "The Development of Psychoanalysis in India," in *International Journal of Psychoanalysis* 47 (1966): 427–39). Of course, Freud's exposure to mysticism in general well antedates his meeting with Rolland. Although David Bakan's *Sigmund Freud and the Jewish Mystical Tradition* (New York: Schocken Books, 1969), about the influence of Jewish mysticism on psychoanalysis, has come under attack (see Harry Trosman, *Freud and the Imaginative World* [Hillsdale, N.J.: The Analytic Press, 1985] and Marthe Robert, *From Oedipus to Moses: Freud's Jewish Identity* [Garden City, N.Y.: Anchor Books, 1976]), he convincingly demonstrates that Freud knew of both the Zohar and Chiam Vital. So too can one find references in Freud's corpus to the Persian mystic Rumi, Bergson, monasticism, the noetic knowledge gained in ecstasy, and other persons and themes associated with mysticism. These "pre-Rolland" references to mysticism further support the view that Freud was familiar with the transcendental claims of what we have referred to as the transient mystical experience, and hence his perplexity when presented with the statelike nature of the oceanic feeling.

37. See *The Interpretation of Dreams*, in *Standard Edition* 5:596. Freud thought contrary wishes and thoughts capable of existing side by side without conflict in the unconscious. In this sense, the unconscious is "beyond contradiction."

38. These observations may also shed light on Freud's cryptic reference to mysticism, found in his working notes of 1939 ("Findings, Problems, Ideas" in *Standard Edition* 23), which reads as follows: "Mysticism is the dark self perception of the realm of the id, the realm outside the ego." Here I follow the translation by Paula Heimann as cited by Marion Milner in her *The Suppressed Madness of Sane Men* (London: Tavistock, 1987) p. 272. Heimann argues that Strachey's translation, which renders *dunkel* as *obscure* rather than *dark*, takes away Freud's original, poetic intent: "Having more poetry it is more true. Moreover, the word 'dark' is associated with natural phenomena, whereas 'obscure' suggests something made by men" (pp. 272–3).

Note as well Milner's reference, in the same book, to this quote from Freud: "Later I found another reference to mysticism in Freud's writing, though not mentioned in the index. In Freud, S. (1920) *The Psychogenesis of a Case of Female Homosexuality*. Standard edition 18, on p. 165 this sentence occurs: 'I know, indeed that the craving of mankind for mysticism is ineradicable.' This follows his referring to 'the unconscious, the real centre of our mental life, the part of us that is so much nearer the divine than our poor consciousness.'" (p. 273).

39. I would like to thank Robert Kaplan of Harvard University for making this clear to me.

40. See Freud, *The Ego and the Id* (in *Standard Edition* 19:25) and *Group Psychology and the Analysis of the Ego* (in *Standard Edition* 18: chapter 4). See also Oskar Pfister, "Plato als Vorläufer der Psychoanalyse," in *International Zeitschrift für Psychoanalyse* 7 (1921); Max Nachmansohn, "Freuds Libidotheorie verglichten mit der Eroslehre Platos," in *Internationale Zeitschrift für Psychoanalyse* 3 (1915); Gerasimos Santas, *Plato and Freud* (New York: Basil Blackwell, 1988).

## Chapter 3

1. *Essai sur la mystique et l'action de l'Inde vivante: La vie de Ramakrishna* (Paris, Librairie Stock, 1929); *Essai sur la mystique et l'action de l'Inde vivante: La vie de Vivekananda et l'evangile universel* (Paris, Librairie Stock, 1930). References, unless otherwise noted, will be to the English translation: *The Life of Ramakrishna* (Calcutta: Advaita Ashrama, 1965); *The Life of Vivekananda and the Universal Gospel* (Calcutta: Advaita Ashrama, 1988).

2. For example, see Fisher, "Sigmund Freud and Romain Rolland: The Terrestrial Animal and His Great Oceanic Friend," p. 29, and Werman, "Sigmund Freud and Romain Rolland," p. 236ff.

3. On the last page of *The Life of Vivekananda*, Rolland appends the date April 1929. In his journal *Inde* (Paris: Éditions Vineta, 1951), in which he jotted down all the contacts and dealings he had with the East from 1915 to 1943, Rolland states that he finished with the last typographical revisions for the publisher on May 22, 1929 (p. 216). According to Strachey's introduction to *Civilization and Its Discontents* in *The Standard Edition* 22, the latter came out in December of 1929. The first mention Rolland makes of it is on December 28, 1929, in a letter to Stefan Zweig (see Fisher, "Sigmund Freud and Romain Rolland: The Terrestrial Animal and His Great Oceanic Friend," p. 35). In *Inde*, Rolland states that the last volume of the biographies was publicly issued on January 6, 1930 (p. 219).

4. For an overview of Freud's *Totem and Taboo* and anthropological criticisms of it, see E. Wallace, *Freud and Anthropology* (New York: International Universities Press, 1983).

5. See, for example, P. Homans, *Jung in Context* (Chicago: University of Chicago Press, 1979); S. Kakar, *The Inner World: A Psycho-Analytic Study of Childhood and Society in India* (Delhi: Oxford University Press, 1981); S. Kurtz, *All the Mothers Are One* (New York: Columbia University Press, 1992); A. Parsons, "Is the Oedipus Complex Universal?" in *Man and His Culture: Psychoanalytic Anthropology after "Totem and Taboo,"* ed. W. Muensterberger (New York: Taplinger, 1970) pp. 331–384.

6. Max Weber, in his *The Protestant Ethic and the Spirit of Capitalism* (New York: Charles Scribner's Sons, 1958), draws a rather stark contrast between the magical, enchanted worldview of the typical Catholic and the lonely, disenchanted religious worldview of the typical Protestant. Following Weber, Rieff shows how this shift in Christian doctrine prepared the Protestant in a psychological sense for Freud's "message" (see "The American Transference: From Calvin to Freud," *Atlantic* 208, July 1961, 105–7).

7. Rolland, *Journey Within*, p. 74.

8. My aim in what follows concerning the "two religions" of Romain's youth is solely to establish their maternal core. For a more detailed overview and analysis of the content of these religions, see chapters 5 and 7.

9. Rolland, *The Forerunners*, trans. Eden and Cedar Paul (New York: Harcourt, Brace, and Howe, 1920), p. 32.

10. Rolland, *Journey Within*, p. 75.

11. See *Romain Rolland and Gandhi Correspondence* (New Delhi: Publications Division, Ministry of Information and Broadcasting, Government of India, 1976), pp. 206–7.

12. From "Le Seuil" in Rolland, *Le Voyage intérieur* (Paris: Éditions Albin Michel, 1959), p. 176.

13. Rolland, *Journey Within*, pp. 11–12.

14. Ibid., pp. 114–15.

15. Ibid., p. 5.

16. Ibid., p. 73.

17. Ibid., p. 13.

18. In Rolland, *Cahiers Romain Rolland 4, Le Cloître ae la rue d'Ulm. Journal de Romain Rolland à l'Ecole Normale (1886–1889)*, pp. 303–4.

19. Rolland, *Journey Within*, p. 89.

20. *Romain Rolland and Gandhi Correspondence*, p. 207.

21. See "Royame de T," in *Le Voyage intérieur* (Paris: Éditions Albin Michel, 1959) p. 204; *Inde*, p. 254.

22. Rolland thought the doctrine of Original Sin unjustly placed the sin of one man on all, sanctified suffering, and took away the responsibility of man (see Rolland, *Au Seuil de la dernière porte* [Paris: Les Éditions de Cerf, 1989], p. 23). So too did he think the confessional excused sin and failed to instill religious behavior (see Rolland's "Royame de T"; *Inde*, p. 254). On Rolland's objections to Catholic dogma, see his "My Confession" in *Au Seuil de la dernière porte*, p. 89ff. See also F. J. Harris, *André Gide and Romain Rolland: Two Men Divided* (New Brunswick, N.J.: Rutgers University Press, 1973), pp. 98–9 and W. Starr, *Romain Rolland: One Against All*, p. 217 passim.

23. See Rolland, *Au Seuil de la dernière porte*, pp. 16, 24. *Above the Battle* and *Journal des années de guerre: 1914–1919* (Paris: Albin Michel, 1952) are also fertile sources for Rolland's views on Christianity during the war.

24. Rolland, *Au Seuil de la dernière porte*, p. 23.

25. See, for example, the introduction to Rolland's *Au Seuil de la dernière porte*.

26. P. Claudel, "La Pensée religieuse de Romain Rolland," *La Revue* (January–February, 1949): pp. 193–211.

27. Rolland, *Au Seuil de la dernière porte*, p. 26.

28. See W. Starr, *Romain Rolland and a World at War*, p. 11.

29. Rolland, "My Confession," in *Au Seuil de la dernière porte*, p. 89ff.

30. Doré and Prévost, eds., *Selected Letters of Romain Rolland* (Delhi: Oxford University Press, 1990), p. 72.

31. Ibid., p. 90.

32. See Rolland, *Au Seuil de la dernière porte*, pp. 128–9.

33. Ibid., p. 129. Compare also Rolland's letter to Freud of May 3, 1931.

34. I do not deny that one can find in this vision, as well as in Rolland's other visions, dreams, and autobiographical reflections, Oedipal elements, just as one can find in Freud's life and thought pre-Oedipal elements. Nevertheless, in every person, as is so well illustrated by the concept of a "character-type," various developmental lines and conflicts tend to preponderate. I highlight the maternal and pre-Oedipal in Rolland on both factual and rhetorical grounds in order to show its complicity in Rolland's advocacy of a mystical psychoanalysis, thereby helping to contrast it with the psychosocial determinants of Freud's cultural works as shown in previous chapters.

35. See Starr, *Romain Rolland: One Against All*, p. 196; Doré and Prévost, eds., *Selected Letters*, p. ix. In his journal at the École Normale, Rolland cited how his friends dubbed him "the musical Buddha of a revolutionary mysticism" (*Cahiers Romain Rolland* 4:323).

36. See Rolland, *The Life of Vivekananda*, p. 176; D. K. Roy, *Among the Great* (Bombay: N.M. Tripathi, Nalanda Publications, 1945), pp. 71–3; Rolland, *Inde*, pp. 43–4.

37. See especially Rolland's comments in *Inde*, 11ff., on Tagore's lectures at the University of Tokyo in 1916. Fisher (*Romain Rolland and the Politics of Intellectual Engagement*, chapter 6) has some interesting observations on Rolland's political activities during this time and their connection with his turn East.

38. Rolland, foreword to Ananda Coomaraswamy, *The Dance of Shiva* (New York: The Sunrise Turn, 1924), p. 3.

39. See *Rolland and Tagore*, ed. A. Aronson and K. R. Kripalani (Calcutta: Visva-Bharati, 1945), p. 84. Many of these concerns were expressed by Rolland in his *The Revolt of the Machines or Invention Run Wild* (Ithaca, N.Y.: The Dragon Press, 1932). Rolland's views suggest at least a cursory acquaintance with the writings of Marx and Weber. According to Fisher (*Romain Rolland and the Politics of Intellectual Engagement*, chapter 10), Rolland did not engage in a systematic fashion the thought of Marx until after 1930. Up until that time, he lacked an awareness of the complex economic and philosophical basis of Marxism, although he was familiar with fundamental concepts such as the notion of alienation, Marx's critique of idealism, and the deep humanism that permeated Marx's early works. However, I have been unable to find evidence that Rolland read Weber.

40. Rolland, foreword, Coomaraswamy, *The Dance of Shiva*, p. i. See also Rolland's biography of Vivekananda, p. 293.

41. See Rolland, *Inde*, pp. 9–12. Coomaraswamy's article appeared in *The New Age*, December 24, 1915, and Tagore's in *The Outlook*, August 9, 1916. The fact that the references to these two articles make up the first two entries in Rolland's journal *Inde*, which is well over 400 pages and spans the years 1915–1942, confirms their importance for Rolland's turn to the East.

42. See *Inde* for his correspondence with Coomaraswamy. Rolland's correspondence with Tagore can be found in *Cahiers Romain Rolland* 12, *Rabindranath Tagore et Romain Rolland. Lettres et autres écrits*, and in *Rolland and Tagore*. Interesting reflections on Sri Aurobindo can be found in the French edition of *The Life of Vivekananda* (in the appendix, "Le Réveil de l'Inde après Vivekananda"). For Rolland's correspondence with Gandhi, see *Cahiers Romain Rolland* 19, *Gandhi et Romain Rolland. Correspondance, extraits du Journal et texts divers*, and Rolland's biography of Gandhi, *Mahatma Gandhi: The Man who Became One with the Universal Being*, trans. C. Groth (New York: Century, 1924).

43. Letter, Rolland to Tagore, June 11, 1923, in *Rolland and Tagore*, p. 43. Rolland's correspondence with Tagore also reveals his attempts to establish an international university and an East–West journal.

44. See Fisher, *Romain Rolland and the Politics of Intellectual Engagement*, chap. 4. Rolland's efforts to establish an international review were only partially realized in the journal *Europe* (see W. Starr, *Romain Rolland: One Against All*, chapter 13).

45. Ibid., pp. 116–18. See also Alex Aronson, *Europe Looks at India* (Calcutta: Riddhi-India 1979), pp. 138–48.

46. E. Said, *Orientalism* (New York: Vintage, 1979), pp. 250–51; Fisher, *Romain Rolland and the Politics of Intellectual Engagement*, pp. 117–18.

47. Fisher, *Romain Rolland and the Politics of Intellectual Engagement*, pp. 116–18.

48. Ibid., p. 117.

49. Cited in Aronson, *Europe looks at India*, p. 140.

50. Rolland's description of the lives and worldview of the Hindu saints was certainly adequate given the state of comparative studies of his day. But in light of recent studies, it is rendered a historical fossil. For more on the studies by Sil, Kakar and Kripal, see chapter 6.

51. Rolland, *The Life of Ramakrishna*, p. 4.

52. Rolland, *The Life of Vivekananda*, pp. 287–90.

53. Rolland, *The Life of Ramakrishna*, p. 8.

54. See Rolland's foreword to Coomaraswamy's *Dance of Shiva*.

55. See especially Note 3 in the appendix of the biography of Vivekananda.

56. Rolland, *The Life of Ramakrishna*, p. 9.

57. Most of these sources and their influence on Rolland can be found in his journal *Inde* and his biographies of the Hindu saints. The reader is referred to chapter 6 for an in-depth examination of Rolland's participation in the comparative study of mysticism of his day.

58. Rolland, *The Life of Vivekananda*, pt. 2, chapter 4.

59. See especially pt. 1, chapter 4 and note 3 in *The Life of Vivekananda*.

60. Ibid., p. 348, ft. 1.

61. See Schwab, *The Oriental Renaissance*, pp. 466ff.

62. Rolland, *The Life of Vivekananda*, p. 309.

63. Ibid., pp. 304–10.

64. See especially Rolland's comments on the Brahmo Samaj in the chapter entitled "The Builders of Unity" in *The Life of Ramakrishna*.

65. Rolland, *The Life of Ramakrishna*, p. 7.

66. See, for example, Rolland's journal *Inde*, p. 177.

67. Rolland, *The Life of Ramakrishna*, p. 6.

68. Ibid., p. 4.

69. Ibid., pp. 4–5. See also the first two appendixes in *The Life of Vivekananda*.

70. Rolland, *Life of Vivekananda*, pp. 346–47.

71. Ibid., p. 224, ft. 2; pp. 258–60.

72. A good overview of this period can be found in Benjamin Beit-Hallahmi, "Psychology of Religion 1880–1930: The Rise and Fall of a Psychological Movement," *Journal of the History of Behavioral Sciences* 10 (1974):84–90. The most detailed historical work on the psychology and religion movement is to be found in David Wulff, *Psychology of Religion: Classic and Contemporary Views.*

73. For the best studies penned by these authors, see; James, *The Varieties of Religious Experience*; G. S. Hall, *Adolescence: Its psychology and its relation to physiology, anthropology, sociology, sex, crime, religion and education* (New York: Appleton, 1915–1916); Edwin Starbuck, *The Psychology of Religion* (London: Walter Scott, 1914); James Leuba, *The Psychology of Religious Mysticism* (New York: Harcourt, Brace, 1926); George Coe, *The Psychology of Religion* (Chicago: University of Chicago Press, 1916); W. E. Hocking, *The Meaning of God in Human Experience* (New Haven: Yale University Press, 1912).

74. In particular, James was indebted to Myers' notion of the "subliminal self" in formulating the conclusions in his *Varieties*, whereas Leuba cited the influence exercised on him by Janet (*The Psychology of Religious Mysticism*, x–xi). The latter, in turn, hailed Leuba, along with Durkheim, as the greatest figures in the scientific study of religion (for Janet's views on mysticism see Rev. Walter M. Horton, "The Origin and Psychological Function of Religion According to Pierre Janet," *American Journal of Psychology*, 35 [1924]:20; H. Ellenberger, *The Discovery of the Unconscious* [N.Y.: Basic Books, 1970] chapter 6). In contrast to James, Leuba thought psychoanalysis to be so entirely lacking in scientific accuracy that "it may not long endure in the form given it by its author" (*The Psychology of Religious Mysticism*, p. 321). E. I. Schaub ("The Psychology of Religion in America During the Past Quarter Century," *Journal of Religion* 6 [1926]:113–34) cites a book by E. D. Martin, *The Mystery of Religion*, as being the first American book applying

psychoanalytic method to religion. Homans, in his article "Psychology and Religion," has pointed out that it was not until the second "period" of the psychology and religion movement (1930–1960) that psychoanalysis exercised a powerful appeal in the United States. Even then, however, the debate was not over the issue of mysticism but those of ethics, existentialism, and pastoral counseling.

75. See E. I. Schaub, "The Psychology of Religion in America during the Past Quarter Century"; J. B. Pratt, "The Psychology of Religion," *Harvard Theological Review* 1 (1908):435–54. Many of the "psychologists" in France, most obvious in the case of Maréchal, also donned the hat of philosopher and theologian. The same could be said of James and Hocking. The term *psychology of religion*, then, should be here understood in the relatively wide sense it had at that period in history.

76. H. Delacroix, *Études d'histoire et de psychologie du mysticisme: Le grands mystiques chrétiens* (Paris: Alcan, 1908); J. Pacheu, *L'Expérience mystique et l'activité subconsciente* (Paris: Perrin, 1911); J. Maréchal, *Studies in the Psychology of the Mystics* (Albany, N.Y.: Magi Books, 1964).

77. F. Alexander, "Buddhistic Training as Artificial Catatonia"; F. Morel "Essai sur l'introversion mystique."

78. This is not because of a dearth of knowledge concerning psychoanalysis. Maréchal, for example, wrote a two-part article on psychoanalysis ("Les Lignes essentiales du Freudisme" in *Nouvelle Revue Theologique* 52 [1925]:537–51; 577–605, and 53 [1926]:13–50) detailing its major tenets and applications. However, in his famous work, *Studies in the Psychology of the Mystics*, it was in the main Leuba, James, and Delacroix with whom he was conversing. This may well have been because Freud spent so little time on mysticism whereas the American psychologists clearly made it one of the centerpieces of their agenda. Freud may also have been too reductionistic for Maréchal, who, in the final analysis, felt only philosophical and theological hypotheses could account for certain aspects of mysticism, such as the "intellectual intuitions" of the great Christian mystics. Finally, it should be noted once again that at this point in history psychoanalysis had not yet reached the popularity it was later to enjoy both on the Continent and in the United States. The lack of receptivity in France to psychoanalysis was not lost on Freud. "Among European countries," he wrote, "France has hitherto shown itself the least disposed to welcome psychoanalysis. . . . In Paris itself, a conviction still seems to reign . . . that everything good in psychoanalysis is a repetition of Janet's views with insignificant modifications, and that everything else in it is bad" (Freud, *On the History of the Psychoanalytic Movement*, in *Standard Edition* 14:32). This seems to corroborate Rolland's statement that he was one of the very first to have not only read but appreciated Freud in France.

79. The books cited in this study by Hocking, Flournoy, Leuba, and Maréchal are excellent examples of this. Unfortunately, despite an enormous amount of evidence indicating how dependent the psychology of religion was on an international exchange of ideas, it has yet to be fully detailed in what complex ways scholars on both continents influenced each other's thoughts through correspondences, collaborations, and international conferences, as well as through articles and books. Some examples of the enormous contact between people on the two continents that have been well noted are as follows: Leuba wrote some of his articles for French journals; French books were regularly reviewed in journals like *The Psychological Bulletin* by leading scholars in the United States; James engaged in a substantial correspondence with Flournoy and was president of the British-based Society for Psychical Research, which was started by Myers (who also deeply influenced Flournoy); in at least one of the international conferences held in Germany, Janet, Leuba, and the psychoanalyst Ernest Jones were the major

speakers; articles and books in both France and the United States were filled with references and criticisms of the other countries' studies, and so forth. However, I know of no study that has cataloged this exchange, particularly with respect to mysticism, in a systematic way and with respect to its importance to the shape of the emerging psychology of religion movement.

80. Pratt, "The Psychology of Religion," p. 449.

81. Ibid., pp. 449–54. It should once again be emphasized that France did not, at least during Rolland's lifetime, accord to psychoanalysis a favorable reception. The reasons for this are many. Freud himself referred to the "national character" of France (*The Freud–Jung Letters*, p. 65). It also seems to be the case that psychoanalysis has a better cultural "fit" with Protestantism (see Rieff, "The American Transference: From Calvin to Freud"). France, of course, has traditionally been more Catholic than Protestant. Catholicism, with its strong maternal presence, would be a better cultural fit with Jung or pre-Oedipal psychology. Along these lines, one could also cite the therapeutic dimension of Catholicism—its rituals, particularly the confession, stress on a maternal presence, and mediated relationship to God—as so effective as to delay the need for psychoanalytic therapy.

82. See Rolland, *Life of Ramakrishna*, p. 34, ft. 2, and *Life of Vivekananda*, p. 87, ft. 1; p. 346, ft. 1.

83. See Masson, *The Oceanic Feeling*, p. 47. Rolland did not seem to be aware of the exchange between Leuba and Maréchal over the nature of the "intellectual intuitions" of mystics (see Maréchal, *Studies in the Psychology of the Mystics*, especially pp. 124–135). This is unfortunate, for it would have been interesting to see if and how this awareness would have been used by Rolland in his critique of Morel's analysis of the "unmitigated" form of mysticism.

84. Rolland, *Life of Ramakrishna*, p. 5.

85. Rolland, *Life of Vivekananda*, p. 346, ft. 1.

86. The term *psychologia perennis*, defined and then elaborated as a continuation and development of the perennial philosophy, was introduced by Ken Wilber in his "Psychologia Perennis: The Spectrum of Consciousness," *Journal of Transpersonal Psychology* 7 (1975):105–132 (see especially p. 105). It would be accurate, I think, to see the Freud–Rolland correspondence as one of the historical sources for that aspect of the psychology and religion movement which I will from here on refer to as the "perennial psychology."

87. Most of Rolland's comments on Yoga can be found in part II of his biography of Vivekananda, particularly the chapter entitled "The Great Paths."

88. See *The Life of Vivekananda*, p. 186, ft. 1; pp. 240–56.

89. Ibid., p. 238, ft. 4; p. 239.

90. Ibid., p. 233, ft. 3.

91. Ibid., pp. 231–2, 183–4. See also p. 183, ft. 2.

92. Ibid., pp. 178–85; 214.

93. Ibid., pp. 240–56.

94. Ibid., p. 222. Rolland included himself as an "instinctive" practitioner of Yoga (pp. 230–1).

95. One can find evidence of this throughout chaps. 2–4 of Part 2 in *The Life of Vivekananda*.

96. Ibid., p. 345.

97. This lays to rest Masson's claim (*The Oceanic Feeling*, pp. 47–8, ft. 13) that Rolland never read, nor would he have wanted to read, Morel's study. No extant work on the Freud–Rolland correspondence has noted the importance of Morel's work for Rolland's

appendix. Fisher notes that Rolland read Morel and summarizes, as does Werman, some of Rolland's more salient passages which deal with his criticisms of Morel's use of psychological models in interpreting mysticism (see Werman, "Sigmund Freud and Romain Rolland," p. 238; Fisher, "Sigmund Freud and Romain Rolland: The Terrestrial Animal and His Great Oceanic Friend," pp. 29–35). However, neither seems to understand that Rolland is responding in the appendix to Morel and Morel only. Indeed, both Werman and Fisher seem to be under the impression that Rolland was responding in some measure to Freud's interpretation of the oceanic feeling in *Civilization and Its Discontents*. Fisher, for example, states that Rolland answered "Freud's critique of mysticism in the introduction and appendix of the work" (p. 29). This is clearly impossible since Freud wrote nothing substantial on mysticism before he responded to Rolland in *Civilization and Its Discontents*—and at this time Rolland had not yet read the latter. In fact, if one looks at Morel's *Essai sur l'Introversion mystique* carefully (especially pp. 11–14; 19–20), one finds that all of Rolland's references to Freud in this appendix were verbatim quotes taken directly from Morel's work. In sum, neither Fisher nor Werman seeks to coordinate Rolland's criticisms of psychoanalysis with Morel's use of it in *Essai sur l'Introversion mystique*, a fact which has led to important omissions and errors in their respective analyses. As a result, in this section I have endeavored to put Rolland's arguments in proper context. Only then can one arrive at an accurate understanding of the historical roots of the emerging psychoanalytic theory of mysticism.

98. Morel gives a detailed summary of precisely how he is utilizing these theorists in the introduction of his work (pp. 5–29). The "Freud" Morel cites is for the most part the early Freud: one pivotal book (*Three Essays on Sexuality*), two metapsychological papers (*Two Principles of Mental Functioning*; *On Narcissism*) and several early papers.

99. The source of Morel's understanding of Jung and the concept of "introversion" lies in his *Symbols of Transformation* (see Morel, pp. 21–2. See also Carl Jung, *Psychology of the Unconscious* [New York: Dodd, 1916]:486–7, ft. 15).

100. See Morel, *Essai sur l'introversion mystique*, pp. 293–336.

101. Rolland, *Life of Vivekananda*, pp. 333, ft. 4.

102. Ibid., p. 333–5. Rolland's analysis of the mitigated form of introversion can be found on pp. 333–38; that of its unmitigated form on pp. 338–45.

103. Rolland, *Life of Vivekananda*, p. 338.

104. Ibid., pp. 337–8; 344, ft. 3. Baudouin's article is entitled "La Régression et les phénomènes de recul en psychologie" (*Journal de Psychologie*, vol. 25 [November–December 1928]:795–823).

105. Ibid., p. 345.

106. Here I agree with Fisher that Rolland anticipated revisions in psychoanalytic theory ("Sigmund Freud and Romain Rolland: The Terrestrial Animal and His Great Oceanic Friend," p. 31). Fisher, however, links Rolland to Norman O. Brown and Herbert Marcuse while I link him, through Baudouin, to the ego-psychologists.

107. E. Kris, *Psychoanalytic Explorations in Art* (New York: Schocken Books, 1952), cf. Werman, "Sigmund Freud and Romain Rolland," p. 239.

108. H. Hartmann, *Ego Psychology and the Problem of Adaptation* (New York: International Universities Press, 1958), pp. 36–7. Of relevance here are Rolland's observations concerning the adaptive nature of Ramakrishna's visions. See *Life of Ramakrishna*, p. 38.

109. Erik Erikson, *Young Man Luther* (New York: W. W. Norton, 1962).

110. Rolland, *Life of Vivekananda*, pp. 335–6. Cf. Fisher, "Sigmund Freud and Romain Rolland," pp. 33–5. Again, let me emphasize that Rolland's characterizations of Janet and Freud are taken directly from the introduction to Morel's book (compare in the latter pp. 11–14; 19–20). In other words, Rolland was not relying on any outside texts, cer-

tainly not *Civilization and Its Discontents*, for his information on the psychologists he was critiquing. This led to an uncritical blending of the ideas of Janet, Freud, and Jung, a point Freud was to pick up on in his letter of January 19, 1930, to Rolland.

111. Rolland, *Life of Vivekananda*, pp. 343; 339; 344.

112. Ibid., p. 344.

113. Rolland, *Life of Ramakrishna*, p. 25.

114. Rolland, *Life of Vivekananda*, p. 338.

115. Ibid., p. 240.

116. Ibid., pp. 234–56. Rolland also gave voice to this "deeper" area of the unconscious in poetic terms in numerous works. See, for example, chap. 4 of *Journey Within* (pp. 108ff.) and the last volume of *The Soul Enchanted* (entitled *A World in Birth*, trans. Amalia de Alberti [New York: Henry Holt, 1934], chapter 28, pp. 218–19). We shall come back to these works in chapter 5.

117. Rolland, *The Life of Vivekananda*, pp. 246, ft. 1; p. 333; p. 338, ft. 2; p. 342, ft. 3. In the beginning of the appendix (p. 333, ft. 1), Rolland lauds the studies in the Bergsonian tradition that attempted to rehabilitate intuition on scientific grounds. Later, he explicitly cites Bergson's disciple E. LeRoy's article "La Discipline de l'intuition" (in the review *Vers l'Unite* [1925] pp. 35–6) as reflective of his own views on the matter. Rolland goes on to make an unjustified and easy equation between LeRoy and Yoga (*The Life of Vivekananda*, pp. 343–4, ft. 3) and implies a virtual equivalence between views of intuition in the Bergsonian tradition and those espoused by Sri Aurobindo. Although not apparent in the biographies, it is the case that Rolland was first exposed to the concept of intuition through Spinoza (see chapter 5 of this work). Interesting enough, despite seeming similarities between Bergson's vitalistic philosophy and Rolland's dynamic conception of the "oceanic feeling," Rolland did not have anything particularly revealing to say about the influence of Bergson on his philosophy. Because both were French and contemporaries, this strikes me as surprising. As Cheval (*L'Allemagne et la guerre*, p. 87, ft. 2) has pointed out, there are few allusions to Bergson in the written corpus of Rolland. One could certainly say that vitalism was "in the air." It should also be noted that Rolland himself attributed the vitalistic dimension in his philosophy to the pre-Socratic philosophers Heraclitus and Empedocles and to his interest in the Italian Renaissance (see R. Wilson, *The Pre-War Biographies of Romain Rolland* [New York: Oxford University Press, 1939], p. 122 and chapter 5).

118. Rolland, *Life of Vivekananda*, p. 341.

119. Ibid., p. 341. The phrase of which Rolland speaks comes from the *Tao Te Ching* ("Thirty spokes are united around the hub to make a wheel, But it is on its non-being that the utility of the carriage depends"). See Wing Tsit Chan, *A Source Book in Chinese Philosophy* (Princeton, N.J.: Princeton University Press, 1963, p. 144). Rolland also cited the advances of modern physics, especially Einstein's theory of relativity, as coming close to the Hindu mystical worldview (p. 243).

120. Ibid., p. 342.

121. Letter to Bruno Scanferla, September 7, 1927, in *Selected Letters of Romain Rolland*, pp. 83–4. See also *Life of Vivekananda*, p. 342, ft. 1. On p. 344, ft. 2, Rolland also pointed out the chemist Jean Perrin, author of *The Atoms* (see especially the *Introduction* to that work) as another, Western promoter of the "intuitive method." For Rolland's contact and friendship with Bose, see his journal *Inde*.

122. Letter to Bruno Scanferla, September 7, 1927, in *Selected Letters*, pp. 83–4.

123. Rolland was familiar with the writings of Aurobindo through the journal *Arya*.

124. Rolland, *The Life of Vivekananda*, pp. 342–3.

125. Ibid., p. 246, ft. 1.

126. Ibid., p. 342, ft. 1; p. 342, ft. 3. See also Doré and Prévost, eds., *Selected Letters*, p. 84.

127. Ibid., p. 344; p. 246, ft. 1. Also see in this regard Rolland's crucial letter of November 14, 1913, to Sophia Bertolini (in *Cahiers Romain Rolland, Chère Sofia. Choix de lettres de Romain Rolland à Sophia Bertolini Guerrieri-Gonzaga* (1909–1932). 11:187 ff.)

128. For a comparison between Bergson's and Aurobindo's concepts of intuition, see S. K. Maitra, *The Meeting of East and West in Sri Aurobindo's Philosophy* (Pondicherry, India: Sri Aurobindo Ashram, 1956), chapter 2.

## Chapter 4

1. For an interesting response of Rolland to Freud's analysis of the oceanic feeling, see his letter to Zweig of December 30, 1929, in *Romain Rolland/Stefan Zweig Briefwechsel* (Berlin: Rütten and Loening, 1987), 2:348–9.

2. In a letter of March 13, 1930, to Charles Baudouin, Rolland commented on this letter, remarking that Freud's reference to Jung "smells of excommunication" (Cornubert, "Freud et Romain Rolland," p. 36). Fisher, in his "Sigmund Freud and Romain Rolland: The Terrestrial Animal and His Great Oceanic Friend," adds that there is no evidence that Rolland knew of the Freud–Jung split (see p. 40). This letter also undermines Masson's assertion that Freud never read Rolland's biographies (see Masson, *The Oceanic Feeling*, p. 44, ft. 1).

3. Freud, *Introductory Lectures on Psychoanalysis*, in *Standard Edition* 16: lecture 23. In distinguishing his use of the term *introversion* from that of Jung, note that Freud understood Jung's use of the term to be used exclusively with respect to *dementia praecox.*

4. Ibid. See also Freud's *Formulations on The Two Principles on Mental Functioning, Standard Edition* 12:213–26. Of course many of Freud's views on art were given greater metapsychological clarity and sophistication by ego psychologists like Hartmann, Kris, and Erikson.

5. Freud, *The Future of an Illusion, Standard Edition* 21:28.

6. Ibid., pp. 31–2.

7. Once again, while I am indebted to the studies by Cornubert and Fisher for unearthing many of the letters and texts of what I call the late period of the Freud–Rolland correspondence, our interpretation of these letters and texts varies. For example, with regard to this letter (of January 19, 1930), my major point of difference with Fisher stems from our varying analysis of Rolland's engagement with Morel (see Fisher, "Sigmund Freud and Romain Rolland," pp. 35–39). In contrast to Fisher, I attempt to show the continuity between Freud's letter, *The Future of an Illusion*, and Rolland's distinction between "mitigated" and "unmitigated" kinds of intuition—a distinction lost on Fisher but crucial for the psychoanalytic theory of mysticism. I also link this letter to my earlier sociological observations on Roland's status as interlocuter.

8. Cited in Cornubert, "Freud et Romain Rolland," p. 37; Fisher, "Sigmund Freud and Romain Rolland," p. 40.

9. The "open letter" to Rolland was written in 1936. Although the *New Introductory Lectures* (in *Standard Edition* 22:1–182) came out in 1933, Freud had finished writing them in May of 1932.

10. Freud, *New Introductory Lectures*, Lecture 31.

11. Bruno Bettelheim, *Freud and Man's Soul* (New York: Vintage, 1984), pp. 61–4.

12. I wish to thank Professor Samuel Jaffe of the University of Chicago for alerting me to the grammatical structure and religious significance of what I have referred to as

the psychoanalytic motto. He is, of course, not responsible for any errors I may have made by interpreting it with respect to the Freud–Rolland correspondence.

13. This is the title which is used most commonly in referring to Freud's analysis of his feeling of "derealization" which occurred on the Acropolis in 1904. The German title is "Brief an Romain Rolland" (*"Eine Errinerungsstörung auf der Akropolis"*).

14. See Maynard Solomon, "Freud's Father on the Acropolis," *American Imago* 30 (1973):142–56; William Niederland, "Freud's 'Déjà Vu' on the Acropolis," *American Imago* 26 (1969):373–8.

15. See Solomon, "Freud's Father on the Acropolis," pp. 143–5, for an indication of precisely how varied the perspectives employed and theories generated have been.

16. The single study that has treated Freud's essay as one concerning mysticism is by J. M. Masson and T. C. Masson, "Buried Memories on the Acropolis: Freud's Response to Mysticism and Anti-Semitism," in *International Journal of Psychoanalysis* 59 (1978): 199–208. In their attempts to formulate a general theory of mysticism, they conclude that Freud saw mystical phenomena as defenses against deeply repressed traumatic memories and that the paper on the Acropolis attempted to articulate that view. My analysis differs in both emphasis and interpretation, seeking as I do to contextualize the "open letter" more specifically with respect to Rolland's biographies and the "late period" of the Freud–Rolland correspondence. The Massons do not think Freud ever read the biographies by Rolland, hence they fail to see the Acropolis paper in context.

17. Freud, *The Future of an Illusion, Standard Edition* 21:25.

18. Ibid.

19. Jones, *The Life and Work of Sigmund Freud* 2:24.

20. Two other studies have briefly noted the connection between this passage and Freud's correspondence with Rolland: Mark Kanzer, "Sigmund and Alexander Freud on the Acropolis," *American Imago,* 26 (1969):346 and Irving Harrison, "On Freud's View of the Mother–Infant Relationship and of the Oceanic Feeling: Some Subjective Influences," *Journal of the American Psychoanalytic Association* 27 (1979):399–419.

21. E. Freud, *Letters,* pp. 182–3.

22. John Gedo, "Freud's Self-Analysis and his Scientific Ideas," in *Freud: The Fusion of Science and Humanism: The Intellectual History of Psychoanalysis,* ed. J. Gedo and George Pollock (New York: International Universities Press, 1976), p. 296.

23. Freud, "A Disturbance of Memory on the Acropolis," in *Standard Edition* 22:247.

24. No one has followed up this particular avenue of Freud's ruminations on mysticism better than Ben-Ami Scharfstein in chapter 8 ("Freud's Psychoanalysis and Patanjali's Yoga") of his *Mystical Experience* (Indianapolis, Ind.: Bobbs-Merrill, 1973). See also J. M. Masson, *The Oceanic Feeling.*

25. Freud, "A Disturbance of Memory on the Acropolis," in *Standard Edition* 22:247.

26. Masson and Masson, "Buried Memories on the Acropolis: Freud's Response to Mysticism and Anti-Semitism," p. 199; Kanzer, "Sigmund and Alexander Freud on the Acropolis," p. 341, ft. 4. See also Meissner, *Psychoanalysis and Religious Experience,* pp. 47–8 and compare Solomon, "Freud's Father on the Acropolis."

## Chapter 5

1. Rolland, *Journey Within,* p. 5.
2. Rolland, *Le Voyage intérieur,* p. 203.
3. Ibid.

4. Louis Beirnaert, "Romain Rolland, Les Dernières Etapes du voyage intérieur," in *Études* vol. 144 (1945):250–6. This is taken from a letter Rolland wrote to him in 1929.

5. On this point there is a slight discrepancy between the *Mémoires* and the letter to Beirnaert on the one hand and *Journey Within* on the other. In the *Mémoires* (p. 23), Rolland appends the date 1881, which is consistent with the letter to Beirnaert, whereas in *Journey Within* the date reads 1882 (p. 13). The discrepancy would be resolved if there was any indication that Rolland was referring to two different "éclairs." However, in his *Mémoires* Rolland explicitly states that he is referring to the experience he wrote about in *Journey Within*. The discrepancy is understandable considering Rolland's advanced age and poor health.

6. Rolland, *Journey Within*, pp. 14–15.

7. Compare Hebrews 9; Exodus 26; Matthew 27:51.

8. Rolland, *Mémoires et fragments du Journal* (Paris: Albin Michel, 1956), p. 23.

9. Ibid.

10. Ibid.

11. Ibid.

12. Rolland, *Journey Within*, pp. 30–1. Rolland also mentions this episode in a letter to Sophia Bertolini in *Cahiers Romain Rolland 10 Chère Sophia. Choix de lettres de Romain Rolland à Sophia Bertolini Guerrieri-Gonzaga (1901–1908)*, pp. 26ff.

13. Rolland, *Jean-Christophe*, trans. G. Cannan (New York: The Modern Library, 1913). See pp. 252–3.

14. Rolland, *Mémoires*, pp. 23–5.

15. See *Cahiers Romain Rolland*, 4:30–3.

16. Rolland, *Journey Within*, p. 16.

17. Ibid., p. 19. On page 17 Rolland says he read a copy of Spinoza's *Ethics* translated by Emile Saisset, with critical introduction (New Edition, revised and augmented, Paris: Charpentier, 1872, in 3 volumes). What especially appealed to him were the following: *Ethic* Part 1: Definitions 2–6 and the Explanation; Propositions 15, 16 and 29. *Ethic* Part 2: Definition 6; Lemma 7, particularly the Scholia. *Ethic* Part 4: Propositions 40–42 and 45. Rolland also cites Spinoza's *Treatise on the Improvement of the Understanding* and a few letters (to Oldenburg, Schuller, and Mayer).

18. Rolland, *Journey Within*, p. 21. Rolland is quoting here from *Ethic* 1, Scholia to Proposition 29.

19. Ibid. Rolland is quoting from *Ethic* 1, Proposition 15.

20. Ibid.

21. Ibid., p. 22.

22. Ibid., p. 23. Rolland here is quoting from *Ethic* Part 4, Proposition 40–42 and 45 and *Treatise on the Improvement of the Understanding*.

23. Ibid. One cannot overestimate the significance of Spinoza for Rolland's life. As late as 1924, Rolland said that Spinoza "still remains sacred to me, like the Holy Scriptures for those who believe in them; and I never touch those volumes except with reverence" (*Journey Within*, p. 17).

24. Rolland, *The Life of Vivekananda*, p. 341, ft. 2.

25. Rolland, *Journey Within*, p. 20.

26. Ibid., p. 19.

27. Ibid., p. 25.

28. The *Credo* did not receive its final essay form until May 24, 1888, the date Rolland appended on the title page. However, Rolland felt that the conceptual battle had been essentially won in April of 1887. The English translation of *Voyage intérieur*, quoted

above, mistakenly has the date April 11, 1888 (compare *Mémoires*, p. 47; Starr, *Romain Rolland: One Against All*, p. 32; *Voyage intérieur*, p. 40; *Cahiers Romain Rolland*, 4:73–81). In the above quote, I have corrected the error.

29. The *Credo quia verum* can be found at the end of volume 4 of *Cahiers Romain Rolland* and should be compared to Rolland's notes during the academic year 1886–1887 (found in the same volume). At this date it remains untranslated. I would like to thank Dan Bertsche of the Department of Romance Languages at the University of Chicago for his help in translating sections of the *Credo*. Of course, I take full responsibility for the final translation as it appears in these pages.

30. Rolland, *Credo quia verum*, Preface, p. 351.

31. Ibid., section 1, p. 356.

32. Ibid., the only footnote of the section entitled "The Being," p. 359.

33. Ibid., "The Being," p. 359.

34. Ibid., section 1, p. 357.

35. Ibid., "On Intuition," p. 360.

36. Ibid. See also *Journey Within*, p. 22. Surely this is the origin of Rolland's later interest in the studies on intuition by LeRoy and Aurobindo that we discussed in chapter 3. Theologians may wonder whether Rolland ever read Schleiermacher. The early Schleiermacher of the *Speeches* and *Soliloquies* emphasized, like Rolland, a religious a priori that consisted of feeling and intuition and a religious life the essence of which consisted in "becoming." Unfortunately I have been unable to document that Rolland read or knew of Schleiermacher. The similarity between the two may come from the fact that both were influenced by Romanticism and Spinoza. Certainly Rolland's comparative agenda (see chapter 6) espoused the same "modern" approach found in the early Schleiermacher. So too can one argue that Rolland's gravitation toward psychoanalysis was prepared by his exposure to Romanticism.

37. *Cahiers Romain Rolland*, 4:75–6.

38. Rolland, *Credo quia verum*, "Beings," p. 361.

39. *Cahiers Romain Rolland*, 4:77.

40. Ibid., pp. 77–8.

41. Ibid., p. 89.

42. It should be noted that one can find at least one reference within *War and Peace* to the "ocean of humanity" (Part 3, chap. 8). See also *Journey Within*, p. 27, where Rolland uses oceanic metaphors in describing *War and Peace*.

43. Starr, *Romain Rolland: One Against All*, p. 196; Doré and Prévost, eds., *Selected Letters*, p. ix. In his journal at the École Normale, Rolland cited how his friends dubbed him "the musical Bouddha of a revolutionary mysticism" (*Cahiers Romain Rolland*, 4:323).

44. Masson, *The Oceanic Feeling*, pp. 36ff. Masson also cites a passage from Saradananda's biography of Ramakrishna, from which he thinks Rolland derived the term "oceanic feeling." It appears that Masson did not know of the *Credo* or Rolland's early mystical experiences.

45. Sudhir Kakar, *The Analyst and the Mystic*, p. 6. Note that Kakar cites a different passage from Saradananda's biography, the "Salt Doll" metaphor.

46. Rolland, *Credo quia verum*, "The Being" and "On Communion of Souls in God." For documentation of Rolland's knowledge of and interest in writing about Ramakriskna, see his journal *Inde*, pp. 141ff. (entry of October 4, 1926).

47. Rolland, *Journey Within*, pp. 16–17.

48. Rolland, *Empédocle d'Agrigente, suivi de l'Éclair de Spinoza* (Paris: Le Sablier, 1931), pp. 49–50.

49. Rolland, *Credo quia verum*, "Beings" p. 361; see also *Cahiers Romain Rolland*, 4:77.

50. Ibid., "How to Live Love." p. 374.

51. Ibid., "On the Outside World," p. 370. The metaphor of individuality as a "role," as well as musical metaphors, can be found in mystical literature. In Rolland's case, we should entertain the possibility that he devised them from nonmystical literary sources. For example, as a boy in Clamency, Rolland was exposed to and dearly loved Shakespeare (see *Compagnons de route* [Paris: Éditions du Sablier, 1936]). Shakespearean characters, while not evident in the above quotes, were cited in the *Credo* in conjunction with the "roles" the individual plays. Rolland was also trained in the piano at an early age and developed a love for Beethoven well before his move to Paris. This interest sustained him throughout his life, as is evinced by the fact that he became professor of musicology at the Sorbonne.

52. Ibid., "On Communion of Souls in God," p. 363.

53. Ibid., pp. 364–65.

54. Ibid. See also the section entitled "Appendix to Paragraph ix." Later, in his *Journey Within* (p. 105), Rolland emphasized how this Spinozistic Being was the transcendental source of creativity by once again utilizing the Cartesian formula: "I create; therefore I exist."

55. Ibid., "On Communion of Souls in God," pp. 364–65.

56. Ibid.

57. Ibid., "Appendix to Paragraph ix," pp. 375–76.

58. Ibid., "How to Live Irony," pp. 371–73.

59. Ibid.

60. Ibid.

61. Ibid, p. 372. See also *Cahiers Romain Rolland*, 4:88.

62. Rolland, *Credo quia verum*, "How to Live Irony," pp. 37–73.

63. Ibid., "How to Live Love," p. 374.

64. Ibid., "How to Live Irony," p. 372.

65. Ibid., p. 373.

66. Ibid., "How to Live Love"; see also *Cahiers Romain Rolland*, 4:89.

67. Rolland, *Credo quia verum*, "How to Live Love," p. 375.

68. Ibid., "Rules of a Provisional Morality," pp. 368–69.

69. Rolland, *Mémoires*, p. 24. Here Rolland is referring to the Breithorn experience. See also *Journey Within*, p. 14.

70. See *Cahiers Romain Rolland*, 4:111 ("perpétuel devenir") and the *Credo*, the last sentence in the section "On the Communion of Souls in God" ("developpement eternel," p. 365).

71. See *Journey Within*, p. 147; *Compagnons de route*, p. 9. Undoubtedly it was magnified through the influence of his close association with Malwida von Meysenbug, a woman Rolland referred to as his "second mother," who spoke with him endlessly about her relationship with men like Nietzsche and encouraged his early artistic efforts (see in particular Rolland's letters to her in *Cahiers Romain Rolland 1, Choix de lettres à Malwida von Meysenbug*, and *Journey Within*, chapter 5).

72. See Rolland's *Credo*, "How to Live Love" pp. 373–75. See also Rolland's *Compagnons de route*, pp. 9; 30–40, and the essay on Goethe; Wilson, *The Pre-War Biographies of Romain Rolland*, pp. 120–22. As late as 1936 Rolland gave primacy to the Italian Renaissance and the pre-Socratics as the source responsible for his dynamic conception of life (in Wilson pp. 121–22 and the appendix, letter of June 29, 1936, from Rolland to R. Wilson). The pre-Socratics played little role in the *Credo* despite the fact that Rolland

had been introduced to their thought as a young man (see *Journey Within*, pp. 16–17). However, they played a definitive role in imparting a passionate life to Rolland during his stay in Italy in 1889–1891 (see *Journey Within*, chapter 5) and during the Great War.

73. See Fisher's comments on Rolland's "optimism of the will" in the conclusion of his *Romain Rolland and the Politics of Intellectual Engagement.*

74. See Rolland's diatribe against "false" idealism in *Compagnons de route* ("Le poison idealiste," pp. 17–22).

75. This is evident throughout his biographies on the Hindu saints, where Rolland, in combating the European stereotype of Indian passiveness, characterized Vivekananda as endowed with a sharp intellect and overpowering will. It is interesting to note that Freud as well noted Rolland's embodiment of willpower (see the letter to Rolland of January 29, 1926).

76. See *Journey Within* (chapter 5); W. T. Starr, *Romain Rolland: One Against All* (chapter 4); R. Wilson, *The Pre-War Biographies of Romain Rolland* (chapters 1 and 2). Wilson's book is still the best study available for the meaning and import of Rolland's biographies, his "Vies."

77. See Wilson, *The Pre-War Biographies of Romain Rolland*, especially pp. 125ff.

78. See Ellen Key, "Romain Rolland," in *La Revue*, vol. 106 (January–February 1914):171–81.

79. Rolland, *Credo Quia Verum*, "On Liberty," p. 366.

80. Ibid., "On Liberty," p. 367.

81. See Starr, *Romain Rolland and a World at War*, pp. 20–1; Starr, *Romain Rolland: One Against All*, chapter 14.

82. Rolland, *The Life of Vivekananda*, p. 344. For the influence of Renan on Rolland, see *Compagnons de route*, pp. 139–48 and also Jouvre, *Romain Rolland vivant*, pp. 300ff. Rolland adopted Shakespeare's policy of transmitting the truth indirectly to the masses through art (see *Compagnons de route*, pp. 44ff.).

83. See René Cheval, *L'Allemagne et la guerre*, p. 138. Lerch sees Rolland as a disciple of Nietzsche, a point disputed by Wilson. The best treatment of Rolland and Nietzsche can be found in Cheval, "Romain Rolland et Nietzsche" (*Deutschland–Frankreich*, vol. 2, Stuttgart, Deutsche Verlags-Anstalt [1957]:292–308). Rolland was introduced to Nietzsche through a series of essays written about the latter in France in 1882 (see Wilson, *The Pre-War Biographies of Romain Rolland*, p. 122, ft. 3). Rolland thought *The Birth of Tragedy* to be the best of Nietzsche's works (Cheval, "Romain Rolland et Nietzsche," p. 298). Rolland clearly admired Nietzsche's ideal of the *Übermensch*, his independence and free spirit, his search for the truth and exposé of social mendacity. On the other hand, he thought Nietzsche lacked an appreciation of the communal nature of man, the need for charity and even weakness. "It is good to be an overman," said Rolland, but "it is better and more difficult to be human." One gets the impression Rolland attempted to combine the best of Nietzsche with the best of a Christian ethos—a strained and formidable task. Rolland was also deeply fearful of what the thought of a Nietzsche could do to a Europe pervaded by social malaise. His deepest fears were realized when Nietzsche's sister wrote a letter to Mussolini extolling him as the paradigmatic *Übermensch*. Rolland immediately resigned his membership in the Nietzsche-Gesellschaft by way of a letter strongly condemning the perversion of Nietzsche's thought and its association with fascism.

84. Rolland, *Above the Battle*, p. 42.

85. Ibid. *L'Un contre tous* was the original title of Rolland's *Clerambault*, the story of a free conscience during the war.

86. See Rolland's letters of December 5, 1927, and May 3, 1931. Note in this last let-

ter Rolland's citation of Montaigne's "Que Sais Je?" and his feeling of moral closeness with Freud as one who, like himself and Montaigne, sought for truth "without desire, without hope, without fear."

87. See Rolland's letters to Sophia of November 14, 1913 (*Cahiers Romain Rolland* 11) p. 187ff. and July 30, 1912 (*Cahiers Romain Rolland* 11) p. 159.

88. Rolland, *Credo Quia Verum*, "How to Live Love," pp. 373–74.

89. Ibid., "Rules of a Provisional Morality," p. 368.

90. Rolland, *The Life of Ramakrishna*, p. 4.

91. Rolland, *Journey Within*, p. 10.

92. Ibid., pp. 10–11.

93. Rolland's stress on the teleological nature of the "subconscious" once again brings him close to the thought of Jung.

94. *Journey Within*, pp. 24–5.

95. D. K. Roy, *Among the Great*, pp. 71–3. A similar statement can be found in Rolland's journal *Inde*, pp. 43–4.

96. See Rolland, *The Life Ramakrishna*, pp. 5, 10–11; *The Life of Vivekananda*, pp. 176–7. Also see footnote 2 on p. 176.

97. See Rolland, *The Life of Vivekananda*, p. 57, ft. 2; p. 60.

98. Ibid., p. 252.

99. Ibid., p. 178.

100. Ibid., pp. 178–85.

101. Ibid., p. 253.

102. Ibid., p. 252.

103. Ibid., p. 176.

104. Ibid., p. 256.

105. See W. T. Starr, *Romain Rolland: One Against All*, p. 186. The volumes are entitled: *Annette and Sylvia*, trans. B. R. Redman (New York: Henry Holt, 1925); *Summer*, trans. E. Stinson and V. W. Brooks (New York: Henry Holt, 1925); *Mother and Son*, trans. V. W. Brooks (New York: Henry Holt, 1927); *The Death of a World*, trans. Amalia de Alberti (New York: Henry Holt, 1933); *A World in Birth*, trans. Amalia de Alberti (New York: Henry Holt, 1934).

106. See Fisher, *Romain Rolland and the Politics of Intellectual Engagement*, pp. 170–6.

107. Rolland, *Herman Hesse and Romain Rolland*, trans. M. L. Hesse (London: Oswald Wolff, 1978), p. 91. The relation between Rolland and Hesse, which began in 1915, is an interesting one. Hesse dedicated the first part of *Siddhartha* to Rolland in 1921 (see pp. 62–63, 81). In turn, Rolland called it "one of the most profound works a European has ever written on (and in the spirit of) Hindu philosophy." The two also exchanged thoughts on Eastern religion (Taoism, Buddhism, Hinduism). One can also find in the correspondence Hesse's many reviews of Rolland's books.

108. Starr, *Romain Rolland: One Against All*, p. 186.

109. Rolland, *Annette and Sylvie*, pp. 11–12.

110. See Georges Buraud, "Romain Rolland créateur de valeurs," in Doisey, *Hommage à Romain Rolland* (Lausanne: Éditions de Mont-Blanc, 1945, pp. 36–48); Starr, *Romain Rolland: One Against All*, p. 195.

111. Starr, *Romain Rolland: One Against All*, p. 194; cf. *A World in Birth*, pp. 431–40, 565–6.

112. *A World in Birth*, pp. 431–40.

113. Ibid.

Chapter 6

1. Rolland refers to his correspondence with Bremond in a few of the letters in *Au Seuil de la dernière porte* (see, for example, pp. 43, 69). Apparently the correspondence was not substantial. In his journal *Inde* (entry of July 1930, p. 230), Rolland reveals his high opinion of Bremond and remarks that he reacted favorably to the biographies of the Hindu saints. Later in life, after his debate with Freud, Rolland showed evidence of an increased interest in Christian theological perspectives on mysticism (see Rolland's *Au seuil de la dernière porte*).

2. For an overview of the French material, see McGinn, *The Foundations of Mysticism* (pp. 277–80, 297–310). McGinn further provides an excellent bibliography for those who wish to study this period further.

3. To name just some: with respect to scripture, one finds a range from the Upanishads and the Bhagavad Gita to various Buddhist sutras and the works of Lao-tzu; with respect to mystic authors, Plato, Empedocles, Heraclitus, Philo, Plotinus, Dionysius, Eckhart, Suso, Tauler, Ruysboreck, Bonaventure, St. Teresa, St. John, a host of French Catholic mystics, and "nature" mystics like Emerson, Whitman, and Thoreau, and, of course, a number of Hindu mystics.

4. Rolland had in general negative comments on Oldenberg and Levi (see *Inde*, pp. 68, 237) and on the Catholic response to India (see for example *The Life of Vivekananda*, p. 358). Rolland was far more sympathetic of Masson-Oursel (see *Inde* and Masson-Oursel's tribute to Rolland's researches into India in *Hommage à Romain Rolland*).

5. See Rolland, *The Life of Vivekananda*, pp. 346–82.

6. Ibid., pp. 346–7.

7. Huxley, *The Perennial Philosophy* (New York: Harper and Row, 1945).

8. See for example S. Radhirkrishnan, *East and West in Religion* (London: Allen and Unwin, 1933); N. Smart, "Interpretation and Mystical Experience" in *Understanding Mysticism*, pp. 78–91.

9. R. C. Zaehner, *Mysticism Sacred and Profane*. In delineating these categories I follow for the most part the strategies laid down by Almond (*Mystical Experience and Religious Doctrine* [Berlin and New York: Mouton, 1982] chapter 1 and pp. 128ff.) and Katz (see his *Mysticism and Philosophical Analysis*, pp. 23–5). It is debatable whether Zaehner should be classified as a "common-core" theorist. I acknowledge that Zaehner goes beyond classic "common-core" theories in his postulation of three "cores." Nonetheless, the fact he has such universal cores (relative to Katz's stress on much greater diversity) is reason enough in my mind to include him in this group.

10. Rolland, *The Life of Vivekananda*, pp. 346–7.

11. Ibid., pp. 348–9.

12. Ibid., p. 348.

13. Ibid., p. 349.

14. Ibid.

15. Ibid., pp. 378–82.

16. Ibid.

17. Ibid., p. 348, ft. 1.

18. Rolland, *The Life of Ramakrishna*, p. 33.

19. Ibid., pp. 33–4.

20. Rolland, *The Life of Vivekananda*, p. 378.

21. This is not to say Rolland was not aware of others who advocated the perennialist position, such as Radhikrishnan (see his journal *Inde*, p. 409, the first entry of 1939).

Rather, it is to emphasize that of the early perennialists, Otto and James seemed to have had the most discernible impact.

22. Rolland belongs to the bulk of scholarship that reads James in such a fashion. Such a view needs qualification in light of the recent study by Barnard. See G. William Barnard, "William James and the Origins of Mystical Experience," in Robert K. C. Forman, ed., *The Innate Capacity* (New York: Oxford University Press, 1998).

23. See Rolland, *The Life of Vivekananda*, p. 348. It should be noted that, although Otto did speak of a "uniform nature of mysticism," his analysis was much more detailed and specific than Rolland's. As for the correspondence, Ursula King (in *Towards a New Mysticism* [New York: The Seabury Press, 1981], p. 95, and personal communication) has stated that Rolland engaged in a correspondence with Otto and that a plan was afoot to publish it along with an introduction by Teilhard de Chardin. Unfortunately, this book was never published. I have not been able to learn the whereabouts of the Rolland–Otto correspondence—one which would certainly be of importance in evaluating Rolland as comparativist. The introduction by de Chardin may be in the hands of Jeanne Mortier, as King thinks, but it is apparently not as yet publicly accessible.

24. Rudolph Otto, *Mysticism East and West*, trans. R. L. Bracey and R. C. Payne (New York: Macmillan, 1970). See pp. 57–72.

25. Ibid., pp. 59–60.

26. Ibid., pp. 60–72. See also Almond's valuable analysis in *Mystical Experience and Religious Doctrine*, pp. 94–105.

27. Rolland, *Life of Vivekananda*, pp. 354, 366–7.

28. Ibid., pp. 362, 367.

29. Ibid., p. 372.

30. Ibid., p. 60.

31. Ibid., p. 347, ft. 1; p. 357, ft. 1.

32. Rolland, *Life of Ramakrishna*, p. 5.

33. See, for example, his letter to Kalida Nag of June 17, 1922 (in Doré and Prévost, eds., *Selected Letters*, pp. 33–5); letter to D. K. Roy of October 1, 1924 (in *Among the Great*, pp. 71–3); *The Life of Ramakrishna*, pp. 9–11; *The Life of Vivekananda*, p. 176.

34. Rolland, *Life of Vivekananda*, p. 348, ft. 1.

35. See Swami Ashokananda, *The Influence of Indian Thought on the West* (Calcutta: Advaita Ashrama Mayavati, 1930).

36. See D. K. Roy, *Yogi Sri Krishnaprem* (Bombay: Bharatiya Vidya Bhavan, 1968), pp. 120–1; 123.

37. Katz, *Mysticism and Philosophical Analysis*, p. 26.

38. See A. Perovitch, "Does the Philosophy of Mysticism Rest on a Mistake?" in Robert K. C. Forman, ed., *The Problem of Pure Consciousness* (New York: Oxford University Press, 1990).

39. Katz, *Mysticism and Philosophical Analysis*, pp. 58–9.

40. Rufus Jones, *Studies in Mystical Religion* (New York: Russell and Russell, 1909), p. xxxiv.

41. See Katz, *Mysticism and Philosophical Analysis*, p. 27. Almond refers to these three stages as "incorporated," "reflexive," and "retrospective" (*Mystical Experience and Religious Doctrine*, p. 162).

42. Ibid., pp. 53–6, 62–3.

43. The term is Almond's (see *Mystical Experience and Religious Doctrine*, p. 128).

44. Having said this, let me admit to one qualification. The essentialist argument of mysticism, as promoted by Robert K. C. Forman and others, which, in its briefest form, points to the existence of "pure consciousness," of wholly deconstructed states of mystical

consciousness, strikes me as legitimate. As Forman notes, this moment occurs during the mystical "event," which allows for shaping before and after it. Furthermore, as Forman again notes, it is in need of epistemological justification. Moreover, such pure experiences are but one kind of mystical experience, many of which as in the case of the "intellectual visions" of Christian mystics, are in need of epistemological justification. For example, St. Paul's ascent to the third heaven and Paradise is hardly a moment of Advaitic pure consciousness. Finally, it should be noted that the value of pure consciousness varies from tradition to tradition. For example, one can isolate such moments of "forgetting" in Mansion 5 of St. Teresa's *The Interior Castle*. But they are hardly seen as the pinnacle of mystical development, as indeed seems to be the case in someone like Sri Ramana Maharshi. In other words, even "PCE's" must be seen "in context."

45. John E. Smith, "William James's Account of Mysticism," in S. Katz, ed., *Mysticism and Religious Traditions* (New York: Oxford University Press, 1983), p. 253.

46. James, *The Varieties of Religious Experience*, p. 391.

47. Ibid., p. 396.

48. Ibid., p. 403.

49. L. Dupré, "The Mystical Experience of the Self and Its Philosophical Significance," in Woods, *Understanding Mysticism*, p. 460. Dupré's reference is specifically to Joseph Maréchal, the early French Catholic psychologist of mysticism who engaged in a long debate with his contemporaries (particularly James Leuba) in America. However, Dupré also includes Otto and Maritain in this school of thought.

50. A. Perovitch, "Does the Philosophy of Mysticism Rest on a Mistake?" pp. 246–9.

51. In the next chapter I will illustrate this approach by utilizing Arthur Diekman's concept of deautomatization in conjunction with a Jamesian epistemology. I do not hold, however, that this epistemological framework accounts for all forms of mystical experience.

52. See Cavendish Moxon, "Mystical Ecstasy and Hysterical Dream-States," *Journal of Abnormal Psychology* 15 (1920):329–34; Theodore Schroeder, "Prenatal Psychisms and Mystical Pantheism," *International Journal of Psychoanalysis* 3 (1922):445–66.

53. See E. Jones, *Papers on Psychoanalysis* (Boston: Beacon Press, 1948) pp. 273–41; Federn, *Ego Psychology and the Psychoses* (New York: Basic Books, 1952) pp. 283–322; Franz Alexander, "Buddhistic Training as an Artificial Catatonia," *The Psychoanalytic Review* 18, 2 (1931):129–41.

54. Richard Sterba, "Remarks on Mystic States," *American Imago*, 25 (1968):77–85; Bertram Lewin, *The Psychoanalysis of Elation* (New York: The Psychoanalytic Quarterly, 1961); Ben-Ami Scharfstein, *Mystical Experience*; C. Kligerman, "A Psychoanalytic Study of the Confessions of St. Augustine," *Journal of the American Psychoanalytic Association*, 5 (1957):469–84.

55. J. Masson and T. C. Masson, "The Study of Mysticism: A Criticism of W. T. Stace," in *Journal of Indian Philosophy* 4 (1976):109–25. See p. 109.

56. Ibid.

57. Masson and Hanly, "A Critical Examination of the New Narcissism," in *International Journal of Psychoanalysis* 57 (1976):59–60. See also Masson's other works on this topic: "Sex and Yoga: Psychoanalysis and the Indian Religious Experience," in *Journal of Indian Philosophy* 2 (1984):315–16; "Indian Psychotherapy?" in *Journal of Indian Philosophy* 7 (1979):330; *The Oceanic Feeling*, chapter 1.

58. See Masson, "Indian Psychotherapy?"

59. Masson, *The Oceanic Feeling*, chapter 1.

60. N. Sil, *Ramakrishna Paramahamsa: A Psychological Profile*.

61. The accepted translation of M's biography is Swami Nikhilananda's *The Gospel*

*of Sri Ramakrishna* (New York: Ramakrishna-Vivekananda Center, 1984); that of Saran-dananda's biography is Swami Jagananda's *The Great Master* (Mylapore, India: Sri Ramakrishna Math, 1978).

62. Sil, *Ramakrishna Paramahamsa*, p. 168.

63. Ibid., p. 5.

65. Ibid., p. 118.

65. Masson and Masson, "The Study of Mysticism: A Criticism of W. T. Stace," p. 114.

66. Sil, *Ramakrishna Paramahamsa*, p. 34.

67. The term is Masson's (see Masson, "Indian Psychotherapy?" p. 125).

68. See Sudhir Kakar, "Reflections on Psychoanalysis, Indian Culture and Mysticism," in *Journal of Indian Philosophy* 20 (1982):289–97.

69. For an illuminating study of Adjun Mun, see T. Tambiah, *The Buddhist Saints of the Forest and the Cult of Amulets* (Cambridge: Cambridge University Press, 1984). I should add that the psychological literature that treats mysticism as a form of schizophrenia makes for fascinating reading. Alexander's article is a good example of the classic schools' perspective in this regard. While not psychoanalytic, being indebted to the positive view of schizophrenia promoted by Laing and others in the sixties, Kenneth Wapnick's "Mysticism and Schizophrenia" (in Woods, ed., *Understanding Mysticism*, pp. 321–337) promotes an adaptive view. Another decidedly unpsychoanalytic study which nevertheless promotes that perspective I have called transformative can be found in Jess Hollenback's *Mysticism: Experience, Response, and Empowerment* (University Park, Pa: Penn State Press, 1996, pp. 120–30).

70. See Wilber, Engler, Brown, eds., *Transformations of Consciousness* (especially chapter 1).

71. Kohut, *The Analysis of the Self* (New York: International Universities Press, 1971); C. Lasch, *The Culture of Narcissism* (New York: Warner Books, 1979).

72. Richard Gombrich's review of Masson's *The Oceanic Feeling* can be found in *Journal of the Royal Asiatic Society* 1 (1982):75–8; Halbfass's in *Journal of Asian Studies* 41 (1982):387–8. Others have critiqued Masson's unnuanced use of psychobiography. See, for example, Kakar, "Reflections on Psychoanalysis, Indian Culture and Mysticism." In his review of Masson's *The Oceanic Feeling*, Wilhelm Halbfass intimates that Masson's analysis of Indian mysticism is betrayed by countertransference. The same, I think, holds true for Sil's study of Ramakrishna. In speaking of attempts by scholars such as McDaniel, Olson, and Sharma to analyze Indian mysticism, Sil finds them possessed by a "naive enchantment," adding that he finds their attempts "frankly obscene" (*Ramakrishna Paramahamsa*, p. 6). I also find Masson's equation of Buddhist views on "suffering" with clinical depression to be a parody of what is meant by the first noble truth. See, for example, Wapola Rahula, *What the Buddha Taught* (New York: Grove Press, 1974) chapter 2.

73. A. Roland, *In Search of Self in India and Japan* (Princeton, N.J.: Princeton University Press, 1988); Kakar, *The Inner World*; S. Kurtz, *All the Mothers Are One*.

74. Meissner, *Ignatius of Loyola*; Kakar, *The Analyst and the Mystic*; Kripal, *Kali's Child*; Wilber, Engler, Brown, eds., *Transformations of Consciousness*; Jeffrey B. Rubin, *Psychotherapy and Buddhism* (New York: Plenum Press, 1996).

75. This theme was later elaborated by her analysand Harold Kelman. See Rubin, *Psychotherapy and Buddhism*, pp. 38–9.

76. Erikson, *Young Man Luther*, pp. 177, 248. Interestingly enough, in a passage that lies outside his correspondence with Rolland, Freud observes that a monastic adept does not "necessarily display any pathogenic disposition," for he is capable of sublimating erotic impulses "to a heightened interest in the divine, in nature, or in the animal king-

dom without his libido having undergone introversion to his phantasies or retrogression to his ego" (in "On Narcissism," in *Standard Edition* 14:80–1).

77. Erich Fromm, D. T. Suzuki, Richard De Martino, eds. *Zen Buddhism and Psychoanalysis* (New York: Harper Colophon, 1960).

78. See Fromm's article "Psychoanalysis and Zen Buddhism," in *Zen Buddhism and Psychoanalysis*, pp. 77–141.

79. See Fingarette, *The Self in Transformation*, chap. 7. This chapter was first published in *Psychoanalysis and the Psychoanalytic Review*, 45, 1 (1958):5–41.

80. The paper by Prince and Savage was first published in 1966 in *Psychedelic Review* and can be found in *The Highest State of Consciousness*, ed. John White, pp. 114–34.

81. Horton, "The Mystical Experience: Substance of an Illusion"; M. Milner, *The Suppressed Madness of Sane Men*; Mohammad Shafii, "Silence in the Service of the Ego: Psychoanalytic Study of Meditation," *International Journal of Psychoanalysis* 54 (1973):431–44; K. Fateaux, *The Recovery of the Self* (Mahweh, N.J.: Paulist Press, 1994). Also see *Mysticism: Spiritual Quest or Psychic Disorder?* (New York: Group for Advancement of Psychiatry, 1976); David Aberbach, "Grief and Mysticism," *International Review of Psychoanalysis* 14 (1987):509–26; David Werman, "On the Nature of the Oceanic Experience," *The Journal of Psychoanalytic Anthropology* 9 (1986):339–58; Daniel Merkur, "Unitive Experiences and the State of Trance." W. W. Meissner's earlier work, *Psychoanalysis and Religious Experience*, gives a brief overview of interpretations of mysticism from ego-adaptive and object-relations perspectives. His more recent work on Ignatius is really a study of mysticism. In a detailed and very rich analysis of the Christian categories of corporeal, imaginary, and intellectual visions, Meissner points out the pathological elements in the mysticism of Ignatius yet concludes with an adaptive reading championing how his visions led to the "transvaluation of all values." The cultural ambiance of this period was also a factor in giving rise to studies by Bakan and McClelland, who argued for continuities between psychoanalysis and Jewish mysticism (David Bakan, *Sigmund Freud and the Jewish Mystical Tradition*; David McClelland, *Psychoanalysis and Religious Mysticism* [Wallingford, Penn: Pendle Hill Pamphlets, 1959]).

82. See Merkur, "Unitive Experiences and the State of Trance."

83. Meissner, *Ignatius of Loyola*, chapter 20.

84. Kakar, *The Analyst and the Mystic*, pp. ix–x.

85. Merkur, "Unitive Experiences and the State of Trance," p. 152.

86. See R. Jones, "Jung and Eastern Religions," p. 150.

87. The term is used by Suzanne Kirschner in her *The Religious and Romantic Origins of Psychoanalysis* (Cambridge: Cambridge University Press, 1996), p. 15.

88. See Kakar, "Reflections on Psychoanalysis, Indian Culture and Mysticism."

89. Suzanne Kirschner, *The Religious and Romantic Origins of Psychoanalysis*, p. 17. Kirshner's study seeks to show the continuity between the developmental narrative that animates psychoanalytic theory and those found in biblical theology, neo-Platonism, Protestant mysticism, and Romanticism. As such, she argues against those social theorists who see a break between psychoanalysis and its Western past.

90. Kurtz, *All the Mothers Are One*. See particularly the conclusion.

91. A. Roland, *In Search of Self in India and Japan*, chap. 9.

92. Kakar, *The Inner World*, chapter 2; *Shamans, Mystics and Doctors: A Psychological Inquiry into India and Its Healing Traditions* (New York: Knopf, 1982), chapter 6. Kakar draws on a number of theorists in defining the relation between culture and psyche. Earlier works like *The Inner World* draw heavily on Erikson. *Shamans, Mystics and Doctors* draw on the individual/dividual dichotomy as fashioned by McKim Mariott. In more recent works, such as his essay "Clinical Work and Cultural Imagination" (*Psycho-*

*analytic Quarterly*, vol. LXIV (1995):265–81), I see the influence of Kurtz. See also Kakar's "Psychoanalysis and Non-Western Cultures," *International Review of Psychoanalysis*, 12 (1985):441–2.

93. Kakar, *The Analyst and the Mystic*, p. 27.

94. Ibid.

95. Ibid., p. 18.

96. Ibid., p. 29.

97. Ibid., p. 34.

98. Some may object that certain adaptive studies, notably those by Meissner and Kakar, do, in fact, accept a religious dimension to mysticism. For example, although Meissner promotes the view that the mystical experiences and spiritual transformation of Ignatius can be conceptualized in terms of those normal psychological capacities, structures, and functions mapped by psychoanalysis, he goes on to point out that from a faith-based perspective, the remarkable ego strength displayed by Ignatius in overcoming and directing developmental vicissitudes is ultimately the work of grace. Thus the transformation of Ignatius "can be regarded as an effect of grace that found expression through powerful and dynamic psychological processes" (Meissner, *Ignatius of Loloya*, pp. 347, 398). However, what is of direct concern to this study is that Meissner, even in his dialogue with theologians like Egan over the problem of causality in infused visions, never directly addresses the epistemological problems of mystical noesis in other than developmental terms (see chapters 18–20). His view of mystical subjectivity is that it is capable of being captured by classic–adaptive models.

In the case of Kakar, one could argue that his use of Lacan indicates acceptance of a bona fide mystical dimension to the personality. However, if one looks closely, Kakar's flirtation with Lacan is brief and exists solely to justify the mystic *intent* to seek the Real. Ultimately, Kakar's conclusion displaces the primacy of extraordinary metaphysical insight in favor of the Winnicottian emphasis on adaptive creativity. Again, Kakar also draws attention to how Bion's concept of "O," clearly a mystical, religious concept, approximates the Yogic ideal of moksha. However, having noted this, Kakar then draws back: "My own stance does not go as far as Wilfred Bion . . . for whom the goals of psychoanalysis are mystical goals, and who deliberately takes recourse to religious terminology to describe what happens in a psychoanalysis" (p. 68).

99. See Erikson's *Young Man Luther*, p. 246; "The Galilean Sayings and the Sense of 'I'" (The Yale Review 70 [1981]):321–62. See also Hetty Zock, *A Psychology of Ultimate Concern* (Amsterdam: Rodopi, 1990), pp. 100ff.

100. W. Bion, *Attention and Interpretation* (New York: Jason Aronson, 1983), p. 26.

101. Lacan, "God and the Jouissance of Women," in J. Mitchell and J. Rose, eds., *Feminine Sexuality: Jacques Lacan and the École Freudian* (New York: W. W. Norton, 1982), p. 147.

102. R. Webb and M. Sells, "Lacan and Bion: Psychoanalysis and the Mystical Language of Unsaying," in *Theory and Psychology*, 5, no. 2 (1995):195–15. My thanks to Professor Amy Hollywood of Dartmouth College for drawing my attention to this line of argument. Hollywood is presently researching the relation between psychoanalysis, mysticism, and gender in the writings of Lacan, Irigaray, and Bataille (see her forthcoming *Sensible Ecstasy: Mysticism and Sexual Difference in Twentieth Century French Thought*).

103. See M. de Certeau, *The Mystic Fable: Volume One, The Sixteenth and Seventeenth Centuries* (Chicago: The University of Chicago Press, 1992); J. Kristeva, *Revolution in Poetic Language* (Translated by Margaret Walker. New York: Columbia University Press, 1984).

104. In the next chapter I will utilize both of these metapsychological concepts in my analysis of Rolland's mysticism.

105. See E. Wolfson, *Through the Speculum that Shines: Vision and Imagination in Medieval Jewish Mysticism* (Princeton, N.J.: Princeton University Press, 1994); M. Frolich, *The Intersubjectivity of the Mystic: A Study of St. Teresa of Avila's Interior Castle* (Atlanta: Scholars' Press, 1993); K. Ewing, *Arguing Sainthood: Modernity, Psychoanalysis, and Islam* (Durham: Duke University Press, 1997).

106. See Wilber, Engler, Brown, eds., *Transformations of Consciousness*.

107. Ibid., p. 49.

108. Ibid., p. 51.

109. Kripal, *Kali's Child*, p. 358, ft. 71.

110. Ibid., p. 24.

111. Ibid., p. 23.

112. Ibid., p. 326.

113. Ibid., pp. 323–24.

114. Ibid., p. 43.

115. See in particular Jeffrey Rubin's critique of Engler in *Psychotherapy and Buddhism*, pp. 43–44, 86–89, and passim. For an evaluation of Rubin's work, see Harvey Aronson's review in *Journal of Buddhist Ethics*, vol. 5, 1998.

116. Kripal, *Kali's Child*, p. 83.

## Chapter 7

1. See, for example, Almond, *Mystical Experience and Religious Doctrine*, chap. 2; Katz, *Mysticism and Philosophical Analysis*, pp. 30–2; Smart, "Interpretation and Mystical Experience"; McGinn, *The Foundations of Mysticism* (pp. 338ff). Zaehner adopts a developmental stage approach to mysticism which similarly betrays his Catholic bias. This becomes clear when he states that his evaluative criteria for nature mystics is the extent to which their panenhenic experiences promote "individuation"—a Jungian term which, in its most actualized form, Zaehner thinks is commensurate with Oscar Wilde's "true personality of man" and the Christian view of Adam before the Fall. Zaehner then makes it equally clear that individuation is but the first stage on the mystic's path to his ultimate destination, union with God: "If our analysis of the data has been at all correct, the normal progress of the mystic from ordinary ego-consciousness to 'deification' would seem to be approximately as follows. First comes personal integration which belongs to the realm of psychology, then isolation which must be achieved by asceticism. . . . [I]n the case of the monistic mystic this will be the final stage. . . . [I]t is only at this point, however, that God starts to operate directly: the soul is led out of its isolation and is slowly transmuted into the substance of the Deity like a log of wood which is gradually assimilated to the fire. . . . This denoted the 'deification' of the soul" (p. 150). Whereas nature mysticism promotes individuation and can be interpreted through a Jungian psychological model, theistic mysticism presupposes individuation and is dependent on a transcendent Therapist beyond our control. Thus it is that alongside Zaehner's phenomenological distinctions between nature, monistic, and theistic mysticism lies a religio-ethical stage theory of mysticism that, while incorporating and utilizing Jungian psychology, ultimately reserves an explanation of its highest stages for that conceptual scheme endemic to traditional religious, theistic modes of apprehension.

2. Zaehner, *Mysticism Sacred and Profane*, p. 38.

3. For Rolland's relationship with Malwida, see *Journey Within* and *Letters of Ro-*

main *Rolland and Malwida von Meysenbug, 1890–1891*, trans. T. Wilson (New York: Henry Holt, 1933). As with Werman ("Sigmund Freud and Romain Rolland," p. 238), who also notes Malwida's mystical experiences', I have not found any evidence to indicate the two conversed about their oceanic feelings.

4. Zaehner, *Mysticism Sacred and Profane*, pp. 40–1.

5. Ibid., pp. 38–9.

6. Ibid., pp. 6–7.

7. Ibid., p. 41.

8. Ibid., chapter 1 (see especially p. 12); pp. 97ff.

9. Ibid., pp. 93–4.

10. Ibid., pp. 36–7.

11. Ibid., pp. 51–61.

12. Ibid., p. 57, ft. 1.

13. Ibid., pp. 110–11.

14. Ibid., chapters 1 and 2.

15. Ibid., p. 43, 65.

16. Ibid., p. 45, 62.

17. Ibid., chapter 4 and p. 63.

18. Ibid., chapter 5.

19. For Zaehner's views on Spinoza as nature mystic, see pp. 34, 66, 116–17.

20. Both experiences are cited in *Memories, Dreams, Reflections* and read as follows: "I was wafted into an entirely new and unexpected state of consciousness. There was no longer any inside or outside, no longer an 'I' and the 'others,' No. 1 and No. 2 were no more; caution and timidity were gone, and the earth and sky, the universe and everything in it that creeps and flies, revolves, rises, or falls, had all become one" (p. 77); "We shy away from the word 'eternal,' but I can describe the experience only as the ecstasy of a non-temporal state in which present, past and future are one. Everything that happens in time had been brought together into a concrete whole. Nothing was distributed over time, nothing could be measured by temporal concepts. The experience may best be described as a state of feeling, but one which cannot be produced by the imagination. How can I imagine that I exist simultaneously the day before yesterday, today, and the day after tomorrow? . . . . One is interwoven into an indescribable whole and yet observes it with complete objectivity" (pp. 295–96). Jung also refers to this experience and the objectivity attained as "part of a completed individuation" (p. 256). See chapters 3, 10, and 11 of the same book for more of Jung's autobiographical accounts of his visions and experiences.

21. See Coward, *Jung and Eastern Thought* (Albany: State University of New York Press, 1985); Clarke, *Jung and Eastern Thought: A Dialogue with the Orient* (London: Routledge, 1994).

22. On this point see Zaehner's essay "A New Buddha and a New Tao," in R. C. Zaehner, ed., *The Concise Encyclopedia of Living Faiths* (New York: Hawthorn Books, 1959), pp. 402–12.

23. Zaehner, *Mysticism Sacred and Profane*, pp. 32, 198–9.

24. Ibid., pp. 94, 106, 118, 148.

25. Ibid., pp. 110–11.

26. Ibid., pp. 110–11; cf. pp. 60–1, 102.

27. Ibid., pp. 60, 79, 110.

28. The studies I have relied on come from proponents of both psychoanalysis and Jung's analytic psychology. For a general survey of Jungians who promote this synthesis,

see Andrew Samuels, *Jung and the Post-Jungians* (London: Routledge and Kegal Paul, 1985), especially chapter 1. For more specialized studies, good introductions can be found in works by Mario Jacoby, *Individuation and Narcissism: The Psychology of Self in Jung and Kohut* (London: Routledge, 1990), and "Reflections on H. Kohut's Concept of Narcissism," *Journal of Analytic Psychology* 26, no. 1 (1981):19–32. For studies from the camp of revisionist psychoanalysis, see Peter Homans, *Jung in Context*, and "Narcissism in the Jung–Freud Confrontations," *American Imago* 38 (1981):81–95.

29. See J. Van Herik, "'Thick Description' and the Psychology of Religion," in F. Reynolds and B. Moore, eds., *Anthropology and the Study of Religion* (Chicago: Center for the Scientific Study of Religion, 1985); Susan E. Henking, "Placing the Social Sciences: Cases at the Intersection of the Histories of Disciplines and Religions"; Peter Homans, *The Ability to Mourn*.

30. See Peter Homans, *The Ability to Mourn* (particularly the introduction); *Jung in Context*; "Psychoanalysis East and West: A Psychoanalytic Essay on Religion, Mourning and Healing," *History of Religions* 24, no. 2 (1984):133–54. For a useful summary of his key concepts, see W. Parsons, "The Ability to Mourn: Disillusionment and the Social Origins of Psychoanalysis: A Conversation with Peter Homans," *Criterion*, 30, no. 2 (Spring 1991):2–8.

31. From "Le Seuil" in Rolland, *Le Voyage Interieur*, p. 176.

32. See the discussion in chapter 5.

33. See chapter 3.

34. See Rolland, *Journey Within*, pp. 2–3; 75–80.

35. Ibid., pp. 3–4.

36. Ibid., p. 81.

37. Ibid., p. 80.

38. Ibid., p. 3.

39. Ibid., p. 82.

40. See chapter 5.

41. *Journey Within*, p. 3.

42. Ibid., p. 5.

43. See Theodore Zeldin, *France 1848–1945* (Oxford: Oxford University Press, 1973), 1:43–52.

44. Rolland, *Journey Within*, p. 83.

45. Ibid., p. 37.

46. Ibid.

47. Ibid., p. 42.

48. Ibid., pp. 48–9.

49. Ibid., p. 44.

50. See Wilson, *The Pre-War Biographies of Romain Rolland*, pp. 17–20.

51. See Rolland, *Compagnons de route*, chapter 2. In the latter Rolland exalted as one of Shakespeare's most noble characters the figure of Coriolanus, who Rolland described as a Nietzschean *Übermensch*, "the hero absolutely free, standing single against the whole world, and whose every breath breathes a world of truth." (pp. 40, 49–50). My thanks to Robert Parsons, M. F. A., of the Theater Department of Solano College, for making this clear to me.

52. From Rolland, *The Forerunners*, p. 52. See also *Journey Within*, pp. 49–50.

53. Rolland, *Au Seuil de la dernière porte*, p. 129. See also chapter 3.

54. Rolland, *Journey Within*, p. 68.

55. Ibid., p. 86.

56. Ibid., p. 83.

57. See Rolland, *Mémoires*, p. 23, and also his letter to Malwida von Meysenbug of February 26, 1894, in *Cahiers Romain Rolland*, pp. 111–12.

58. Rolland, *Journey Within*, p. 85.

59. Ibid.

60. Ibid, p. 88.

61. See Rolland, *Compagnons de route*, chapter 6.

62. See Wilson, *The Pre-War Biographies of Romain Rolland*, pp. 17–20.

63. Rolland, *Mémoires*, p. 23.

64. Rolland, *Journey Within*, pp. 85–7.

65. Rolland, *Mémoires*, p. 23.

66. Masson, *The Oceanic Feeling*. See especially chapter 3.

67. D. Fisher, "Reading Freud's Civilization and Its Discontents," pp. 267–8.

68. Rolland, *Mémoires*, p. 24.

69. This is notable in lieu of the fact that Rolland's fellow educated, mystically inclined contemporaries like Sri Aurobindo ("it is difficult to take psychoanalysis seriously . . . one cannot discover the meaning of the lotus by analyzing the secrets of the mud in which it grows") and Charan Singh were altogether dismissive of psychoanalytic interpretations of mysticism. (Quote taken from S. Kakar, "Reflections on Psychoanalysis, Indian Culture and Mysticism," p. 293.)

70. Masson, *The Oceanic Feeling*, p. 48, ft. 13.

71. Paul Horton, "The Mystical Experience: Substance of an Illusion."

72. See D. W. Winnicott, *Playing and Reality* (Harmondsworth: Penguin, 1980), especially chapters 1 and 7.

73. Ana-Maria Rizzuto, *The Birth of the Living God*, p. 47.

74. Ibid., pp. 46, 48–9. See also chapters 1–3.

75. Rolland's first letter to Tolstoy, dated April 16, 1887, starts out as follows: "I should not dare write to you if I had to express only my passionate admiration for your works; it seems to me that I know you too well through your novels to send banal compliments, which your great spirit scorns, and which would really be impertinent on the part of a boy, such as I. But I am impelled by a burning desire to know how to live my life; and from you alone I can expect a reply, for you alone have asked the questions which bother me" (Doré and Prévost, eds., *Selected Letters*, p. 1. Other letters can be found in *Cahiers Romain Rolland* 24, *Monsieur le Conte. Romain Rolland et Léon Tolstoy texts*). For Rolland's later comments on Tolstoy's influence, see his *Tolstoy*, trans. B. Miall (London: Kennikat Press, 1972) and *The Forerunners*.

76. Rolland, *Journey Within*, p. 26.

77. See Rolland, *The Life of Vivekananda*, p. 338.

78. Ibid., p. 338, ft. 2.

79. Ibid., p. 341, ft. 2.

80. Freud, "Dreams and Occultism," in *New Introductory Lectures, Standard Edition* 22:55. While outside the Freud-Rolland Correspondence, this passage can be adduced as Canonical justification for the further reflections of the transformative school.

81. Kohut, "Forms and Transformations of Narcissism," in *The Search for the Self*, 1:453.

82. Kakar, *The Inner World*, p. 19.

83. See M. Gill and W. Brenman, *Hypnosis and Related States: Psychoanalytic Studies in Regression* (New York: International Universities Press, 1959); Deikman, "Deuautomatization and the Mystic Experience," in Woods, ed., *Understanding Mysticism*.

84. Deikman, "Deautomatization and the Mystic Experience," p. 256.

85. While I endorse Deikman's concept of deautomatization, I should note that his article is problematic on both comparativist and epistemological grounds. For example, Deikman states that all mystical phenomena can be classified under three rubrics: untrained sensate, trained sensate, and trained transcendent. The difference between the first two is negligible, as Deikman states that they are essentially the same. In illustrating this, Deikman draws on drug-induced mystical experiences (untrained sensate) and a text from the famed Christian woman mystic, Julian of Norwich (trained sensate). The latter text, however, consists of a vision containing what Christian mystics refer to as "imaginary" and "intellectual" elements. The latter is thus felt inwardly to the exclusion of the outer world, is infused, hence passively received through grace, and requires epistemological justification, being a form of mystical noesis transcending the ordinary channels of knowledge. It cannot, then, be wholly classified as being under a "sensate" category. Moreover, it is—in a phenomenological, epistemological, and theological sense—vastly different from a nature mystical experience as induced by drugs.

Deikman also seems ignorant of the complexity of the problem of mystical noesis and the various ways different religious traditions have sought to explain them. Deikman claims that meditation involves the process of deautomatization, hence providing access to and cultivation of dormant, mystical modes of knowing. This is a psychologically significant theory that I accept. But I add that it is here that the dialogue with philosophical and theological reflection on those modes of knowing begins. Deikman cuts short the need for this dialogue by simply stating that deautomatization accounts for the forms of mystical noesis activated in mergings with nature and in the apophatic apprehensions of pure consciousness found in mystics East and West. Only on a purely psychological level is this true, granted that deautomatization is operative in both types of mystical experience. However, further dialogue is needed, as the actual faculty of knowing as well as the knowledge gleaned may well be different in the two types of mystical knowing he cites.

In the case of Rolland, we have seen that, in his efforts to go beyond Kant, Rolland drew on the theories of intuition as found in Aurobindo and LeRoy and on James's view of the subconscious. Without endorsing the following, I think that Rolland would most likely gravitate towards linking the psychological process of deautomatization with James's view of mystical intuition as it has recently been elaborated by G. William Barnard in his article "William James and the Origins of Mystical Experience" (in Forman, ed., *The Innate Capacity*). Barnard's analysis provides an avenue that goes beyond Kant and links philosophical views on intuition with deautomatized modes of consciousness in a way commensurate with Rolland's approach. Briefly put, Barnard shows that, in contrast to Kant, who saw the "something" the mystic intuits as unknowable chaotic manifold which becomes intelligible only through being subjected to the shaping process of a priori categories, James held that the "something" or "More," although in some sense ineffable, contains germs of meaningful patterns that can be unpacked and elaborated. This preformed and partially structured transcendent content is accessed through that intuitive immediacy James refers to as "knowledge-by-acquaintance." He further thought the content of intuition could vary from person to person. As Barnard convincingly demonstrates, the "received view" of James, which characterizes him as a "common-core" theorist, is misleading. Drawing on James's advocacy of a pluralistic universe and field theory of self and reality, Barnard shows how James allows for the possibility that what the mystic intuits as the Reality of the More is as complex and pluralistic as our own. Practically applied, a Jamesian epistemology would see Rolland's attraction to Spinoza in particular (as opposed to the numerous other mystical authors available to him) as reflective of that particular preformed content given to him in his mystical intuitions. At the same time, it would hold that Spinoza and other forms of ideation contained in Rolland's

*Credo* helped him further explicate and render meaningful the deeper, more ineffable aspects of those experiences.

86. From *The Symposium* in Plato, *The Collected Dialogues*, edited by E. Hamilton and H. Cairns (Princeton, N.J.: Princeton University Press), pp. 562–3. Note that this is one of earliest uses of "oceanic" imagery to describe mystical experience.

87. See Augustine's *Confessions*, particularly VII:10–17; IX:10.

88. In this regard see Robert K. C. Forman's comparativist attempt, in his *Meister Eckhart* (Rockport, Mass.: Element, 1991) to correlate Rolland's oceanic feeling with what he perceives to be the developmental stages of Eckhart's journey to the Godhead.

89. See Rolland, *Above the Battle*, p. 110.

90. Ibid., pp. 48–9.

91. Cited in Starr, *Romain Rolland and a World at War*, pp. 175–6.

92. See chap. 5 and *Au Seuil de la dernière porte*, p. 23.

93. Kohut, *The Search for the Self*, 1:456.

94. Ibid., pp. 454–5.

95. Ibid., p. 458.

96. Ibid., p. 455.

97. Kohut, *Self-Psychology and the Humanities* (New York: W. W. Norton, 1985) pp. 70–1. For Hammarskjöld's mysticism, see Henry Van Dusen, *Dag Hammarskjöld: The Statesman and His Faith* (New York: Harper and Row, 1967) and Hammarskjöld's *Markings*, trans. Leif Sjöberg and W. H. Auden (New York: Knopf, 1964).

## Conclusion

1. See Homans's preface to the second edition of his *Jung in Context*, pp. xii ff.

2. Cited in Kakar, "Reflections on Psychoanalysis, Indian Culture and Mysticism," p. 293.

3. See Rubin, *Psychotherapy and Buddhism*; R. Fields, *How the Swans Came to the Lake*.

4. James, "A Suggestion about Mysticism," in Woods, ed., *Understanding Mysticism*, p. 221.

## Appendix

All of the letters cited in this appendix can be found (in French) in Henri and Madeleine Vermorel, *Sigmund Freud et Romain Rolland: Correspondance 1923–1936* (Paris: Presses Universitaires de France, 1993). Many of these letters can be found in part or in whole in other studies. In citing the latter sources I will use the following abbreviations:

(**C**) Colette Cornubert, "Freud et Rolland: Essai sur la découverte de la pénsee psychoanalytique par quelques écrivains Français." (**F**) David Fisher, "Sigmund Freud and Romain Rolland: The Terrestrial Animal and His Great Oceanic Friend." (**L**) Sigmund Freud, *The Letters of Sigmund Freud* (edited by E. Freud). (**B**) Sigmund Freud, *Briefe 1873–1939* (edited by E. Freud. These contain Freud's letters to Rolland in German). (**SL**) Romain Rolland, *The Selected Letters of Romain Rolland* (edited by F. Doré and M. Prévost). (**RR**) Romain Rolland, *Cahiers Romain Rolland*, vol. 17.

The studies by Fisher, Cornubert, and the Vermorels are based on the original French documents in Archives Romain Rolland, now housed in the Bibliothèque Nationale in Paris. For those of Rolland's letters that remain untranslated, I have used the reproductions in the studies by Cornubert and the Vermorels' as the basis for the English translations provided here. I would like to thank Dan Bertsche of the University of Chicago for his help in translating selected letters from the French. Of course, I take full responsibility for the final product.

1. Reference to a request made by Freud to Edouard Monod-Hertzen (letter, Freud to Monod-Hertzen of February 9, 1923, in (L) #199, p. 341) to "pass along a word of respect" to Rolland. This letter can only be found in the French original (see (C), pp. 12–13).

2. See (L) #200, pp. 341–42; (B) p. 359.

3. Rolland had sent Freud *Liluli* shortly after Freud's letter of March 4, 1923. See (F) p. 7.

4. Rolland's dedication read "To Freud the Destroyer of Illusions."

5. In (F) p. 10.

6. Reference to Rolland's biography of Gandhi, *Mahatma Gandhi: The Man Who Became One with the Universal Being.*

7. Reference to the lunch Freud and Rolland had together (with Stefan Zweig as interpreter) on May 14, 1924.

8. This letter was written for *Liber Amicorum Romain Rolland* (ed. Maxim Gorki, Georges Duhamel, Stefan Zweig. Rothapfel-Verlag, Zurich, 1926). It is reproduced in the *Standard Edition*, vol. 20, under the title "To Romain Rolland." See also (L) #217 p. 364; (B) p. 379.

9. Written on the occasion of Freud's seventieth birthday. See (C) p. 20.

10. Written in response to Rolland's telegram honoring Freud's seventieth birthday (Jones, *The Life and Work of Sigmund Freud,* 3:123). See (L) #223 p. 370; (B) p. 385.

11. This is the most crucial letter of the Freud–Rolland debate on mysticism. It can be found in (C) pp. 25–26; (RR) pp. 264–66; (F) pp. 20–22; (SL) pp. 86–88. The latter is reproduced here.

12. The reference is to *The Future of an Illusion.*

13. The "two nearly contemporary personalities" are Ramakrishna and Vivekananda, to whom Rolland devoted book-length studies in 1929 and 1930.

14. See (L) #241 p. 388; (B) pp. 405–06.

15. Cornubert, who cites the French version of this letter, has the sentence as follows: "It happens in a new work which lies before me yet uncompleted, I profit from the intellectual excitation you have brought me, mention the 'oceanic' feeling and try to interpret it from the point of view of our psychology."

16. See (C) pp. 29–30; (SL) p. 95. The latter is reproduced here.

17. The reference is to Bremond's massive work, A *Literary History of Religious Thought in France from the Wars of Religion Down to Our Own Times.*

18. See (L) #242 p. 389; (B) p. 406.

19. This letter can be found only in the French original. See (C) p. 33.

20. Rolland wrote this sentence in Greek.

21. See (L) #246 pp. 392–393; (B) p. 410.

22. This is a reference to Rolland's biographies of Ramakrishna and Vivekananda.

23. This letter can only be found in the French original. See (C) pp. 37–39.

24. Freud had sent Rolland a copy of the second edition of *Civilization and Its Discontents* on March 18, 1931, with the dedication: "The Landtier to his great Oceanic Friend." See (F) p. 40.

25. See (L) #261 p. 406; (B) p. 424.

26. Telegram sent on the occasion of Rolland's seventieth birthday. See (C) p. 41; (F) p. 48. Freud also sent Rolland his "open letter" analyzing his experience on the Acropolis for this event.

27. For the French original see (C) p. 41.

28. This was in response to Rolland's autographed note, which had been elicited by Stefan Zweig for Freud's birthday. Freud added: "I cannot tell you how glad I was to receive your autographed note. I am far from being as insensitive to praise and blame as I would like to appear through natural self-defense" (in [F] pp. 56–57). On January 22, 1937, Freud wrote to Rolland's wife, Marie, who had asked Freud for copies of signed manuscripts which could be auctioned for money for the Spanish Republicans. Freud responded: "Herewith two samples of my handwritten production. Do you truly believe people would give money for that? My cordial regards to you and Romain Rolland" (in [F] p. 57).

# Bibliography

Aberbach, D. "Grief and Mysticism." *International Review of Psychoanalysis* 14, (1987):509–26.

Alexander, F. "Buddhistic Training as an Artificial Catatonia." *The Psychoanalytic Review* 18, no. 2 (1931):129–41.

Almond, P. *Mystical Experience and Religious Doctrine*. Berlin and New York: Mouton, 1982.

Anzieu, Didier. *Freud's Self-Analysis*. London: The Hogarth Press and the Institute of Psycho-analysis, 1986.

Aronson, Alex. *Europe Looks at India*. Calcutta: Riddhi-India, 1979.

——— . *Romain Rolland: The Story of a Conscience*. Bombay: Padma, 1944.

Aronson, A. and Kripalani, K. R., eds., *Rolland and Tagore*. Calcutta: Visva-Bharati, 1945.

Aronson, H. Review of *Psychotherapy and Buddhism* by J. Rubin. *Journal of Buddhist Ethics*, vol. 5, 1998.

Ashokananda, Swami. *The Influence of Indian Thought on the West*. Calcutta: Advaita Ashrama Mayavati, 1930.

Aurobindo, Sri. *The Life Divine*. Pondicherry, India: Sri Aurobindo Ashram, 1970.

Bakan, David. *Sigmund Freud and the Jewish Mystical Tradition*. New York: Schocken Books, 1969.

Barnard, G. William. "William James and the Origins of Mystical Experience." In Robert K. C. Forman, ed., *The Innate Capacity*. New York: Oxford University Press, 1998.

Baudouin, C. "La Régression et les phénomènes de recul en psychologie." *Journal de Psychologie*, vol. 25 [Nov.–Dec., 1928]:795–823.

Beers, William. *Women and Sacrifice: Male Narcissism and the Psychology of Religion*. Detroit: Wayne State Press, 1992.

Beirnaert, L. "Romain Rolland, Les Dernières Etapes du voyage intérieur." *Études*, vol. 144 (1945):250–6.

Beit-Hallahmi, B. "Psychology of Religion 1880–1930: The Rise and Fall of a Psychological Movement." *Journal of the History of Behavioral Sciences* 10 (1974):84–90.

———. *Psychoanalysis and Religion: A Bibliography.* Norwood, Pa.: Norwood Editions, 1978.

Bettelheim, Bruno. *Freud and Man's Soul.* New York: Vintage, 1984.

Bion, W. *Attention and Interpretation.* New York: Jason Aronson, 1983.

Bouyer, L. "Mysticism: An Essay on the History of the Word." In *Understanding Mysticism,* edited by Richard Woods. Garden City, N.Y.: Image, 1980, pp. 42–56.

Bremond, Henri. *A Literary History of Religious Thought in France from the Wars of Religion Down to Our Own Times.* Vol. 1. Translated by K. L. Montgomery. New York: Macmillan, 1928.

Browning, Don. *Religious Thought and the Modern Psychologies.* Philadelphia: Fortress Press, 1987.

Bucke, R. M. *Cosmic Consciousness.* New York: Citadel Press, 1993.

Buraud, G. "Romain Rolland créateur de valeurs." In Doisey, M. *Hommage à Romain Rolland.* Lausanne: Éditions de Mont-Blanc, 1945, pp. 36–48.

Campbell, J. *The Hero with a Thousand Faces.* Princeton, N.J.: Princeton University Press, 1972.

Capps, D. and J. E. Dittes, eds. *The Hunger of the Heart: Reflections on the Confessions of Augustine.* West Lafayette, IN: Society for the Scientific Study of Religion, Monograph Series, no. 8, 1990.

Capps, Don, Lewis Rambo, and Paul Ransohoff, eds. *Psychology of Religion: A Guide to Information Sources.* Detroit: Gale, 1976.

Carmody, Denise, and John Carmody, *Mysticism: Holiness East and West.* New York: Oxford University Press, 1996.

Carroll, Michael. *The Cult of the Virgin Mary: Psychological Origins.* Princeton, N.J.: Princeton University Press, 1986.

Carver, A. "Primary Identification and Mysticism." *British Journal of Medical Psychology* 4 (1924):102–14.

Chan, W. T. *A Source Book in Chinese Philosophy.* Princeton, N.J.: Princeton University Press, 1963.

Cheval, René. "Romain Rolland et Nietzsche." *Deutschland–Frankreich.* Vol. 2. Stuttgart: Deutsche Verlags-Anstalt (1957):292–308.

———. *L'Allemagne et la guerre.* Paris: Presses Universitaires de France, 1963.

Clark, J. J. *Jung and Eastern Thought: A Dialogue with the Orient.* London: Routledge, 1994.

Claudel, Paul. "La Pensée religieuse de Romain Rolland." *La Revue* January–February (1949):193–211.

Coe, George A. *The Psychology of Religion.* Chicago: University of Chicago Press, 1916.

Coomarasway, A. "A World Policy for India." *The New Age,* December 24, 1915.

———. *The Dance of Shiva.* New York: The Sunrise Turn, 1924.

Cornubert, Colette. *Freud et Rolland: Essai sur la découverte de la pensée psychoanalytique par quelques écrivains Français.* Thèse No. 453 pour Le Doctorat en Médecine. Paris, Faculté de Médecine de Paris, 1966.

Coward, H. *Jung and Eastern Thought.* Albany: State University of New York Press, 1985.

de Certeau, Michel. "'Mystique' au XVIIe siècle: Le problème du langage 'mystique.'" In *L'Homme devant Dieu: Mélanges offerts au Père Henri de Lubac.* Paris: Aubier, 1964. 2:267–91.

———. *The Mystic Fable: Volume One, the Sixteenth and Seventeenth Centuries.* Chicago: University of Chicago Press, 1992.

Deikman, A. "Deautomatization and the Mystic Experience." In *Understanding Mys-*

*ticism,* edited by Richard Woods. Garden City, N.Y.: Image Books, 1980, pp. 240–60.

Delacroix, H. *Études d'histoire et de psychologie du mysticisme: Le grands mystiques chrétiens.* Paris: Alcan, 1908.

DiCenso, James. "Religion as Illusion: Reversing the Freudian Hermeneutic." *Journal of Religion* 71 (1991):167–79.

Doisey, Marcel. *Hommage à Romain Rolland.* Lausanne: Éditions de Mont-Blanc, 1945.

——— . *Romain Rolland.* Brussels: Editions La Boétie, 1945.

Doré, F. and Prévost, M., eds. *Selected Letters of Romain Rolland.* Delhi: Oxford University Press, 1990.

Dupré, Louis. "The Mystical Experience of the Self and Its Philosophical Significance." In *Understanding Mysticism,* edited by Richard Woods. Garden City, N.Y.: Image Books, 1980, pp. 449–66.

Eliade, Mircea. *Myths, Dreams and Mysteries.* New York: Harper and Row, 1960.

Eliade, Mircea, ed. *The Encyclopedia of Religion.* New York: Macmillan, 1987.

Ellenberger, Henri. *The Discovery of the Unconscious.* New York: Basic Books, 1970.

Erikson, Erik. *Young Man Luther.* New York: W. W. Norton, 1962.

——— . "The Galilean Sayings and the Sense of 'I'." *The Yale Review* 70 [1981]:321–62.

Ewing, K. *Arguing Sainthood: Modernity, Psychoanalysis, and Islam.* Durham: Duke University Press, 1997.

Fateaux, K. *The Recovery of the Self.* Mahweh, N.J.: Paulist Press, 1994.

Federn, P. *Ego Psychology and the Psychoses.* New York: Basic Books, 1952.

Fields, R. *How the Swans Came to the Lake.* Boston: Shambhala, 1992.

Fingarette, H. *The Self in Transformation.* New York: Harper and Row, 1965.

Fisher, David. "Sigmund Freud and Romain Rolland: The Terrestrial Animal and His Great Oceanic Friend." *American Imago* 33 (1976):1–59.

——— . "Reading Freud's *Civilization and Its Discontents.*" In *Modern European Intellectual History: Reappraisals and New Perspectives,* edited by Dominick LaCapra and Stephen L. Kaplan. Ithaca, N.Y.: Cornell University Press, 1982, pp. 251–79.

——— . *Romain Rolland and the Politics of Intellectual Engagement.* Berkeley: University of California Press, 1988.

Flournoy, T. "Une Mystique moderne." *Archives de Psychologie* 15 (1928), pp. 1–224.

Forman, Robert K. C., ed. *The Problem of Pure Consciousness.* New York: Oxford University Press, 1990.

——— . *Meister Eckhart.* Rockport, Mass.: Element, 1991.

——— , ed. *The Innate Capacity.* New York: Oxford University Press, 1998.

Fowler, James. *Stages of Faith.* San Francisco: Harper and Row, 1981.

Freud, E., ed. *The Letters of Sigmund Freud.* Translated by Taria and James Stern. New York: Basic Books, 1960.

——— . *Briefe 1873–1939.* Frankfurt am Main: S. Fisher, 1968.

——— , ed. *The Letters of Sigmund Freud and Arnold Zweig.* Translated by Elaine and William Robson-Scott. New York: New York University Press, 1970.

Freud, Sigmund. (1900) *The Interpretation of Dreams.* In *Standard Edition,* 4–5.

——— . (1901) *The Psychopathology of Everyday Life.* In *Standard Edition,* 6.

——— . (1910) "The Psychoanalytic View of Psychogenic Disturbance of Vision." In *Standard Edition,* 11:209–18.

——— . (1911) "Formulations on the Two Principles of Mental Functioning." In *Standard Edition,* 12:213–26.

——— . (1912–13) "Totem and Taboo." In *Standard Edition,* 13:1–161.

——— . (1914a). "On the History of the Psychoanalytic Movement." In *Standard Edition,* 14:1–66.

———. (1914). "On Narcissism." In *Standard Edition*, 14:67–102.

———. (1915) "Thoughts for the Times on War and Death." In *Standard Edition*, 14:274–300.

———. (1916) "On Transience." In *Standard Edition*, 14:303–08.

———. (1920) "Beyond the Pleasure Principle." In *Standard Edition*, 18:1–64.

———. (1921) "Group Psychology and the Analysis of the Ego." In *Standard Edition*, 18:65–144.

———. (1923) "The Ego and the Id." In *Standard Edition*, 19:1–59.

———. (1925) "An Autobiographical Study." In *Standard Edition*, 20:1–70.

———. (1927) "The Future of an Illusion." In *Standard Edition*, 21:1–56.

———. (1928) "Dostoevsky and Parricide." In *Standard Edition*, 21:173–94.

———. (1930) "Civilization and Its Discontents." In *Standard Edition*, 21:57–146.

———. (1930). "The Goethe Prize." In *Standard Edition*, 21:208–12.

———. (1933). "New Introductory Lectures on Psycho-Analysis." In *Standard Edition*, 22:1–182.

———. (1933) "Why War?" In *Standard Edition*, 22:195–218.

———. (1936) "A Disturbance of Memory on the Acropolis." In *Standard Edition*, 22:239–48.

———. (1937) "Analysis Terminable and Interminable." In *Standard Edition*, 23:209–53.

———. *The Origins of Psychoanalysis: Letters to Wilhelm Fliess, Drafts and Notes*, 1887–1902. Edited by Marie Bonaparte, Anna Freud, and Ernst Kris. New York: Basic Books, 1954.

———. *The Diary of Sigmund Freud*. New York: Scribner's, 1992.

Freud, Sigmund and Lou Andreas-Salomé. *Sigmund Freud and Lou Andreas-Salomé: Letters*. Translated by Elaine and William Robson-Scott. New York: W. W. Norton, 1966.

Freud, Sigmund and Carl Jung. *The Freud–Jung Letters*. Edited by William McGuire. Translated by R. Manheim and R. F. C. Hull. Princeton, N.J.: Princeton University Press, 1979.

Freud, Sigmund and Oskar Pfister. *Psychoanalysis and Faith: Dialogues with the Reverend Oskar Pfister*. Edited by H. Meng and E. L. Freud. New York: Basic Books, 1963.

Frohlich, Mary. *The Intersubjectivity of the Mystic: A Study of Teresa of Avila's Interior Castle*. Atlanta, Ga.: Scholars Press, 1993.

Fromm, Erich, D. T. Suzuki, and Richard De Martino, eds. *Zen Buddhism and Psychoanalysis*, New York: Harper Colophon, 1960.

Furse, M. *Experience and Certainty: William Ernest Hocking and Philosophical Mysticism*. Atlanta, Ga.: Scholar's Press, 1988.

Furst, S. et al. *Mysticism: Spiritual Quest or Psychic Disorder?* New York: Group for the Advancement of Psychiatry, Committee of Psychiatry and Religion, vol. IX, no. 97, 1976.

Gay, Peter. *Freud: A Life for Our Time*. New York: W. W. Norton, 1988.

Gill, M., and Breman, W. *Hypnosis and Related States: Psychoanalytic Studies in Regression*. New York: International Universities Press, 1959.

Gimello, R. "Mysticism and Meditation." In *Mysticism and Philosophical Analysis*, edited by S. Katz. New York: Oxford University Press, 1978, pp. 170–199.

Goetz, Bruno. "Erinnerungen an Sigmund Freud." *Neue Schweitzer Rundschau* 20 (1952):3–11.

———. "That Is All I Have to Say About Freud: Bruno Goetz's Reminiscences of Sigmund Freud." Translated by Shirley E. Jones. *International Review of Psychoanalysis* 2 (1975):139–43.

——. "This Is All I Have to Tell About Freud: Reminiscences of Sigmund Freud." Translated, with an Introduction, by Martin Grotjahn, M.D., and Ernest S. Wolf, M.D. *Annual of Psychoanalysis* 10 (1982):281–91.

Gombrich, R. Review of *The Oceanic Feeling*, by Jeffrey Masson. *Journal of the Royal Asiatic Society* 1 (1982):75–8.

Gómez, L. "Oriental Wisdom and the Cure of Souls: Jung and the Indian East." In Donald S. Lopez Jr., ed., *Curators of the Buddha: The Study of Buddhism under Colonialism*. Chicago: The University of Chicago Press, 1995, pp. 197–250.

Grigg, Kenneth. "'All Roads Lead to Rome': The Role of the Nursemaid in Freud's Dreams." *Journal of the American Psychoanalytic Association* 21 (1973):108–26.

Grinstein, Alex. *Sigmund Freud's Dreams*. New York: International Universities Press, 1980.

Guttman, Samuel, Randall L. Jones, and Stephen M. Parish, eds. *The Concordance to The Standard Edition of the Complete Psychological Works of Sigmund Freud*. New York: International Universities Press, 1984.

Halbfass, W. Review of *The Oceanic Feeling*, by Jeffrey Masson. *Journal of Asian Studies* 41 (1982):387–8.

Hall, G. S. *Adolescence: Its psychology and its relation to physiology, anthropology, sociology, sex, crime, religion and education*. New York: Appleton, 1915–16.

Hammarskjöld, D. *Markings*. Translated from the Swedish by Leif Sjöberg and W. H. Auden. New York: Knopf, 1964.

Happold, F. C. *Mysticism: A Study and an Anthology*. Harmondsworth, England: Penguin Books, 1963.

Harris, F. J. *André Gide and Romain Rolland: Two Men Divided*. New Brunswick, N.J.: Rutgers University Press, 1973.

Harrison, Irving. "On the Maternal Origins of Awe." *Psychoanalytic Study of the Child* 30 (1975):181–96.

——. "On Freud's View of the Infant–Mother Relationship and of the Oceanic Feeling: Some Subjective Influences." *Journal of the American Psychoanalytic Association* 27 (1979): 399–419.

Hartmann, H. *Ego Psychology and the Problem of Adaptation*. New York: International Universities Press, 1958.

Henking, S. "Placing the Social Sciences: Cases at the Intersection of the Histories of Disciplines and Religions." *Religious Studies Review*, 19 (1993):116–26.

Hocking, W. E. *The Meaning of God in Human Experience*. New Haven: Yale University Press, 1912.

——. "The Meaning of Mysticism as Seen Through Its Psychology." In *Understanding Mysticism*, edited by R. Woods. Garden City, N.Y.: Image Books, 1980, pp. 223–40.

Hollenback, J. *Mysticism: Experience, Response, and Empowerment*. University Park, Pa: Penn State Press, 1996.

Homans, Peter. *Theology After Freud*. Indianapolis, Ind.: Bobbs-Merrill, 1970.

——. *Jung in Context*. Chicago: University of Chicago Press, 1979.

——. "Narcissism in the Jung–Freud Confrontations." *American Imago* 38 (1981): 81–95.

——. "Psychoanalysis East and West: A Psychoanalytic Essay on Religion, Mourning and Healing." *History of Religions* 24 (1984):33–54.

——. "The Psychology and Religion Movement." In *The Encyclopedia of Religion*, edited by Mircea Eliade. New York: Macmillan, 1987, 12:66–74.

——. *The Ability to Mourn*. Chicago: University of Chicago Press, 1989.

Hood, Ralph, Jr. "Conceptual Criticisms of Regressive Explanations of Mysticism." *Review of Religious Research* 17, no. 3 (1976):179–88.

Horton, P. "The Mystical Experience: Substance of an Illusion." *Journal of the American Psychoanalytic Association* 22 (1974):364–80.

Horton, W. "The Origin and Psychological Function of Religion According to Pierre Janet." *American Journal of Psychology* 35 (1924):16–52.

Huxley, A. *The Perennial Philosophy.* New York: Harper and Row, 1945.

Idel, M. *Kabbalah: New Perspectives,* New Haven, Conn.: Yale University Press, 1988.

——— . "Universalization and Integration: Two Conceptions of Mystical Union in Jewish Mysticism." In *Mystical Union and Monotheistic Faith,* edited by M. Idel and B. McGinn. New York: Macmillan, 1989, pp. 27–55.

Idel, M. and McGinn, B., eds. *Mystical Union and Monotheistic Faith.* New York: Macmillan, 1989.

Jacoby, Mario. "Reflections on H. Kohut's Concept of Narcissism." *Journal of Analytical Psychology* 26 (1981):19–32.

——— . *Individuation and Narcissism: The Psychology of Self in Jung and Kohut.* London: Routledge, 1990.

James, William. *The Varieties of Religious Experience.* New York: Modern Library, 1936.

——— . "A Suggestion about Mysticism." In *Understanding Mysticism,* edited by R. Woods. Garden City, N.J.: Image Books, 1980, pp. 215–23.

Janet, P. *De l'Angoisse à l'extase.* 2 vols. Paris: Félix Alcan, 1926–1928.

John of the Cross, St., *Selected Writings.* Edited by Kieran Kavanaugh. New York: Paulist Press, 1987.

Jones, Ernest. *Papers on Psychoanalysis.* Boston: Beacon Press, 1948.

——— . *The Life and Work of Sigmund Freud.* 3 vols. New York: Basic Books, 1953–1957.

Jones, Richard H. "Jung and Eastern Religious Traditions." *Religion* 9 (1979):141–55.

Jones, Rufus. *Studies in Mystical Religion.* New York: Russell and Russell, 1909.

Jonte-Pace, D. "Feminist Transformations in the Psychology of Religion: New Developments in Method and Theory." *Method and Theory in the Study of Religion.* (forthcoming).

Jouvre, Pierre-Jean. *Romain Rolland vivant (1914–1919).* Paris: Ollendorff, 1920.

Jung, Carl. *Psychology of the Unconscious.* New York: Dodd, 1916.

——— . *Memories, Dreams, Reflections.* New York: Vintage, 1963.

——— . *Symbols of Transformation.* Princeton, N.J.: Princeton University Press, 1967.

Kakar, Sudhir. "Relative Realities: Images of Adulthood in Psychoanalysis and the Yogas." In *Identity and Adulthood,* edited by S. Kakar. Delhi: Oxford University Press, 1979, pp. 118–31.

——— . *The Inner World: A Psycho-Analytic Study of Childhood and Society in India.* Delhi: Oxford University Press, 1981.

——— . "Reflections on Psychoanalysis, Indian Culture and Mysticism." *Journal of Indian Philosophy* 20 (1982):289–97.

——— . *Shamans, Mystics and Doctors: A Psychological Inquiry into India and Its Healing Traditions.* New York: Knopf, 1982.

——— . *The Analyst and the Mystic.* Chicago: University of Chicago Press, 1991.

——— . "Clinical Work and Cultural Imagination." *Psychoanalytic Quarterly,* 64 (1995):265–81.

——— . "Psychoanalysis and Non-Western Cultures." *International Review of Psychoanalysis* 12 (1985):441–48.

Kanzer, Mark. "Sigmund and Alexander Freud on the Acropolis." *American Imago* 26 (1969):324–54.

Kaplan, Robert. "Plato, Kant, Nietzsche and Wittgenstein: Antidotes for the Mystically Insane." 1970. Unpublished manuscript.

Katz, Steven, ed. *Mysticism and Philosophical Analysis.* New York: Oxford University Press, 1978.

——— . *Mysticism and Religious Traditions.* New York: Oxford University Press, 1983.

Key, Ellen. "Romain Rolland." *La Revue* 106 (January–February 1914):171–81.

King, U. *Towards a New Mysticism.* New York: The Seabury Press, 1980.

Kirschner, S. *The Religious and Romantic Origins of Psychoanalysis.* Cambridge: Cambridge University Press, 1996.

Klein, Dennis B. *Jewish Origins of the Psychoanalytic Movement.* New York: Praeger Publishers, 1981.

Kligerman, C. "A Psychoanalytic study of the Confessions of St. Augustine." *Journal of the American Psychoanalytic Association* 5 (1957):469–84.

Kohut, Heinz. *The Analysis of the Self.* New York: International Universities Press, 1971.

——— . *The Search for the Self: Selected Writings of Heinz Kohut, 1950–1978.* Edited by Paul Ornstein. 2 vols. New York: International Universities Press, 1978.

——— . *Self Psychology and the Humanities.* Edited by Charles B. Strozier. New York: W. W. Norton, 1985.

Kohut, Heinz and Ernest Wolf. "The Disorders of the Self and Their Treatment: An Outline." *International Journal of Psychoanalysis* 59 (1978):413–25.

Kripal, Jeffrey J. *Kali's Child: The Mystical and the Erotic in the Life and Teachings of Ramakrishna.* Chicago: University of Chicago Press, 1995.

Kris, Ernst. *Psychoanalytic Explorations in Art.* New York: Schocken Books, 1952.

Kristeva, J. *Revolution in Poetic Language,* tr. Margaret Walker. New York: Columbia University Press, 1984.

Kurtz, S. *All the Mothers Are One.* New York: Columbia University Press, 1992.

Lacan, J. "God and the Jouissance of Women." In *Feminine Sexuality: Jacques Lacan and the École Freudian,* edited by J. Mitchell and J. Rose. New York: W. W. Norton, 1982.

LaCapra, D. and Kaplan S., eds. *Modern European Intellectual History: Reappraisals and New Perspectives.* Ithaca, N. Y.: Cornell University Press, 1982.

Lasch, C. *The Culture of Narcissism.* New York: Warner Books, 1979.

Lerch, E. *Romain Rolland und die Erneuerung der Lesinnung.* Munich: M. Huebner, 1926.

LeRoy, E. "La Discipline de l'intuition." *Vers l'unité* 35–6 (1925):23–26.

Leuba, J. *The Psychology of Religious Mysticism.* New York: Harcourt, Brace, 1926.

Lewin, B. *The Psychoanalysis of Elation.* New York: The Psychoanalytic Quarterly, 1961.

Lopez, D. *Curators of the Buddha: The Study of Buddhism Under Colonialism.* Chicago: The University of Chicago Press, 1995.

Maitra, S. K. *The Meeting of East and West in Sri Aurobindo's Philosophy.* Pondicherry, India: Sri Aurobindo Ashram, 1956.

March, Harold. *Romain Rolland.* New York: Twayne Publishers, 1971.

Maréchal, Joseph. "Les Lignes essentiales du Freudisme." *Nouvelle Revue Theologique* 52 (1925):537–51, 577–605; 53 (1926):13–50.

——— . *Studies in the Psychology of the Mystics.* Albany, N. Y.: Magi Books, 1964.

Masson, J. "Sex and Yoga: Psychoanalysis and the Indian Religious Experience." *Journal of Indian Philosophy* 2 (1974):307–20.

———. "The Psychology of the Ascetic." *Journal of Asian Studies* 35 (1976):611–25.

———. "Indian Psychotherapy?" *Journal of Indian Philosophy* 7 (1979): 327–32.

———. *The Oceanic Feeling: The Origin of the Religious Sentiment in Ancient India.* Dordrecht, Netherlands: D. Reidel, 1980.

Masson, J., and C. Hanly. "A Critical Examination of the New Narcissism". *International Journal of Psychoanalysis* 57 (1976):49–66.

Masson, J., and T. C. Masson. "The Study of Mysticism: A Criticism of W. T. Stace". *Journal of Indian Philosophy* 4 (1976):109–25.

———. "Buried Memories on the Acropolis: Freud's Response to Mysticism and Anti-Semitism." *International Journal of Psychoanalysis* 59 (1978):199–208.

McClelland, D. *Psychoanalysis and Religious Mysticism.* Wallingford, Penn.: Pendle Hill Pamphlets, 1959.

McGinn, Bernard. *The Foundations of Mysticism: Origins to the Fifth Century.* New York: Crossroad, 1991.

McGrath, William. "Freud as Hannibal: The Politics of the Brother Band." *Central European History* 7 (1974):31–57.

Meissner, W. W. *Annotated Bibliography in Religion and Psychology.* New York: Academy of Religion and Mental Health, 1961.

———. *Psychoanalysis and Religious Experience.* New Haven, Conn.: Yale University Press, 1984.

———. *Ignatius of Loyola: The Psychology of a Saint.* New Haven, Conn.: Yale University Press, 1992.

Merkur, D. "Unitive Experiences and the State of Trance." In *Mystical Union and Monotheistic Faith,* edited by M. Idel and B. McGinn. New York: Macmillan, 1989, pp. 125–57.

Milner, M. *The Suppressed Madness of Sane Men.* London: Tavistock, 1987.

Moller, H. "Affective Mysticism in Western Civilization." *The Psychoanalytic Review* 52 (1965):15–30.

Moloney, J. "Mother, God and Superego." *Journal of the American Psychoanalytic Association* 2 (1954):120–51.

Morel, F. *Essai sur l'introversion mystique.* Geneva: Kundig, 1918.

Mott, L. *Ernest Renan.* New York: D. Appleton, 1921.

Moxon, C. "Mystical Ecstasy and Hysterical Dream-States." *Journal of Abnormal Psychology* 15 (1920):329–34.

Muensterberger, W., ed. *Man and His Culture: Psychoanalytic Anthropology after "Totem and Taboo."* New York: Taplinger, 1970.

Nachmansohn, M. "Freuds Libidotheorie verglichten mit der Eroslehre Platos." *Internationale Zeitschrift für Psychoanalyse* 3 (1915).

Neumann, Erich. "Mystical Man." In *The Mystic Vision: Papers from the Eranos Yearbooks.* Edited by Joseph Campbell. Princeton, N.J.: Princeton University Press, 1968, 30:375–415.

Niederland, William. "Freud's 'Déjà Vu' on the Acropolis." *American Imago* 26 (1969):373–78.

Obeyesekere, G. *Medusa's Hair.* Chicago: The University of Chicago Press, 1981.

———. *The Work of Culture: Symbolic Transformation in Psychoanalysis and Anthropology.* Chicago: The University of Chicago Press, 1990.

O'Flaherty, W. Doniger. *Women, Androgynes and Other Mythical Beasts.* Chicago: The University of Chicago Press, 1980.

Oliner, Marion. *Cultivating Freud's Garden in France*. Northvale, New Jersey: Jason Aronson, 1988.

Ornstein, R. *The Psychology of Consciousness*. San Francisco: W. H. Freeman, 1972.

Osborne, A. *Ramana Maharshi and the Path of Self-Knowledge*. New York: Samuel Weiser, 1973.

Otto, Rudolf. *Mysticism East and West*. Translated by R. L. Bracey and R. C. Payne. New York: Macmillan, 1970.

Pacheu, J. *L'Expérience mystique et l'activité subconsciente*. Paris: Perrin, 1911.

Papini, G. "A Visit to Freud." *Review of Existential Psychology and Psychiatry* 9 (1969):130–4.

Parrinder, Geoffrey. *Mysticism in the World's Religions*. New York: Oxford University Press, 1976.

Parsons, A. "Is the Oedipus Complex Universal?" *Man and His Culture: Psychoanalytic Anthropology After "Totem and Taboo,"* edited by W. Muensterberger. New York: Taplinger, 1970:331–84.

Parsons, W. B. "The Ability to Mourn: Disillusionment and the Social Origins of Psychoanalysis: A Conversation with Peter Homans." *Criterion*, 30 (1991):2–8.

Paul, Robert A. *Moses and Civilization: The Meaning Behind Freud's Myth*. New Haven, Conn.: Yale University Press, 1996.

Perovitch, A. "Does the Philosophy of Mysticism Rest on a Mistake?" in *The Problem of Pure Consciousness*, edited by Robert K. C. Forman. New York: Oxford University Press, 1990.

Pfister, O. "Plato als Vorläufer der Psychoanalyse." *Internationale Zeitschrift für Psychoanalyse* 7 (1921).

Plato. *The Symposium*. In Plato, *The Collected Dialogues*, edited by E. Hamilton and H. Cairns. Princeton, N.J.: Princeton University Press, 1961, pp. 526–574.

Pratt, J. B. "The Psychology of Religion." In *Harvard Theological Review* 1 (1908):435–54.

——— . *The Religious Consciousness*. New York: Macmillan, 1920.

Prince, R., and C. Savage. "Mystical States and the Concept of Regression." In *The Highest State of Consciousness*, edited by John White. Garden City, N.Y.: Doubleday Anchor Books, 1972, pp. 114–34.

Radhikrishnan, S. *East and West in Religion*. London: Allen and Unwin, 1933.

Rahula, W. *What the Buddha Taught*. New York: Grove Press, 1974.

Reynolds, F. and Moore, B., eds. *Anthropology and the Study of Religion*. Chicago: Center for the Scientific Study of Religion, 1984.

Rieff, P. "The American Transference: From Calvin to Freud." *Atlantic* 208 (1961), 105–07.

——— . *The Triumph of the Therapeutic*. New York: Harper and Row, 1966.

——— . *Freud: The Mind of the Moralist*. Chicago: University of Chicago Press, 1979.

Rizzuto, Ana-Maria. *The Birth of the Living God*. Chicago: University of Chicago Press, 1979.

Robert, Marthe. *From Oedipus to Moses: Freud's Jewish Identity* Garden City, N.Y.: Anchor Books, 1976.

Roland, A. *In Search of Self in India and Japan*. Princeton, N.J.: Princeton University Press, 1988.

Rolland, Romain. *The Life of Michelangelo*. Translated by F. Lees. London: Heine Heinemann, 1912.

——— . *Jean-Christophe*. Translated by G. Cannan. New York: The Modern Library, 1913.

———. *Above the Battle*. Translated by C. K. Ogden. Chicago: Open Court, 1916.

———. *The Forerunners*. Translated by Eden and Cedar Paul. New York: Harcourt, Brace and Howe, 1920.

———. *Liluli*. New York: Boni and Liveright, 1920.

———. *Mahatma Gandhi: The Man Who Became One with the Universal Being*. Translated by C. Groth. New York: Century, 1924.

———. *The Soul Enchanted*. New York: Holt, 1925–34. 5 vols.

———. *Annette and Sylvia*. Vol. 1 of *The Soul Enchanted*. Translated by B. R. Redman. New York: Henry Holt, 1925.

———. *Summer*. Vol. 2 of *The Soul Enchanted*. Translated by E. Stimson and V. W. Brooks. New York: Henry Holt, 1925.

———. *Mother and Son*. Vol. 3 of *The Soul Enchanted*. Translated by V. W. Brooks. New York: Henry Holt, 1927.

———. *Essai sur la mystique et l'action de l'Inde vivante: La vie de Ramakrishna*. Paris: Librairie Stock, 1929.

———. *Essai sur la mystique et l'action de l'Inde vivante: La vie de Vivekananda et l'evangile universel*. Paris: Librairie Stock, 1930.

———. *Empédocle d'Agrigente, suivi de l'Éclair de Spinoza*. Paris: Le Sablier, 1931.

———. *The Revolt of the Machines or Invention Run Wild*. Ithaca, N.Y.: The Dragon Press, 1932.

———. *The Death of a World*. Vol. 4 of *The Soul Enchanted*. Translated by Amalia de Alberti. New York: Henry Holt, 1933.

———. *Letters of Romain Rolland and Malwida von Meysenbug, 1890–1891*. Translated by Thomas J. Wilson. New York: Henry Holt, 1933.

———. *A World in Birth*. Vol. 5 of *The Soul Enchanted*. Translated by Amalia de Alberti. New York: Henry Holt, 1934.

———. *Compagnons de route*. Paris: Éditions du Sablier, 1936.

———. *I Will Not Rest*. New York: Liveright, 1937.

———. *Rolland and Tagore*. Edited by A. Aronson and K. Kripalani. Calcutta: Visva-Bharati, 1945.

———. *Journey Within*. New York: Philosophical Library, 1947.

———. *Cahiers Romain Rolland*. Paris: Albin Michel. 28 vols. 1948–91.

———. *Choix de lettres à Malwida von Meysenbug*. In *Cahiers Romain Rolland*, Vol. 1. Paris: Éditions Albin Michel, 1948.

———. *Correspondance entre Louis Gillet et Romain Rolland*. In *Cahiers Romain Rolland*, Vol. 2. Paris: Éditions Albin Michel, 1949.

———. *Inde*. Paris: Éditions Vineta, 1951.

———. *Journal des années de guerre: 1914–1919*. Paris: Albin Michel, 1952.

———. *Le Cloître de la rue d'Ulm. Journal de Romain Rolland à l'Ecole Normale (1886–1889)*. *Cahiers Romain Rolland*, Vol. 4. Paris: Éditions Albin Michel, 1952.

———. *Mémoires et fragments du Journal*. Paris: Albin Michel, 1956.

———. *Chère Sofia. Choix de lettres de Romain Rolland à Sophia Bertolini Guerrieri-Gonzaga (1901–1908)*. *Cahiers Romain Rolland*, Vol. 10. Paris: Éditions Albin Michel, 1959.

———. *Le Voyage intérieur*. Paris: Éditions Albin Michel, 1959.

———. *Chère Sofia. Choix de lettres de Romain Rolland à Sophia Bertolini Guerrieri-Gonzaga (1909–1932)*. *Cahiers Romain Rolland*, Vol. 11. Paris: Éditions Albin Michel, 1960.

———. *Rabindranath Tagore et Romain Rolland. Lettres et autres écrits*. In *Cahiers Romain Rolland*, Vol. 12. Paris: Éditions Albin Michel, 1961.

———. *The Life of Ramakrishna*. Calcutta: Advaita Ashrama, 1965.

———. *Gandhi et Romain Rolland. Correspondance, extraits du journal et texts divers.* Cahiers Romain Rolland, Vol. 19. Paris: Éditions Albin Michel, 1969.

———. *Tolstoy*. Translated by B. Miall. London: Kennikat Press, 1972.

———. *Romain Rolland and Gandhi Correspondence*. New Delhi: Publications Division, Ministry of Information and Broadcasting, Government of India, 1976.

———. *Herman Hesse and Romain Rolland*. Translated from the French by M. G. Hesse. London: Oswald Wolff, 1978.

———. *Monsieur le Compte. Romain Rolland et Léon Tolstoy texts. Cahiers Romain Rolland,* Vol. 24. Paris: Éditions Albin Michel, 1981.

———. *Romain Rolland/Stefan Zweig Briefwechsel*. Vol. 2. Berlin: Rütten und Loening, 1987.

———. *The Life of Vivekananda and the Universal Gospel*. Calcutta: Advaita Ashrama, 1988.

———. *Au Seuil de la dernière porte*. Paris: Les Éditions du Cerf, 1989.

Roudinesco, E. *Jacques Lacan & Co.: A History of Psychoanalysis in France, 1925–1985.* Chicago: University of Chicago Press, 1990.

Roy, D. K. *Among the Great*. Bombay: N. M. Tripathi, Nalanda Publications, 1945.

———. *Yogi Sri Krishnaprem*. Bombay: Bharatiya Vidya Bhavan, 1968.

Rubin, J. *Psychotherapy and Buddhism*. New York: Plenum Press, 1996.

Said, E. *Orientalism*. New York: Vintage, 1979.

Samuels, Andrew. *Jung and the Post-Jungians*. London: Routledge and Kegan Paul, 1985.

Santas, G. *Plato and Freud*. New York: Basil Blackwell, 1988.

Scharfstein, Ben-Ami. *Mystical Experience*. Indianapolis, Ind.: Bobbs-Merrill, 1977.

Schaub, E. I. "The Psychology of Religion in America During the Past Quarter Century." *Journal of Religion* 6 (1926):113–34.

Schimmel, A. *Mystical Dimensions of Islam*. Chapel Hill: University of North Carolina Press, 1975.

Scholem, G. *Major Trends in Jewish Mysticism*. New York: Schocken Books, 1961.

Schorske, Carl. *Fin-de-Siècle Vienna: Politics and Culture*. New York: Vintage, 1981.

Schroeder, T. "Prenatal Psychisms and Mystical Pantheism." *International Journal of Psychoanalysis* 3 (1922):445–66.

Schur, M. "The Background of Freud's 'Disturbance' on the Acropolis." *American Imago* 26 (1969):303–23.

———. *Freud: Living and Dying*. New York: International Universities Press, Inc., 1972.

Schwab, R. *The Oriental Renaissance: Europe's Rediscovery of India and the East, 1680–1880.* Translated by Gene Patterson-Black and Victor Reinking. New York: Columbia University Press, 1984.

Seippel, Paul. *Romain Rolland, l'homme et l'oeuvre*. Paris: Ollendorff, 1913.

Sénéchal, Christian. *Romain Rolland*. Paris: Éditions de la Caravelle, 1933.

Sil, N. *Ramakrishna Paramahamsa: A Psychological Profile*. Leiden, Netherlands: Brill, 1991.

Sinha, T. C. "The Development of Psychoanalysis in India." *International Journal of Psychoanalysis* 47 (1966): 427–39.

Smart, Ninian. "Interpretation and Mystical Experience." In *Understanding Mysticism,* edited by R. Woods. Garden City, N.Y.: Image Books, 1980, pp. 78–91.

Smith, John E. "William James's Account of Mysticism." In *Mysticism and Religious Traditions,* edited by S. Katz. New York: Oxford University Press, 1983, pp. 247–79.

Solomon, M. "Freud's Father on the Acropolis." *American Imago* 30 (1973):142–56.

Spencer, Sidney. *Mysticism in World Religion*. Baltimore: Penguin Books, 1963.

Stace, W. T. *Mysticism and Philosophy.* London: Macmillan, 1960.

Starbuck, E. D. *The Psychology of Religion.* London: Walter Scott, 1914.

Starr, William. *A Critical Bibliography of the Published Writings of Romain Rolland.* Evanston, Ill.: Northwestern University Press, 1950.

——. *Romain Rolland and a World at War.* Evanston, Ill.: Northwestern University Press, 1956.

——. *Romain Rolland: One Against All.* The Hague: Mouton, 1971.

Sterba, R. "Remarks on Mystic States." *American Imago* 25 (1968):77–85.

Suleiman, E. *Private Power and Centralization in France: The Notaries and the State.* Princeton, N.J.: Princeton University Press, 1987.

Tagore, R. "India's Message to Japan." *The Outlook,* August 9, 1916, pp. 856–8.

——. *The Religion of Man.* Boston: Beacon Press, 1961.

Tambiah, S. *The Buddhist Saints of the Forest and the Cult of Amulets.* Cambridge: Cambridge University Press, 1984.

Teresa of Avila, St. *The Interior Castle.* Translated by Kieran Kavanaugh and Otilio Rodriguez. New York: Paulist Press, 1979.

Tillich, Paul. *The Protestant Era.* Chicago: The University of Chicago Press, 1948.

——. *The Courage to Be.* New Haven, Conn.: Yale University Press, 1952.

——. *The Meaning of Health.* Chicago: Exploration Press, 1984.

Trosman, Harry. *Freud and the Imaginative World.* Hillsdale, N.J.: The Analytic Press, 1985.

Tweed, T. *The American Encounter with Buddhism, 1844–1912: Victorian Culture and the Limits of Dissent.* Bloomington: Indiana University Press, 1992.

Van Duesen, H. *Dag Hammarskjöld: The Statesman and His Faith.* New York: Harper and Row, 1967.

Van Herik, J. "'Thick Description' and the Psychology of Religion." In F. Reynolds and B. Moore, eds., *Anthropology and the Study of Religion.* Chicago: Center for the Scientific Study of Religion, 1985, pp. 56–74.

Versluis, A. *American Transcendentalism and Asian Religions.* New York: Oxford University Press, 1993.

Vermorel, Henri, and Madeleine Vermorel. *Sigmund Freud et Romain Rolland Correspondance 1923–1936.* Paris: Presses Universitaries de France, 1993.

Wallace, E. *Freud and Anthropology.* New York: International Universities Press, 1983.

Wallwork, E. "Thou Shalt Love Thy Neighbor as Thyself: The Freudian Critique." *Journal of Religious Ethics* 10 (1982):264–308.

——. *Psychoanalysis and Ethics.* New Haven, Conn.: Yale University Press, 1991.

Wapnick, K. "Mysticism and Schizophrenia." In Richard Woods, ed., *Understanding Mysticism,* pp. 321–371.

Webb, R., and M. Sells, "Lacan and Bion: Psychoanalysis and the Mystical Language of Unsaying." *Theory and Psychology* 5, 2 (1995):195–215.

Weber, Max. *The Protestant Ethic and the Spirit of Capitalism.* New York: Charles Scribner's Sons, 1958.

Welbon, G. *The Buddhist Nirvana and Its Western Interpreters.* Chicago: University of Chicago Press, 1968.

Werman, David. "Sigmund Freud and Romain Rolland." *International Review of Psychoanalysis* 4 (1977):225–43.

——. "On the Nature of the Oceanic Experience." *The Journal of Psychoanalytic Anthropology* 9 (1986):339–58.

White, John, ed. *The Highest State of Consciousness.* Garden City, N.Y.: Anchor Books, 1972.

Wilber, K., J. Engler, and D. Brown, eds. *Transformations of Consciousness.* Boston: Shambhala, 1986.

Wilber, K. "Psychologia Perennis: The Spectrum of Consciousness." *Journal of Transpersonal Psychology* 7 (1975):105–32.

Washburn, M. *The Ego and the Dynamic Ground.* Albany: State University Press of New York, 1988.

Williams, R. *Teresa of Avila.* Harrisburg, Pa.: Morehouse Publishing, 1991.

Wilson, Ronald. *The Pre-War Biographies of Romain Rolland.* New York: Oxford University Press, 1939.

Winnicott, D. W. *Playing and Reality.* Harmondsworth: Penguin, 1980.

Wittels, F. "A Neglected Boundary of Psychoanalysis." *Psychoanalytic Quarterly* 18 (1949):44–59.

Wolfson, E. *Through a Speculum That Shines: Vision and Imagination in Medieval Jewish Mysticism.* Princeton, N.J.: Princeton University Press, 1994.

Woods, Richard. *Understanding Mysticism.* Garden City, N.Y.: Image, 1980.

Wulff, David M. *Psychology of Religion: Classic and Contemporary Views.* New York: Wiley, 1991.

Zaehner, R. C. *Mysticism Sacred and Profane.* New York: Oxford University Press, 1961.

——— . "A New Buddha and a New Tao." In R. C. Zaehner, ed., *The Concise Encyclopedia of Living Faiths.* New York: Hawthorn Books, 1959, pp. 402–12.

Zeldin, T. *France 1848–1945.* Vol. 1. Oxford: Oxford University Press, 1973.

Zilboorg, G. *Psychoanalysis and Religion.* New York: Farrar, Strauss and Cudahy, 1962.

Zock, H. *A Psychology of Ultimate Concern.* Amsterdam: Rodopi, 1990.

Zweig, S. *Romain Rolland: The Man and His Work.* New York: Thomas Seltzer, 1921.

# Index